CHAMBER OF COMMERCE
RESEARCH ACTIVITIES

CHAMBER OF RESEARCH

ACCRA Editorial Committee

COMMERCE
ACTIVITIES

Edited by

Howard N. Martin

Director of Research
Houston Chamber of Commerce

Published by

AMERICAN CHAMBER
OF COMMERCE
RESEARCHERS ASSOCIATION

Distributed by

AMERICAN CHAMBER
OF COMMERCE EXECUTIVES

1133 15th St., N.W. Washington, D.C. 20005

Revised Edition

International Standard Book Number: 0-9600852-1-1

Library of Congress Catalog Card Number: 74-33239

Printed in the United States of America

Kaufmann Graphics, Inc.
Washington, D.C.

CONTRIBUTORS

The persons whose names are shown in this list prepared papers that were used in writing preliminary drafts of chapters for this manual. The listing for each person includes the researcher's title and organization affiliation on the date that he or she submitted material relating to one or more chapters of this publication.

Kurt P. Alverson, Director
Research & Marketing Services
 Department
Buffalo Area Chamber of
 Commerce
Buffalo, New York

Michael D. Baird, Assistant Manager
Research Department
Houston Chamber of Commerce
Houston, Texas

Robert S. Barr, Director
Research Bureau
Greater Philadelphia Chamber of
 Commerce
Philadelphia, Pennsylvania

Don W. Belcher, Director of
 Research
Nashville Area Chamber of
 Commerce
Nashville, Tennessee

Edward J. Bowman, Director
Taxation Department
Indiana State Chamber of
 Commerce
Indianapolis, Indiana

Frank A. Brady, Jr., Director
Government Finance & Research
 Department
New York Chamber of Commerce
 & Industry
New York, New York

Donald E. Chafey, Research
 Director
Greater Trenton Chamber of
 Commerce
Trenton, New Jersey

Robert L. Chaffin, Manager
Economic Research Division
Jackson Chamber of Commerce
Jackson, Mississippi

Peggy Chambers, Manager
Department of Business Research
Tulsa Chamber of Commerce
Tulsa, Oklahoma

Byron E. Cowart, Director
Business Research
Colorado Springs Chamber of
 Commerce
Colorado Springs, Colorado

James W. Cowart, Director
Research Department
Oakland Chamber of Commerce
Oakland, California

R. S. Crowder, Manager
Research Department
Birmingham Area Chamber of
Commerce
Birmingham, Alabama

Earle L. Elmore, Managing
Director
West Virginia Chamber of
Commerce
Charleston, West Virginia

Jack D. Englar, Manager
Business Research Department
Chamber of Commerce of
Metropolitan Baltimore
Baltimore, Maryland

John M. Fabrey, Director
Legislative & Economic Research
Department
Rochester Chamber of Commerce
Rochester, New York

Leslie M. Gravlin, Manager
Research Department
Greater Hartford Chamber of
Commerce
Hartford, Connecticut

John G. Hagen, Manager
Business Research Division
Metropolitan Milwaukee
Association of Commerce
Milwaukee, Wisconsin

Richard K. Harb, Director
Research Division
Louisville Area Chamber of
Commerce
Louisville, Kentucky

Russell Heflin, Manager
Government Operations
Department
Illinois State Chamber of
Commerce
Springfield, Illinois

Bill Hendrie, Manager
Research Department
Fresno County & City Chamber of
Commerce
Fresno, California

Robert Hibbard, Assistant
Executive Director
Pennsylvania State Chamber of
Commerce
Harrisburg, Pennsylvania

Dewayne Hollin, Assistant Manager
Research Department
Houston Chamber of Commerce
Houston, Texas

Gerald T. Horton, Director of
Research
Atlanta Chamber of Commerce
Atlanta, Georgia

Ken Howard, Manager
Research & Central Records
Dallas Chamber of Commerce
Dallas, Texas

Arthur C. Jordan, Research Analyst
Economic Development & Research
California State Chamber of
Commerce
Sacramento, California

William Julius, Research Analyst
Chamber of Commerce of
Metropolitan St. Louis
St. Louis, Missouri

Charles Kenyon, Manager
Research Department
Albany Area Chamber of
Commerce
Albany, New York

Evelyne Kieler, Research Associate
Greater Des Moines Chamber of
  Commerce
Des Moines, Iowa

E. L. Kimmel, Research Analyst
Chamber of Commerce of
  Metropolitan St. Louis
St. Louis, Missouri

Alice M. Klein, Economic Research
  Manager
Louisville Area Chamber of
  Commerce
Louisville, Kentucky

Jan Knoop, Director of Research
Colorado State Chamber of
  Commerce
Denver, Colorado

Stanley R. Kowalsky, Manager
Research Department
Memphis Area Chamber of
  Commerce
Memphis, Tennessee

Charles Kramer, General Manager
Greater Cincinnati Chamber of
  Commerce
Cincinnati, Ohio

Paul Latture, Manager
Chamber of Commerce
Fort Smith, Arkansas

James H. Lewis, Manager
Management Planning & Research
Los Angeles Area Chamber of
  Commerce
Los Angeles, California

C. J. Libbey, Assistant Manager
Lake Charles Chamber of
  Commerce
Lake Charles, Louisiana

W. F. Limpp, Manager
Business Research Department
Omaha Chamber of Commerce
Omaha, Nebraska

John J. Mackin, Research Director
Columbus Area Chamber of
  Commerce
Columbus, Ohio

Robert S. Marshall, Manager
Research Department
Greater Kansas City Chamber of
  Commerce
Kansas City, Missouri

Craig L. Mason, Director
Research Department
Mobile Area Chamber of
  Commerce
Mobile, Alabama

Frederick McCarthy, Director
Governmental Research
  Department
Indianapolis Chamber of
  Commerce
Indianapolis, Indiana

Lawrence B. McGee, Chief—
  Technical Service Section
Department of Conservation &
  Development
Raleigh, North Carolina

Thomas L. McGrath, Manager
Research & Development
  Department
Greater Boston Chamber of
  Commerce
Boston, Massachusetts

Jessie McMullen, Manager
Research Department
Cincinnati Chamber of Commerce
Cincinnati, Ohio

John F. Moon, Research Director
Minneapolis Chamber of
  Commerce
Minneapolis, Minnesota

Lucille Mortimer, Manager
Research Department
San Diego Chamber of Commerce
San Diego, California

Leland L. Narr, Director
Research Department
Tallahassee Area Chamber of
　Commerce
Tallahassee, Florida

Gene Neeley, Manager
Research & Transportation
San Antonio Chamber of
　Commerce
San Antonio, Texas

Ruth Ann Nickel
Research & Statistics
Chamber of Commerce of Greater
　Pittsburgh
Pittsburgh, Pennsylvania

Harry A. Noren, Manager
Business Research & Survey
Denver Chamber of Commerce
Denver, Colorado

Thomas A. Olberding, Manager
Business Research Department
Dayton Area Chamber of
　Commerce
Dayton, Ohio

James E. O'Leary, Fiscal Specialist
Ohio Chamber of Commerce
Columbus, Ohio

William K. Opdyke, Manager
Research Department
Los Angeles Chamber of Commerce
Los Angeles, California

Robert W. Palmer, Director
Economic Research & World Trade
Indianapolis Chamber of
　Commerce
Indianapolis, Indiana

Wallace O. Parker, Research
　Director
Jacksonville Chamber of Commerce
Jacksonville, Florida

Thomas L. Pickard, Research
　Manager
Greensboro Chamber of Commerce
Greensboro, North Carolina

Margaret A. Poling, Research
　Director
West Virginia Chamber of
　Commerce
Charleston, West Virginia

Fred J. Reinhardt, General
　Manager
Department of Development
County of Riverside
Riverside, California

Forest L. St. Pierre, Research
　Associate
Greater Boston Chamber of
　Commerce
Boston, Massachusetts

George Sawyer
General Manager - Program
California Chamber of Commerce
Sacramento, California

DeVer Sholes, Director
Research & Statistics Division
Chicago Association of Commerce
　& Industry
Chicago, Illinois

Eldon W. Sneeringer, Manager
Research &Taxation Department
Michigan State Chamber of
　Commerce
Lansing, Michigan

Paul W. Spain, Manager
Economic Development
  Department
Greater Winston-Salem Chamber
  of Commerce
Winston-Salem, North Carolina

John F. Spragins, Jr., Director of
  Research
Fort Worth Chamber of Commerce
Fort Worth, Texas

Robert R. Statham, Director
Taxation Department
Indiana State Chamber of
  Commerce
Indianapolis, Indiana

John R. Steiner, Manager
Economics & Research Department
Greater Detroit Chamber of
  Commerce
Detroit, Michigan

Jack Suiter, Assistant Director
Business Development Department
Miami-Dade County Chamber of
  Commerce
Miami, Florida

Hal Tinker, Research Associate
El Paso Chamber of Commerce
El Paso, Texas

James I. Tucker, Manager
Economic Development & Research
  Department
Fresno County & City Chamber of
  Commerce
Fresno, California

J. W. Vanden Bosch, Business
  Analyst
Cleveland Chamber of Commerce
Cleveland, Ohio

Thomas N. Watkins, Director
Research & Industrial Development
Kentucky Chamber of Commerce
Louisville, Kentucky

Paul A. Willax, Director
Research & Education
Buffalo Area Chamber of
  Commerce
Buffalo, New York

Richard L. Wilson, Manager
Research Department
Louisville Area Chamber of
  Commerce
Louisville, Kentucky

David E. Wolvin, Director of
  Research
Lincoln Chamber of Commerce
Lincoln, Nebraska

PREFACE

In recent years, the entire field of Chamber of Commerce management has metamorphosized to meet the demands of a world characterized by increasingly complex social and economic conditions. In this new era, the ability to use the techniques of modern economic and social research effectively is essential to every Chamber's service role.

The contemporary Chamber of Commerce executive is constantly called upon to analyze, evaluate, and recommend projects of considerable importance to his community. If he lacks a basic understanding of how research can be usefully applied to these issues, he is severely handicapped in making decisions about the Chamber of Commerce program, and consequently diminishes his Chamber's influence and usefulness.

Chamber of Commerce Research Activities is about research functions in Chambers of all sizes. It deals concretely and comprehensively with the way researchers work and the techniques by which they can most effectively fulfill their responsibilities. This book serves a dual function: it presents a framework for organizing and solving research problems, and it provides a step-by-step "how-to-do-it" manual of Chamber of Commerce research—a primer for the Chamber executive or staff member who wishes to strengthen his Chamber's research program. In brief, our intention is both to aid the researcher in enhancing his skills and to provide a reference for other Chamber personnel who wish, without becoming specialists, to develop a working knowledge of how research can best be used in the local Chamber of Commerce program.

The choice of material has been difficult. Selective rather than encyclopedic, this book covers those topics regarded as having the greatest importance and interest. The dominant goal is to illuminate the more basic and commonly-used tools, techniques, and methods, rather than try to anticipate every research contingency. To have included each research procedure now in use would have lengthened the present book intolerably and would have destroyed a greater part of its utility. Hence experienced researchers hopefully will accept the absence of some useful but more esoteric techniques.

Although various statistical tools and techniques are discussed, this manual has not been conceived to serve as a statistics textbook. Rather it complements statistics textbooks by showing how certain analytical procedures are applied to Chamber of Commerce research specifically. Its focus is the characteristic activities of Chamber of Commerce researchers—those staff members who are responsible for the real world applied research necessary for decision-making and problem-solving in a local Chamber of Commerce program. The Chamber researcher is advised to use this book in conjunction with one or more standard statistics textbooks, turning to them for detailed background material on specific procedures.

Special effort has been made to present material in a manner that will personally involve the reader in the problems, decisions, and activities of Chamber of Commerce researchers in a world of uncertainty. I have attempted to cover essential research principles and practices without resorting to more technical and theoretical aspects of mathematics. For additional information about technical aspects of the subject matter in this manual, the reader should refer to the specialized books and articles mentioned in footnotes and listed at the ends of chapters. These references were selected to provide both breadth and depth for the conscientious researcher who wishes to delve further into a subject.

Reading one book will not turn anyone into an expert researcher, but the effort to produce this manual must be considered successful if it helps the reader to:

1. Acquire an appreciation of research as a fundamental and essential process for solving problems;
2. Develop a critical awareness of the strength and weakness of research procedures;
3. Design and execute valid research projects of moderate dimensions and difficulty;
4. Become more adept at evaluating the research results he encounters, at judging their validity, and at recognizing their limits of inference, applicability, and precision.

Chamber of Commerce Research Activities has been organized on the principle that the basic prerequisite of an understandable research manual is the logical arrangement and clear exposition of subject matter. This manual starts with first things first. Part I, "Organizing for Research," centers on significance of the research process and the step-by-step development of a research program. To assist researchers in selecting activities for their respective programs, Appendix A presents a comprehensive list of research activities. Combined with Appendix B, it serves as a guide to Chambers of Commerce whose personnel have experience in specific areas of Chamber research.

Part II, "Information Systems," treats information sources and some of the tools, techniques, and methods commonly used by Chamber of Commerce researchers. Chapter 4 reflects my conviction that data management on a small-area basis is especially significant to researchers and merits detailed treatment. Chapter 5 deals with the utility and applicability of electronic data processing in Chamber of Commerce operations. Instead of including a survey of sampling procedures in Chapter 6, this material purposely is detailed in a separate chapter.

It is a basic tenet of this book that a researcher should never figuratively isolate himself in a remote corner of the Chamber of Commerce organization, waiting for someone to call on him for information or other assistance. He should be an aggressive member of the Chamber of Commerce team, originating activity suggestions and participating significantly in the organization's decision-making process. Part III, "Spotlighting Business Conditions and Trends," sets forth certain areas of Research Department initiative. These chapters describe selected activities through which a researcher can (1) keep his fingers on the community's economic pulse; (2) provide significant data for problem identification, problem prevention, and problem solving within the local area; and (3) focus attention upon the continuing value of the Chamber's research program.

While most chapters of Part III relate to characteristics and current status of the economy in local areas, Chapter 11 represents a "change of pace." It is an introduction to predicting future economic conditions of the United States. The emphasis in this chapter is upon *future* rather than *current* economic conditions, and the geographic scope is widened from local community to the entire nation. The role of Chapter 11 in Part III is crucial because the prospects of a local community are substantially determined by the general level of economic activity. Trends and expectations of the economy as a whole are of vital significance to its constituent parts. The local Chamber of Commerce executive therefore should be concerned with and understand the state of the national economy as well as economic trends in the community which he serves.

As this is essentially a "how-to-do-it" rather than a "what-to-do-it-for" book, the chapters in Part IV, "Research for Economic Development," assume a commonality of Chamber of Commerce objectives and do not attempt to describe the organization of Chamber programs for industrial development and trade promotion. Instead, these chapters concentrate upon a few types of research projects that will be most useful in the local Chamber's economic development program. Additional research activities for economic development are listed in Appendix A.

Part V, "Demographic and Social Research," introduces the subject matter and methods of demography — an area of major importance in both social and economic research. Demographic methods are used with increasing frequency in economic research, since population changes tend to occur more irregularly and to involve alterations in structure. The two chapters appearing in Part V are not intended to constitute a complete survey of demography — one topic whose omission will be noted is population projection — but they cover those aspects of demography most pertinent to Chamber research. Other chapters in this manual (including Chapters 4, 6, and 7) contain additional material related to demographic procedures.

Chamber of Commerce members are demanding stronger action on legislative issues at the local, state, and national levels. Government-oriented problems go beyond the scope of research, but research plays a vital part in activities related to these problems. Suggestions for the application of research in an effective governmental affairs program are presented in Part VI, "Governmental Research."

The proposal to publish a manual for Chamber of Commerce researchers was discussed originally during a meeting, attended by six researchers from various cities, in the offices of the Los Angeles Chamber of Commerce on June 22, 1961. This meeting had been called to exchange research experiences and to discuss the formation of a permanent organization for this specialty group. The publication of a research manual was presented as one of the reasons for organizing the American Chamber of Commerce Researchers Association, or ACCRA, as the organization generally is known.

During the early years of its existence ACCRA developed its organizational structure and expanded in membership. At the ACCRA national meeting in June, 1965, Richard K. Harb, research director of the Louisville, Kentucky, Chamber of Commerce, presented the results of a survey in which Chamber of Commerce executives throughout the United States expressed a need for a research manual. Immediately thereafter the ACCRA board of directors voted to initiate work on a manual and organized a committee for this purpose.

On June 2, 1966, the manual committee reported at the ACCRA national meeting that a list of suggested chapters had been prepared and that researchers had been invited to submit material for use in writing various chapters. During the next two years the papers related to each chapter were combined into a preliminary draft of that chapter. Since 1968 all of these chapters have evolved steadily through a continuous series of revisions.

A book so long in the making naturally incorporates the work of many people besides the editor. It simply is not possible to acknowledge fully the aid and encouragement that many individuals have given me, both directly and indirectly, during the years this manual was in preparation. My greatest obligation is to the members of the ACCRA editorial committee who assisted in preparing early revisions of chapters for this publication and who gave me the benefit of their knowledge and suggestions.

Secondly, I am very grateful to the researchers who prepared papers used in writing preliminary chapter drafts. Let me make it clear that they cannot be held responsible for any of the content or style of the book. Considerable editing, rewriting, and supplementation were done in the interests of uniformity of style and treatment and to eliminate gaps and duplications in coverage.

I am indebted to the Chamber of Commerce of the United States for permission to reprint "Introduction to Business and Economic Forecasting" in Chapter 11. This chapter was written by Dr. Carl H. Madden, Chief

Economist, and Dr. James R. Morris, Senior Associate, in the National Chamber's Economic Analysis and Study Group.

The following chapters were prepared partially or in their entirety by staff members of the U.S. Bureau of the Census: Chapter 4 (Sections B through F) by Gerald L. O'Donnell, Data Access and Use Laboratory, Data User Services Office; Chapter 18 by Michael G. Garland, Chief, Data Access and Use Laboratory, Data User Services Office; and Chapter 19 (Section B) by Donald E. Starsinic, Chief, State and Local Population Estimates and Projections Branch, Population Division. I am grateful for their contribution to this work.

Other representatives of the Census Bureau provided materials used in the production of this manual, and I am pleased to acknowledge the assistance of Dr. Conrad E. Taeuber, formerly Associate Director for Demographic Fields (retired); William T. Fay, formerly Chief, Geography Division (retired); Meyer Zitter, Chief, Population Division; Morton A. Meyer, Chief, Geography Division; Jacob Silver, Acting Assistant Chief for Operations, Geography Division; Dr. Robert C. Klove, Geographic Research Advisor, Statistical Research Division (formerly Assistant Chief for Research and Development, Geography Division); Toshi Toki, Geographic Statistical Areas Branch, Geography Division (formerly Chief, Census Tract Branch, Geography Division); and Ann D. Casey, Data Access and Use Laboratory, Data User Services Office.

The American Chamber of Commerce Executives provided liaison with the printer, and I am grateful especially to Ronald R. Rumbaugh, President, and Paul J. Greeley, Jr., Manager, Council Operations, for their assistance.

I cannot forbear saying a word of very sincere appreciation to the Houston Chamber of Commerce as an institution, to the two successive chief executive officers, W. Marvin Hurley and Louie Welch, and to Leonard S. Patillo, Executive Vice President and General Manager. They have provided much needed help and have encouraged me to follow my path wherever it led, even though that meant numerous revisions of chapters and repeated postponements of completion.

While working on this book I received assistance from other associates at the Houston Chamber of Commerce. I am indebted to Marsha E. Carr, editor of *Houston Magazine,* for a thorough and penetrating critique, both microscopic and macroscopic, of the last pre-publication chapter revisions. Her suggestions have been used throughout this book, and there can be no doubt that the manual has benefitted immeasurably by them. Frank R. Kenfield, Manager, Public Affairs/Freight Traffic Department, developed very effective materials which are used in illustrations for the chapters in Part VI. Members of the Houston Chamber's Research Department staff provided a wide variety and large number of services in the preparation of the manuscript. Dewayne Hollin and

Michael D. Baird helped in writing parts of several chapters and in handling a general fact-checking assignment. Charles A. Kasdorf III assisted in preparing final revisions of all chapters and the index. Most of the burden of computing, typing, and proofreading has been executed neatly by Katherine Slocum, Ernestine Lloyd, Alice Barnes, and Norma Salas, who met reasonable and unreasonable demands with equal promptness and pleasantness. Among a number of competent and conscientious typists of the manuscript, Maria Carla Figueredo, Linda Roberts, Catherine Brown, Irene Garces, and Vivienne Lester deserve special thanks.

Carole Jacobs of Omnibook, Washington, D.C., provided typographic design, went over the manuscript line by line, and contributed invaluable aid, ranging from advisory opinions on basic content to countless clarifications of thought and phraseology.

My wife, Valerie, has graciously and patiently endured those exigencies of life associated with a husband's efforts in trying to haul a book over the long road from preliminary planning to final publication.

The efforts of those mentioned above have been directed toward improving the contents of this manual and helping to remove errors and misstatements. I shall share happily with them credit for any strengths in this book; but, needless to say, the reverse does not hold true—I cannot share with them the responsibility for flaws. Along with my thanks for their assistance, I must absolve them of blame for those inadequacies that remain, which are solely my responsibility.

Howard N. Martin
Houston, Texas

CONTENTS

PART IV: RESEARCH FOR ECONOMIC DEVELOPMENT

PART V: DEMOGRAPHIC AND SOCIAL RESEARCH

PART VI: GOVERNMENTAL RESEARCH

APPENDIXES

Part I

ORGANIZING

FOR RESEARCH

1 THE ROLE OF RESEARCH IN THE CHAMBER OF COMMERCE PROGRAM

A. INTRODUCTION

For years authors of articles in Chamber of Commerce-generated publications and reports, as well as speakers at meetings, have called for better research tools and procedures to assist decision-makers in understanding and solving their problems. Massive shifts of population to urbanized areas, kaleidoscopic mobility of population, mechanization, the growing complexity of urban life, large-scale organization, and the information explosion have created new social and economic environments in which the dynamics of change make the new of today the obsolete of tomorrow.

The challenge to Chamber of Commerce decision-makers has been greatly magnified and complicated by the impact of these and similar developments. While the use of research in the decision-making process has grown in recent years, it still is applied on a very limited scale when compared to the magnitude of management decisions and the capacity of research to aid in making these decisions.

It is an encouraging step forward when Chamber of Commerce organizations turn the spotlight on research in an attempt to determine the practical application of research to management decisions. There are, however, broader potential applications underlying the current emphasis upon research.

1. Urban Problems

The rapid changes occurring in urbanized areas call for the constant collection of facts into a local data management system for continuous use in the prevention, delineation and solving of problems.

2. The Sophistication of Member Firms

Chamber of Commerce members are increasingly becoming aware of the importance of good data management systems for their firms and com-

3

panies, and they expect the local Chamber to demonstrate corresponding efficiency in establishing and maintaining a data management system for the community.

3. Community Image

Analysts, industrial and commercial site locators, consultants and other data users are increasingly sophisticated in their search for information. The local Chamber of Commerce researcher, with the quality and quantity of his resources, helps to shape the opinion which these information-seekers form about the community.

Veterans in the industrial development field have indicated that, on initial information-requesting visits to a Chamber of Commerce office, a site locator usually prefers to keep the purpose of his visits confidential. The tendency is to bypass the chief executive officer and economic development manager, going instead directly to the Research Department or, in smaller organizations, to the person whose staff assignments include those of the researcher.

Readily available answers to the site locator's inquiries show that the Chamber has kept its finger on the community's pulse and has maintained an awareness of shifts and trends within its market area. Negative or inadequate responses from the researcher, on the other hand, could result in doubts about the community's alertness, its procedures for discovering problems, and its program of planning for future economic progress and a higher quality of life.

In short, the researcher can play a very important positive role — or be a definite liability — in a community sales program.

4. Meeting the Competition

The competition of federally-funded planning, research and economic development agencies — plus privately-funded urban research organizations — calls for an ongoing concerted effort by the local Chamber of Commerce to maintain and expand its leadership position in the community.

If the Chamber's research department is recognized throughout the community as both a reliable source of accurate data and the focal point for community-oriented research, that research capability can be a means of focusing attention upon the local Chamber of Commerce and preventing erosion of membership support.

5. The Decision-Making Role

The nature and role of this activity — research — are not generally understood. The most common Chamber definition states that "Economic Research is nothing more than fact-finding." Although a substantial portion of research activity does relate to fact-finding, research in its broader framework is cast in a far more significant decision-making mold.

B. DEFINITION OF RESEARCH

The objective of *basic* or *pure* research is to advance human knowledge—to discover, develop and verify that knowledge. It provides the explanations which allow observers to better understand phenomena. Concomitantly, basic research attempts to develop hypotheses and theories.

Applied research prescribes procedures and/or techniques for solving operational problems and/or offers solutions to these problems. It is concerned with objectives for managing things and people—how to employ knowledge to build useful devices.

The type of research described in the work programs of this nation's Chambers of Commerce is classified as *applied*—rather than basic or pure—and serves as the operational "tool kit" for solving a community's problems. The definition of research, as it is used to describe Chamber activity, consists of five principal parts: Problem Delineation, Data Collection, Analysis and Interpretation, Publication, and Implementation.[1]

The Chamber of Commerce researcher uses knowledge to produce useful solutions to definite problems *as rapidly as possible*. Researchers are not engaged in the business of producing theories directly, although the results of applied research may be used in theoretical research.

C. DEVELOPING CHAMBER RESEARCH CAPABILITIES

1. The Geographic Framework

In preparing to do a better job in research, the first step should be to mark out a *geographic framework for collecting and retrieving data on a small-area basis*. Aggregate information about an entire Standard Metropolitan Statistical Area, a county or even an incorporated area, has very little applicability to most of the problems demanding attention in urbanized areas. Many urban problems relate to small parts of the urbanized area, and information from and about these small areas is needed for problem solving.

By 1960 individual small-area data frameworks—known as census tract plans—were in existence for nearly all standard metropolitan areas in the United States. Information compiled by census tract was useful in

---

[1] Each of the five parts of this definition is described in Chapter 2.

locating problem areas or areas of opportunity, dividing a city or metropolitan area into sections for particular purposes, evaluating a given site
for appropriate use, locating new facilities, evaluating market or service
potential, and helping to plan for the future.

Prior to the Census of 1970, the census tract framework for the
nation's SMSA's was upgraded from a census tract plan to the computerized Address Coding Guide and DIME[2] data linkage systems, which
permit amazing flexibility in delineating an area to be studied and in
retrieving data related *only* to the area delineated, which may be much
smaller than a census tract.

Chamber of Commerce researchers should take the lead in developing
the data management framework for their respective communities—keeping up with trends and advances in this activity area—and be prepared to
use it effectively.

2. The Data Management System

The second step in advancing research is to *develop a basic data
management system for the community with continuous collection and
processing of information.*

It can start as a simple system which produces:

   a. Files of information on a wide variety of subjects relating to the
      community,
   b. A monthly summary of business indicators,
   c. An image brochure for the community, and
   d. An economic handbook for new business and industrial prospects.

Each item of information (with an address, where applicable) in the
data management system should be linked to the geographic framework
for the area (for example, indicate the census tract corresponding to the
address of the information item). Data items in this category include
population and housing information from censuses plus such locally-
generated information as construction, demolitions, vital statistics, industrial and commercial location, crimes, diseases, accidents, customers,
subscribers.

There are good reasons for Chamber involvement in developing and
operating a community data system, whether that system is very simple in
structure and data input or is in the more advanced category. These
advantages lie in the functions of:

   a. Providing early warning—or trend alerts—for problem avoidance,
   b. Assisting in defining problems,
   c. Helping to shape the program of work of the local Chamber of
      Commerce,

---

[2]DIME is an acronym for Dual Independent Map Encoding.

    d. Maintaining control over the customization, accuracy and timeliness of community-oriented data input, and

    e. Creating dependency on the local Chamber's Research Department as the community's primary source of reliable data.

3. Expanding Research Boundaries

The third step is to *expand the subject matter boundaries of research*. In the past, much of the Chamber of Commerce research effort was centered around economic development. The fast-changing, complex communities in which Chambers must operate call for a balanced program in which research on economic, demographic and governmental subjects should be represented.

4. The Use of Computer Technology

Increasing quantities of data will be manageable due to rapid advances in computer technology. Electronic data processing equipment and applications are the most important developments in the field of data management to date. Most of the progressive sophistication of Chamber research will relate to applications of this amazing invention.

Many potential users of Electronic Data Processing seem to be partially blinded by the glamor of the output phase of a computerized project, in which buttons are pushed and printouts of tabulations and calculations magically appear. Unfortunately, some of these potential users are disappointed when they encounter the grim realities of the input side of the computerized project—the large volume of very unglamorous, tedious work necessary in the processing of data that is to emerge later as "glamorous" printouts.

The computer began rather humbly as a bookkeeper, mechanizing such tedious chores as payroll preparation and billing. It graduated quickly to more sophisticated levels of application, and now is classified as one of the most important innovations in our history.

Many Chambers of Commerce are already using computers extensively. Some of these applications are little more than modest bookkeeping procedures, while others are quite sophisticated. A partial listing of computer uses by Chambers of Commerce includes: membership records (storage, retrieval, billing, financial accounting, etc.), production of commercial and industrial directories, surveys of membership opinion, analysis of committee membership, population estimates by census tract; preparation of monthly summaries of business indicators, magazine records (addressing mail-labels, circulation control, cost-control and budgeting, advertising-account "aging" and analysis), housing studies, development of business indexes, and use of the Bureau of the Census computer packages for the Address Coding Guide and DIME programs.

Free computer service is usually available to Chambers of Commerce from such member firms as banks and utilities. Getting the job done when you want it, however, is another problem when operating on a borrowed-time basis.

Most Chambers process data to a certain stage themselves, then call in service bureaus—companies that, for a fee, make available their own computer hardware and the skill and planning necessary to operate the computer—to complete the operation.

Computers are a "must" in present Chamber of Commerce work and will be even more so in the future.

5. Planning for the Future

Future studies will become increasingly important in program of work development. The accelerating rate of change makes it imperative to plan farther ahead. To provide a sound data-base for future studies, Chamber researchers should be constantly revising demographic and economic projections.

Most communities include professionals whose fundamental interests lie in anticipating future needs: forecasters for utilities, planners of postal services and schools, transportation planners, and municipal-services developers. If these specialists are organized into a division of the Chamber's Research Committee, they can provide information for and coordinate a future-studies program.

Time-series data can plot past-to-present trend-lines with 10-year projections within the variable framework of "discontinuities" which make trend-bending impacts and disturb the continuity of trend-lines by altering the direction and rate of change. Maintaining credibility will be a continuing concern, but Chambers of Commerce must accept this challenge.

Community leadership in the years ahead will require future-studies programs inclusive of careful—and frequently updated—projections. Projections should be indicated clearly; limitations should be stated plainly. But only through self-critical use can the procedures and the data be improved, thereby increasing the effectiveness of future studies in structuring Chamber of Commerce programs of work.

6. Applications of Systems Analysis

Progress is being made in the development of a new problem-solving game plan, labeled *Systems Approach to Problems of an Urbanized Area.*

Programmers and others associated with computers use a term *"Recursive Optimization"*—which simply means starting with an objective, and then working backward to determine the steps to achieve the objective most efficiently. The Systems Approach, an expansion of this procedure, is defined as an attempt to consider simultaneously as many variables as possible relating to a problem, and then anticipating the long-run consequences of individual decisions.

The Systems Approach warrants more attention from Chambers of Commerce, and the future products of research will be important factors in this management technique.

D. SUGGESTIONS RELATING TO THE RESEARCH STAFF

It is good to raise local Chamber sights as to the future use of research—to broaden the horizons of its objectives—to visualize additional use of computers and other electronic equipment. But, in looking ahead to Chamber of Commerce research that will be required in the future, plans should be formulated now to determine the scope of this research activity and the adequacy of the research staff needed to function most effectively with its assignments.

1. Centralization of Research

The first suggestion is to *maximize Chamber of Commerce efficiency by assigning the Chamber's researcher to do the research work for all the other departments of the organization.*

"Buzz" words popular among economists include "achieving economy of scale." Paraphrased slightly, a desirable goal of a Chamber of Commerce should be to "achieve economy of specialized research skill."

Research done by staff members in each of the other departments too frequently suffers from both the insufficiency of the time that staff members can devote to research activities and their lack of familiarity with the various resource materials which would be helpful in the research project.

For additional clarification: In football why spend all the time and effort necessary to train the quarterback to pass the ball, if, during the game, all the other team members—the running specialists, the blocking specialists, the receivers—alternate at throwing passes?

If the specialized staff researcher undertakes all the research for the other staff members, the organization not only maximizes the researcher's skill but also maximizes the skills of the other staff specialists—by freeing them of the responsibility for doing research so that they may concentrate upon their respective fields of activity.

2. Utilizing In-House Personnel

The next staff suggestion is to *increase the experience and capability of the Chamber of Commerce researcher rather than hire outside specialists.*

A question that arises frequently is: Should we enlarge our research staff or hire outside specialists for the occasional jobs? If "in-house" researchers are assigned to these jobs, the Chamber staffers will:

    a. Learn more about the community,

    b. Discover additional information sources,

    c. Make new contacts with suppliers of information and prospective committee personnel,

    d. Gain experience with problem-solving techniques,

    e. Direct attention to the Chamber of Commerce as the community leader in research capability — which helps in membership maintenance and increases, and

    f. Last, but perhaps as important as any other benefit from "do-it-yourself" research: with the additional experience and research capability gained, the staff member is available immediately when the organization needs him in other similar projects.

On the other hand, if the Chamber chooses to employ outside specialists, the organization may not get what is needed when it is needed, and Chamber of Commerce funds are spent to underwrite the training and experience of other organizations that may compete with the local Chamber for operating funds in the future.

At stake is a vital issue: Should the research capability of local Chambers of Commerce be increased, or should these Chambers contribute to increasing the research capability of outside organizations? If the latter alternative is selected, the research functions required for community problem-solving will be performed by non-Chamber organizations and the local Chamber of Commerce will ultimately be reduced to the status of broker for the research done by these outside organizations. The practice of depending upon outsiders for research products is not conducive to stabilized, long-range planning and operation.

3. Allocation of Resources

The final suggestion is to recognize that *upgrading and expanding the local Chamber's research program will probably require some reallocation of the organization's resources.*

This is a painful fact to present, but any Chamber seriously intending to do a better job in research will have to provide adequate staff and funding for this activity. Something more will have to be done than to select a staff member and say, "Joe, you are responsible for Civic Affairs, World Trade, Transportation, Governmental Affairs — and, if you have time, serve as the organization's researcher."

Chambers are at the crossroads in relation to increasing their research effectiveness. Are additional funds available for this purpose? Can organizations afford to reallocate already scarce resources in order to do a better job in research? On the other hand, can they afford *not* to reallocate resources for this purpose — if the failure to do so means lagging behind aggressive competing organizations or even the Chamber's own members?

E. SUMMARY

In the past, changes in the communities served by Chambers of Commerce — changes in our programs of activities and changes in the operational tools available to us — were slow to materialize. They occurred over periods of years. And somehow they were taken into account — without unusual concentration or effort — during the preparation of Chamber of Commerce plans. Too often many of us adopted a complacent, "stay-in-the-rut" approach to planning.

Today the winds of change, blowing in subject areas of significance to Chambers of Commerce, are reaching gale proportions. They already present a constant challenge within our field of organizational service. Unless we adapt quickly and successfully to the changing times and conditions under which we operate, they will seriously threaten our Chamber of Commerce leadership images.

Reflection on the need for new techniques and procedures prompted Malcolm Hatch, executive vice president of the Pawtucket (Rhode Island) Chamber of Commerce, to write in July of 1968: "It is quite clear that in coming years local Chambers will be forced to make a decision on whether to step aside and play a relatively insignificant role in the life of the community along the traditional lines of the past, or whether they want to reassess the problems of the community and determine what they need by the way of objectives, organization, and program to achieve meaningful results."

Recent developments indicate that Chambers of Commerce are, indeed, adjusting to meet new challenges. Research has moved away from its previously limited scope of activities as a gatherer of facts to emphasize the significance and application of these facts in decision-oriented, action-oriented, problem-solving research. These changes in the structure of research functions reflect a much more widely-reported phenomenon: a shifting emphasis and orientation of Chamber programs in general to a concentration upon the new and more complex problems arising in this nation's urban areas.

Although a substantial portion of the Chamber researcher's activities continues to relate to fact gathering, research now is much broader, not only providing data, but also indicating the significance of the data, interpreting the data, and pointing the way for using this information in decision-making. It is a basic set of procedures and methods for developing solutions to community problems.

Selected Reading References

Ackoff, Russell L. *Scientific Method: Optimizing Applied Research Decisions.* New York, N.Y.: John Wiley & Sons, Inc., 1962.

American Chamber of Commerce Executives, Research Monographs. *No. 1: What is Chamber of Commerce Research?; No. 2: Chamber of Commerce Solutions Through Research; No. 3: Mobilizing Manpower for Research.* Washington, D.C.: ACCE, 1965.

Anshen, Melvin. "Fundamental and Applied Research in Marketing." *The Journal of Marketing.* Vol. 19, No. 3: 233-243.

Archer, Harry C. "Computers: Future Uses for Associations." *Association Management,* (May, 1971), 34-38.

Bower, Joseph L. "Systems Analysis for Social Decisions." *Computers and Automation,* (March, 1970), 38-42.

Brown, Hugh H. "A Technique for Estimating the Population of Counties." *American Statistical Association Journal,* (June, 1955), 323-343.

Business Management Magazine. "The Five Pillars of Long-Range Planning." (March, 1970), 18-20, 36.

Business Management Magazine. "Is There a Computer Service Bureau in Your Future?" (May 27, 1970), 26-29.

Churchman, C. West. *The Systems Approach.* New York, N.Y.: Dell Publishing Co., 1968.

Cochran, William G., Frederick Mosteller, and John W. Tukey. "Principles of Sampling." *Journal of the American Statistical Association,* Vol. 49 (March, 1954), 13-35.

Coman, Edwin T., Jr. *Sources of Business Information.* Berkeley and Los Angeles, Calif.: University of California Press, 1964.

Council of Planning Librarians. *Planning and Urban Affairs Library Manual.* Monticello, Ill.: 1970.

Dean, Neal J. "The Computer Comes of Age." *Harvard Business Review,* (January-February, 1968), 83-91.

Dearden, John. "How to Organize Information Systems." *Harvard Business Review,* (March-April, 1965), 65-73.

Erber, Ernest. *Urban Planning in Transition.* New York, N.Y.: Grossman Publishers, 1970.

Fiock, L. R., Jr. "Seven Deadly Dangers in EDP." *Harvard Business Review,* (May-June, 1962), 88-96.

Forrester, Jay W. "What's Wrong with Today's Research?" *Management Review,* (April, 1966), 51-55.

Gruenberger, Fred. *Expanding Use of Computers in the 70's.* Englewood Cliffs, N.J.: Prentice-Hall, Inc., 1971.

Hajnal, John. "The Prospects for Population Forecasts." *American Statistical Association Journal,* (June, 1955), 309-322.

Hartley, Harry J. "12 Hurdles To Clear Before You Take On Systems Analysis." *Journal of Systems Management,* (June, 1969), 28-29.

Head, Robert V. "Information Systems: The Changing Scene." *Journal of Systems Management,* (April, 1969), 40-41.

Herrmann, Cyril C. "Systems Approach to City Planning." *Harvard Business Review,* (September-October, 1966), 71-80.

Hofer, Charles W. "Emerging EDP Pattern." *Harvard Business Review,* (March-April, 1970), 16-18, 20-22, 26-31, 169-171.

Holm, Bart E. *How to Manage Your Information.* New York, N.Y.: Reinhold Book Corporation, 1968.

Johnson, John W. *Associations and the Computer.* Washington, D.C.: Chamber of Commerce of the United States, 1970.

Liston, David, Jr. "Information Systems: What They Do, How They Work." *Management Review,* (September, 1966), 68-72.

Luck, David J. "Education for Marketing Research." *The Journal of Marketing,* Vol. 14, No. 3: 385-390.

MacLean, John D. "Choosing Between In-House and Service Bureau." *Management Controls,* (September, 1970).

National Association of Business Economists, Committee on Recruitment and Placement. *Business Economics Careers.* Washington, D.C.: NABE, 1968.

Population Reference Bureau, Inc. *The World Population Dilemma.* Washington, D.C.: Columbia Books, Inc., 1972.

Rigby, Paul H. *Conceptual Foundations of Business Research.* New York, N.Y.: John Wiley & Sons, Inc., 1965.

Shaeffer, Ruth G. "Systems in Managing Change." *The Conference Board Record,* (August, 1970), 48-51.

Shorter, Edward. *The Historian and the Computer*. Englewood Cliffs,
N.J.: Prentice-Hall, Inc., 1971.

Silk, Leonard S., and M. Louise Curley. *A Primer on Business Forecasting*. New York, N.Y.: Random House, Inc., 1970.

Smalter, Donald J., and Rudy L. Ruggles, Jr. "Six Business Lessons
from the Pentagon." *Harvard Business Review*, (March-April, 1966),
64-75.

Stich, Robert S. "Pitfalls To Systems Management." *Management
International Review*, 1970, Vol. 10, No. 1: 19-22.

Stockton, John R., and Charles T. Clark. *Introduction to Business and
Economic Statistics*. 4th Edition. Cincinnati, Ohio: South-Western
Publishing Co., 1971.

System Development Corporation. *A Geographic Base File for Urban
Data Systems*. Santa Monica, Calif.: SDC, 1969.

Thimm, Alfred L. "General Systems Theory: A Tool for Social Analysis." *Journal of Systems Management*, (October, 1970), 16-21.

U.S. Bureau of the Census. *Handbook of Statistical Methods for Demographers*, by A. J. Jaffe. Washington, D.C.: U.S. Government
Printing Office, 1951.

U.S. Bureau of the Census. *Census Tract Manual*, Fifth Edition. Washington, D.C.: U.S. Government Printing Office, 1966.

U.S. Bureau of the Census. *Some Uses of Census Tracts in Private
Business*, by Wilbur McCann. Washington, D.C.: U.S. Government
Printing Office, 1967.

U.S. Bureau of the Census. *1970 Census Users' Guide*. Washington,
D.C.: U.S. Government Printing Office, 1970.

U.S. Bureau of the Census. *Census Use Study: Data Uses in Urban
Planning*, Report No. 9. Washington, D.C.: U.S. Government
Printing Office, 1970.

U.S. Department of Commerce, Economic Development Administration.
*A Bibliography of Resource Materials in the Field of Regional
Economic Development*. Washington, D.C.: U.S. Government Print-
ing Office, 1966.

U.S. Department of Health, Education and Welfare. *Handbook of Sta-
tistical Procedures for Long-Range Projections of Public Enrollment*,
Office of Education Technical Monograph OE-2417, by A. J. Jaffe.
Washington, D.C.: U.S. Government Printing Office, 1969.

Wilemon, David. "Transferring Space-Age Management Technology." *The Conference Board Record*, (October, 1970), 50-55.

2 RESEARCH PROGRAMS FOR LOCAL CHAMBERS OF COMMERCE

A. INTRODUCTION

Almost all research programs in Chambers of Commerce throughout the country have suffered the conflicts of identity crisis. Why is it here? What is it supposed to be doing? How can it be done? It is from this uncertainty—not knowing where to start—that some researchers have been sidetracked as mere fact gatherers, isolated in remote corners of the organizational program. For others, these questions have led to programs in areas of research nonexistent 20 years ago and continue to stimulate development of newer and better tools, techniques, methods—and research applications.

The effective research program is an active effort, generating projects and information that contribute prominently to decisions made relative to community growth and expansion—be it planning for the future, problem identification, problem solving, or presenting a profile of the community to prospective business and industrial residents. The crucial point is that there is a great deal more to research than operating an answering service. But the optimal role of research cannot be fulfilled without a well-defined, carefully-constructed research program.

There exists no single comprehensive research program that is universally applicable to all Chambers of Commerce. Problems and their respective solutions are unique to each community; no two are identical. Among the variable factors distinguishing one region from another are each city's age, size, demography, government, resources, attitudes, and geography, to mention but a few. The particular combination of assets and liabilities in each region will distinguish it from any other, thereby making the Chamber's corresponding duties unique.

The problems of the nation's eastern industrial centers, for example, differ considerably from those of the relatively younger communities of the South, Southwest, and Far West. In the East, the critical problems requiring continuous solution are population congestion, economic stagnation,

17

traffic strangulation, lack of usable land area for expansion, and the inherent problems of aging cities. In the newer cities of the Southwest and Far West, these problems are in more embryonic stages and can be minimized over the longer term, and the cities have time to incorporate preventive solutions in their growth and to take appropriate action. Even with the "breathing room" afforded by this time lag, however, the need for these cities to keep up with the surging population growth and plan for the future is immediate.

In addition to the continuing growing pains every city feels, there are the sporadic, unpredictable crises which affect every community at one time or another; these, too, need solutions. When they arise, the local Chamber of Commerce must call upon all of its available resources, human and otherwise, in an effort to build an adjusted program that can contribute to the solutions of these unexpected problems. Such problems could be the impending removal of an important government facility, the loss of a contract by a company important to the community, or proposed state legislation which could harm the local economy. Whatever problems may arise, the Chamber should have an organized framework within which it can work for a solution.

In order to begin the discussion of procedures involved in establishing a workable program of research, assume that you, a new staff member of a local Chamber of Commerce, have been assigned the task of developing the research program from the ground up. Where do you begin? What are you attempting to achieve and how will you do it? What are the steps, and in what order should you take them?

B. STEP-BY-STEP DEVELOPMENT OF A RESEARCH PROGRAM

1. Study Your Own Chamber of Commerce

In your position as the Chamber researcher, you are a member of the organizational crew—a synergistic system in which all components work together to produce results. To understand your role in the performance of the total Chamber duties, you must have a solid conception of how the components function individually and how they work together as a Chamber of Commerce. It is also necessary to have an over-view of the organization's goals, objectives, strengths, and weaknesses. Part of this knowledge will come with time and exposure, but a great deal can be learned by the kind of comprehensive study which is requisite to properly carrying out future duties.

Once you, the researcher, are aware of the overall goals and program of the Chamber, you can develop some idea of how best to contribute to the achievement of the stated organizational goals. The research department should be tailor-made to work well within the confines of the organizational structure and to supplement the activities of the entire staff.

2. Study the Community Served by the Local Chamber of Commerce

Know your community. This procedural step is obvious, but it is so important that it must be reiterated frequently. For a Chamber to actually fill a need, its staff must be intimately aware of community goals and capabilities and must try to achieve some kind of harmony with them. This approach applies to providing business services and promotional information as well as to working in civic and cultural affairs, education and welfare, community planning, governmental activities, and other areas of interest to various segments of the community.

While the Chamber is funded through memberships from the business community, it is becoming widely recognized that the Chamber has obligations beyond those to any limited group or sector. In this age of rising interest in consumer rights, social welfare responsibilities, and ecological concern, Chambers of Commerce must not allow themselves to become labeled as responsive to only one segment of the population. To neglect broader considerations is to sacrifice their credibility. This is not to say that Chambers should not devote much of their time and effort to business and economic considerations, but, rather, they also have other responsibilities which cannot be ignored.

The shift in community emphasis has put yet more pressure on the researcher to broaden his research activities. Whereas he could once limit himself to studies in a particular field, he must now serve different and often opposing interests and objectively reconcile the differences as best he can. This task demands a thorough knowledge of community needs and a sensitivity to public attitude.

3. Prepare a Preliminary Program of Research Activities

An early phase in the development of a work program for the research department is preparation of a preliminary written activity outline. A common practice used by some researchers in embarking upon their own programs is to contact other Chamber research managers and examine the programs which have worked elsewhere and the specific component activities of these programs. While this method provides an excellent approach to program development, it has its built-in pitfalls. The inherent individuality of each city's problems and assets should be recognized. Those projects and studies which benefit economic or community development in one city might be totally ineffective in another, and are expensive in opportunity costs besides. Chambers operate with limited staffs and budgets, and every project or activity attempted means at least three or four others must be neglected for lack of time and facilities. The Chamber researcher must insure that every activity undertaken by his staff is tailored to community needs and that it will be productive as well as rewarding in terms of costs and benefits.

The preparation of a preliminary program of research activities is only the start of creating an operative research program. The researcher's program will certainly need to be revised as it becomes functional and as the abilities and limitations of the research committee and the research staff— plus requirements of the local Chamber and the community—become apparent. The idea of this step is not to produce a massive list of departmental activities, but merely to give direction to the staff and committee members. Once the department actually begins working toward completion of early projects, the program can be modified to more closely specify its objectives and the goals may be either broadened or narrowed as circumstances indicate.

4. Begin to Assemble Reference Materials Needed in the Research Program

An important preliminary step in the implementation of a research program is the assembly of a research library. This activity is described in Chapter Three, and its significance cannot be too strongly emphasized.

Since your role as a researcher is to develop information that can effectively answer most questions your department will receive, you will need all the data you can obtain. Though a search of published material is the usual method employed in obtaining information essential to research operations, there are times when data must be obtained by other means. Such methods include surveys, contacts with compilers of various types of community-oriented data, and correspondence with persons or organizations who are familiar with the subject being researched.

Another significant activity—one recommended for early scheduling— is planning for the continuous compilation of raw data and basic facts about the community. This information should be stored within the Chamber's Research Department, thus establishing the Chamber as an authoritative information clearinghouse for the whole community and the surrounding region. The types of information that should be collected include: bank data, building permits, new residential electrical connections, electric and gas sales, payrolls, department store sales, retail and wholesale sales, motor vehicle registrations, telephone data, transportation and traffic data, cost of living index, employment and unemployment statistics, population characteristics, school enrollments, taxes and valuations, vital statistics (births, deaths, marriages), and public welfare expenditures.

5. Organize a Research Committee

Chamber research operations are influenced by the area or region they serve and by the recognition, direction and support provided by the rest of the organization and the community. These same influences also help to determine the composition and direction of the Research Committee.

For a Research Committee to make a meaningful contribution to the organization, it should be of modest size, usually around 15 to 25 members for the smaller and medium-sized Chambers. The size of the committee will of course vary with the size of the community, and may reach 75 or 100 members for the larger cities. Too many members will make the Committee unwieldy to operate, and too few will not give a good performance or an adequate cross-sectional representation.

Despite a tendency among Chambers of Commerce to seek widespread participation from their membership, the Research Committee should be restricted to those persons possessing professional backgrounds in economics, finance, statistics, report writing, and business analysis. Quality, rather than quantity, should be the prime criterion for this important segment of your operations — and productivity should be the goal.

The recognized professional authorities from within a Chamber's membership can be the best initial talent source for committee participation. The membership criterion should not be rigid, however, since other qualified candidates may be drawn from such non-Chamber sources as state and federal agencies. Experience indicates that research directors of banks, insurance companies, universities, utilities and consulting firms are also excellent candidates. The committee structure should also include expert representation from each major economic sector in the local community, such as a port authority or a particularly concentrated industry.

Although a Research Committee serving a local Chamber is primarily an advisory group, it should also be adaptable, able to take on special projects that may create a heavy staff workload or require a particular expertise. Such a need might arise for the preparation of location proposals for a government, industrial, or commercial center. Other projects beyond department capabilities will arise periodically, and the Committee should be available as needed.

In the normal course of activities, the Research Committee will provide the staff with advice, experience, and direction for the completion of the research program. The committee as a whole can also serve as editor of department publications. Materials for such reviews usually should be distributed to the committee members in advance of their next meeting so that comments and revisions can be offered at that gathering.

The Research Committee is a sounding board for the Research Department on priority projects. The members' reactions and advice can save many wasted hours and dollars on projects which would not have been worthy of a major investment. The members can also bring to light other subjects more deserving of the staff's attention. These and other roles for the committee will be evident as the program develops from its formative stages.

6. Intensify Efforts to Develop a Research Information System

Once the groundwork for research activities has been laid, it is advisable to begin construction of a total information system which will perform the functions mentioned in Chapter 1. After the geographic framework for researching the data on a small-area basis has been determined, the researcher should next begin collecting information and assembling files on subjects of special interest to the community. More complete lists of subjects about which data may eventually be collected can be found in Chapter Eight, "Monthly Summary of Business Indicators," and Chapter 13, "Economic Handbook." Remember that these are *suggested* subjects, ones which might only eventually be studied and included in the total system after the staff has developed some expertise in research and as the need arises.

7. With Assistance of the Research Committee, Revise the Research Program of Work

The building of a Chamber of Commerce work program is nothing more or less than community planning, in which the local organization should keep pace with, if not stay ahead of, public thinking.[1] This is especially true in the functioning of a Research Department, where the Chamber researcher must stay ahead of public thinking and the concomitant information requirements. His mission: lead the course of change, rather than being led by it. It is the researcher who must decide which facts will be of most use to the Chamber membership and to the rest of the community in analysis, planning, and decision-making. It may be stated generally that the specific objectives of a written program of research activities include:

   a. *Charting the future course of research activities.* By establishing certain guideposts and directing the thinking energies of the staff, a program can eliminate much lost motion. This planning can also help cut out digressive efforts that stray outside the area of original Chamber interest.

   b. *Providing a checklist for research performance.* The final value of

---

[1]W. Marvin Hurley, *Chamber of Commerce Administration,* Chicago: National Institute for Commercial and Trade Organization Executives, Second Printing 1947, p. 31.

research is measured by what it actually accomplishes for community betterment. On a year-to-year basis, a research program of work may be balanced against realized accomplishments as a measure of departmental achievement.

c. *Helping to sell the Chamber of Commerce to its membership.* Without planning and organization, each of the departments and, ultimately, the Chamber itself will become inefficient and ineffectual. An organization which fragments its efforts will not survive long. A carefully delineated research program, with recognizable and achievable goals, which establishes a framework for its own operation, is an excellent incentive for community support and involvement, and will convince many hardened disbelievers that the Chamber is a worthwhile, functioning organization.

Finally, it must be remembered that in planning the work program, as in all other Research Department activities, flexibility is mandatory. The purpose of a work program is to set guideposts for performance, not merely to specify certain projects and techniques which cannot later be changed. As a researcher, you must be able to shuffle priorities as needed to deal with problems as they arise—and problems will arise because of the nature of the work. Circumstances seldom reflect expectations, as it is impossible to foresee all of the special projects and answers to information requests that must be provided. The researcher must be able to concentrate his efforts on a single problem, follow it through as best he can, and then go on to something else. This process will certainly be a lot easier if allowances have been made for it in the structuring of the total work program.

In addition to building flexibility into the program, the researcher should structure the program so that it can be reviewed, and—if necessary—revised or refined on a periodic basis. Annual review allows readjustment of the goals and activities of the staff to follow changes in organization and community direction. While some research department efforts will be directed toward completion of long-term, continuing projects which will appear in the program from year to year, there must be sufficient latitude for addition or deletion of supplementary activities as needed. The Research Committee will play an especially important part in this process, as its inputs are a catalyst for change. Without community participation from committee members, there is a danger of the department becoming isolated and unresponsive to community trends, locked into providing unused or out-dated services.

For an example of the *suggested format* of a research program for a local Chamber of Commerce, please refer to Exhibit 2-A. This combination of activities is not necessarily recommended for any local Chamber. This program is presented as a guideline or suggested outline for writing a program of research activities.

8. Plan Your Research Strategy

The Chamber of Commerce researcher works with a variety of research tools, techniques, and methods. The distinction of terms here may seem inconsequential, but has been made to emphasize the logical procedure that must be followed in the course of a study from its inception to its completion. For example: an adding machine, a filing system, a library, and a computer are all tools. Each might have a system, but each is ultimately a tool. The use of the computer to collect and compute adjusted time-series data, the collection of community data on separate sheets for later use, and the employment of formulas, such as those for retail trade area delineation (see Chapter 15), are all techniques. The application of computerized seasonally adjusted information to the preparation of a local business index, the assembling of an economic handbook from separate data sheets, and the collection of statistics into a monthly summary are all methods. The method represents a larger sector — than tools and techniques — of the researcher's problem-solving strategy.

Each of these seemingly arbitrary categories plays an important part in the development and enactment of a research program. Though the methods or approaches are decided upon first in response to a need, they cannot become reality without foundation techniques whose existence is predicated upon the existence of research tools. As a kingdom was lost for want of a nail, so too can a research program be lost for want of proper basic tools. The tools and techniques of a program are highly-significant factors in a research project.

The sum of the researcher's total activities in pursuit of an answer to a problem has been defined variously as the research design, the research process, or the research approach. The Chamber researcher should develop a general pattern of activity — whatever he calls it — to serve as a guide for completion of his projects. Any steps taken by him, any procedures followed, should not be performed randomly, but should fit into a logical sequence of events in a master plan or model for the conduct of an investigation.

A five-part definition of Chamber of Commerce research is mentioned in Chapter One. The components of this definition are described here to emphasize their importance as guidelines for the Chamber researcher as he plans his research strategy — the steps to be followed in a research project.

a. *Problem formulation*

A problem of concern to the Research Department may have existed for some time, it may be one of the "pop up" or "crash" nature that needs resolving immediately, or it may be one that has only recently become recognized through examination of the accumulating data in the research information system. Regardless of its origin, clearly outlining a problem's nature and the purpose of its study is a very important first step in undertaking a research project focused on it. The problem should be delineated carefully, along with the circumstances which brought attention to it and the means by which it could be resolved. What are you trying to attain by this research project? What are your specific goals?

A good way to begin a study is by finding out what is already known about the problem and what information is available that might save time and mistakes in a similar study of your own. Surveying literature for guidance and assistance should involve examination of both internal and external sources. Internal sources are those available in your own library, or which have already been prepared by other staff members of the local Chamber for use in a related study.

External sources include other organizations and agencies which have collected associated data. Theses written by graduate students in nearby universities will be helpful. Another valuable source includes published materials — books, monographs, articles — in libraries available to you.

The researcher's next task is to identify the components of his problem. This phase involves making sure that he understands the parameters of the problem, that he has in mind a profile of the problem environment, and that he has listed the variables which may affect the outcome of his investigation.

At this stage of his problem formulation the researcher should plan courses of action. What are the alternatives? What should be done to achieve his objectives? It is recommended that the researcher outline his procedure, step-by-step, to produce a research design, a framework, or model for guidance in subsequent investigation.

b. Data collection

The next major activity phase on the researcher's outline of his investigation is to compile data relating to the problem, the decision to be made, or the results to be achieved. Fact-gathering should be methodically organized. Information collected should relate to the investigative framework referred to in the preceding discussion of problem formulation.

There are two general types of data — secondary and primary. Secondary, or data already available, include published materials, government statistics, unpublished reports, and internal statistics and records. Secondary materials should be explored first, since this type of information, in most instances, will reduce the cost of the study considerably.

If secondary data are not available, then the researcher must turn to primary data — which he must assemble from original sources. This type of information is collected through mail questionnaires, personal and telephone interviews, observations and experiments.

A mass of unorganized information will have limited value in a research design. The collected data, therefore, should be systematized — arranged into groups on the basis of a specific type of relationship. The items included in one group will share certain characteristics that separate them from the items in other groups. There are numerous ways in which data may be classified, including these common groups: chronological (time-series), geographical, alphabetical, magnitude (size of item), differences of kind or type, and differences of degree of a characteristic (quantitative).

c. Analysis and interpretation

At this point the researchers are separated from the fact-gatherers. The processing of the data might include sampling, adjusting for seasonal variation, preparing index numbers, measuring relationships by computing coefficients of correlation, preparing link relatives, using the "least squares" principle in time-series analysis, or involvement in any other procedures that may be appropriate. The significance of the processed data should be illustrated by means of visual aids (charts, graphs, slides, etc.) and narrative comments.

d. Publication

Publish the results of this project and make sure that the research report is directed to the attention of appropriate decision-makers. A suggested outline for this report might include the following features:

(1) Title page;
(2) Letter of transmittal, foreword or preface — including a brief summary of the results of the study;
(3) Description of the framework of the investigation, including
    (a) Objectives,
    (b) Variables (that may affect outcome of the investigation),
    (c) Courses of action (steps taken in the investigation),
    (d) Data collection and usage,
    (e) Application of research tools, techniques, and methods,
    (f) Analysis and interpretation of data;
(4) Detailed presentation of findings;
(5) Recommendations; and
(6) Technical appendices and supplementary tables.

e. Implementation

The researcher's responsibility does not end with the completion of a report on his research. Just as an architect is a vital factor in implementing his plans for a building, so must the researcher fulfill his obligation to implement the results of his study. The researcher knows how the investigation was done, what information was used, and how the results were achieved. He understands the results and can be uniquely useful in the implementation of his research project.

At this point the researcher becomes a consultant. Actions in applying the results of his research could include:

(1) Assisting the chief executive officer or other staff personnel to

select the most appropriate alternative course(s) developed by his research;

(2) Helping the chief executive officer shape the general program of the local Chamber of Commerce; and

(3) Consulting with businessmen and others who visit the local Chamber's office to seek the researcher's guidance in decision-making activities.

9. Select Activities for a Research Program

Your written research program of work serves as a chart for future activities. To help you prepare this program, a list of suggested research activities is presented in Appendix A.

There are three important points to keep in mind while using this list. First, the items listed constitute *only a few* of the "things to do" that might have been included here. Second, these items have been *selected* to *represent* the types of research activities.

The third point is that none of the items in this list *necessarily* involves the use of all of the five parts of the Research Process described in Step Eight. Some of these items relate to the preparation of research tools and techniques; many involve several parts of the Research Process. For example, the publication of a Directory of Manufacturers will involve problem formulation, data collection, and publication. The published directory may then be used by the researcher, or another member of the Chamber staff, in analysis and interpretation and — ultimately — implementation, to sell a prospect on locating in the local area.

For another illustration, note that a Population Characteristics Study involves problem formulation, data collection, analysis and interpretation, and publication. Additional analysis and interpretation may precede the implementation of this completed study in a wide variety of people-oriented problems.

Additionally the preparation of a Local Business Index involves the first four parts of the Research Process. In the implementation stage it may be used in many types of decisions related to business conditions and trends.

An appropriate description applicable to most of the items shown on this list might be "research expediters." Nearly all of these items involve part of the Research Process and are themselves used at certain stages in various types of research projects.

Examine the *selected, representative* activities shown in Appendix A and pick out the items that seem most appropriate for your program. Begin your research program slowly, of course, and do not try to initiate too many activities too soon. It is better to do a good job with a few activities and expand your program gradually.

EXHIBIT 2-A
SUGGESTED FORMAT OF A PROGRAM
OF RESEARCH ACTIVITIES

Note: This program of research activities is not necessarily applicable to any local Chamber of Commerce. It is shown here only to suggest the outline or format for writing a program of this type.

CENTRAL CITY CHAMBER OF COMMERCE
RESEARCH COMMITTEE PROGRAM OF WORK
1974

COMMITTEE MISSION

Collect, organize, interpret and publish information relating to the Central City region economy. This information has many uses in planning and decision-making for environmental improvement, and in expanding and strengthening this region's industrial and commercial fabric.

TEN-YEAR OBJECTIVES

- Maximize flexibility in activities of the committee and departmental staff to meet new requirements for research in the Seventies and to assist other Chamber of Commerce committees that may need research in their respective areas of activity.
- Provide leadership in the establishment and operation of a regional data bank that will expedite the collecting and retrieving of needed information.
- Develop electronic data processing capabilities and systems within the departmental offices, including the installation of small computers.
- Expand departmental capabilities to provide for special emphasis upon the preparation of major directories and other publications.

CENSUS TRACT DIVISION

Act as coordinator for a special census data-users conference to be held in early spring.

> Objective: Since the use of data by small areas is essential in various types of community analysis and problem-solving activities, users of the data must be informed of the many features of recent computerized censuses.

CONSTRUCTION DIVISION

Through a series of meetings, provide a forum for the exchange of important information related to developments and trends in the construction industry in the Central City region. Publish the following periodical reports on a definite time schedule: New Residential Building Permits by Census

Tract, Frequency Distribution of New Residential Building Permits by Permit Value, and New Residential Electrical Connections by Census Tract.

>Objective: These reports are published monthly. They provide new and comparative data related to Central City's current economic activity by small areas for use in business planning and operations. The meetings of this Division furnish a clearinghouse for timely information pertaining to new investment in Central City's expanding economy.

ECONOMIC NEWSLETTER DIVISION

Provide data for the Economic Newsletter that appears monthly in Central City Magazine.

>Objective: Provide specialized information. This feature of the Central City Magazine provides analysis and interpretation of Central City economic news to increase the utility of this information for planning purposes.

ECONOMIC OUTLOOK DIVISION

Organize the "Central City Outlook '75" Conference (January, 1975).

>Objective: Forecast Central City-area economic conditions and trends for 1975.

MANUFACTURING DIVISION

Publish a 1974-75 edition of the Central City Area Manufacturers Directory.

>Objective: Provide a complete inventory of manufacturing operations in the eight-county, Central City-centered industrial complex. Compiled by a firm-by-firm survey by the Research Committee, the listings of producing plants in this directory will be the most complete and accurate available for analysis of manufacturing in the Central City area.

MARKETING DIVISION

Compile and publish reports from the latest decennial Census data.

>Objective: Improve availability of information. Use of data by small areas is essential in various types of community analyses and problem-solving activities.

Report Central City prices for the ACCRA Inter-City Cost of Living Index.

>Objective: The American Chamber of Commerce Researchers Association, with the cooperation of local Chambers of Commerce, publishes an Inter-city Cost of Living Index as a meaningful measurement of differences in living costs between cities. Reports of the Index are available through subscriptions.

POPULATION DIVISION

Continue the annual population studies in cooperation with the independent school districts in Central County.

Objective: All of the school districts in Central County participate in this annual study. Population information provided by the school districts is used in preparing population estimates by census tract.

OTHER ACTIVITIES

Plan for the additional use of electronic data processing equipment in the work of the Research Committee.

Objective: A fast reaction capability with information. In the Seventies, individuals and organizations in various sectors of local socio-economic activity will perform unprecedented services in relating social statistical measurements to economic data in planning and problem-solving projects. Reduction of time lag between occurrence of social and economic activity and the publication of relating indicators will be more desirable. This need for a timely flow of significant data will require additional utilization of electronic data processing and the installation of small computers in the Chamber of Commerce offices.

Prepare briefs and exhibits to document Central City's position in various types of proceedings, such as air service cases.

Objective: Enhance Central City's interests. This is one of the Research Department's most challenging responsibilities. In blueprinting a program of activities, therefore, this department practices flexibility in organization and activities so that the departmental staff and facilities may be concentrated on the preparation of supporting briefs and exhibits when the need arises.

Publish a 1974 edition of the Central City Facts Brochure.

Objective: Disseminate information about Central City. The Research Department presents thumbnail facts about a wide range of Central City area subjects in this brochure. Copies are mailed to those who write to the Central City Chamber of Commerce requesting general information about Central City.

Publish summaries of general industrial and commercial development data.

Objective: Provide summary data on the economic growth of the Central City area. The reports will highlight developments occurring over a 10-year period.

Publish a Directory of Research Publications.

Objective: Catalog research publications as a convenient guide to the most recent Central City-area economic data.

Part II

INFORMATION
SYSTEMS

3 RESEARCH LIBRARY

A. INTRODUCTION

In this age of revolution in technological development and managerial skills, business and industrial leaders are intensifying their search to learn more about their own operations and those of their competitors at home and abroad, and in so doing have created an information explosion that is rocking library science. Vast quantities of information which has been sorted, catalogued, microfilmed, and computerized for quick and easy retrieval by the busy executive are now being generated as well as collected by highly specialized libraries. Thus a new era in library technology has sprung up in the last decade, paralleling the sophistication of technologies in almost every conceivable business and industry.

There are four general classifications of libraries: school libraries, college and university libraries, public libraries and special libraries. A special library is one which is established to meet the complex and sophisticated informational needs of a specific organization. Special libraries exist in industry, banks, trade and professional organizations and government. Despite the diversity of their parent institutions, they have in common a limited subject scope and a size small by public library standards. The research library of a Chamber of Commerce is a special library.

With the tremendous growth of economic and statistical research, more and more business organizations have found it necessary to establish and maintain access to sources of economic information. In some cases companies have developed large research operations capable of handling most questions. Other companies maintain much smaller research staffs which compile limited collections of reference works. Many of the companies unable to afford any research staff of their own have found that membership in their Chamber of Commerce is an open door to the stores of information they might need. While the primary responsibility of a local Chamber's research library is to serve internal research personnel and other staff representatives, Chambers of Commerce generally have welcomed the opportunity to accept responsibilities as community consultants. This job is not, however, an easy one.

As is emphasized in Chapters 2 and 13 and is implicit in this book as a whole, a Chamber of Commerce Research Department—or the researcher in a smaller Chamber—must maintain a continuing and workable research information system to adequately fulfill its assigned responsibilities. The research library, in conducting the collection and transfer of resource materials, is the hub of this information system. Its effectiveness is maximized by the particularity of its clientele, but it is still the task of the researcher to maintain this effectiveness by building a collection of the most useful source materials his budget will allow.

As used throughout this chapter, the term "library" is applicable to library sizes (volume count) varying from a shelf or two of books in the office of the Chamber of Commerce with a one-man staff up the scale to the very large Chamber with a separately housed research library.

B. NEED FOR RESEARCH LIBRARY

The person who answers questions for a small organization may face numerous inquiries on a wide range of subjects. It is only realistic to admit that he will be able to extemporaneously answer no more than a small number of the questions that come to him. Answering the remainder can be time-consuming and extremely expensive in terms of man-hours and opportunity costs. To complicate the problem further, the researcher frequently acts as such only on a part-time basis, his other duties thus constantly being balanced against time expended in handling inquiries. It is critical that he have orderly access to a variety of information resources.

It can be assumed that in every city there is an increasing demand for the services provided by the Chamber research library. It is expected to function as a repository for information which serves its business and industrial members effectively and to be of use to the citizens of the community. Chamber officers, committees, and staff, industry and commerce, civic organizations, and—in many instances—government offices and private individuals depend upon the Chamber research library for complete, updated, accurate information in many fields with which they are—or possibly will be—concerned. The library collection, to be of value, must be kept current in pertinent areas of immediate and future Chamber interest.

The success of the library entirely depends upon the quality and volume of the information available and its accessibility to users. In a general research library, inquiries reflect wide variations in subject, depth of interest, approach, and familiarity with library materials and methods, making the overall library function that of a bibliographic apparatus which assists in identifying relevant materials. It is this apparatus, along with a reference service to aid inquirers in using resource materials, that makes the library a viable extension of the Chamber into the community.

Obviously, there is a tremendous demand for efficient operation. Efficiency in furnishing information requires two capacities: knowledge of available sources of information and maintenance of access to these sources. It is generally a longer and harder job to find out where the information is than to obtain it once it has been located; hence, the emphasis in this chapter is on the information sources and how to use them.

Assuming that the researcher may not have the facilities for making an original statistical study to answer each specific question, he has two possible choices in handling the inquiry. (1) He may answer from his own knowledge — the ideal solution, but also the most unlikely. (2) He may seek the answer from sources in his possession. It is in this latter respect that the well-prepared researcher can best establish his department's credibility as a data bank. The better equipped and the better organized his library, the more likely the researcher is to successfully answer these questions. No Chamber can expect to have enough references to answer every question. The degree of formality and extent of the information collection depends entirely upon the size of the Chamber membership, the staff size, the needs of both — plus budgeted funds. But with some careful planning the researcher can get the most mileage out of his budget.

The research library is the very heart of a research information system. Before any information can be collected, categorized, assembled, printed, distributed, and implemented by any or all of the other Chamber departments, it first must be centrally located and sufficiently well arranged for anyone to be able to use the available data with minimum trouble.

It is no secret that the most inexpensive way to obtain information is to read it. Every Chamber has a collection of helpful handbooks, catalogs, magazines, and books throughout its offices — but herein the problem. There is a need to find this information quickly. Frequently, in answering the numerous questions daily coming into the offices, staff members remember seeing some item that would give them the information they seek but do not recall where the information is or who may have it. This problem could be solved quickly and simply if the Chamber were to have a research library in which information, even if it were not catalogued, would at least be collected in a single area and thus made more available to those who need it.

A catalogued library saves costs by eliminating duplicated research. A competent librarian — or a regular staff member who serves that function part-time — who is aware of Chamber operation is able to prepare abstracts for the different departments in anticipation of their needs. A central information specialist can expedite staff research work in several ways. He serves as a clearinghouse for information so that time will not be wasted performing a study someone else has already done. He stays current on what other Chambers are doing in certain areas and uses this knowledge to improve his organization's information system.

C. DESIGNATED RESEARCH LIBRARIAN

A research library without a librarian — part-time, at least — or someone is familiar with the information it contains is merely a collection of materials. It is the librarian who makes the collection meaningful. His job involves selection, arrangement and classification of materials, subject indexing, and devising a method by which to keep track of various publications so that they are readily available to the other departments and members.

The designated research librarian[1] can supply answers to the majority of inquiries and maintain contact with the most frequent users and suppliers of information. For a small Chamber, the part-time librarian might, in addition to his non-library duties, simply see that publications are ordered as needed, catalogued, and stored in some central location. In a larger Chamber, the librarian should review publishers' announcements and distribute them to the interested staff. To facilitate access to the collection, he should catalogue material as it is received. He could prepare announcements of new acquisitions, compile selective bibliographies of titles which form a cohesive collection of material on a particular subject, and maintain such special collections as maps, films, and documents.

The librarian's functions under ideal circumstances may be summarized as follows:

1. To maintain current familiarity with the material in his collection.
2. To have knowledge of the sources from which information may be collected.
3. To keep in touch with other Chamber libraries and sources of information in order to fill requests for materials in other fields.
4. To see that staff members have the information they need when it is requested.

---

[1]For convenience the term "librarian" is used in this chapter in referring generally to the personnel responsible for operating Chamber of Commerce research libraries. A librarian may be the Chamber manager who is the only staff member in his organization or a Research Department staffer with either part-time or full-time library responsibilities.

D. ESTABLISHING A LIBRARY

When planning the library, the Chamber researcher must be aware of the types of information the staff and members will want. A daily log of inquiries should be kept and reviewed on a reasonably regular schedule so that certain basic research materials can be anticipated, maintained, and updated.

Generally speaking, it is almost impossible to gather *too much* research information on the area your Chamber is serving. It is a rare day when a Chamber answers all of the inquiries in its files. However, the worth of any material must be continually measured in light of its purchase and storage expense.

The research library, large or small, requires the following:

1. Adequate space, centrally located and convenient to all the staff. If at all feasible, room should be left for expansion. Any library, to do its job, must grow.
2. Equipment such as shelves, filing cabinets, and typewriters.
3. A budget allotment for books, periodicals, and supplies.
4. A librarian — part-time or full-time — to care for the library, at least during assigned hours.
5. A definite set of rules and regulations for the use of the library.

It is recommended to avoid "over-gathering" material in the beginning. Research library materials must be geared to fit the Chamber's needs, so the initial information must be collected, ordered, assimilated and made ready for use before more is acquired.

Chamber research, at any level, is based partially on knowing where to obtain required information. This is why Chambers get more inquiries about more subjects than any other kind of organization, private or public. People have need for varied information, but have little knowledge of where to find it.

It is advisable for persons who conduct research to make periodic inspections of their research material in order that they can be totally familiar with the content and quality. The more systematically the researcher arranges his information sources, the more quickly he can get his answers. This does not necessarily mean cross-indexing the library, because in a small library such a detail is often superfluous. It does mean systematically maintaining files of frequently used material.

E. OUTLINE OF REFERENCE MATERIALS FOR A RESEARCH LIBRARY

Since the library collection reflects the past, current and future interests of the local Chamber's membership, officers and staff, the librarian should keep a constant incoming flow of materials in the areas of traffic and transportation, civic affairs, business and industrial development, world trade, governmental affairs, and other activity areas represented in the Chamber's program of work. Lists of suggested publications useful in developing a Chamber research library are presented in Exhibits 3-A and 3-B. The materials listed in Exhibit 3-A constitute a minimum or beginning library for a research program. Exhibit 3-B is a supplementary list of bibliographies and publications catalogs in which the researcher will find lists of reference books and other source materials that may be added as needed for expansions in the Chamber's program of research activities.

Statistical material published in books and magazines is generally at least a few weeks old. More current material is available from newspapers, press releases, and similar sources. A systematic filing system can be a great help in keeping abreast of this material. For example, the weekly wholesale price index is published every Friday in *The New York Times* and other papers. If clipped, pasted on uniform sheets, and filed, the latest figures are always available. Similarly, the weekly supplement to the *Survey of Current Business* should be kept in a loose-leaf binder rather than allowed to lie among a pile of papers with a routing slip attached.

Frequently, an inquirer will come up with a question like, "How is the average consumer dollar spent?" The answer will not appear in any regular current source, but the researcher may recall vaguely having seen a pie chart in a newspaper or magazine which gave the exact information—if only he knew *where* he had seen it. Many a wasted hour of searching will be saved if newspaper and magazine articles giving useful information not regularly obtainable are clipped and filed. The researcher will, of course, have to use his best judgment as to what material is likely to prove useful since it is obviously impossible to file more than a small proportion of the vast flow of information appearing in periodicals.

Information sources outside the office should be recorded also. If, after a diligent search, the researcher finds that Mr. Jones of the Central City National Bank is the man to call for cotton ginning figures, he would do well to note that fact under an appropriate heading. One question on a subject is very likely to be followed by more and, in handling numerous inquiries on varied subjects, it is almost impossible to remember where specific answers were obtained.

The librarian should request that the Research Department's library be placed on certain mailing lists in order to receive information on source materials on an automatic, continuing basis. These lists include those of the Superintendent of Documents, Government Printing Office, U.S. Department of Commerce, U.S. Department of Labor, Census Bureau, area Federal Reserve Bank, state officials who issue informational materials, the business research bureaus of state and local universities, and local government and civic agencies which prepare their own studies. Specific references to many of these sources are shown in Exhibits 3-A and 3-B. Publishing houses usually need not be contacted, since they will find their way to the librarian with a volume of catalogs. These, of course, should be reviewed for new source materials.

The New York City Public Library and many other local libraries issue bibliographies of new materials. These can be obtained free of charge by requesting that the Chamber be added to their mailing lists. Publications directories from the Chamber of Commerce of the United States, the State Chamber of Commerce, and the U.S. Council of the International Chamber of Commerce, as well as those from the Tax Foundation, Inc., the American Iron & Steel Institute, the Committee for Economic Development, and others should be included on the shelf of sources for acquisitions.

F. INDEXING

An index helps the user of an information system retrieve the data or documents he wants. Many small research libraries are finding that simple indexing systems may serve their purpose better than elaborate systems. Some individual ingenuity may be required in adapting a system to the needs of the particular Chamber and its interests, since these vary with size of the city or town and other factors.

Whatever system is used, it must be flexible. It should have an index flexible enough to conform to the ever-changing needs of the Chamber membership and staff. Such an index can be used in the various departments of the Chamber in order to organize file material under a modified central file system designed to provide uniformity in locating materials in both the library and separate offices.

After the index has been adopted, the books must be catalogued. It is debatable whether or not to catalogue pamphlets, especially since many of these quickly become outdated and are usually subject to a retention schedule. The appearance of the pamphlet titles on the acquisition records and the retention calendar should be enough. The books should be triple-catalogued according to title, author, and subject.

G. REFERENCE SERVICE

The Research Department's reference service primarily involves exploitation of the materials collected and made accessible in the research library. The principal types of this reference service include the following:

1. *Special-subject research:* Within the limitations of the library and its staff, library research is done on subjects requested by Chamber members and other staff personnel, by other Chambers of Commerce, and by business and research organizations. If the information

is easily available, it should be dispensed freely and graciously. If the requests require detailed research, it is up to the librarian's discretion whether there should be a charge for the service.

2. *Consultation by telephone:* Answering telephone calls is a part of the Research Department's free consulting service within the scope of source materials in the research library.

3. *Replies to letters:* Answering letters is another important function of the consulting service provided by the research library. Letters received by the Research Department should be acknowledged if possible. If they cannot be answered, they should be referred to another appropriate agency. Inquirers should always be informed — whether they contact the Research Department by telephone or by letter — that their requests have not been ignored but have been referred to another organization or agency.

4. *Conferences with inquirers:* Personal contacts with staff personnel, Chamber members, and the public who come in to use the research library are probably the most important part of the Research Department's reference service. Complete help in locating and interpreting statistical data and other materials should be given to each person who requests it. Face-to-face contact with the public is extremely significant: it is an excellent channel through which to project the service image of the local Chamber and its Research Department. Users should be offered the reference materials, shown how to use them, and then left to perform their own research. Questions should be answered courteously, but all-out efforts on the part of the staff in helping visitors do their studies put too great a strain on the resources and staff of most Research Departments.

The quantitative and qualitative services offered must be dictated by the capabilities of each Research Department, with consideration being given also to the needs of the local Chamber and the community it serves. Reference services can be expanded for larger Research Departments and reduced for smaller ones.

EXHIBIT 3-A:
BASIC REFERENCE MATERIALS
FOR THE RESEARCH LIBRARY

The following list contains reference sources that have been especially useful to Chamber of Commerce researchers. By no means all-inclusive, it is intended only to suggest a beginning library. Each researcher should supplement this basic library by adding other references relating to his expanding program of activities.

1. A copy of each census report—published by the U.S. Bureau of the Census and listed below, a-g—*for your state.* To purchase copies of these reports, write to Superintendent of Documents, U.S. Government Printing Office, Washington, D.C. 20402. Copies may also be ordered from the nearest GPO bookstore. Prices vary for individual state reports.
    a. *Census of Agriculture.* Quinquennial (published for years ending in 4 and 9).
    b. *Census of Business.* (Retail and Wholesale Trade and Selected Services). Quinquennial (to be taken for years ending in 2 and 7).
    c. *Census of Housing.* Decennial (published for years ending in 0).
    d. *Census of Manufactures.* Quinquennial (to be taken for years ending in 2 and 7).
    e. *Census of Mineral Industries.* Quinquennial (to be taken for years ending in 2 and 7).
    f. *Census of Population.* Decennial (published for years ending in 0).
    g. *Census of Transportation.* Quinquennial (to be taken for years ending in 2 and 7).
2. *World Almanac and Book of Facts.* New York: Newspaper Enterprise Association, Inc. Annual. $2.00.
    The most comprehensive and useful of American almanacs of general information. A general index is one of its most outstanding features.
3. *Statistical Abstract of the United States.* Published annually by the U.S. Bureau of the Census. Washington, D.C.: U.S. Government Printing Office. $6.30.
    This publication is the standard source for national statistics on income, population, trade, agriculture, employment, and a wide variety of other subjects. Not only are all the important governmental statistical agencies represented, but many of the commonly-used private agencies' statistics are included as well. Source notes provide keys to

detailed tables summarized here. Also included is a "Guide to Sources of Statistics."

4. *County Business Patterns.* Published annually by the U.S. Bureau of the Census. Washington, D.C.: U.S. Government Printing Office. $12.20.

This series of reports is released annually for individual states and represents a variety of data that businessmen, market researchers, and industrial and civic planners need for states, SMSA's and counties. It is a statistical by-product derived from employment and payroll information reported by firms whose employees are subject to Social Security tax withholdings; this information is supplemented by a special survey of multi-unit companies. Principal data items are presented by specific industry for states and counties and by major industry groups for SMSA's. Industry groups included are agricultural services, forestry, fisheries, mining, contract construction, manufacturing, transportation, wholesale and retail trades, finance, insurance, real estate, and selected services.

5. *County and City Data Book.* U.S. Bureau of the Census. Washington, D.C.: U.S. Government Printing Office. $12.20.

New statistics for counties, cities, and standard metropolitan statistical areas (SMSA's) are issued in this publication at the completion of each group of major censuses. This book presents local area data from each of the most recent censuses as well as statistics from other governmental and private agencies.

6. *Sales Management Survey of Buying Power.* New York: Bill Brothers Publishing Corporation. Annual. $15.00.

For states, counties, cities and metropolitan areas, current population estimates are given, based on *Sales Management's* own figures. Additional data include current estimates on sales, income, and buying power. Updated each year, these figures serve as a useful guide to anticipated growth as well as a means of establishing trends, both local and regional. Introductory chapters explain *Sales Management's* data-gathering methods as well as various uses for the statistical series. Useful for anyone attempting market analysis.

7. *Survey of Current Business.* U.S. Department of Commerce, Business Economics Office. Washington, D.C.: U.S. Government Printing Office. Monthly. $20.00 per year.

Each month over 2,000 statistical series are presented updating some of the information in the annual *Statistical Abstract.* This is an important source of current data and provides a quick, overall survey of the economy. Statistics of interest in this report include: employment and earnings data, inventories, gross national product, national income, prices of selected commodities and products, and a wide variety of figures on specific industries.

8. *Federal Reserve Bulletin.* Published monthly by the Board of Governors, Federal Reserve System, Washington, D.C. $6.00 per year.
One of the best sources of information on aggregate financial activity. Provides leading current data on money and banking; stock market credit; real estate mortgage and consumer credit; Federal Reserve indexes of industrial production; department stores; flow of funds; consumer finance data and analyses; and international financial statistics. Analyses of current economic developments and special articles on financial subjects. Includes list of Federal Reserve publications.

9. *The Marketing Information Guide.* Washington, D.C.: Trade Marketing Information Guide, Inc. Monthly. $10.00 per year.
This is a useful annotated listing of current material in the fields of marketing, industry development, foreign trade, and other areas of economic activity.

10. *Economic Indicators.* Prepared for the Joint Economic Committee by the Council of Economic Advisers, Executive Office of the President. Washington, D.C.: U.S. Government Printing Office. Monthly. $2.50 per year.
Presents basic statistical series on: Total output, income, and spending; employment, unemployment and wages; production and business activity; prices, currency, credit, and security markets; and Federal finance. A *Historical and Descriptive Supplement to Economic Indicators,* prepared by the Office of Statistical Standards, Bureau of the Budget, and the committee staff, contains historical data and a description of each series, technical procedures, relation to other series, uses and limitations, and references.

11. *Small-Area Data Notes.* U.S. Bureau of the Census. Washington, D.C.: U.S. Government Printing Office.
Issued monthly, this periodical provides highlights concerning new developments in Census Bureau programs, including 1970 Census products and services. Items included cover a wide range of subjects and are directed toward an audience of users of small-area data at state, regional, and local levels. Articles are selected for publication on the basis of their possible interest to state and local officials, planning personnel, and leaders in the civic, educational, and business sectors.
A subscription package will include 12 monthly issues of *SAD Notes* and four to six issues of *Data Access Descriptions* for an annual subscription price of $5.50. For additional information write to the Data Access and Use Laboratory, Data User Services Office, Bureau of the Census, Washington, D.C. 20233.

12. *Data Access Descriptions.* Washington D.C.: U.S. Government Printing Office. Issued occasionally by Data Access and Use Laboratory, Data User Services Office, Bureau of the Census. (See Item 11 for price.)

This publication was introduced in 1967 to provide information on means of access to unpublished data of the Census Bureau for persons with data requirements not fully met by the printed reports. Essentially, it provides convenient answers to questions generated by the Bureau and their subsequent exploration of Bureau data for particular research purposes. The full range of Census Bureau products and services, and occasional advance information on the contents and schedules of forthcoming printed reports, are covered in this series of publications.

13. *Standard Industrial Classification Manual.* Prepared by Statistical Policy Division, Office of Management and Budget, Executive Office of President. Washington, D.C.: U.S. Government Printing Office, 1972. Price $6.75.

    Classification of establishments by type of activity in which engaged. This classification is being used extensively in government and industry.

14. *Historical Statistics of the United States, Colonial Times to 1957.* U.S. Bureau of the Census, 1960. $8.25. Continuation to 1962 and revisions, 1965. $1.50. Washington, D.C.: U.S. Government Printing Office.

    A remarkable collection of aggregate time-series data covering almost every field of interest. About 6,000 statistical series, largely annual, extending back to the earliest year for which the data are available, with specific source notes, definitions of terms, and descriptive text. Primary edition and supplements contain information on population, farm mortgages, exports, imports, natural gas consumption, federal expenditures, and other types of activity. It is supplemented in part by the yearly *Statistical Abstract.*

15. *1970 Census Users' Guide.* U.S. Bureau of the Census. Washington, D.C.: U.S. Government Printing Office.

    Developed by the Data Access and Use Laboratory, the *1970 Census Users' Guide* is a general reference manual covering 1970 Census content, procedures, products, and uses. It has been designed to provide data users with information about the 1970 Census of Population and Housing. Procedures for collecting and processing census data are complex; data products and services are numerous and greatly varied in their characteristics; terminology is often uniquely associated with census programs or tabulations. The *Users' Guide* furnishes the information which data users need in order to understand and use the 1970 Census to best advantage.

    The Guide is organized into two separately bound sections:

    > *Part I,* including the text and three appendices — 1970 Census Users' Dictionary, Comparison of Printed Reports and Summary Tapes, and Glossary. Price: $2.10.

Part II, including seven appendices—Technical Conventions, Character Set, First through Fourth Count Technical Documentation. Price: $3.70.

16. *Business Service Checklist*. U.S. Department of Commerce. Washington, D.C.: U.S. Government Printing Office. Weekly. $5.50 a year.
This is a weekly guide to U.S. Department of Commerce publications plus key business indicators. Data shown include personal income, labor force, consumer price index, and gross national product, all presented on an aggregate basis.

17. *Consumer Price Index*. Bureau of Labor Statistics, U.S. Department of Labor. Monthly.
By means of index numbers, changes in prices of selected goods and services are shown for the United States and for metropolitan areas. (Also, see Chapter 12, ACCRA Cost of Living Index)

18. *Business Conditions Digest*. U.S. Bureau of the Census. Washington, D.C.: U.S. Government Printing Office.
A wide variety of indicators of business activity is covered. These are grouped under "leading indicators" or those that run ahead of business trends; "coincident indicators" that more or less run with the business cycle; and "lagging indicators" that run behind general business trends. Features compilation of data presented from the viewpoint of the business cycles analyst.

19. *Minerals Yearbook*. U.S. Department of the Interior, Bureau of Washington, D.C.: U.S. Government Printing Office. Annual (3 volumes: minerals, mineral fuels, and area reports).
General tables give mineral products by year, quantity, value, and state; also employment and injuries, including injury rates and trends of injury rates. Separate chapters on each mineral, mineral fuel, and state and territory give such data as production and shipments, principal mines, average value, prices, consumption, stocks, foreign trade, reserves, mining by state, employment and injuries, and world production.

20. *Current Population Reports*. U.S. Bureau of the Census. Monthly and annually.
The Bureau of the Census collects current data on the population in its current population survey—a monthly canvass of a scientifically selected sample of households in selected areas. The data are collected by Census Bureau enumerators who visit households and obtain information on population characteristics (such as marital status, school enrollment, household characteristics, internal migration, fertility, etc.), on individual and family incomes, and on the labor force activity of each member of the household 14 years of age or older. The survey yields continuing monthly data on the labor force and annual or less frequent data on other characteristics of the population. Results are

published in the various series of *Current Population Reports* issued by the Bureau of the Census. Among these reports are current estimates of the size of the population and occasional population projections, data on selected population characteristics, estimates of the farm population issued jointly with the Agricultural Marketing Service, and results of special censuses taken at the request and expense of local governments.

21. Newsletters of the Federal Reserve Bank serving your district. Frequent statistical releases show conditions of member banks in the district, types of loans made and amounts. Irregular publications of the bank's Research Department include income data, reports on the economy, and similar topics. Once on the mailing list, you receive all publications as issued.

22. Lists of various types of trade, business, and professional associations in your state. These listings may be used to determine which organization or association is likely to have data not otherwise available. Often a letter to the manager or executive director will bring detailed information not available in published form.

23. Labor Market Information. Releases by your state employment security commission.

24. Monthly business review of your state, usually published by the Bureau of Business Research in a state university.

25. Almanac or fact book for your state.

26. Maps. (a) Street map of your city; (b) census tract map of the local SMSA; (c) map of your state.

27. Directory of manufacturers in your state.

28. Budgets for all levels of government.

29. City ordinances.

30. Bills introduced in the state legislature.

31. Tax information for your area (municipal, special district, county, state).

32. Files of research-oriented information produced by the Chamber of Commerce of the United States and the American Chamber of Commerce Executives.

33. Standard dictionary.

34. Statistics textbook for an introductory, college-level statistics course.

35. *Style Manual.* Revised edition. Washington, D.C.: U.S. Government Printing Office, 1973. Buckram: $4.70; paper cover: $2.95.

36. *The MLA Style Sheet.* Second Edition. New York: Modern Language Association, 1971.

37. *A Manual of Style.* Twelfth Edition, Revised. Chicago: The University of Chicago Press, 1972.

38. Guides for writing research reports:
   a. *Research Papers,* by William Coyle. Second Edition. New York: The Odyssey Press, 1965.
   b. *Student's Guide for Writing College Papers,* by Kate L. Turabian. Second Edition, Revised. Chicago: The University of Chicago Press, 1972.

EXHIBIT 3-B:
GUIDES TO ADDITIONAL REFERENCE
MATERIALS FOR THE RESEARCH LIBRARY

Barton, Mary N., and Marion V. Bell. *Reference Books: A Brief Guide.* Baltimore: Enoch Pratt Free Library, 1970.

Business Periodicals Index. New York: H.W. Wilson Co.

Coman, Edwin T., Jr. *Sources of Business Information.* Berkeley and Los Angeles, Calif.: University of California Press, 1964.

Daniells, Lorna M. *Business Reference Sources.* Boston: Baker Library, Graduate School of Business Administration, Harvard University, 1971.

Johnson, H. Webster. *How to Use the Business Library with Sources of Business Information.* Cincinnati: South-Western Publishing Co., 1972.

Manley, Marian Catherine. *Business Information, How to Find It.* New York: Harper, 1955.

Schmeckebier, Laurence F., and Roy B. Eastin. *Government Publications and Their Use.* Washington, D.C.: The Brookings Institution, 1961.

U.S. Bureau of the Census. *Bureau of the Census Catalog.* Washington, D.C.: U.S. Government Printing Office. Quarterly. $6.50 a year.

U.S. Bureau of the Census. *Census Bureau Programs and Publications: Area and Subject Guide.* Washington, D.C.: U.S. Government Printing Office.

U.S. Bureau of the Census. *Directory of Federal Statistics for Local Areas: 1966.* Washington, D.C.: U.S. Government Printing Office, 1966.

U.S. Bureau of the Census. *Directory of Federal Statistics for States: 1967.* Washington, D.C.: U.S. Government Printing Office, 1967.

U.S. Bureau of the Census. *Directory of Non-Federal Statistics for States and Local Areas: 1969.* Washington, D.C.: U.S. Government Printing Office, 1969.

U.S. Bureau of the Census. *Guide to Census Bureau Data Files and Special Tabulations.* Washington, D.C.: U.S. Government Printing Office.

U.S. Bureau of the Census. *Guide to Foreign Trade Statistics.* Washington, D.C.: U.S. Government Printing Office, 1972.

U.S. Bureau of the Census. *Guide to Recurrent and Special Governmental Statistics*. Washington, D.C.: U.S. Government Printing Office, 1972.

U.S. Bureau of the Census. *Index to 1970 Census Summary Tapes*. Washington, D.C.: U.S. Government Printing Office, 1973.

U.S. Bureau of the Census. *Special and Technical Services from the Bureau of the Census, Available to State and Local Governments*. Washington, D.C.: U.S. Government Printing Office, 1970.

U.S. Department of Commerce. *A Bibliography of Resource Materials in the Field of Regional Economic Development*. Washington, D.C.: U.S. Government Printing Office, 1966.

U.S. Department of Commerce. *Measuring Markets: A Guide to the Use of Federal and State Statistical Data*. Washington, D.C.: U.S. Government Printing Office, 1966.

U.S. Executive Office of the President, Office of Management and Budget. *Statistical Services of the United States Government*. Washington, D.C.: U.S. Government Printing Office, 1959.

U.S. Small Business Administration. *A Survey of Federal Government Publications of Interest to Small Business*. Washington, D.C.: U.S. Government Printing Office, 1965.

U.S. Small Business Administration. *Basic Library Reference Sources for Business Use*. Washington, D.C.: U.S. Government Printing Office, 1966.

U.S. Superintendent of Documents. *List of Selected United States Government Publications*. Washington, D.C.: U.S. Government Printing Office. Semimonthly.

U.S. Superintendent of Documents, *United States Government Publications Monthly Catalog*. Washington, D.C.: U.S. Government Printing Office.

U.S. Superintendent of Documents. *Price Lists of Government Publications*. Washington, D.C.: U.S. Government Printing Office.

Wasserman, Paul, Eleanor Allen, and Charlotte Goergi. *Statistics Sources*. Detroit, Michigan: Gale Research Co., 1971.

Winchell, Constance M. *Guide to Reference Books*. Chicago, Ill.: American Library Association, 1967.

Wynar, Bohdan S. *Reference Books in Paperback*. Littleton, Colo.: Libraries Unlimited, Inc., 1972.

SELECTED REFERENCES RELATING TO LIBRARY ORGANIZATION AND OPERATION

A Classification Index for an Urban Collection. Washington, D.C.: National League of Cities and U.S. Conference of Mayors, 1968.

Anglo-American Cataloging Rules. Chicago, Ill.: American Library Association, 1967.

Baer, Mark. "Planning the New Library." *Special Libraries,* (December, 1963).

Bourne, Charles P. *Methods of Information Handling.* New York: John Wiley & Sons, 1963.

Collison, Robert L. *Indexès and Indexing.* London: Ernest Benn, Ltd., 1959.

Collison, Robert. *Indexing Books.* New York, N.Y.: John De Graff, Inc., 1962.

"Designs for the Company Library." *Administrative Management,* (October, 1964).

Dunkin, Paul S. *Cataloging U.S.A.* Chicago, Ill.: American Library Association, 1969.

Evans, Marshall K., and Lou R. Hague. "Master Plan for Information Systems." *Harvard Business Review,* (January-February, 1962), 92-103.

Gates, Jean Key. *Guide to the Use of Books and Libraries.* New York: McGraw-Hill, 1969.

Glidden, Sopyia H., and Dorothy Marchus. *A Library Classification for Public Administration Materials.* Chicago, Illinois: Public Administration Service and the American Library Association, 1942.

Holm, Bart E. *How to Manage Your Information.* New York: Reinhold Book Corporation, 1968.

Hutchins, Margaret. *Introduction to Reference Work.* Chicago: American Library Association, 1944.

Hutson, Kathryn V. "Needed: Data. Prime Source: Company Library." *Administrative Management,* (February, 1971), 53-55.

Knobbe, Mary L., and Janice W. Lessel. *Planning and Urban Affairs Library Manual.* Monticello, Illinois: Council of Planning Librarians, 1970.

Library of Congress. *Rules for Descriptive Cataloging in the Library of Congress.* Washington, D.C.: U.S. Government Printing Office, 1949.

Liston, David, Jr. "Information Systems." *Machine Design,* (July 21, 1966), 190-197.

McCrum, Blanche Prichard, and Helen Dudenbostel Jones. *Bibliographical Procedures & Style.* Washington, D.C.: The Library of Congress, 1954.

Metcalfe, John. *Information Indexing and Subject Cataloging.* New York, N.Y.: The Scarecrow Press, Inc., 1957.

Public Administration Service. *The Administration of a Public Affairs Library: A Report on the JRL Collection.* Chicago, Illinois: Public Administration Service, 1971.

Rescoe, A. Stan. *Cataloging Made Easy.* New York, N.Y.: The Scarecrow Press, Inc., 1962.

Schimmelpfeng, Richard H., and C. Donald Cook. *The Use of Library of Congress Classification.* Chicago, Ill.: American Library Association, 1968.

Seely, Pauline A. *ALA Rules for Filing Catalog Cards.* Chicago, Ill.: American Library Association, 1972.

Weeks, Bertha M. *How to File and Index.* New York, N.Y.: Ronald Press, 1956.

Wellisch, Hans, and Thomas D. Wilson. *Subject Retrieval in the Seventies.* Westport, Conn.: Greenwood Publishing Co., 1972.

"What Management Expects of the Library." *Special Libraries,* (February, 1964).

Wheeler, Marion Thorne. *New York State Library Indexing: Principles, Rules and Examples.* Albany, N.Y.: University of the State of New York Press, 1957.

Ziskind, Sylvia. *Reference Readings — A Manual for Librarians and Students.* Hamden, Conn.: The Shoe String Press, Inc., 1971.

4 GEOGRAPHIC TOOLS FOR DATA COMPILATION AND RETRIEVAL

A. INTRODUCTION

The development and use of geographic tools has been directly responsible for widening the possibilities and applications of small-area data analysis in economic and demographic research. Chamber of Commerce researchers are continually realizing benefits from increasingly sophisticated techniques of small-area data compilation, linkage, and retrieval.

Aggregate information about an entire SMSA, a county, or an incorporated area has little value in answering a majority of the specific problems demanding our attention. Geographic considerations—through use of neighborhood-by-neighborhood profiles—can be life-supports in handling today's urban concerns. Consider the role geography plays in:

1. Differentiating the inner city from the suburbs;
2. Establishing electoral districts;
3. Establishing program service areas such as police beats, fire zones, and health districts;
4. Locating businesses and public facilities;
5. Focusing neighborhood-oriented programs, such as Model Cities; and
6. Isolating areas of specific problems, such as unemployment, that differ across the city.

The concerns listed above—like so many others—relate to small parts of the urbanized area, each with its own community identity that is characteristically different from all others making up the city, each with its own problems calling for individual solutions.

Fundamental to economic, demographic, and governmental planning and analysis is the geographic location of activities, facilities, and conditions throughout the urbanized area. Small-area data systems developed by the U.S. Bureau of the Census provide tools for compiling and linking data to small geographic areas — constructing a framework for a comprehensive information system on the local area.

Ideally, Chamber of Commerce researchers should be leaders in developing the small-area data framework in their respective communities, keeping up with trends and advances in this activity area, and they should be prepared to use it effectively.

A majority of research activities requiring applications of small-area data will involve the use of census tracts. The features of a census tract plan which are especially significant to Chamber of Commerce researchers include the ready availability and relatively low cost of printed reports for census tracts.

Census tracts are small, permanently established, geographical areas into which cities and their environs in metropolitan areas are divided for purposes of statistical monitoring. Tracts averaging about 4,000 persons are laid out with attention to achieving some uniformity of population characteristics, economic status, and living conditions. Boundaries follow such permanent and easily recognized features as streets, railroads, waterways, or other natural barriers.

In each decennial census, the Bureau of the Census tabulates population and housing information for each tract to permit statistical comparisons from census to census on social, ethnic, and economic changes. The value of census information increases as local groups tabulate locally collected data, allowing statistical comparisons to be made from year to year to show changes within a community.

Development of a census tract plan, whether for a previously untracted area or as a revision of an existing tract plan, must be accomplished from within the community. Thus it should be the responsibility of the local Chamber of Commerce researcher to recognize the value of tracting for his community, take the lead in developing a tract plan, and serve as an integral part of census tract promotion. Additional information about census tracts is presented in Section G of this chapter.

B. 1970 CENSUS GEOGRAPHIC AREAS

Geography played a crucial role in every stage of planning, enumerating, and tabulating the 1970 Census of Population and Housing.[1] Identification of geographic areas was the basis for administrative control in taking the 1970 Census and processing the returned questionnaires. Census tabulations were prepared for specific geographic areas — whether the entire United States or a city block. Without the ability to assign or relate data

---

[1]Sections B through F of this chapter were prepared by Gerald L. O'Donnell, Data Access and Use Laboratory, Data User Services Office, Bureau of the Census, Washington, D.C.

to specific areas, the data collected from a census would be of little value other than for furnishing national totals. It is those statistics presenting characteristics for states, counties, cities, and smaller areas which make the censuses important to most data users.

The geographic work for a census basically involves determining boundaries, coding geographic areas, and preparing maps. Additional geographic work was required for the 1970 Census in the development of mailing lists of residential addresses for the metropolitan areas which were enumerated by mail rather than by census takers. Work relating to geography resulted in several products—such as new types of census maps, geographic code schemes, and address coding guides—which are of value to census data users as well as the Bureau of the Census.

In the 1970 Census substantial improvements were made in providing tabulations for small geographic areas. Small-area census data are used by the Federal government in the development of national policies and by state and local governments for planning and implementing many of their programs. Semi-public agencies, university faculties, and the business community also are interested in small-area census data.

Boundaries of the geographic areas for which the Bureau of the Census collected and tabulated 1970 Census data were established in several ways. Boundaries of political areas—states, congressional districts, counties, minor civil divisions, incorporated places, and city wards—are based on information received from the appropriate authorities. Boundaries of statistical areas are determined by groups with special expertise, often with the advice and assistance of the Bureau of the Census. For example, the Office of Management and Budget of the Executive Office of the President, with the assistance of other Federal agencies, defines standard metropolitan statistical areas. Boundaries of functional or administrative areas are defined outside the Census Bureau by the appropriate agencies, such as the ZIP code areas defined by the U.S. Postal Service. In addition, the Bureau of the Census established the boundaries of several kinds of geographic areas for which it tabulated 1970 Census data—urbanized areas, census county divisions, unincorporated places, census tracts (in cooperation with local census tract committees), enumeration districts, block groups, and blocks. Census county divisions and unincorporated places are defined with local assistance at several levels of government.

To meet the processing and tabulation requirements of the 1970 Census, numeric codes were used in lieu of names to identify areas for which census data were summarized. The geographic codes were derived primarily from a master coding scheme prepared by the Bureau, and they appear on the 1970 Census summary tapes and related geographic products. Each level in the census geographic hierarchy, from the state down to the block, has an associated code scheme, with individual codes ranging in length from one to six digits.

C. GEOGRAPHIC REFERENCE PRODUCTS

A number of geographic reference products have emerged from the 1970 Census. These products are essential to the effective use of small-area data. For example, census maps show the boundaries of each census tract, enumeration district, and block. Geographic code schemes are required to permit identification of census geographic areas contained on the summary tapes. Address coding guides and geographic base (DIME)[2] files provide a means of relating local data to census geographic areas. Descriptions of the various geographic reference products are presented below.

1. Maps

Census Maps are necessary for virtually all uses of small-area census data; they are needed in locating specific census geographic areas and in analyzing their areal relationships. There are basically five kinds of census maps which delineate small-areas: The Metropolitan Map Series, county maps, place maps, county subdivision maps, and tract outline maps.

The *Metropolitan Map Series* (MMS) generally covers the urbanized areas of standard metropolitan statistical areas and shows, in great detail, the location of place and MCD/CCD boundaries, census tracts, enumeration districts, and blocks, and identifies the features which form the boundaries of these areas. These maps are at a common scale of 1 inch = 2,000 feet, with portions of some sheets enlarged to 1 inch = 800 feet. There are approximately 200 map sets in the series (one or more urbanized areas may be in a map set) comprising approximately 3,200 map sheets (each sheet including an area of 5 by 7 miles); the number of sheets in a set range from 2 to 144. The Metropolitan Map Series covers approximately a 110,000-square-mile total area. This coverage includes about two-thirds of the nation's population. The series is available as part of the *Block Statistics* reports for urbanized areas, series HC(3) of the 1970 Census reports. Each report is accompanied by a set of metropolitan maps for the urbanized area concerned. An HC(3) report for a medium-size urbanized area can be purchased for less than $5 from the Superintendent of Documents, U.S. Government Printing Office, Washington, D.C. 20402. The metropolitan maps contained in the HC(3) reports use color and shading to emphasize selected boundaries.

The *county maps,* which generally are reproductions of standard state highway department maps, show the boundaries of minor civil divisions or census county divisions, places, tracts, and enumeration districts for portions of counties not covered by the Metropolitan Map Series, as well as for all counties outside of SMSA's. County maps generally have a scale of

---

[2]DIME is an acronym for Dual Independent Map Encoding.

1 inch = 2 miles. There are usually one or two map sheets for each county except for those counties larger in area. County maps are not published in any census reports. Copies may be obtained at a price of $1 and up for each sheet from the Data User Services Office, Bureau of the Census, Washington, D.C. 20233.

Place maps are available for every incorporated and unincorporated place reported in the 1970 Census but not included in the Metropolitan Map Series. Usually reproductions of maps supplied to the Bureau of the Census by local agencies, these maps identify streets and show boundaries for enumeration districts, tracts where applicable, and blocks for places which contracted with the Bureau for preparation of block statistics. Place maps ordinarily vary in scale from 1 inch = 400 feet to 1 inch = 1,500 feet. There is normally one map sheet for each place. Most place maps are not a part of any census report. They are sold individually by the Data User Services Office at a price of $1.50 or more per map sheet, depending upon the size of the sheet. Place maps appear in the HC(3) reports for places participating in the contract block statistics program; however, these maps do not show ED's.

County subdivision maps of states show boundaries for counties and subdivisions of counties (minor civil divisions or census county divisions) as well as the location of all places recognized in the 1970 Census. There is normally one map sheet for each state with the exception of those few states that have been combined on one sheet. The scale used for most of the county subdivision maps is 1 inch = 12 miles. The maps are priced at 20 cents per state and may be obtained from the U.S. Government Printing Office. Copies of the county subdivision maps on a smaller scale appear in sectionalized form in *Number of Inhabitants,* series PC(1)-A, of the 1970 Census reports.

Tract outline maps show the boundaries of census tracts, counties, and all places with populations of 25,000 or more. The scale of tract outline maps varies according to the size and complexity of the SMSA and may range from 1 inch = ½ mile to 1 inch = 10 miles. Generally, there are two tract outline map sheets per SMSA. These maps are included as part of the Census Tract reports for SMSA's, series PHC(1) of the 1970 Census reports. Most PHC(1) reports cost less than $2 and are available from the U.S. Government Printing Office.

In addition to the census maps already described in this section, there are two kinds of maps published by the Bureau of the Census which should be mentioned briefly. These are the urbanized area maps and the United States Maps.

Urbanized area maps show the extent and components of urbanization through shading. Copies of these maps, at a scale of 1 inch = 4 miles, appear in *Number of Inhabitants,* series PC(1)-A, and in *General Housing Characteristics,* series HC(1)-A, reports, obtainable from the U.S. Government Printing Office. These maps can only be obtained by purchasing the reports. More detailed information on urbanized area boundaries can be found in the Metropolitan Map Series.

The *United States Maps* (the GE-50 map series) are statistical maps showing geographic distribution, by county, of various social and economic data from the 1970 Census as well as from earlier censuses. Different boundaries are easily seen through the color. Each map is a single sheet (generally 42" × 30" in size) at an approximate scale of 1 inch = 80 miles. Copies of these maps sell for 25 to 50 cents each. An order form listing the various maps in the GE-50 series is available upon request from the Publications Distribution Section, Social and Economic Statistics Administration, Washington, D.C. 20233.

To facilitate map acquisition, the Bureau of the Census has compiled an inventory of the Metropolitan Map Series, county maps, and place maps. The *census map inventory* lists the cost and the required number of map sheets for each state, county, and place for maps maintained and sold by the Bureau. Names and the relevant geographic codes for these areas are included. The inventory covers all 50 states and the District of Columbia, making it easy to determine the required map sheets and their cost. The inventory is most useful when ordering place maps and county maps containing enumeration district and other census boundary designations that are not found in any 1970 Census reports.

The U.S. Department of Commerce District Offices, along with the Census Bureau and its regional Data Collection Centers, have the census map inventory for the entire nation on hand to assist users. The inventory can be purchased at a price of $2 for individual states and $75 for the complete set from the Data User Services Office. Users who submit frequent census map orders or copy and distribute large quantities of these maps will find the inventory valuable.

2. Geographic Code Schemes

All geographic areas represented on the 1970 Census computer tape products are identified only by their numeric codes; names are not used. Users require some form of geographic code scheme to associate the codes for geographic areas with their area names. Codes and the corresponding names for census geographic areas are contained in the Census Bureau's Master Enumeration District List and Geographic Identification Code Scheme.

The *Master Enumeration District List,* or MEDList, is a listing of the names of political and statistical subdivisions and related geographic codes from the state down to the county subdivisions and place level. It also provides codes for unnamed areas below the county subdivision level — tracts, enumeration districts (ED's), and block groups — as well as population and housing total counts for most areas. The MEDList is designed to serve the two basic purposes of: (1) furnishing area and place names corresponding to the geographic codes which are used on the 1970 Census summary tapes, and (2) providing official population and housing unit counts for enumeration districts, block groups, and other areas.

A special version of the MEDList containing the latitude and longitude coordinates for the estimated population center points for each of 242,000 enumeration districts and block groups has also been prepared by the Bureau of the Census. The center points, or centroids, were visually estimated from census maps. Coordinate values were then assigned to the points by a machine called a digitizer. The coordinates are expressed in decimal degrees carried to four places. The MEDList without coordinates is available for the United States on three reels of tape for $210; the MEDList with coordinates is sold on a state by state basis (one tape reel for each state) at a cost of $70 per reel. Both products are available from the Data User Services Office, Bureau of the Census.

The *1970 Geographic Identification Code Scheme* (GICS) is a four-volume guide to the geographic codes for the component parts (county subdivisions and larger areas) of each state. Each volume reports on a different region of the country (Northeast, North Central, South, and West). The information published in the GICS is also available from the MEDList computer tapes. For each state within a region the GICS presents two tables. The first table is arranged by counties, county subdivisions, and places: state, county, SMSA, MCD or CCD, place, place description, and place size. The second table presents alphabetically all the places within the state with their corresponding county, county subdivisions, and place codes. A third table, shown once for each volume, presents SMSA and urbanized area codes for the entire United States. Copies of the GICS may be purchased from the U.S. Government Printing Office for the following prices: Northeast, $1; North Central, $1.75; South, $1.50; and West, 60 cents.

Some of the codes included in the MEDList, GACI, and GICS have been standardized for use by all Federal agencies in the exchange of computer-readable information. The Federal standard codes in the Bureau products noted above include state, SMSA, county and congressional district. The Bureau of the Census includes this last code only in the MEDList. These codes are published by the National Bureau of Standards, U.S. Department of Commerce, in a series known as the Federal Information Processing Standards Publications (FIPS PUB) and are sold by the U.S. Government Printing Office. The designations and titles of these reports are: FIPS PUB 5-1, State Codes; FIPS PUB 6-1, County Codes; FIPS PUB 8-2, SMSA Codes; FIPS PUB 9, Congressional District Codes.

For some users, the FIPS PUB series might be more suitable as a source of geographic codes than the Census Bureau's geographic code schemes, especially if a user is interested in only one set of codes (such as codes for all counties in the nation) rather than several sets of codes for each state and its component parts (SMSA, minor civil division, and place).

3. Address Coding Guides

In conducting the 1970 Census of Population and Housing, two different enumeration methods were used: the mail-out/mail-back type of canvass, taken primarily in the large urban areas of the country, and the conventional house-to-house visit by enumerators.

In 145 of the then 233 standard metropolitan statistical areas and in certain adjoining areas the mail-out/mail-back procedure was used. Approximately 60 percent of the nation's population was canvassed by mail rather than by an enumerator's visit. Householders were asked to complete the census questionnaire in the privacy of their own homes and to mail it back to a local Census Bureau office. The remainder of the country was enumerated by the conventional house-to-house canvassing procedure, which closely resembled enumeration methods of the 1960 and earlier censuses. Census takers visited every housing unit in their assigned ED's and obtained the information required on the questionnaires. Census geographic codes for each household were determined and coded on the questionnaire by the enumerator.

In the 145 SMSA's in which the mail-out/mail-back technique was used, a method of assigning specific census geographic codes to a mailing list address was needed. The solution decided upon entailed the development of a master computer file for each area which would contain the information necessary to "geocode" the addresses. The file developed for this purpose was named the Address Coding Guide (ACG). The ACG, in essence, performed one of the functions of an enumerator by providing the "census geography" of each address.

Address Coding Guides are simply computer listings which contain block face records for all streets within the city postal delivery area (which roughly corresponds to the urbanized area) of an SMSA. A block face is one side of a street between two intersections; a block face for a dead-end street is one side of a street from its beginning intersection to the dead end. Features such as municipal boundaries, rivers, and railroad tracks were not included since there were no housing addresses for units associated with them. Each ACG record identifies a single block face by street name; a range of addresses; the block number; and tract, place, and other geographic codes.

To create Address Coding Guides for the 145 SMSA's in the mail census, the Census Bureau first prepared a preliminary "skeleton" ACG from a commercial mailing list and city directories. The preliminary ACG's were then sent to cooperating local agencies for review and correction, after which they were returned to the Bureau for computer processing. After several stages of computer and clerical edits, the ACG's were made available to the public and used in Bureau activities.

Census data users have found the Address Coding Guide valuable as a reference source for assigning census geographic codes to local records containing addresses. This geographic coding employs a program which matches individual addresses contained in local record files to address ranges in the ACG after a local record has been linked to its appropriate ACG record file. This operation represents computerization of the manual process of looking up geographic codes in a printed street index and posting appropriate codes to locally-generated records. For example, crime incidence records may be coded to census tracts, which would permit a correlation study between crime and census socio-economic data for tracts. The ADMATCH program would match each individual address of crime occurrence to the correct address range in the ACG and, upon a match, assign the appropriate census tract code contained in the ACG to the crime incidence record.

The ACG can be used in the assignment of codes other than census geographic codes. If local areas (i.e., police precincts, planning districts, neighborhoods) are defined in terms of blocks and/or tracts, codes for these local areas can be added to the ACG. The addition of local area codes to the ACG is the responsibility of local users. The ADMATCH program will assign the local area codes to records containing addresses in the same manner that it assigns census geographic codes.

Address Coding Guides are available on computer tape (IBM-compatible format) at $70 per tape reel from the Data User Services Office, Bureau of the Census. Most areas covered by the ACG are on one or two reels. The ACG's also are available as computer printed listings on 11- by 14-inch paper. No pricing has been established for the printout version; however, the cost is normally two to three times that for tape versions.

4. Geographic Base (DIME) Files

After preparation of the Address Coding Guides was well under way and the 1970 Census date was too near to permit a change in the system, an improved version of the ACG was developed by the Census Use Study, a small-area data research group in the Census Bureau. This innovation — known as a geographic base file — uses a technique called "DIME," an acronym for "Dual Independent Map Encoding." The geographic base (DIME) file, commonly referred to as GBF/DIME, is characterized by (1) an editing capability which improves the accuracy of the files, and (2) an increased utility to local users as a result of added features.

The concept underlying the creation of the GBF/DIME files is derived from graph theory. Each street, river, railroad track, municipal boundary, etc., that bounds a census block can be considered as one or

more straight line segments; curved streets or other features can be divided
into series of straight line segments. Where streets or other features inter-
sect or change direction, node points are identified. While an Address
Coding Guide is constructed on a block face basis, a GBF/DIME file is
constructed on a street segment basis. Therefore, while each ACG record
contains the appropriate census geographic codes for *one* side of a street
between two intersections, the GBF/DIME segment record contains the
appropriate codes for *both* sides of a street between two nodes. The unique
identification of each segment (including segments that are not along
streets), each node point, and their geographic relationships provides a
capacity for geographic descriptions which can be checked by computer for
accuracy. By digitizing the node points (that is, assigning x-y coordinates),
graphic outputs in either geographic data display or map image form can
be produced by applying computer mapping techniques.

The construction of a GBF/DIME file involves the transcription by
local agencies of geographic information (i.e., street patterns, address
ranges, area identifiers) from metropolitan maps and other sources into a
form that can be read and manipulated by computer. Clerks enter the
various types of geographic information on worksheets which are then key-
punched and entered into the computer. After the computer editing, appropriate correction, and insertion of coordinates, the GBF/DIME file is
ready for use.

Essentially the same information is contained in both the ACG and
GBF/DIME files: Street name, address ranges, block numbers, tract,
place, and other geographic codes. The GBF/DIME file has three additional codes: (1) the left-right orientation code separating the census geographic codes for areas on each side of the street segment, (2) the identification numbers of the node points at each end of the segment, and (3) the x-y
coordinates of each node point expressed in state plane coordinates (measured in feet relative to the state plane grid system), latitude and longitude
(measured in degrees and ten-thousandths of a degree based on distance
from the equator), and map-set miles (measured in miles and thousandths
of a mile from an arbitrary point at the southwest corner of the Metropolitan Map Series sheets). The GBF/DIME file also contains block
boundaries that do not follow streets; these are not contained in the
ACG's.

Originally, GBF/DIME files were created for 79 of the 88 non-mail
SMSA's. Their projected use lay in assigning tract and block numbers to
the workplace responses from the place of work question on the 1970 Census
questionnaire. The Census Bureau and other federal and local agencies
recognized that it would be desirable to add the GBF/DIME features to the
already existing ACG's. Each of the 145 SMSA's included in the original
ACG program was contacted and invited to participate in the development
of a GBF/DIME file; 115 SMSA's agreed to do so. In total, 194 SMSA's

(plus part of the San Juan, Puerto Rico SMSA and the new SMSA of Appleton-Oshkosh, Wis.) participated in the Census Bureau program to develop such files. Of the remaining SMSA's, 32 participated only in the original ACG program and 6 did not participate in either the ACG or GBF/DIME programs.

In addition to the geocoding capability described for the ACG's, the GBF/DIME files have the expanded applications demonstrated in the following examples: (1) Since a GBF/DIME file associates coordinates with computerized geographic records, it provides one of the essential elements for computer mapping. Regardless of the computer mapping system being used, spatial identifiers such as the coordinates found in the file are required. (2) A GBF/DIME file can be used in street network analysis. Street networks of varying degrees of detail are required for computerized study and design of routes for garbage trucks, ambulances, and other service vehicles. (3) Computer programs that are designed to allocate resources to facilities can also take advantage of a GBF/DIME file. For example, the file can be used in assigning people to community fallout shelters or children to schools, determining logical service areas for community health facilities, and evaluating alternative sites for new retail outlets.

The GBF/DIME files are available on computer tape (IBM-compatible format) at $70 per tape reel, with most areas on one or two reels. These tape reels can be purchased from the Data User Services Office, Bureau of the Census. Printed listings of the files can also be obtained on a cost reimbursable basis—the cost is normally two to three times that for tape versions.

D. THE CUE PROGRAM
FOR GBF/DIME FILE MANAGEMENT

The GBF/DIME files contain a large amount of geographic information. Unfortunately, they have some errors in them and like the associated source maps (Metropolitan Map Series) from which the files were constructed, they are becoming out-of-date. Both of these products reflect local urban geography as it existed immediately prior to the 1970 Census. To be of most use to local agencies and the Census Bureau, the files and appropriate maps must be updated as well as corrected. To accomplish this, the Bureau has established the CUE program, referring to the Correction, Update, and Extension of the GBF/DIME file.

The purposes of the CUE program are:

1. To make corrections as necessary to produce a complete and accurate GBF/DIME file and Metropolitan Map Series (MMS) for the SMSA's having an existing file,
2. To extend the GBF/DIME files and MMS to cover the entire

SMSA (at present only the urban cores of SMSA's are covered),
3. To establish GBF/DIME files and MMS for those SMSA's for which GBF/DIME files and MMS do not currently exist,
4. To develop procedures by which each SMSA can systematically maintain a current and accurate GBF/DIME file and MMS series.

Parts of the CUE program are now operational and many local agencies are beginning to correct and update their GBF/DIME files using computer programs developed by the Census Bureau. Further information on the CUE program can be obtained from the Geography Division, Bureau of the Census, Washington, D.C. 20233.

E. COMPUTER PROGRAMS FOR GEOGRAPHIC APPLICATIONS

A number of computer programs for geographic applications, most of which pertain to effective use of the geographic base (DIME) files, are available from the Bureau of the Census in addition to the 1970 Census geographic reference materials previously described. Descriptions of these computer programs are presented in this section. All of these computer programs are available from the Data User Services Office, Bureau of the Census, Washington, D.C. 20233. Unless otherwise stated, the programs are sold on computer tape for $70.

1. DIME (Dual Independent Map Encoding)

DIME is a computer program package designed to aid local users in the creation of GBF/DIME files for non-metropolitan cities. The package consists of a clerical procedures manual and a set of computer programs for file creation.

The manual supplies complete information on the clerical coding operation including personnel and space requirements, materials, training and supervising of coders, coding procedures, and problem resolutions. The set of computer programs converts the coded data to a master file for machine use, validates the completeness and accuracy of the clerical work, modifies the master file to correct errors and omissions, and inserts coordinates into the file. The programs are written in ANSI standard FORTRAN IV for users of almost any computer system with a minimum core storage of 100K bytes.

2. ADMATCH (Address Matching)

ADMATCH is a package of computer programs and documentation designed to assist in the assignment of geographic codes to computerized data records containing street addresses. Geographic codes for areas such as census tracts and blocks can be readily assigned to records in local data files using ADMATCH. ADMATCH compares the individual street addresses of local data files to the address ranges in the ACG or GBF/DIME records, and upon a match, attaches the desired geographic codes contained in these files to the local data records. Local data records on crime incidence, school dropouts, new construction, or other matters can then be aggregated to census geographic areas for study in relation to the census data available for these areas.

Users need not be restricted to studying only census geographic areas. By creating equivalency tables that relate census tracts or blocks to local areas such as health districts, traffic zones, and school districts, the codes for these local areas can be added to an ACG or GBF/DIME file. Then ADMATCH can be used to assign these local area codes to records in local files in the same manner that it assigns census geographic codes.

The ADMATCH program package is written in IBM System/360 Assembler Language. Separate versions are available for use under 16K Disk or Tape Operating Systems (DOS or TOS) and under the Operating System (OS). The minimum core storage requirement is 32K bytes, and a line printer and three magnetic tape or disk units are needed.

3. NICKLE

The NICKLE program is designed to split the street segment records of the GBF/DIME file into block face records. (To use ADMATCH or any other type of computer matching program, individual block face records rather than street segment records are required.) The program reads the GBF/DIME file, drops the non-street records, and then splits the segment records, thus creating a record for each side of the street (block face) much like records in the Address Coding Guide. The block face records may then be used for input to the ADMATCH program.

NICKLE is written for the IBM 360/40 (DOS) in COBOL. A program listing and record layout for the resulting NICKLE film can be obtained at no cost.

4. T-GUIDE

The T-GUIDE program was developed to produce a street index at the census tract level from a GBF/DIME file. The index produced from applying T-GUIDE consists of all streets within each census tract included in the GBF/DIME file, indicating low and high address ranges for each side of the street. The program reads the file, drops all non-street records (such as railroad tracks, streams, etc.), and splits the street segment records, thus creating a record for each side of the block. The address ranges of the block side record along the length of the street within each census tract are then collapsed. This results in an approximate 60-percent reduction in the size of the GBF/DIME files and thereby allows for manual, as well as speedier mechanical, geocoding of census tracts to local data records.

The T-GUIDE program is written for the IBM 360/40 (DOS) in COBOL. A program listing and record layout for the resulting T-GUIDE file can be obtained at no cost.

5. FIXDIME

The FIXDIME program was developed in conjunction with the Bureau's CUE program. FIXDIME enables local agencies to perform correction operations in existing records and to add new records. All items in the files, with the exception of coordinate values, may be corrected.

The FIXDIME program is written in COBOL Level D for the IBM 360 system under DOS.

6. UPDIME

Once the GBF/DIME files have been corrected using FIXDIME, the updating process of the CUE program can begin. As with the correction process, updating the files can only be carried out by the local agencies. To assist the local agencies in this effort, the Bureau has prepared a FORTRAN IV program called UPDIME. UPDIME makes possible the addition to the file of new street segments as well as the x-y coordinates for the new segments. It also contains a block chaining edit which detects the structural defects (e.g., missing street segments) in the GBF/DIME file.

7. GRIDS

The Grid Related Information Display System (GRIDS) is a generalized computer graphics system capable of performing a wide variety of mapping tasks. It produces density, shading, and value maps within a grid pattern. A routine supplied with the system allows GBF/DIME file street networks to be printed displaying segments, city and census tract boundaries, and nodes. GRIDS is written in ASA Basic FORTRAN IV and will run on any computer system with a suitable FORTRAN compiler and sufficient storage, regardless of computer word size or operating system. GRIDS will operate on a machine as small as an IBM System/360 Model 30 computer with 32K bytes of storage.

8. C-MAP (Choropleth Mapping)

C-MAP is a simplified FORTRAN computer mapping program distributed by the Census Bureau to users who have small computers. Data for geographic areas (i.e., states, counties, census tracts) are printed on the map according to a classification of their statistical values. The user specifies the number and limits of the statistical classes and their respective printer characters. Shading is achieved by overprinting two or more printer characters.

Punchcards are presently the input medium; however, the program can be modified for computer tape or disk input. A program listing and the procedures for preparing the necessary punchcards for the input process are available at no cost.

9. DAUList

A series of computer programs, DAUList 1 through 5, displays population and housing tabulations from the first five counts of the 1970 Census summary tapes. The DAUList programs "read" the summary tapes and print out the census tabulations with table descriptions and the appropriate geographic codes. Users of the programs may select the geographic areas that are of interest to them and display any or all tables for these areas. In addition to displaying selected data, the DAUList 3 and DAUList 4 programs for the Third Count and Fourth Count Summary Tapes, respectively, aggregate data from different geographic areas such as blocks or census tracts. The other DAUList programs do not have this aggregation capability.

The DAUList programs are written variously in COBOL and FORTRAN. The minimum core storage varies according to the program, but most programs require 48K.

F. REFERENCE MATERIALS

Several series of publications issued by the Bureau of the Census provide additional information on the Bureau's geographic programs and activities and keep data users informed of new developments, applications, and products.

The results of extensive research conducted by the Bureau's Census Use Study are presented in a series of reports covering such topics as geographic base (DIME) file development, computer mapping, and address matching. An order form listing the various Census Use Study report topics can be obtained from the Publications Distribution Section, Social and Economic Statistics Administration, Washington, D.C. 20233.

The publication series GE-40, *Census Tract Papers,* makes available to all census data users the papers presented at the Census Tract Conferences held periodically to discuss the problems and uses of census tract and related small-area data. Another series of publications, the GE-60 series, *Computerized Geographic Coding,* presents the proceedings of several conferences which were devoted to the local uses of ACG and GBF/DIME files. This series provides insight into what local agencies are doing or plan to do with their files. Order forms for both publications are available from the Publication Distribution Section.

The *1970 Census Users' Guide* is a two-part general reference manual. Part I contains information on census content, data products, geographic materials, and uses, as well as a dictionary of census terms and a comparison of printed reports and summary tapes. Part II contains information specifically relating to the use of summary tapes. The Guide can be purchased from the U.S. Government Printing Office at the following prices: Part I, $2.10; Part II, $3.70; Parts I and II, $5.80.

The monthly newsletter, *Small-Area Data Notes,* highlights Bureau of the Census activities, products, and services in the field of small-area census data. It provides information on new publications, the release of data in both printed reports and summary tapes, upcoming surveys and censuses, developments in census geography, and local applications of census data. *Small-Area Data Notes* is available as part of a subscription package with *Data Access Descriptions* for $5.50 per year. Orders should be sent to the Publications Distribution Section.

G. CENSUS TRACTS

1. General Values of Tract Statistics

a. Geographic comparability[3]

When a metropolitan area is divided into many census tracts for which important statistical data are available, one can readily determine the significant differences between the city's parts. For many purposes it is necessary to be able to distinguish the areas with many aged persons from those with large numbers of children, the areas where the professionally and technically employed live from the areas of the unskilled, the college-educated group from the poorly educated, the single-family homes from the multi-family structures and rooming houses, the high income from the low income, and the crowded from the uncrowded, to mention only a few characteristics. In between the extremes are many different combinations of these characteristics. To divide a city or metropolitan area into many parts with known differences is necessary for the solution of its many different problems.

b. Historical comparability

When an area has been tracted for two or more censuses, the data for the census tracts can be compared for the two dates and the amount of change that has occurred can be measured. Is the population larger or smaller? Are the people richer or poorer? Are housing conditions better or

---

[3]U.S. Bureau of the Census, *Census Tract Manual,* Fifth Edition, Washington, D.C.: U.S. Government Printing Office, 1966, 10-11.

worse? To know the trend over time for an area is of great help in understanding the present, in projecting the future, and in deciding what steps
need to be taken to change the future pattern of development, if it appears desirable.

c. The value of local data

To make more than minimum use of the census tract system of areas,
data should be collected for the census tracts by local organizations.
Against the background of population and housing information from the
censuses, local data by tracts can be analyzed. These may include vital
statistics and data on business licenses, accidents, fires, crimes, land use,
construction and demolition, sales, customers, patients, clients, members,
and subscribers, to mention only a few. Some of these data may be used
also to update as well as to supplement the Census Bureau's tract statistics.

d. Provision for a common small-area base system

The establishment of census tracts in a metropolitan area provides a
common set of small areas for data collection and use. The advantage of
small-area data lies in making it possible to relate the results of one study
by small areas to another and thus to build results upon results.

This is not to say that the census tracts form a perfect system of areas
for all specific purposes. A school enrollment district, a fire protection district, a police precinct, and a neighborhood planning unit are not likely to
cover the same area and perhaps none will coincide with census tracts. Yet
the census tracts will provide relevant data for each.

e. From census tracts to larger areas or smaller areas

For the user interested in somewhat larger areas than the census tract,
it may be possible to combine the data for several tracts to fit the areas
needed. For the user interested in smaller areas than the census tract or
areas composed of parts of several census tracts, other data from the
Census Bureau for small areas, such as enumeration districts and blocks,
are available. Admittedly, there are fewer statistics tabulated for these
areas, but, using what is available, useful estimates can be made for several
kinds of data. In many cases the estimates can be supported by inexpensive
field surveys carried out locally.

2. Census Tract Uses

a. Location of problem areas or areas of opportunity [4]

This is one of the simpler uses of tracts. The planner wishes to identify
areas of population growth and decline and associated demographic char-

---

[4] U.S. Bureau of the Census, *Census Tract Manual*, 12-13.

acteristics. The marketer needs to know where his products are selling or not selling and where the higher income areas are. The public health scientist is interested in the areas with higher and lower incidence of disease. Each of these activities soon leads into more complex studies to determine the socio-economic characteristics of these tracts that may help to explain the distributions.

b. Division of a city or metropolitan area into sections for a particular purpose

The local government agency defines its service areas; the businessman, sales and distribution areas; the transportation planner, traffic zones; the city planner, neighborhoods and communities; and the state legislator, senatorial and representative districts—again to mention only examples. The boundaries of these areas do not always follow tract boundaries exactly, but the availability of all kinds of data for the tracts makes them most useful for area delineation.

c. Evaluation of appropriate site use

The population and housing characteristics in the area tributary to a given site aid the analyst in determining the best possible use for that site. The government agency, the private property owner, the zoning board, the realtor, and the mortgage banker all have a stake in the answer to the question, "Which of a variety of possible uses is best for this site?"

d. Location of new facilities

Today, the use of census tract data has become essential to many public and private agencies and particularly to business. The city or county planner wants to locate new parks; the board of education, new schools; the social welfare agency, a service center; a religious denomination, new churches; the department store, a new branch; and the investor, a shopping center or an office building. Each user estimates the demand for facilities at a series of different sites in order to determine the best one.

e. Evaluation of market or service potential

In this case the facility or service center already exists, but the problem is to determine how effectively it is doing its job. Is the library serving the kind of people that live in its area? Is the Community Chest getting the contributions it should from the different parts of the city? Are the dealers or sales agencies in the different parts of the city selling as much as they should in terms of the kind of population they serve? Is current performance meeting the potential?

f. Contribution to planning for the future

Government and business must look and plan ahead to meet future needs, and the projection of small area data such as those for census tracts can help to achieve their aims. Accurate projections for small areas are most difficult to make, but the availability of census tract data for several decades can be of great help.

3. Areas Eligible for Census Tracts

All standard metropolitan statistical areas (SMSA's) in the United States and Puerto Rico are eligible for census tracts.[5] The tracting of entire standard metropolitan statistical areas is strongly encouraged.

The Bureau of the Census also will permit the establishment of census tracts in the following types of areas:

   a. A densely populated area in a non-SMSA county or town that is adjacent to another heavily-settled area in a county or town presently in an SMSA.
   b. A county with a city that is approaching the qualifying population of 50,000 and that reasonably may be expected to attain 50,000 by the time of the next population census. If it does not achieve SMSA status, a tract report will not be published for this area but tabulations will be available.
   c. A county with a population of 100,000 or more and with more than half of its population classified as urban. Publication will occur only if the county achieves SMSA status.

4. Small-Area Data Framework for Cities with Less than 50,000 Population

With a few exceptions, cities under 50,000 population not located within SMSA's will have to take special steps to get small-area statistics below the level of city totals. The exceptions are cities which entered into special contracts with the Census Bureau prior to the 1970 Census.

Printed 1970 Census reports for small cities contain city-wide totals only, but much more is needed in the problem-solving efforts of these communities. Enumeration district totals from First Count tapes constitute the only other type of information linked to areas within small cities. The Bureau of the Census defines enumeration districts (ED's) as areas with small population which are delineated and used by the Census Bureau for the collection and tabulation of data. Each enumeration district is assigned to one enumerator to canvass. They are the smallest areas for which data are tabulated, with the exception of the blocks used in larger cities. No data are published for enumeration districts.

Each enumeration district includes about 750 people, and approximately 400 data items are available on tape for each of these small districts. To obtain computer printouts of 1970 Census data by enumeration district,

---

[5] U.S. Bureau of the Census, *Census Tract Manual*, 26.

contact the Data Access and Use Laboratory, Data User Services Office, U.S. Bureau of the Census, Washington, D.C.

5. Organizing for a Tracting Project

So far in Section G we have dealt with an explanation of census tracts and their uses. It should be emphasized that the development of a tract plan is entirely up to the local community and that the background information necessary to guide census tracting work is described fully in the U.S. Bureau of the Census publication, *Census Tract Manual.*

Many Chamber researchers in the future will be faced with the problem of developing a census tract plan for a previously-untracted area or revising an already-adopted plan. The population of cities may approach or exceed the 50,000-person minimum. Also, as SMSA's are enlarged, with SMSA delineations changed and new counties added, these additional counties should be tracted.

With the establishment of a census tract committee, the actual job of laying out the census tracts, studying reference material and delineating boundaries will fall to various subcommittees or individuals, depending upon the amount of research time available and the ingenuity of the persons doing the job. Often in such cases a sub-group of two or three can accomplish more than a large group. Or the entire job might logically be broken down into several parts with different sub-groups (or individuals) working separate areas.

When entire counties are to be tracted in larger SMSA's, it may be advantageous to have separate tracting committees for each county, but experience has shown that the job can be done faster and more efficiently by a small, select group of conscientious, capable workers who have a thorough working knowledge of the areas to be tracted and who can devote time to field review.

6. Tracting New Areas

Tracting should begin with the central city and work outward to the remainder of the central county. Where townships are still a recognized unit of government, tracting can be done by these townships without regard to the corporate limits of the central city.

Where the SMSA consists of several counties, each county should be tracted separately. Fringe counties within an SMSA are often sparsely settled, with clusters of population concentration in isolated cities and towns, county seats or small suburban residential communities. Tracting these counties can be accomplished in most cases by grouping townships for desired population concentrations.

The most difficult job of the entire project is delineating tracts in the high-density urban areas. As explained earlier, tracts are useful only if they can define areas of uniform socio-economic conditions. A great amount of detail work is absolutely necessary to achieve as much uniformity as possible; this means a great amount of field work.

Before starting the task, it is imperative to gather such material as:
a. Maps and enumeration district data from the Census Bureau.
b. Current locally-produced maps, as large in scale as possible, from planning departments, utilities, highway department or private sources such as engineering firms.
c. Locally-produced data from utilities or governmental taxing units which might provide numbers of housing units or address locations of family units, and public and parochial school data which can be formulated to provide estimates of total population by school districts. Ward statistics on voter registrations are another possible source.

Because tract areas will remain constant for some time to come, future planning for areas should be determined so that changes in land use within the foreseeable future can be incorporated in the present tract plan. Drawing census tract boundaries will vary from city to city and from tract to tract, but the primary ideas to keep in mind while tracting are:
a. Tracts should average at least 4,000 population. If a county area has 120,000 estimated population, then it should be divided into approximately 30 tracts.
b. Tract boundaries should be major streets, railroads, or natural barriers for permanent delineation.
c. Social and economic homogeneity is very desirable in defining tracts. For example, avoid high and low income areas within the same tract, because statistics for the tract as a whole would not reflect the condition of either group. Keep in mind the end use of the data and its effectiveness.

7. Revising Census Tracts

To obtain comparable data from one period to another, tract boundaries should not change. However, because of major changes in land use within an established tract, such as large apartment complexes or location of a new freeway, the social or economic character may be altered significantly enough to warrant division of that tract into two or more tracts.

8. Census Tract Boundary Descriptions

It is also necessary to prepare a written description of the boundary of each census tract, beginning in the northwest corner of each tract and proceeding clockwise around the tract to the point of beginning, naming each street, road, railroad, stream, etc. (See Exhibit 4-A).

9. Numbering Census Tracts

Tracts should be identified by consecutive numbers (1, 2, 3, etc.). Start numbering in the central business district and continue in a spiral or serpentine pattern out to the perimeter of the county (See Exhibit 4-B).

If census tracts do not observe city limits in their boundaries, as is permissible, the numbering should be continuous within the county and no distinction in numbering should be observed between central city and county. In this case also, either the serpentine or the spiral numbering plans may be used.

Where there is more than one county in a standard metropolitan statistical area, the tracts in each county should be numbered separately and in a distinct series, for example, County A beginning with 101, County B beginning with 201, etc.

The basic census tract number may have no more than 4 digits. These may be followed, where necessary, by 2 decimal digits to indicate tract splits or subdivisions. The possible range of numbers is from 1 to 9999.99. Prefix and suffix letters no longer may be used for tract identification. A short, all-numeric tract identification is very desirable for modern computer use.

Duplication of numbers within an SMSA should be avoided. Exceptions are possible in very large SMSA's, but duplication within a county is not permissible.[6]

10. Census Tract Base Maps

The following types of base maps showing census tract boundaries should be available for area studies in tracted areas[7]:

a. A large-scale, street map of the city and its adjacent built-up area showing tract boundaries and numbers. Such a map is useful to all agencies that collect data by street addresses and allocate them by tracts.

b. A smaller-scale census tract outline map with names of boundary streets and tract numbers. It is similar to the map published by the Bureau in the census tract reports.

11. Census Tract Street Index

Users need a census tract street index to assign to specific tracts data such as those on births, deaths, crimes, delinquencies, building permits, sales, etc., which are identified by street address. The census tract street index shows the census tract number for every house address located in it.

---

[6] U.S. Bureau of the Census, *Census Tract Manual*, 42-43.

[7] U.S. Bureau of the Census, *Census Tract Manual*, 50.

This coding index is essential if data collected by local groups are to be tabulated by tracts.[8]

As the first step in constructing this index, a card should be made for each street, avenue, boulevard, named alley, or other thoroughfare, and the range of the possible address numbers within each census tract listed on the card opposite the census tract. The tract street index is made up from these cards arranged in alphabetical order (See Exhibit 4-C).

12. Assistance from the U.S. Bureau of the Census

Several citations to material in the Census Bureau's *Census Tract Manual* appear in this chapter. This comprehensive manual is published by the Geography Division of the Bureau of the Census and is written in layman's language. It details the necessary rules, regulations, definitions, criteria, and procedures for establishing census tracts. The Census Bureau will supply copies of this manual for free distribution as needed by a local census tract committee. All materials in this manual should be studied thoroughly to acquire a clear understanding of the basic procedures. It is *must* reading before you begin the preparation of census tracts for your local area.

Every Chamber of Commerce research executive should be aware of the value of census tract data and its promotion to his business community. If his community is eligible and has not been tracted, he should take the lead in tracting the local area. If his area is already tracted, he should take the responsibility to make sure that the local census tract committee is active and that the Chamber is an integral part of the tract committee's program.

The development and updating of any community's census tract program is the responsibility of the local community — especially the local Chamber's researcher. The Bureau of the Census generously works with any community to aid and counsel in census tract development.

---

[8] U.S. Bureau of the Census, *Census Tract Manual*, 51.

EXHIBIT 4-A: DESCRIPTIONS OF CENSUS TRACT BOUNDARIES

CT No.

1001 — Beginning at intersection of Montgomery, San Jacinto County and Liberty Co. boundaries; northeast on Liberty-San Jacinto Co. boundary to Southern Pacific R.R.; southeast on Southern Pacific R.R. to Montgomery Co. line; northwest on Liberty-Montgomery Co. boundary to point of beginning.

1002 — Beginning at intersection of San Jacinto-Liberty Co. boundary with Southern Pacific R.R.; northeast on San Jacinto-Liberty Co. boundary to Tarkington Bayou; south on Tarkington Bayou to Luce Bayou; southwest on Luce Bayou to Montgomery-Liberty Co. boundary; northwest on Montgomery-Liberty Co. boundary to Southern Pacific R.R.; northeast on Southern Pacific R.R. to point of beginning.

1003 — Beginning at intersection of State Highway 105 and Tarkington Bayou; east on State Highway 105 to Farm Road 2518; south on Farm Road 2518 to Farm Road 162; southeast on Farm Road 162 to Trinity River; south on Trinity River and west on an imaginary line to oil surfaced road west of confluence with Greens Bayou; northwest and west on oil surfaced road to Gillen Bayou; north and west on Gillen Bayou to Farm Road 1008; south on Farm Road 1008 to Luce Bayou; west on Luce Bayou to Tarkington Bayou; north, northwest on Tarkington Bayou to point of beginning.

1004 — Beginning at intersection of Tarkington Bayou and San Jacinto-Liberty Co. boundary; northeast on San Jacinto-Liberty Co. boundary to Trinity River; south on Trinity River to Farm Road 162; northwest on Farm Road 162 to Farm Road 2518; north on Farm Road 2518 to State Highway 105; west on State Highway 105 to Tarkington Bayou; north on Tarkington Bayou to point of beginning.

EXHIBIT 4-B: NUMBERING CENSUS TRACTS

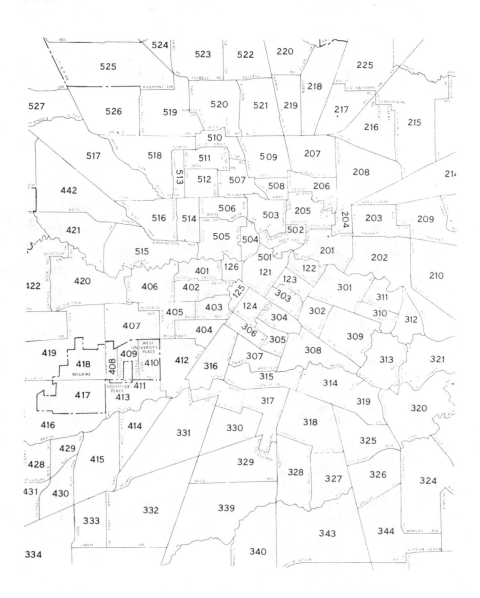

EXHIBIT 4-C: CENSUS TRACT STREET INDEX

Street Address Range		CT Number
Angua		
7800 - 7998	even	215
7801 - 7999	odd	215
Anice		
1500 - 2898	even	240
1501 - 2999	odd	241
Anita		
300 - 998	even	125
301 - 999	odd	125
1000 - 2098	even	124
1001 - 2099	odd	124
2400 - 4098	even	304
2401 - 4099	odd	304
4100 - 4198	even	308
4101 - 4199	odd	308
Ann		
1000 - 1298	even	349
1001 - 1299	odd	355
2200 - 2598	even	122
2201 - 2599	odd	122
12100 - 12598	even	541
12101 - 12599	odd	541
Ann Arbor		
2800 - 3998	even	523
2801 - 3999	odd	523
Ann Louise Rd.		
12500 - 13798	even	539
12501 - 13799	odd	547

5 ELECTRONIC DATA PROCESSING

A. INTRODUCTION

Computers—those electronic wonder machines that absorb information, manipulate it for problem solving and ultimately produce new data—have been described as one of the greatest inventions in the past 500 years. The magnitude of computer technology's impact has led some historians to claim that its effects on mankind are as profound as the development of language . . . and that we are still seeing only its primitive stages.

In spite of its relative youth, Electronic Data Processing (EDP)—of which the computer is the major component—has become such an acceptable and necessary management tool in the business world that it is no longer questionable whether EDP can be applied to Chamber of Commerce activities. Rather, the question centers on how to determine which activities merit EDP. This chapter will explore specific applications of EDP to Chamber activities and at the same time attempt to provide a basis for individual Chamber decisions on the advantages of EDP as related to their programs.

Each year more and more Chambers of Commerce have opted for EDP. Although previously limited to use by relatively large Chambers, a recent survey has revealed that 41% of the Chambers were actively using EDP in their operations and that another 15% were considering using it in one or more applications. Since EDP is primarily a means of handling information through several developmental stages, its utility is independent of the Chamber's size. Any Chamber of Commerce can now enjoy the advantages of rapid data handling without a large investment in expensive equipment. Small Chambers may consider the issues in this chapter as pertinent to their operations, while the larger Chambers should consider this discussion as a point of departure in the analysis of their EDP requirements.

Data processing systems consist of two major components, hardware and software. The former term is used for actual physical equipment employed, and the latter refers to the design of the operations, the computer language used, and the programming. Since hardware devices may aid in creating optimal software procedures, and vice versa, the two terms are not mutually exclusive in functional operations and are used mainly for convenience. When data processing is mentioned, the layman tends to think first of hardware, specifically the computer. Yet in terms of the time and preparation involved in an EDP operation, the software side of processing information — making a computer "package" — is the more pronounced and visible.

The major element in EDP is, of course, the handling of raw information by machines for workup as a finished product once the data have been collected. In order to utilize machine operations, the task given to the computer must be well-structured. Billing, for example, is largely routine and usually one of the first operations to be automated in most organizations. Similar examples would be inventory control, financial analysis, and statistical forecasting. In these cases, the procedures are so well defined that EDP operates in exactly the same manner as would manual manipulation, i.e., according to precise mathematical rules and procedures.

Generally, the Chamber executive who plans to use EDP is attempting to increase the productivity of his staff and/or improve procedures for organizing and reporting data. Whatever the case, the executive must increase his knowledge of EDP and the different approaches available for implementing such a change in procedure. The adaptation of each EDP phase should be preceded by an objective efficiency analysis to determine whether computerization is justifiable or whether greater benefits could perhaps be derived from maintaining any of the steps of the project as manual operations. Decisions about the use of computers should be made on the basis of profitability — not on the basis of capability alone.

B. GENERAL OUTLINE OF AN EDP PROJECT

A typical data-handling project — utilizing EDP — consists of three distinct phases: input, processing, output. For illustrative purposes, assume that data going in one door of a building are the input; inside the building (or computer) it is processed; and the processed data emerge from a door on the opposite side of the building as the output, or desired product. The input could be membership lists, name and address files, census data, primary or secondary economic data. The processing phase may involve mathematical manipulation, sorting, or other appropriate procedures. The output could be calculations, statistical tabulations, reports — whatever the system has been designed to produce.

The step-by-step method of the EDP project involves an analysis called "recursive optimization." This term refers to a procedure in which one starts with the destination or the results desired and works backward to the present situation in order to find the best, most efficient way to solve a problem.

For example, suppose that three people want to travel from New York to San Francisco, each for a different reason. One wishes to arrive in a hurry to complete an important business deal, so money is not an important consideration. He will fly non-stop to arrive as soon as possible. The second person is a student who would like to get home soon but does not have much money. His best alternative is to fly stand-by on a flight that makes stops in Cleveland and Kansas City, and which will cost him about half the regular fare. The third person is retired and is traveling to visit friends, but wants to travel at a leisurely pace and enjoy the scenery. She will ride the train, which is slower and no less costly than flying, but will offer her the advantages of seeing parts of the country which she has never before seen.

Each of these three people had basically the same problem, i.e., traveling from one city to another. Analysis of the problem included consideration of transportation facilities available, travel routes, costs, and objectives of the respective journeys. Each person chose a different alternative solution in accordance with his or her needs, capabilities and interests. This same recursive optimization process — examining desired results and then working backward through the possibilities for achieving those results — should be incorporated into the Chamber of Commerce decision-maker's activity in selecting an EDP system for his organization.

It is essential that any researcher seriously considering implementing an EDP system should examine the project parameters within which he is working and the time and money constraints upon him before evaluating systems as possible solutions to his problems. Implicit in the statement of recursive optimization are two assumptions which should not be overlooked. The first, obviously, is that the researcher must know exactly what it is he wants to achieve. That is, he must know exactly what outputs are desired of the system, whether it be membership lists, address files, or manipulations of primary, secondary, or tertiary data.

The second requisite for a sound comparative analysis of alternative EDP or manual systems is that the researcher know what his critical variables are. While there are usually several solutions to any problem, each will differ in the advantages it offers. One EDP system might be quicker to install and operate, but at a prohibitively high cost; one might be quite economical in terms of purchase price, but time-consuming and needful of more personnel; one system might be very reliable, but designed to provide answers or results only in an inflexible, narrowly usable form; and one might be both cheap and easy to operate, but unsuitable because of physical or organizational constraints.

Some of the important considerations in examining any EDP system using recursive techniques are:

1. The types of statistical inputs available for the system.
2. The personal managerial time required to supervise installation and operation of the system.
3. The costs of the system, including purchase and installation costs, maintenance costs, personnel training costs, and opportunity costs of other systems.
4. The reliability of the system. Will it break down often, due either to personnel or mechanical problems?
5. The general suitability of the system. Will it provide the information needed and, just as importantly, will it answer *when* the information is needed?
6. Are there organizational constraints involved, such as conflicts with managers of other departments in decisions concerning the uses to which the system will be put?
7. Most importantly, will the system do what you want it to do?

Remember, computers are not the answer to everything. In many cases they simply provide a more costly and complex system for achieving the same results as a manual system which is working fine by itself. Computers are not suited to every task and can not necessarily improve on the performance of every job, so the first question to ask is whether or not the manual system can be improved.

C. RELATIVE ADVANTAGES AND DISADVANTAGES OF EDP SYSTEMS

Once the researcher has isolated those variables which he feels are the most important to his system, his next step is to apply the optimization technique—finding out which is the most efficient way of getting from the available input to the desired output.

There are four basic alternatives available to the decision-maker in selecting a computer processing service. Each has its own benefits and detriments and its own costs. These alternatives are: (1) using an in-house type of computer installation; (2) using a time-sharing system; (3) using others' facilities purchased or donated on a part-time basis, such as those owned by a university, bank, or utility; and (4) using a computer service bureau.

Deciding which of these to use is not an easy matter, especially since the distinctions among them are not always clear. As data management industry and technology change daily, the capabilities and advantages of each alternative are changing, also. Each must be carefully evaluated in light of its cost and potential as well as Chamber organizational needs. In the following discussion some of the advantages and disadvantages of each system will be enumerated, although one of the options clearly seems to be better than the others.

1. In-House EDP System

The choice of an in-house system is obviously the most expensive of the possible alternatives. Not only does this method require acquisition of the data processing equipment — the hardware — it also necessitates personnel recruitment and training for operation.

An in-house installation is most likely to be necessary when the organization requires unique, time-consuming applications. The primary criterion for an in-house installation is the service it provides for the organization. The advantage of such an installation is the full accessibility of all the operating staff for coordinating the data processing effort. Also, the personnel and equipment necessary for special projects are always readily available, and the organization may lease unused computer time to outside companies, thereby recouping some of the original investment.

One of the disadvantages of an in-house installation is that the organization must equip itself with a system that is powerful enough to meet all of its long-term data processing requirements, which are frequently hard to predict. Unless there are many immediate applications, the in-house option is an inefficient way of handling data processing needs, because facilities sufficient to meet maximum needs will go unused for at least part of the time. Secondly, the organization must staff its installation with supervisory and operating personnel, which requires more expense; there are often problems in the development stages of work coordination among the programmers and departments. Finally, dependency on the computer may cause serious trouble if the system breaks down.

2. Time-Sharing EDP

Time-sharing is a rapidly growing sector of the computer industry in which companies or organizations buy access to a large computer through a remote terminal located in their own offices. The time-sharing philosophy — that it is cheaper and easier to buy a small part of a large computer than to buy a small computer — usually means the client will pay an initial fixed cost to cover the installation of the terminal, the manuals, and the services of a company representative to help set up and use the basic programs. Thereafter, the user pays for the lease of the terminal plus only that computer time which it actually uses, although there is usually a minimum monthly charge.

Most time-sharing information retrieval systems are user oriented. The learning time required for an untrained individual will vary, but is usually fairly short, as these time-sharing systems operate using relatively easy computer languages and often provide canned statistical programs which will fit a variety of needs.

A major advantage of a time-sharing system is that the remote terminals can be installed wherever there are electric power and telephone lines. The terminals are relatively simple to use, and service is available when needed. Secondly, programs can be developed much faster than is possible on conventional systems and, when a run is needed, it can be completed in seconds. A remote terminal is easy to install and requires a very low level of fixed investment. Some of the newer programming languages can be mastered in a few hours, and existing programs from the company's library can be used without writing new ones.

One of the disadvantages of the time-sharing systems is that they are the least reliable of any of the alternatives. While most such companies take preventive steps, breakdown problems are bound to occur, and do. Major users often cite unreliability as their primary criticism of this system. Time-sharing, compared with conventional forms of computer power, is expensive, especially in light of the services offered. Additionally, many users feel that time-sharing allows only modest quantities of data to be stored and that the remote terminals are usually noisy, unreliable, and expensive. Also, the basic languages which time-sharing systems are required to use are too simple and lack real power.

3. Universities and Local Firms with Unbooked EDP Time

The third alternative is to employ computer facilities donated or purchased on a part-time basis from a university, bank, utility or other major company in the community. Universities are especially good sources as they usually possess large computers which allow many simultaneous uses.

In choosing this alternative, the greatest time will be spent on learning the system. This is particularly true if the researcher tries to run his programs without the aid of someone who is experienced at that installation. Usually, however, the computer owner provides people whose sole job is to help users.

The advantage of using someone else's system is that it is cheaper than either of the first two alternatives. A disadvantage is that the researcher must know quite a bit about computers himself in order to implement his programs, and many of the smaller Chamber researchers do not have the time or the facilities to acquire this knowledge. Secondly, the turn-around time for this method is greater, i.e., the time from insertion of the input to realization of the output. As another organization's facilities are being used, that group has priority on the computer time. Any programs which are badly needed by the Chamber may have to wait until it is convenient for them to be run.

4. Commercial EDP Service Bureau

The final EDP alternative system appropriate for Chamber of Commerce use is to employ a computer service bureau, which provides electronic data processing on a fee basis. Bureaus of this type make available their internally-installed computers (hardware) and the skill and planning necessary to operate the computers efficiently (software) for a fee. The service bureau accepts the raw data which is provided to them, converts it into a language or code that is meaningful to the computer, and then correlates the data or works with them to produce new information useful to you.

The primary advantage of using a service bureau is that it provides limited access to a computer for a minimum investment in time and money. The expenses involved are the preparation costs of accurate input data and the fee paid the company. In performing computer service, the bureau will provide systems and programming work. The only responsibilities of the user are to provide accurate input to the system and to notify the bureau of any modifications in their requirements.

Service bureaus offer standard systems and programs to their users. These package applications enable the bureau to perform a service for the user at a significantly lower cost since development expenses are spread over a number of users. The charge for any program provided will be a function of its complexity.

The advantages offered by service bureaus are that the responsibility for running the computer installation rests outside the organization, thereby saving time, money, and worry; that the user can devote more of his efforts to ensuring the accuracy of the inputs and controls at his end; that staffing the computer installation with qualified personnel is the responsibility of the bureau; and that as the Chamber realizes new requirements for computer use, they can be easily arranged with the service bureau.

A disadvantage of using a service bureau is that it is often quite expensive. This is to be expected, because the user is essentially buying the management and control of the services as well as the computer time. The bureau takes charge of the whole data problem and handles it from beginning to end—usually for a healthy premium.

Another disadvantage of the bureaus is that there are a large number of local independent companies coming into the business. Some of these have been extremely unreliable and a large number of others have gone out of business. A potential liability to using a service company is that it will breed into the organization an inflexibility in procedures. Once a billing project has been completely turned over to a consultant company, for example, it is easy for the user to lose complete control of it. Some understanding of the process has been relinquished and, if the whole problem were suddenly thrust back into the organization's lap, it would be difficult to re-establish the manual procedures for handling it.

These are only possible disadvantages, however, and do not offset the positive points of using a service bureau. Any company or organization, regardless of size, can now enjoy the competitive advantages of rapid data handling without investing in expensive equipment or acquiring a mass of first-hand computer knowledge. Small companies and organizations, especially, will find that the outside EDP service center provides a practical way of speeding routine clerical jobs.

D. RECOMMENDED EDP SYSTEM

Inasmuch as most Chamber activities do not necessitate massive amounts of data processing, few Chambers have a need to own and operate even the most elementary pieces of hardware; on-going innovations in time-sharing, however, may drastically change the future economics of the situation. Thus much, if not all, of the data processing should be handled by outside firms, of which a service bureau will probably be most appropriate for Chamber needs and the kinds of jobs to be performed. Should this option be chosen, the relationship is one of supervising the subcontractor, and all procedures, methodologies, and questions concerning programming should be resolved before the contract is signed.

E. APPLICATIONS OF EDP
TO CHAMBER OF COMMERCE ACTIVITIES

In considering the activities which would be most profitably handled by EDP methods, Chambers of Commerce enjoy the unique position of being able to draw upon the advice and experience of member firms. Nearly all banks, utilities, insurance companies, and accounting firms, for example, are well versed in the techniques and uses of EDP methods and have accumulated a wealth of experience from which the Chamber executives might benefit. Computer leasing companies, time-sharing operators, and the many local service bureaus, of course, are also excellent sources of information, as are the local technical schools and universities which operate data processing departments. In addition, many of the above mentioned concerns have developed "package" programs in such fields as accounting, auditing, statistics, inventory control, and capital budgeting which may be of particular use in certain Chamber activities.

1. Membership Records

The most common initial application of EDP by a Chamber of Commerce is in accounting and financial analysis. A Chamber's membership data may be transferred to punch cards (or tape) for processing by a service bureau and extracted as required. Data items to be punched into cards might include account number, company name and address, representatives and/or number of memberships, Standard Industrial Classification (SIC) Code, telephone number, year joined and renewal date, employment, billing frequency and amount, description of business, billing name and address (if different from above), special funds subscribed, payment history, and other accounting details.

From this kind of information, billing statements can be produced much more rapidly than if handled by manual operations, and in addition, the mailing labels themselves can be created. Also, certain laborious jobs — for example, an "aging" of accounts receivable or other financial analysis — can be handled at the same time that the billing statements are being prepared.

One of the major advantages of using EDP is that the set of data can be manipulated to serve many functionally different purposes. Membership rosters can be created quickly and updated easily by simply adding or deleting selected items from the punched cards. The Chamber's members can be listed and cross-referenced by types of business, geographic area (e.g., by zip code), and by SIC class. Multiple listings and cross references of this kind would be economically impractical by manual methods.

2. Standard Industrial Classification Comparisons

Beyond the simple listing of members, EDP allows for a wide choice of analytical reports, again from the same set of data mentioned above. For example, the Chamber may want to compare its membership SIC classes to the reported distribution in the Census reports. If the number of employees is included as a data item in the punched cards, the membership can be compared to the distributions known for the particular area that the Chamber represents. The point here is that once the deck of data cards is prepared for a given purpose, the addition of just a few more pieces of information on each member enables the Chamber executive to perform analyses as often and in as much detail as he may desire. These activities can be extremely useful in focusing attention upon the kinds of prospective members who should be sought in membership drives or in other special purpose campaigns.

3. Preparation of Mailing Labels

At present most Chambers probably address their mail with addressograph plates or some variant of this method. When selective mailings are desired, or if the Chamber maintains multiple membership (i.e., the billing accounts break down differently from the assigned memberships), maintenance of semi-automatic mailing lists becomes extremely troublesome. If the mailing labels are created by fully automatic methods, the situation changes entirely. The Chamber executive is able to generate many cross-reference mailing lists, minimizing the total number of pieces of mail required for a particular purpose.

The most obvious example lies in the preparation of questionnaires dealing with a particular topic, which would be sent only to Chamber of Commerce chief executive officers. If the Chamber desires to reach firms of a given size, EDP allows the executive to limit his mailings to just that particular sub-set of his membership. Additionally, the Chamber executive can tabulate the questionnaires and other replies by EDP and, if the need arises, he is in a position to make authoritative statements backed by the statistical findings of his research department.

4. Business and Industrial Directories

Another Chamber activity which is ideal for EDP is the compilation of a business or industrial directory. Such directories are difficult to create and maintain manually on a continuing basis because of the substantial amounts of data handled and the almost constant changing and revising of the pieces of information required to keep the contents current. If all the data are stored on punch cards or tape, the large burden of revising data is greatly reduced, since the individual cards may be inserted, deleted, or altered right up to the time of publication.

The directory itself, excluding any advertising, may be compiled by simply listing the contents of the punch cards, after which the printed output can be pasted up, reduced if needed, and printed by the offset method. Alternatively, the cards may be processed completely by a computer program which correctly aligns the pieces of information and simultaneously creates several cross-reference indexes, as well as a table of contents, all of which emerges as copy "camera-ready" for printing, with or without advertisements. For all but the smallest directories, some variation of this application of EDP is certainly essential if the directory is to be kept as up-to-date as possible on a routine basis.

5. Business Indicators

The fifth potential application of EDP relates to business-indicator research. To report even as few as 10 to 15 data items in time series, with the attendant need for deriving index numbers and/or seasonal adjustment factors, is a time-consuming and error-prone job, all the more so when various percentage changes in the indicators are required as a normal part of the process. So long as the original entries are accurate, computer programs can do the job quickly and accurately each month, freeing the staff members for other kinds of research. In addition, the kind of time series revisions which are commonly done with many types of local economic series and national data can be accomplished by simply updating the punched cards while adding the preliminary figures for the following month.

6. EDP Uses for the Chamber of Commerce Magazine

The magazine departments of certain Chambers use EDP for compiling information on subscribers and in developing reports and other activities. A selected list of these EDP uses by the magazine department includes: sorting subscribers by type of subscription (complimentary, paid life member, member, paid subscription or gift subscription); printing labels for mailings; maintaining up-to-date records on cancellations; using programs based on SIC codes for reader surveys to determine the types of material to be included in magazine readership profiles; and accounting procedures such as circulation control, production-control and budgeting, advertising-account "aging" and analysis.

7. Additional Applications of EDP to Chamber of Commerce Activities

Without too much repetitive discussion, it must be stressed that some type of EDP system can be adapted to facilitate many other areas of Chamber operations. In addition to keeping information on membership and dues, the financial department can use computer services to automate payroll and benefit expenditures and to record total expenses. The membership committee can use an EDP system to perform the very time-consuming analysis of the composition of the membership of the Chamber's various committees. With little trouble, the computer will provide alphabetical lists of members, lists of companies represented, the titles of the members, the years they joined, the companies which are heavily represented, and those that are represented by few, if any, of their employees on Chamber of Commerce committees.

Within the realm of the Research Department specifically, an EDP system will provide valuable assistance in compiling statistics for population estimates. It will also aid in sampling procedures for such special projects as airline cases and ACCRA cost-of-living reports. A computerized record-keeping system can also greatly simplify recurring projects like census tract street indexes and address coding guides, which require tremendous amounts of revision each year.

SELECTED READING REFERENCES

Allen, Brandt. "Time Sharing Takes Off." *Harvard Business Review,* (March-April, 1969), 128-136.

Archer, Harry C. "Computers: Future Uses for Associations." *Association Management,* (May, 1971), 34-38.

Becker, E. C., Jr. "Using an EDP Bureau." *Industrial Marketing,* (September, 1967), 136d.

Bromberg, Howard. "Buying Software." *Association Management,* (May, 1971), 43-47.

"Business Takes A Second Look At Computers." *Business Week,* (June 5, 1971), 59-66.

"Choosing and Using An Outside EDP Center." *Administrative Management,* (January, 1965), 59-60.

Churchman, C. West. *The Systems Approach.* New York, N.Y.: Dell Publishing Co., 1968.

Dean, Neal J. "The Computer Comes of Age." *Harvard Business Review,* (January-February, 1968), 83-91.

Dearden, John. "Can Management Information Be Automated?" *Harvard Business Review,* (March-April, 1964), 128-135.

Dearden, John. "How to Organize Information Systems." *Harvard Business Review,* (March-April, 1965), 65-73.

Dearden, John. "Myth of Real-Time Management Information." *Harvard Business Review,* (May-June, 1966), 123-132.

Diebold, John. "What's Ahead in Information Technology." *Harvard Business Review,* (September-October, 1965), 76-82.

Fiock, L. R., Jr. "Seven Deadly Dangers in EDP." *Harvard Business Review,* (May-June, 1962), 88-96.

"Glossary of Common Computer Terms." *American Gas Journal,* (June, 1965), 32-33.

Gruenberger, Fred. *Expanding Use of Computers in the 70's: Markets — Needs — Technology.* Englewood Cliffs, New Jersey: Prentice-Hall, Inc., 1971.

Hartley, Harry J. "12 Hurdles To Clear Before You Take On Systems Analysis." *Journal of Systems Management,* (June, 1969), 28-29.

Head, Robert V. "Information Systems: The Changing Scene." *Journal of Systems Management,* (April, 1969), 40-41.

Head, Robert V. "Old Myths and New Realities." *Datamation,* (September, 1967), 26-29.

Hill, Richard H. "Data Processing: How To Use Outside Programming Services." *Management Review,* (June, 1966), 31-34.

Hofer, Charles W. "Emerging EDP Pattern." *Harvard Business Review,* (March-April, 1970), 16-31, 169-171.

"Is There a Computer Service Bureau in Your Future?" *Business Management,* (May, 1970), 26-29.

Johnson, John W. *Associations and the Computer.* Washington, D.C.: Chamber of Commerce of the United States, 1970.

Jones, Curtis H. "At Last: Real Computer Power for Decision Makers." *Harvard Business Review,* (September-October, 1970), 75-89.

Lachter, Lewis E. "Time-Sharing: Low-Cost Link to Computer." *Administrative Management,* (September, 1965), 66, 68.

Martin, E. Wainright, Jr. *Electronic Data Processing: An Introduction.* Revised Edition. Homewood, Illinois: Richard D. Irwin, Inc., 1968.

Notaro, Michael R., Jr. "What to Ask — And Expect — of Your Service Bureau." *Administrative Management,* (October, 1966), 28-34.

"Over 700 Areas of Application of Computers." *Computers and Automation,* (June, 1954), 82-84.

Roy, John L. "The Changing Role of the Service Bureau." *Datamation,* (March, 1970), 52-54.

Schwab, Bernhard. "The Economics of Sharing Computers." *Harvard Business Review,* (September-October, 1968), 61-70.

Seewald, Eugene J. "Some Thoughts on Service Bureaus." *Business Automation,* (March, 1969), 70-72.

Shorter, Edward. *The Historian and the Computer.* Englewood Cliffs, New Jersey: Prentice-Hall, Inc., 1971.

Smith, Arnold P. "Choosing a Service Bureau." *Computers and Automation,* (December, 1964), 23-24.

Thomas, Uwe. *Computerized Data Banks in Public Administration.* Paris, France: OECD Publications, 1971.

U.S. Office of the President, Bureau of the Budget. *Automatic Data Processing Glossary.* Washington, D.C.: U.S. Government Printing Office, 1969.

U.S. News & World Report. *The Computer: How It's Changing Our Lives.* Washington, D.C.: U.S. News & World Report, Inc., 1972.

Webster, Fran. "Computers: Toy Train or Productive Tool?" *Michigan Challenge,* Vol. 10, No. 10 (July, 1970), 5-6, 8.

Withington, Frederic G. "Data Processing's Evolving Place in the Organization." *Datamation,* (June, 1969), 58, 65-68.

6 SELECTED STATISTICAL TOOLS AND TECHNIQUES

A. INTRODUCTION

As a basic part of his job the Chamber researcher is required to deal with varied techniques of statistical analysis. These techniques are frequently necessary in computing or interpreting local and national business indicators, in demographic studies, in projections based on historical performance, and in a range of other special or daily projects. The successful completion of these projects depends on the researcher having a working knowledge of elementary statistical terms and procedures.

The intent of this chapter is to provide brief explanations and illustrations of some of those tools and techniques which are used most often. Many of the definitions and techniques mentioned here refer to procedures outlined in other chapters in this book and hopefully will serve as a quick and easy reference for those procedures.

It should not be assumed that this chapter will serve all of your statistical needs. It will not, nor was it designed to do so. What this section will do is serve as a convenient reference for selected terms and techniques used most often by Chamber of Commerce researchers.

There is no substitute for a good statistics textbook. A collection of them is even better. A listing of some of the better books and authors in this field is included in the bibliography to this chapter.

Most researchers interested in analyzing statistical data use one of two techniques in arranging information to make it more meaningful. The technique used depends on the type of data being collected. One method is the *time series*, which is used to demonstrate changes in a particular data series over an extended period of time. An example of time series data is a tabulation of the annual population of a city for each of the last 20 years.

The second type of distribution is the *frequency distribution*, which is an arrangement of numerical data according to types of information. A common example of a frequency distribution is the classification of the

population into age groups. This would not be considered a time series because it is the breakdown of the population at a fixed point in time rather
than on a continuing basis.

B. FREQUENCY DISTRIBUTIONS

Frequency distributions, generally, are organized by classes of statistics rather than by arraying the values from top to bottom. Arranging figures according to magnitude of the numbers gives a rather awkward display
which is difficult to handle in analysis. To determine the characteristics of
a set of data it is usually necessary to have class intervals, especially uniform intervals, into which the data are compressed. For example, the population of the United States can be expressed according to age. Perhaps five-
year intervals will be sufficient for analytical purposes, so that it will take
classifications of "five years and under," "six to 10 years," "11 to 15
years." If this much detail is not necessary, perhaps a 10-year interval
might be used, such as "10 years or under," "11 to 20 years," "21 to 30
years." Some definition of terms is necessary to make the limits of the classification mutually exclusive, such as "age at last birthday" or "age at
nearest birthday" so that no question will be raised as to within which
classification the particular age is included.

To aid analysis, these distributions are often graphed to make the
significance of the data more easily determined. Usually the intervals are
placed on the horizontal axis and the number of entries fall into intervals
located on the vertical axis.

When most frequency distributions are graphed, they will construct a
somewhat bell-shaped curve. This is not always the case, but should be expected in a normal distribution. This propensity for the curve to peak out
somewhere near the middle is called the *central tendency.* The central tendency means that most of the values collected will fall near a central point,
although it may not be the exact center of the distribution. All this is simply
a means of saying that in most collections of data, there will be some point
around which the data will be grouped. For example, if one were to take
all the adults in the country and measure their heights and then graph
them, most adults would fall into a 5'0" to 6'0" range. While there are
many adults either above or below this range, most of the people will be
grouped within it, and the graph would represent this fact by having a peak
somewhere within this interval.

A frequency distribution can be analyzed in many ways. Measures of
central tendency are the mean, the median, and the mode. These are defined by formulas elsewhere in this chapter.

A measure of the variability of the data is called a measure of *dispersion.* This is calculated by such statistical tools as the *average deviation* or
the *standard deviation,* which is an indicator of dispersion in which data

can be analyzed for its departure, or dispersion, from the mean. There are also other formulas to measure skew, the tendency of a frequency distribution to cluster above or below the mean value, and the measure of curvature of the line on a chart which is expressing the distribution in graphic terms. The curvature is measured by a *coefficient of kurtosis* which indicates whether the chart comes up to a sharp peak or is flattened out and does not have any very dense portions in the distribution.

Another technique for analyzing data is *regression analysis* or *correlation*. This type of analysis is used in expressing relationships between variables. For illustrative purposes, an analysis might focus upon the relationship between height and weight where there are observations of many individuals. A technique for determining the meaning of these measures of height and weight is found in regression analysis in which a trend line or a "least squares fit" is used to strike an average performance of the data on a straight line summary. Also available in statistics texts are descriptions of curvilinear relationships, used where a straight line does not display the relation between variables, and multiple regression analysis, used when more than two variables must be considered simultaneously.

C. MEASURES OF CENTRAL TENDENCY

In the preceding section of this chapter it was pointed out that although statistical information usually is distributed over a range of values, it also shows a definite tendency to group itself around a given point. This clustering around a point is called the *central tendency* of the data. Determination of this central tendency is one of the most useful calculations that can be made for interpreting numbers.

There are three commonly-used methods of computing central tendency: the arithmetic mean, the median, and the mode. Each of these methods has its own advantages and disadvantages lending it to use in particular situations.

1. Arithmetic Mean

When people talk about the average of a group of numbers, they are most commonly referring to the arithmetic mean. The mean of a series of numbers or values is the sum of the values divided by the number of separate values. For instance, if three people weigh 130, 145, and 190 pounds, respectively, then their average weight is the sum of their weights (130 + 145 + 190 = 465), divided by the number of people (3): 465 ÷ 3 = 155 pounds.

The advantages of the mean are that it is usually very easy to compute and is widely understood due to common usage. The principal disadvantage is that the mean value is greatly affected by a few extreme values among the numbers being averaged. If the weights of six persons were being averaged, and they weighed 130, 135, 150, 155, 160, and 275 pounds, respectively, then 275 is an extreme figure which will distort the average from the central tendency.

2. Median

The second technique for measuring central tendency involves use of the median. The median is the value of the middle item of a group when the items are arranged according to size. If there is an even number of items then the midpoint between the middle two items usually is considered the median. For example, if temperatures in a city for five days are 88, 86, 90, 91, and 89 degrees, then to find the median arrange the numbers according to size (86, 88, 89, 90, 91) and take the middle term which is 89 degrees. If the sample period were for six days and the temperatures were 88, 86, 90, 91, 89, and 91 degrees, then the median term would be midway between 89 and 90 degrees, or 89.5.

The advantages of the median are that it is easy to compute and will not overemphasize extreme values. A disadvantage of the median is that its value is erratic when the number of items listed is small. Also, it does not lend itself to algebraic computation after it has been figured. For example, if there are four groups of people whose weights have been computed, then the mean weights of each of the groups can be added and divided by four to find a new mean. However, if the median weights of the groups were taken, they could not be averaged as the answer would be unrelated to the original numbers.

3. Mode

The mode is the most frequent or most common value of a group. If there are 10 people in a room and their weights are 115, 123, 135, 117, 126, 135, 127, 117, 130, and 135, then the mode is 135 lbs. because it is the value listed the most often.

The advantages of the mode are that it is entirely independent of extreme values for items; it is the most typical and descriptive of the averages; it is simple to approximate empirically when there are a small number of cases; and it is not necessary to arrange the values if they are relatively few in number. The disadvantages are that in a small number of items the mode may not exist because no values are repeated; the significance of the mode is limited when a large number of values are not available; and the mode often must be approximated. For example, in analyzing the ages of people in a city, it might be necessary to divide the people into brackets, such as

20-23, 24-27, 28-31 years of age, to limit the figures to the workable range. This would make it necessary to approximate the mode, as only the numbers of people in the individual groups are known.

To see how the mean, the median, and the mode might compare in similar situations, suppose that an auto dealer wants to know what age person would be most likely to buy his new style car. For a week he keeps a record of the age of everyone who purchases one of the cars in question. At the end of the week he finds that he has sold 10 cars to persons aged 28, 32, 23, 34, 55, 43, 37, 29, 40, and 29. Adding these ages up and dividing by the number of persons (10), he figures that the arithmetic mean is 35 years old: $350 \div 10 = 35$.

The mode of their ages is 29, as it is the age which appears twice while all the rest of them appear only once.

To compute the median, he arranges the numbers in increasing order and takes the middle term. In order the numbers are $23 - 28 - 29 - 29 - 32 - 34 - 37 - 40 - 43 - 55$. Since there are 10 terms, he must take the midpoint between the fifth and sixth terms for the median. The fifth term is 32, the sixth term is 34; therefore, the median is 33.

Depending on how critical it is to be accurate, the dealer could accept or reject his answers knowing the limitations of each method. The mean age, 35, is probably a little high because it incorporates the 55-year-old purchaser, who is not representative of the group. The mode is also probably not very accurate because of the limited number of items. While there are not enough entries to give a completely dependable median, it is probably the most appropriate because of the deficiencies in the other two methods.

D. RATIOS

A ratio is a number used to show the magnitude of one quantity relative to the magnitude of another quantity. It can be expressed as a fraction, a decimal, or a percent.

Example: In 1971, retail sales in Central City were $300,000.
In 1972, retail sales in Central City were $400,000.

Sales in '72 were $400,000/$300,000 = 4/3 = 1-1/3 times sales in '71. It could otherwise be said that '72 sales were $4/3 = 1.333$ times '71 sales, or that '72 sales were 133% of '71 sales.

Therefore, a ratio is nothing more than a method of expressing a relationship between two numbers. However, the value of using ratios in statistical analysis is belied by the ease with which they are computed.

Link relatives are a valuable tool for various kinds of estimates (see Chapter 16) which rely on the use of a series of ratios. A link relative is a number expressing the relationship of one segment of time series data to the segment immediately preceding it. As an illustration, suppose that retail sales in March in Central City were $50,000 and that in April they rose to $55,000. Expressed as a ratio, this means that April's sales were 1.1 times, 110% of, or 10% greater than March's sales. If, after checking historical records, the researcher found that in the past three years April's sales had run 10%, 9%, and 10% more than March's sales, then he might reasonably expect that next year April's sales would have about the same relationship to those of March, i.e., that they would be approximately 10% greater. Knowing this, once March's sales are known, April's sales can be estimated from them. It is also possible to carry this technique several steps further and estimate time series data three, four, or more months ahead. This process is especially useful for projecting year-end total sales figures when only third quarter data are available.

Chain relatives are a modification of link relatives designed to estimate the magnitude of seasonal variation. While link relatives show the relationship of each month to the previous month, chain relatives show the relationship of each month to all of the rest of the months. To do this it is necessary to convert the link relatives into a series of chain relatives. This is accomplished arbitrarily by setting the value of January's figures, whatever they measure, at 100% and then measuring every month against that figure via a series of relatives.

> Example: Monthly sales figures in Central City are:
> | | |
> |---|---|
> | January | $60,000 |
> | February | $54,000 |
> | March | $56,700 |
> | April | $62,370 |

The link relatives for these months are:

January	cannot be computed without December data
February	$54,000 \div $60,000 = 90%
March	$56,700 \div $54,000 = 105%
April	$62,370 \div $56,700 = 110%

Based on these figures, the computed chain relatives are:

January	100% (arbitrarily set)
February	100% × 90% = 90.00%
March	90% × 105% = 94.50%
April	94.5% × 110% = 103.95%

Naturally, this process would be continued for each of the months in the year. When finished, it produces an index of seasonal variation for each month, with a base of January, and can be used to plan inventories and sales personnel for those months in which sales are either heavy or lax. There are adjustments for trend factors which need to be made in chain relative analysis. Here again it is suggested that the interested researcher acquire a good statistics text and thoroughly review the procedure before attempting the analysis: a text can more completely explain refinements to be made and pitfalls to be avoided.

E. INDEX NUMBERS

An index number has been defined as "a measure of relative value compared with a base figure for the same series." In a time series in index form the base period usually is set equal to 100, and data for other periods are expressed as percentages of the value in the base period. Most indexes published by government agencies are presently expressed in terms of a 1967 = 100 base. Index numbers possess several advantages over the raw data from which they are derived. First, they facilitate analysis by their simplicity. Second, they are a more useful basis for comparison of changes in data originally expressed in dissimilar units. Third, they permit comparisons over time with some common starting period — the index base period.

While absolute figures are essential to statistical analysis, the meaning of the data becomes known only after they have been altered into some interpretable form. For example, to know that the average worker in Central City makes $180.00 a week while the average worker in Midland City makes $200.00 a week is of negligible value. What is needed to make this information more meaningful are the costs of living for the two cities, as well as measures of how fast both income and costs are changing. In this instance, assume that the ACCRA Cost-of-Living Index indicates that the cost in Central City equals the nationwide average, for an index number of 100, and that the cost-of-living index for Midland City is 112. To compare purchasing power, which is what we are trying to find out, we divide the income by the cost-of-living index, expressing the latter as a ratio rather than as a percentage:

Central City	$180/1.00 = $180.00
Midland City	$200/1.12 = $178.57

Thus, by using both income and cost-of-living data, we see that it is better to live in Central City despite the higher wages in Midland City.

Index numbers are quite easy to calculate. All that is needed is a base period to serve as a starting point. The base period is some time period for which the relevant statistical data are set equal to 100. Usually base periods are just calendar years, although in some instances base periods of several years are used, in which case the annual figures are averaged. For example, if Central County produced 50,000 tons of wheat in 1967, and 1967 is arbitrarily chosen as the base period, then 50,000 tons is assumed to equal 100, the scale against which all subsequent years will be measured until the base year is again arbitrarily changed. If, in 1968, the production rose to 60,000 tons, then the index number is computed by comparing that against the base number, e.g.,

$$60,000 \div 50,000 = 1.2; 1.2 \times 100 = 120$$

This is read as saying that 1968's production was 120% of 1967's, or, that there was a 20% increase from 1967 to 1968.

If, in 1969 production fell to 45,000 tons, then the index number is:

$$45,000 \div 50,000 = 0.9; 0.9 \times 100 = 90$$

This means that in 1969 production fell to 90% of 1967's figure.

As a corollary to this, if the period 1967-68 were used as the base period, then the base number would be:

$$\frac{50,000 + 60,000}{2} = 55,000$$

and all succeeding years would be compared against this number as denominator.

It is very important in choosing a base year for an index to pick a year that is representative. A year that had excessive fluctuation either upward or downward provides a poor basis for comparison. In the above example, if in 1967 there were a drought that caused massive crop failure, then it would not be a good base year because it would misrepresent the gains made in each of the subsequent years. Aside from this precaution, there is no real advantage to choosing one base period over another. However, base periods might need to be updated occasionally if there are changes in technology, manufacturing techniques or purchase patterns which have developed since the last base period and could reduce the value of the index for comparative purposes.

There are many governmentally-designated indexes in popular usage. Some of the better known index numbers are the Consumer Price Index of the Bureau of Labor Statistics, the Wholesale Price Index, also from the BLS, and the Index of Industrial Production prepared by the Federal Reserve Board. The Consumer Price Index currently is comparing with the 1967 base equaling 100; the Wholesale Price Index uses the same base, as does the Industrial Production Index. There is no real advantage, generally, in choosing one base over another. It is possible, however, that the index number may become less meaningful after it is removed a considerable distance from the base.

The Consumer Price Index measures the trend in "Costs of Living" over a span of time for each of the reported cities. While it measures the changes in Cost-of-Living for a fairly long period, it measures only the trend within a city and is not usable for intercity comparisons. This is due to the fact that there was no adjustment for comparability between cities in the base period. Because the Bureau of Labor Statistics did not start out with an adjusted relationship between all cities, the Bureau always warns users not to compare cities on this basis. This index measures price change for a "Market Basket" of commodities which has been redefined and studied for many years for improvement. It measures price changes but its overall flaw lies in the difficulty of including in the index any measurement of the qualitative up-grading of the products reported. The BLS has extensive specifications for collecting prices nationwide but no provision for quality change in the ordinary operation of the index. Periodically, the BLS reviews specifications and takes into account some of the new expenditures made by consumers for products which did not exist in prior years. For instance, in the 1950's the BLS had to introduce prices for television sets, which were becoming standard in a large portion of the dwelling units of the country and had never before been priced.

The Wholesale Price Index measures manufacturers' prices primarily for commodities as they leave the manufacturing plant but reports only for the nation as a whole, without any geographic breakdown. A vast number of items are priced — well over 1,000 — and the Index is produced on a monthly basis for nationwide industries.

These two indexes can be obtained both adjusted and unadjusted seasonally, and they are primarily concerned with prices rather than volume of goods. They are meant to measure inflation, not production.

The Industrial Production Index of the Federal Reserve Board also is obtainable in seasonally adjusted or unadjusted form and covers nearly all manufactured products. The Industrial Production Index, unlike the other two mentioned here, sets out to measure physical volume of manufacturing. An index number of this type allows the comparison by industry for the country as a whole of durable manufactures, non-durable manufactures, machinery, paper, chemicals, foods, and other categories of production, as well as mining and utility production. The series used to produce the index comes from a great many governmental sources in which physical volume of production is available. There is, to say the least, a very complicated system of industrial reporting for this index on a monthly basis. Different components come from different sources, but they are put together in an index, or a series of index numbers, in such a way that comparisons can be made. However, not all industries have measures of physical output. In order to measure the production of these industries, the FRB formerly utilized man-hour series for many of its components. It was felt that the number of man-hours worked in an industry measured the output from production workers in manufacturing and mining more closely than any other measure available. In order to weight the individual indexes of specific industries the "Value Added by Manufacture" was utilized, taken usually from the latest *Census* or *Survey of Manufactures.*

In 1971 the FRB Index was revised for a new base—1967—and new weights utilizing the value of products rather than the value added by manufacture. Instead of utilizing "man-hours" for the non-production series throughout the index, electric power consumption by industry has been substituted for many series in the revision.

Many new series have been developed for a total of 227. About 2/3 of the monthly measurements based on man-hours have been replaced by series based on consumption of electric power. New weighting factors have been incorporated and various new measurement features have been added to improve analysis of national economic developments. Revisions have been carried back in detail to 1954, and a more limited revision goes back to 1939. While there has been little experience so far with the new index, it seems to follow the pattern of the old index closely except in plotting somewhat lesser declines for the 1967 and 1958 downturns than the old index. New groupings of sub-indexes are also possible on a SIC basis, which gives more detail than ever before.

The main thrust of index-number preparation is to compare, over time, or at a given moment, industrial performance areas and other socioeconomic characteristics with reference to a given base. As we have seen, the Consumer Price Index measures through time but not between cities. The Wholesale Price Index measures manufacturers' prices without regard to geographic location. The Index of Industrial Production measures physical output, not dollars, without geographic breakdown, but at a frequency of once a month. All of these measures have fairly obvious shortcomings. No index number can do all things for all statistics.

There is one added precaution to using index numbers. It is very important that the person preparing the index know exactly what it is he is trying to measure, and how the various indexes relate to one another, if at all. Very often researchers compile indexes of unrelated statistical series thrown together and loosely tied to each other by an inaccurate system of weights. Such indexes are hard to justify and easy to discredit, often resulting in embarrassment for the researcher using them.

F. TIME SERIES DATA

From the *Dictionary of Economic and Statistical Terms:* "An economic time series is a set of quantitative data collected over regular time intervals (e.g., weekly, monthly, quarterly, annually), which measures some aspect of economic activity." The data may measure a broad aggregate such as GNP, or a narrow segment such as sales of tractors or the price of copper.

In short, time series data can be any information — such as records of sales, production, or prices — kept over a period of time on a regular, recurring basis. These data provide vital information for the control and regulation of business activity, for they make the most effective method of showing the changes taking place in a business, an industry, or an economy. Time series data are especially helpful in making projections of future activity because such forecasts are always based on past performance.

When time series data are plotted graphically, it becomes obvious that there are both long- and short-term fluctuations within them. The changes that occur in this information are usually grouped into four categories, each of which represents a rather well-defined type of economic change. These types of fluctuation are: (1) secular trend, (2) seasonal variation, (3) cyclical fluctuations, and (4) random or erratic fluctuations. The forces affecting time series data might be classified in a number of ways, but the classification presented above is the one that is the most commonly used to distinguish among long-term trends, periodic movements throughout a year, recurring changes that do not necessarily occur in a fixed period of time, and purely random fluctuations.

The first of these movements, secular trend, reflects the effect of forces causing gradual growth or decline of the activity being measured. These forces operate over long periods of time and usually are not subject to sudden reversals in direction. As an illustration, if one were to examine a graph of the agricultural production of the U.S. from 1900 to the present, he would find that there has been a steady overall upward movement of the graph. While the graph would reflect many other fluctuations, the start-to-finish general trend is one of upward movement. This upward tendency is called secular trend.

Some of the changes in industrial production, agricultural output, consumer buying, and price levels are the result of seasonal variations. Crops are produced in a regular annual cycle with some seasons heavier than others; consumer needs vary widely from one season to the next, as in heating oil demands; Christmas gift purchases swell the December retail trade figures, and unregulated prices rise and fall according to seasonal changes in supply and demand. These seasonal movements are usually no cause for concern insofar as businesses anticipate them and compensate accordingly.

Cyclical fluctuations are those representing the natural movements of the business cycle. These movements reflect the periodic swing from prosperity to recession (and sometimes to depression), to recovery, and finally back again to prosperity. While the business cycle seems to be a necessary evil attached to any capitalist economy, it is somewhat predictable despite variance in time of occurrence, length or duration, and intensity of effect. Business cycle movements are certainly troublesome, but the fact that they are recognized and studied allows attempts at their prediction and cure.

All other unusual movements in time series data generally are called residual, accidental, erratic, or random variations. These disturbances result from unexpected sources such as wars, natural disasters, labor strikes, consumer fads, weather deviations, and a host of other non-recurring events. These fluctuations are of the greatest concern to businessmen and research personnel because of their unpredictability and the resulting disruption of normal activities.

How do you remove the seasonal fluctuations? Several techniques are available. The first is the moving average, which is a method of averaging fluctuations over a period of time to obtain a smoother curve.

By averaging on a 12-month basis starting in January and ending in December the mid-year point between June and July will be expressed in terms of the 12-month average. Moving on to February-through-January yields the next month's average, which would fall between July and August. Proceeding with the same process by dropping February and picking up February of the following year creates what is called a "moving average" for the data at hand. This relatively simple method of eliminating seasonal fluctuation always produces a latest figure on the average which is several months behind the latest figure being reported. In cases of this kind you may want to run a three- or six-month or perhaps two-month moving average of the 12-month moving average. An odd number of months has the advantage of providing a mid-month value instead of falling between months as in the case of the 12-month or any even-month moving average.

Another way of covering seasonal fluctuations is to list the values over a period of years, by month. All of the January figures will be listed, and all of the February figures, and then all of the March figures, etc. Taking the mean of the values for each month yields a series of monthly averages which will express the seasonal pattern for the year. Taking the mean of these averages and relating to it each monthly average produces weights for each month of the year, all adding up to 100% of the annual total. These percentages or ratios can then be applied to the numerical data for each month, providing a non-seasonal pattern for the real figures. This will eliminate the periodic fluctuations due to seasonal or regular monthly swings, making it possible to determine the long-term trends of the variable under analysis.

There is a method devised by Julius Shiskin for using a computer program to make seasonal adjustments to any time series mechanically. The methodology was published by the National Bureau of Economic Research (Occasional Paper 57, New York, 1957) and can be obtained through that source. It is widely used for economic forecasting.

G. STATISTICAL TABLES

A statistical table is a systematic arrangement of numerical data presented in a tabular form to simplify comparison and analysis and to provide a ready source of reference.

While there are generally acceptable rules for the construction of statistical tables, the practice does vary somewhat. In a table the data are usually arranged in a series of rows and columns. The table title should be concise and self-explanatory, and should clearly indicate the nature of the data presented, the area covered by the information, and the time period for which it was collected. The title is usually placed above the table in type large enough to be easily read.

The source or sources of any material used should always be acknowl-edged on the table to indicate the authority of the data, to provide a means of verification, and to serve as a reference for additional information. Any notes necessary to explain any of the data in the table should be placed immediately beneath the table but above the source. A footnote should be avoided because it might be interpreted as part of the table.

The arrangement of data in a table should be such that it facilitates reading, analysis, and comparison of the information and allows the em-phasis of selected parts of the data as needed. The items in the columns and rows may be arranged alphabetically, as is most frequently done in general purpose tables; chronologically, or according to the time of occur-rence; geographically, according to location in the customary classifica-tion; or by magnitude according to traditional procedures.

Tables should be set up with the "stub" (the left-hand column which contains the subheadings or classifications on the corresponding lines in the table) clearly stated. Column headings at the top of the table should be separated by lines encompassing the columns to which they refer. If there are no vertical lines in the table, the underscoring of the headings should be as wide as the individual column heading and no wider. There should be a break between each column heading in the underscore line, which should fall between the columns. If several columns fall under an overall heading, the line should be across all the columns referred to by that head-ing.

The preparation of tables can be very involved if a great number of subclassifications are necessary in order to display the basic data. It is usually better to make several tables of extremely complex data rather than to attempt to put everything into one all-inclusive form.

There are display tables which illustrate in themselves a series of data pertinent in the accompanying text. There are also less formal tables, generally called "text tables," which illustrate a portion of the text which is adjacent to the table itself. Text tables may have simple column headings and a simple stub, but are generally less formal than the display tables discussed above.

H. CHARTS AND GRAPHS

Charts and graphs, discussed here synonymously, are a means of pictorially presenting data which cannot be presented adequately by a statistical table. They consist of lines, pictures or other two-dimensional presentations of data allowing the magnitude of change or relationship to be grasped visually. Their advantage and attraction lie in the fact that they can be used to highlight certain facts and relationships, bringing them immediately to the attention of the casual observer. Statistical tables often obscure the real meaning of the data behind a camouflage of numbers.

Charts and graphs are purposely designed to avoid this problem by allowing the gist of the data to be seen and digested at a glance.

There is a variety of charts which can be used to present almost any information in such a way that it becomes readily understandable. Chart types include curves, ratios of change, statistical density, bar charts, pie charts, pictograms, three-dimensional bars, and log and semi-log presentations, to mention only a few. Also, some mapping techniques can be considered as charts.

Linear representations often are made by drawing a line from point to point for a series of years or months or some other unit of measure. Fluctuations in a time series will frequently be so slight that minute differences do not become apparent to the eye. In such cases it is often considered proper to blow up the scale, thereby exaggerating the fluctuations in the variable you are studying. The data thus can be presented in a manner which would make possible a comparison of trends or movements that would otherwise be difficult to ascertain.

Some types of curves are better for charts than are linear measures. Logarithmic charts involving the gradation of horizontal or vertical lines provide for application of raw data in such a manner as to represent plotting the actual logarithms of the numbers used. This is used when ratios are plotted or when percentage relationships are desired. For example, a semi-log chart in which the logarithmic scale runs vertically with a horizontal scale of evenly-spaced intervals can be used for time series in which vertical distances of the same length measure equal percentage changes. This is valuable in some types of analyses, especially those with more than one variable.

Equal vertical distances also will measure equal percentage change, even though the values of each of the lines are considerably different. Plotting them on an arithmetic scale would require a very long vertical scale for the chart on which small fluctuations could not be seen.

Another type of chart is the pie chart, a circle divided into segments representing, generally, percentage distributions of the whole variable.

Bar charts are useful for linear comparisons, using either vertical or horizontal bars. When using a time series, it is often better to employ vertical bars because the dates or years at the bottom of the chart are not long and can be shown easily within the bar width. Horizontal bars should be used only when there is so large a word or phrase to designate each bar that it would be difficult to fit it within the space available on vertical bars. For instance, on a bar chart showing industrial data by segments of the economy such words as "manufacturing," "wholesale and retail trade," "construction," "finance," "insurance," "real estate," etc. can be printed horizontally to the left of a zero line on the chart much more readily than they can be condensed for presentation at the bottom or on top of the chart because of the length of the name.

Pictograms are another charting technique which is sometimes abused. For instance, if a chart were being made to show population of two separate countries with one short man shown as representing one of the countries and a much taller and bigger man shown representing the other country, the difference in the size of the figures is very misleading because it is not apparent whether the chart refers to the heights of the men, to the area covered by the men, or to the volume of the men's bodies. In using pictograms, repeating a pattern of figures such as ships, people, animals, or nearly any object, each representing a certain quantity of the variable being presented, with all the pictorial figures the same size, can make a very interesting charting technique.

Similarly, three-dimensional bars are somewhat confusing because of the necessity to slant the top of the bar to give a perspective of the three dimensions. This can be misleading if it is not clear which part of the top of the bar represents the height being shown. Actually, bar charts, line charts, component lines, and other uses of charting are mainly a graphic presentation of two dimensions: (1) the height of the bar, line, or component versus (2) the x-axis, which may represent time, another variable, or some other measure. The volume idea, discussed above with the two sizes of men, is applicable here to the three-dimensional bar: it is unnecessary and often confusing to present three dimensions in a two-dimensional chart.

Statistical maps are a type of chart which allow presentation with geographically-distributed data. Maps are of several types, including those with boundaries of certain areas such as states or counties. Those depicting density of population, housing, or other geographically-distributed relationships can be expressed by dots, pins, circles, shading, or crosshatching.

SELECTED READING REFERENCES

1. Research-Problem Organization

Ackoff, Russell L. *The Design of Social Research.* Chicago: University of Chicago Press, 1953.

Ackoff, Russell L. *Scientific Method: Optimizing Applied Research Decisions.* New York: John Wiley & Sons, Inc., 1965.

Ailloni-Charles, Dan (Editor). *New Directions in Research Design,* Proceedings of the Second National Conference on Research Design. New York: American Marketing Association, 1965.

American Marketing Association. *The Design of Research Investigations.* Marketing Research Techniques Series, No. 1, 1958.

American Marketing Association. *Problem Definition.* Marketing Research Techniques Series, No. 2, 1958.

Churchman, C. West, and Russell L. Ackoff. *Methods of Inquiry.* St. Louis: Educational Publishers, 1950.

Dewey, John. *Logic: The Theory of Inquiry.* New York: Henry Holt & Co., 1938.

Ferber, Robert, and P. J. Verdoorn. *Research Methods in Economics and Business.* New York: The Macmillan Company, 1962.

Greenwald, Douglass. *McGraw-Hill Dictionary of Modern Economics.* New York: McGraw-Hill Book Company, Inc., 1965.

Huff, Darrell. *How to Lie with Statistics.* New York: W. W. Norton & Company, Inc., 1954.

Kendall, M. G., and W. R. Buckland. *A Dictionary of Statistical Terms.* London: Oliver and Boyd, 1957.

Reichmann, W. J. *Use and Abuse of Statistics.* New York: Oxford University Press, 1962.

Rigby, Paul H. *Conceptual Foundations of Business Research.* New York: John Wiley & Sons, Inc., 1965.

U.S. Department of Commerce, Social and Economic Statistics Administration. *Dictionary of Economic and Statistical Terms.* Washington, D. C.: U.S. Government Printing Office, 1972.

U.S. Department of Labor, Bureau of Labor Statistics. *BLS Handbook of Methods for Surveys and Studies,* Bulletin No. 1711. Washington, D. C.: U.S. Government Printing Office, 1971.

Waldo, Willis H. *Better Report Writing.* New York: Reinhold Publishing Company, 1965.

2. Statistics Textbooks

Clark, Charles T., and Lawrence L. Schkade. *Statistical Methods for Business Decisions.* Cincinnati: South-Western Publishing Co., 1969.

Croxton, Frederick E., Dudley J. Cowden, and Ben W. Bolch. *Practical Business Statistics,* 4th Edition. Englewood Cliffs, New Jersey: Prentice-Hall, Inc., 1969.

Ferber, Robert. *Statistical Techniques in Market Research.* New York: McGraw-Hill Book Company, Inc., 1949.

Freund, John E. *Modern Elementary Statistics.* Englewood Cliffs, New Jersey: Prentice-Hall, Inc., 1973.

Griffin, John I. *Statistics Methods and Applications.* New York: Holt, Rinehart and Winston, 1962.

Hoel, Paul G. *Elementary Statistics,* 3rd Edition. New York: John Wiley & Sons, Inc., 1971.

Lorie, J. H., and H. B. Roberts. *Basic Methods of Marketing Research.* New York: McGraw-Hill Book Company, Inc., 1951.

Miller, Irwin. *A Primer on Statistics for Business and Economics.* New York: Random House, Inc., 1968.

Moore, P. G. *Principles of Statistical Techniques.* Cambridge: Cambridge University Press, 1969. 2nd Edition.

Neter, John, William Wasserman, and G. A. Whitmore. *Fundamental Statistics,* 4th Edition. Boston: Allyn and Bacon, Inc., 1973.

Spurr, William A. *Statistical Analysis for Business Decisions.* Homewood, Illinois: Richard D. Irwin, Inc., 1967.

Stockton, John R., and Charles T. Clark. *Introduction to Business and Economic Statistics,* 4th Edition. Cincinnati: South-Western Publishing Co., 1971.

Wallis, W. Allen, and Harry V. Roberts. *Statistics: A New Approach.* New York: The Free Press of Glencoe, 1964.

Wonnacott, Thomas H., and Ronald J. Wonnacott. *Introductory Statistics.* New York: John Wiley & Sons, Inc., 1969.

3. Statistical Description

American Marketing Association. *Tabulation: Elements of Planning and Techniques.* Marketing Research Techniques Series, No. 5, 1962.

Arkin, Herbert, and Raymond R. Colton. *Tables for Statisticians.* New York: Barnes & Noble, Inc., 1963.

Myers, John H. *Statistical Presentation.* Ames, Iowa: Littlefield, Adams & Co., 1958.

Robinson, Arthur H. *Elements of Cartography.* New York: John Wiley & Sons, 1953.

Schmid, Calvin F. *Handbook of Graphic Presentation.* New York: The Ronald Press Company, 1954.

Spear, Mary Eleanor. *Charting Statistics.* New York: McGraw-Hill Book Company, Inc., 1952.

U.S. Bureau of the Census. *Bureau of the Census Manual of Tabular Presentation,* by Bruce L. Jenkinson. Washington, D.C.: U.S. Government Printing Office, 1949.

4. Sampling

See references presented in Chapter 7.

5. Periodic Analysis and Forecasting

Barton, J. C., Jr. "Adjustment for Seasonal Variation." *Federal Reserve Bulletin,* (June, 1941), 518-528.

Bassie, V. Lewis. *Economic Forecasting.* New York: McGraw-Hill Book Co., 1958.

Bratt, Elmer C. *Business Cycles and Forecasting.* Homewood, Illinois: Richard D. Irwin, Inc., 1961.

Cole, Arthur H. *Measures of Business Change.* Homewood, Illinois: Richard D. Irwin, Inc., 1952.

Frickey, E. *Economic Fluctuations in the United States.* Cambridge, Mass.: Harvard University Press, 1942.

Garvy, George. *The Development of Bank Debits and Clearings and Their Use in Economic Analysis.* Washington, D.C.: Board of Governors of the Federal Reserve System, 1952.

Gordon, Robert A. *Business Fluctuations.* New York: Harper & Brothers, 1952.

Hannan, E. J. *Time Series Analysis.* New York: John Wiley & Sons, Inc., 1960.

Kuznets, Simon. *Seasonal Variations in Industry and Trade.* New York: National Bureau of Economic Research, 1933.

Lewis, John P. *Business Conditions Analysis.* New York: McGraw-Hill Book Co., Inc., 1959.

Lovell, Michael C. "Seasonal Adjustment of Economic Time Series and Multiple Regression Analysis." *Journal of the American Statistical Association,* (Vol. 58, 1963), 993-1010.

Luedicke, Heinz E. *How to Forecast Business Trends.* New York: Journal of Commerce, 1954.

Macaulay, Frederick R. *The Smoothing of Time Series.* New York: National Bureau of Economic Research, 1931.

Maisel, Sherman J. *Fluctuations, Growth and Forecasting.* New York: John Wiley & Sons, Inc., 1957.

Moore, Geoffrey H. *Business Cycle Indicators,* Vol. I & II. Princeton: Princeton University Press, 1961.

Newbury, Frank D. *Business Forecasting: Principles and Practices.* New York: McGraw-Hill Book Co., 1952.

Salzman, Lawrence. *Computerized Economic Analysis.* New York: McGraw-Hill Publishing Co., Inc., 1968.

Shiskin, Julius. *Electronic Computers and Business Indicators,* Occasional Paper No. 57. New York: National Bureau of Economic Research, 1957.

Shiskin, Julius, and Harry Eisenpress. *Seasonal Adjustments by Electronic Computer Methods,* Technical Paper 12. New York: National Bureau of Economic Research, 1958.

Silk, Leonard S. and M. Louise Curley. *A Primer on Business Forecasting.* New York: Random House, Inc., 1970.

Snyder, Richard M. *Measuring Business Changes.* New York: John Wiley & Sons, Inc., 1955.

Steiner, Peter O. *An Introduction to the Analysis of Time Series.* New York: Holt, Rinehart and Winston, 1956.

U.S. Bureau of the Census. *The X-11 Variant of the Census Method II Seasonal Adjustment Program,* Technical Paper No. 15, 4/67:425-0497. Washington, D.C.: U.S. Government Printing Office.

6. Index Numbers

Fisher, Irving. *The Making of Index Numbers.* Boston and New York: Houghton Mifflin Company, 1927.

Gainsbrugh, M. R. and Jules Backman. *Inflation and the Price Indexes.* New York: National Industrial Conference Board, 1966.

Griliches, Zvi. *Price Indexes and Quality Change.* Cambridge, Mass.: Harvard University Press, 1971.

Mudgett, Bruce D. *Index Numbers.* New York: John Wiley & Sons, Inc., 1951.

Tierney, Cecilia. *Financial Reporting of Price Level Changes: The Index Number Problem.* New York: American Institute of Certified Public Accountants, 1963.

U.S. Department of Labor, Bureau of Labor Statistics. *The Making and Using of Index Numbers,* by Wesley C. Mitchell, Bulletin No. 656. Washington, D.C.: U.S. Government Printing Office, 1938.

U.S. Department of Labor. *Wholesale Prices and Price Indexes, January, 1971.* Washington, D.C.: U.S. Government Printing Office, 1971.

7. Demography

Barclay, George W. *Techniques of Population Analysis.* New York: John Wiley & Sons, 1958.

Benjamin, Bernard. *Demographic Analysis.* New York: Frederick A. Praeger, Publishers, 1969.

Blalock, H. M. *Social Statistics.* New York: McGraw-Hill Book Co., 1960.

Bogue, Donald J. *Principles of Demography.* New York: John Wiley & Sons, 1969.

Cox, Peter R. *Demography*. Cambridge, England: Cambridge University Press, 1959.

Dornbusch, Sanford M., and Calvin F. Schmid. *A Primer of Social Statistics*. New York: McGraw-Hill Book Company, Inc., 1955.

Eldridge, Hope T. *The Materials of Demography: A Selected and Annotated Bibliography*. New York: International Union for the Scientific Study of Population and Population Association of America, 1959.

Hauser, Philip M., and Otis Dudley Duncan. *The Study of Population*. Chicago, Ill.: University of Chicago Press, 1959.

Levy, Clifford V. *A Primer for Community Research*. San Francisco: Far West Research, Inc., 1972.

Morrison, Peter A. *Demographic Information For Cities: A Manual for Estimating and Projecting Local Population Characteristics*. A report prepared for U.S. Department of Housing and Urban Development, R-618-HUD. Santa Monica, California: The Rand Corporation, 1971.

Southern Regional Demographic Group. *Research and the 1970 Census*. Oak Ridge, Tenn.: Oak Ridge Associated Universities, Inc., 1971.

Spiegelman, Mortimer. *Introduction to Demography*. Cambridge, Massachusetts: Harvard University Press, 1970.

U.S. Bureau of the Census. *Handbook of Statistical Methods for Demographers*, by A. J. Jaffe. Washington, D.C.: U.S.Government Printing Office, 1951.

U.S. Bureau of the Census. *The Methods and Materials of Demography*, by Henry S. Shryock and Jacob S. Siegel. Washington, D.C.: U.S. Government Printing Office, 1973.

U.S. Bureau of the Census. *Who's Home When*, by Dean Weber and Richard C. Burt (Working Paper No. 37). Washington, D.C.: U.S. Government Printing Office, 1972.

U.S. Department of Health, Education and Welfare. *Handbook of Statistical Procedures for Long-Range Projections of Public Enrollment*. Office of Education Technical Monograph OE-2417, by A. J. Jaffe. Washington, D.C.: U.S. Government Printing Office, 1969.

7 SAMPLING

A. INTRODUCTION

Sampling is a statistical technique for estimating the characteristics of a universe[1] by surveying only a portion, or sample, of that universe. It is an economical procedure that may be used in gathering certain types of information required in Chamber of Commerce planning and decision-making.

In this chapter, "universe" refers to the whole group of businesses or persons about which information is being gathered. Relevant universes for Chamber research might be the population of the city, the list of area manufacturers, or the Chamber membership. The term "sample" refers to a small but representative part of that universe.

One of the primary surveying advantages which Chambers of Commerce have over many other types of organizations is a more or less captive audience, in the form of both individuals and firms. Chamber members, because they are already a part of a voluntary organization, are usually more willing to cooperate in mail or interview surveys than members of many other groups. Another advantage is that a Chamber typically has members from a good cross-section of the area industry, trade, and service establishments which it serves. The Chamber may often be the only organization in a city which encompasses all types of business and industry, as trade associations are too restrictive in their membership to constitute a truly representative sample.

Surveying or sampling of local Chamber members also provides multiple rewards. While it yields information necessary for the planning and execution of various Chamber projects, it also serves as an excellent means

---

[1]The entire group of elements under study. The terms "whole," "mass," "universe" and "population" are used interchangeably throughout this chapter.

of maintaining contact with member firms. A timely, well-designed survey brings to the Chamber member a sense of participation which he may find stimulating; when published, the results of the surveys may provide the member with problem-solving information unavailable elsewhere.

As the principal representative of business in the community, the Chamber is considered to be a source of answers to, or at least information about, complex business and community problems. Survey research provides fundamental facts which enable the Chamber to illuminate its assumed role as community spokesman. Similar survey input of a more technical nature will often provide the answers to community problems about which information may become known only through survey techniques. However, surveys need not be limited to Chamber membership. The universe should be expanded to include any individuals or firms which can provide relevant information. This practice will render the survey and the Chamber itself more credible in its final position.

The results of surveys need not emerge as sterile reporting of statistical tables, but may consist of various types of analyses and presentations which can lead to the implementation of policy decisions. Survey reports give tangible evidence of the research capabilities of the local Chamber of Commerce. If well done, they reflect favorably on the Chamber's work. Reports of survey results, if properly presented, are impressive documents and can be used with little alteration for articles in the Chamber's magazine, newsletter, or news releases. News media frequently devote considerable space and time to Chamber surveys because they come from respected organizations and are well-received by the general public. It is therefore important that the survey and sampling techniques be executed under precautions which maintain true representation and factual results and thereby uphold a hard-earned reputation for objectivity and credibility.

B. WHAT IS SAMPLING?

The objective in sampling is to learn something about the subject in question quickly and with relatively little expenditure of effort. Sampling can be arranged to achieve varying levels of accuracy as needed, with the more sophisticated techniques requiring greater care and expertise. From the sample survey data available a researcher can make very precise estimates of population characteristics, as in the U.S. Census of Population and Housing, or more general analyses, as in the Nielsen television viewer survey.

The basis or justification for sampling procedure is the form of logic known as "inductive reasoning." Inductive reasoning is the process of generalizing about a whole class or group based on information from only a few specific members of that group. This is a common form of reasoning, one which we all use everyday. For example, if a cook tastes a spoonful of soup and finds it too salty, then he assumes that all of it is too salty. If a Chamber researcher finds that a 15% sample of the people in an area are dissatisfied with the bus service, then probably most of the total population in the same area are also dissatisfied with the service.

C. WHY SAMPLE?

The two principal ways of acquiring otherwise unknown information about a population are: (1) by taking a census (complete enumeration) of the population, or (2) by taking a sample of the elements in the population and using this information as the basis for observations about the whole. Naturally, if the time and money are available, then a complete enumeration will be more accurate and desirable; but Chamber personnel are usually operating under constraints in both time and money, which necessitates using sampling techniques. However, these are not the only advantages of a sample. Some of the others are:

1. *A complete enumeration may be impracticable or infeasible if the number of elements in the universe is indefinitely large.* For example, it is not likely that the New York Chamber of Commerce would attempt to survey all of the city's residents on any issue. Regardless of the financial and personnel resources the Chamber might make available for the project, such factors as people moving into and out of the city, changes of residence within the city and the existence of persons with no fixed address would make surveying each resident virtually impossible.

2. *A complete count of the population may yield only infinitesimally more precise results than a properly conducted sample and may thus be unnecessary.* If sample procedures can be sufficiently refined to keep the measurements within acceptable limits of error, then for all practical purposes the sample may be as accurate as a complete canvass.

3. *Sampling as a technique is sufficiently flexible to be adjusted to the precision of information needed.* It is wasteful to produce data more precise than may be required for a specific project. This increase in data precision will definitely increase the project cost but may not result in a proportionate increase in the usefulness of the information.

4. *Sampling reduces the manpower requirements in a data-gathering activity.* Fewer trained people are needed in a sampling than in complete enumeration.

Although sampling is constantly gaining acceptance in Chamber of Commerce research activities, a word of caution is inserted here for prospective samplers. Results obtained from studying a sample cannot be assumed—in all cases—to be exactly the same as those obtainable from an analysis of the entire universe. If the sampling project is structured carefully, however, the sample data may be as useful as the tabulations from a complete enumeration.

D. SAMPLING TECHNIQUES

Several types of sampling procedures are available. The circumstances prevailing in each case determine the particular method which should be selected. Some of the principal sampling methods are outlined in this section. As with most of the analysis in this book, the reader is referred to the more complete statistical texts, listed in the bibliography, which can provide the detailed explanation of techniques not available here.

Sampling methods are generally divided into two broad classifications: *non-probability* and *probability*. The difference between the two is in the method of sample selection. In non-probability sampling some judgmental or subjective method is used to control the sample selection. Probability sampling, on the other hand, involves the use of chance or random distribution in selecting a sample from the universe. Each element in the universe has a computable probability of being included in the sample. But while each member of the population has equal chance of being selected, some relevant characteristics have either greater or lesser probabilities of being selected. For example, if the universe in question consists of 7 women and 3 men, then each *person* has a 1-in-10 chance of being selected at random. However, the chances are 7/3 or 2-1/3 times as great that a woman will be included in the sample instead of a man. It is important to know the demographic composition of the universe so that projections based upon the sample will reflect the area peculiarities in the population distribution.

1. Non-Probability Sampling

Although a non-probability sample is not scientific, it can be a useful expedient. Usually it is sufficiently faster and cheaper than probability sampling to warrant its use under certain conditions. Types of non-probability sampling are:

a. *Using whatever is already available*

Assume that the local Chamber's chief executive desires an indication of opinion from the organization's membership in relation to a local legislative matter. The available data inputs could be letters and phone calls already received in the Chamber office.

b. *Collecting data by the most convenient procedures*

This method might involve distributing questionnaires through the Chamber magazine, newsletter, at meetings, or through "on the street" interviews. The results obtained from these surveys should be used cautiously, as the researcher chooses the places, the occasions, the attractions, and the media, all of which may bias the results.

c. Using information known by the best-qualified persons

A judgment sample is frequently selected when expert opinions are wanted. Such a panel would be useful in a number of ways. The members might be chosen to represent the population as a whole and serve as barometers of the universe. They might be used to analyze the quality of the results from judgment sampling, as its precision cannot be computed mathematically. They might be used to select typical areas within the city or typical individuals to act as representative figures for another sample. As a representative panel they would also influence the operation of the Chamber, such as in preparing the Program of Work.

d. Quota sampling

This is the most systematic approach to obtaining a representative sample of those listed in the non-probability section. Typical techniques involve trying to make the sample similar in a number of ways to the universe. This can be done by scattering the sample over the whole population so it contains the same percentage of elements having certain characteristics as does the total population or by selecting members of the sample in the same numerical relationship as the groups of members in the total population. The steps involved in this process are: (1) dividing the whole population into relevant subgroups or strata, (2) determining the percentage of population in each stratum, (3) allocating similar portions of the strata into the sample, and (4) apportioning the sample among interviewers with instructions about the number of persons falling into each category which he is to contact. It is important that the interviewers be given instructions to avoid building bias into the survey. For example, it would be easy for researchers to interview only attractive people or those in nice houses, but this procedure would probably destroy the validity of the survey. If the interviewer selected people in purely random fashion, the quota sample could be classified as stratified random sampling, but in actual practice the likes, dislikes, and bias of interviewers often subconsciously enter into the selection of sample elements.

2. Probability Sampling

a. Simple or unrestricted random sample

In this type of sample, subjective influence is not allowed to affect the selection of elements for the sample. Each member of the universe or population has an equal chance of being selected for the sample and thus has the same probability of being included. Probability theory can be used in predicting how the element-selection procedure will work and determines the representativeness of the chosen sample.

Simple random sampling is accomplished by assigning a different number to each element of the population. This process naturally requires that the researcher be working with a relatively small universe. Then a table of random numbers, such as Rand Corporation's *A Million Random Digits with 100,000 Normal Deviates,* is used to select a sample. The tables in these books of random numbers consist of series of digits, from 0 to 9. Each digit occurs approximately the same number of times in an order that has been determined as random, usually based on a computer program. The numbers may be used in the order in which they occur in the book, eliminating any duplication, or the researcher may add his own system to the numbers in the book, taking every *N*th value.

b. Systematic sampling

This procedure spreads the sample elements over the total population. A sample is drawn by taking items from the universe list at regular intervals. For example, from a list of 1000 items, an appropriate sample might be every fifth item, or every ninth item.

In actual practice it is better to arrange the items in the universe in some type of order, such as descending height of people standing in a line or persons alphabetized by last name. After this is done, the appropriate sample size must be decided. For a 10% sample of 1000 persons, then a sample of 100 persons would be needed. The members of the universe should be arranged on a list or by cards, numbered beginning with one, and a random number selected as a beginning point. Then the sample will be selected by taking every *N*th unit as required for the sample size. For example, in the 10% sample of 1000 persons, every 10th person would be selected. Beginning at arbitrarily selected number 4, then the 4th, 14th, 24th, 34th, etc., persons would be chosen for the sample.

c. Stratified sampling

This is really random sampling within the parameters of a stratified universe in an attempt to make sure that the variable elements (geographic location, age, sex or other characteristics) of the population are represented in the final sample.

To accomplish stratified sampling the total population is divided into subgroups or strata. Then random samples are taken from each subgroup — that is, each element of the subgroup has the same chance of being chosen — in the same proportion that that subgroup is represented in the total population. For example, if the sample size has been specified at 10%, then 10% of each subgroup should also be taken. In a universe, if there are 400 white collar workers and 600 blue collar workers, then the sample should be stratified accordingly. For a 10% sample, 40 white collar and 60 blue collar workers would be chosen. However, within the separate groups each person would have the same chance of being selected.

d. Area or cluster sampling

A disadvantage of simple random, systematic, and stratified sampling is that the researcher must have a list of the population from which he will draw his sample. In many situations involving the use of sampling, lists of the total population are simply not available. In these cases, area or cluster sampling is the most useful alternative. Area sampling involves dividing the population area into smaller subareas and then sampling the residents of that area. First, the survey area is divided into small areas (usually census tracts or combinations of city blocks) on a map. Then each area is assigned a number. From this list of numbered areas, a random or systematic sample of areas is made. In each of the sample areas chosen another sample of the residents is made (in some cases all of the residents might ultimately be interviewed), this also on a random basis.

The purpose of cluster sampling is to save the interviewer both time and money. Instead of interviewing one family in each of 1000 blocks the researchers can interview ten adjoining families in each of 100 blocks.

E. PLANNING THE SURVEY

As mentioned earlier, there are several methods of obtaining data needed in a survey. The three most common ways are through the use of personal interviews, telephone interviews, and mailed questionnaires.

For those situations in which the researcher has adequate time, staff, and money, the personal interview method can be the most rewarding of the three. This technique requires the staff interviewers to visit sample members and extract in-depth information from them. An advantage of this method is that it allows the interviewer to establish a rapport with the participant through a face-to-face discussion. It also enables the interviewer to explain exactly what the purpose of the survey is and to thereby elicit more exact responses. The primary drawback to this method is that it requires a number of extra trained personnel which most Chambers cannot afford to hire.

Telephone surveys are operationally easier because staff time is saved in removing the necessity of journeying out into the field. However, this method still requires more personnel than the questionnaire system and is usually frustrating and no more reliable as well. It is difficult to deal with people over the phone. For one thing, a feeling of confidentiality is hard to establish. For another, unless specific names are known it is very difficult to find someone who is both willing and able to answer the questions.

Therefore, the most common method used in Chamber operations is the mailed questionnaire. When names are known the questionnaires can be addressed to specific individuals. When they are not known, the intended recipients can often be addressed by title, as the executive vice president of a bank or the treasurer of a company. Also, once the questionnaire has been prepared and mailed, only one person is needed to tabulate the returns. A drawback to the use of mail surveys is that only in a very few cases are all questionnaires returned the first time. Second and third mailings are usually necessary, and these must often be followed by phone calls to the remaining hold-outs.

An outline of the basic steps in a sample survey is as follows:

1. Decide if a survey is actually needed. What is to be the purpose of it? What data will be collected and from whom? How are the data to be used? Will the data to be collected really answer the questions you have in mind? When and where will the survey be conducted? Also arrange for an operating schedule, including time and cost estimates and plans for pre-testing.

2. Examine the universe from which the sample will be drawn. What are the characteristics of the universe?

3. From the universe devise a means of sampling which will extract the best results. What will be the probable size and composition of the sample?

4. Decide what type of survey will best serve the purpose — mail, telephone, personal interview, or some other method. This decision is contingent upon the size and make-up of the sample.

5. Compose a draft of the questionnaire. This is one of the most critical procedures, as the questions must be clearly understood and provide readily quantifiable answers.

6. Determine the desired degree of precision which users should be able to expect from the sample data. Precision can be expressed in terms of permissible error (tolerance) and acceptable risk (confidence). Degree of precision will be a function of the purpose of the survey.

7. Pretest the reporting forms, questionnaires, and instructions on a small scale basis. This has proved to be an indispensable and inexpensive step. The results of this test may indicate that the forms require alteration in order to serve the purpose of the survey properly.

8. Arrange for any extra personnel who will be needed to help conduct the survey. This includes hiring and training.

9. Arrange for editing, coding, and tabulating the results. It will probably be necessary to design forms and procedures to expedite this activity.

10. Decide on the type of analysis to be carried out on the return data. This procedure could involve manual tabular breakdowns or more sophisticated computer analysis.

11. After the survey has been completed, the data collected, and the results analyzed, present a report of your findings, including a description of how it was conducted and the probable limits of reliability, to those persons who would be interested.

F. DESIGNING THE SURVEY QUESTIONNAIRE

Although there are no hard and fast rules for questionnaire development, the questionnaire itself is one of the most critical parts of the whole survey technique. It must be carefully prepared so that the questions will be clearly understood by the respondents. A determination of the information which is needed should be made, and the questionnaire should carefully exclude extraneous queries that will not supply the necessary facts. Before this can be done it is usually desirable to set forth the objectives of the survey in very precise terms so that everyone working with it will know what is to be accomplished.

The questions should be designed so that they neither lead the respondent nor leave room for subjective interpretation. For certain types of questionnaires, multiple choice responses are to be preferred; others might have "yes-no" answers; still others might provide numerical data. The most important point is that the language and the sentences should be simple. Ambiguous questions are to be avoided. Personal and confidential questions should be avoided for most surveys, and definitely should be avoided for all surveys until the respondents have been prepared in some manner and have indicated that they will not be offended by them.

The sequence of questions is also important: each question should be considered and placed in light of both its influence on following questions and the effect of previous questions upon it.

The questionnaire should not be hurriedly created. It should be planned and checked and then pretested to see if it actually does elicit the desired kinds of responses. If it does not, it must be changed and rechanged until it does work. The questionnaire should also be physically designed to present as neat and attractive a form as possible. A good appearance adds a look of professionalism, increases the response rate, and makes the form itself much easier to work with as well. A questionnaire which is too complex can work against itself. Brevity both in the explanatory letter and in the questionnaire itself is a virtue.

Before mailing the questionnaire, it is always wise to pretest it among a small number of persons to see whether the questions you have asked will evoke the proper answers or will be misinterpreted by the respondents. The researcher creating the questionnaire can sometimes get so lost in his own verbiage that only he can understand what information is sought with the questions. This problem can be diagnosed and remedied by a pre-test, which will turn up most of the problem areas. Therefore, a pre-test is an essential element of any survey.

G. SAMPLE ERROR

The results which are obtained from sampling are usually different from the results which come from testing the whole universe. This difference in results between the total population and the sample population is called the sampling error. In formulating and analyzing a sample survey it is necessary to determine the probable magnitude of this sampling error. For a sample survey to be useful one must be able to look at the size of the universe and the size of the sample and determine that there is X% probability that all of the possible responses fall within a determined range. Another way of stating this idea is to say that out of one hundred test cases only Y number will be outside of this given range.

An example of a case where this predictability would be required is in a pricing survey. If a Chamber researcher were interested in knowing how much a loaf of bread costs in his city, he could send questionnaires to a number of the area grocery stores. If he were dealing with 20 stores out of a possible 100, in his report he would not list each of the separate prices indicated on the returned questionnaires. Rather, he would give either an average price or a narrow price range for bread. If he had compiled his data by means of a random sample, he would be able to compute the standard deviation of the sample prices, or the standard error of the mean if average prices were given, and state that X% of all the stores in the city would have bread within this price range.

The statistical techniques applied to determine the precision of the sample are useful in planning a sample as well as in analyzing the results of one already completed. If the researcher wants 90% accuracy, he can compute the number of businesses which would be required in the sample for that degree of accuracy. If he wanted 95% accuracy he could also compute the required sample size for the higher percentage. If the surveying process requires relatively costly personal interviews, then the researcher can weigh the added precision gained by increasing the sample against the added cost of talking to more people. Discussions of mathematical formulas are beyond the scope of this chapter, and researchers requiring this information should use statistics texts such as those listed in the chapter bibliography.

If you are not interested in measurable precision, there are certain guidelines which can be followed to improve the results. A large sample is to be considered more accurate than a small sample because of the greater representation of the universe. If cost reduction is an important consideration, a small cluster or stratified sample which has been well prepared is almost as good as a large random sample which has been poorly planned and executed.

There is also a fairly simple method for checking the accuracy of your survey results, a method which does not require the use of any sophisticated formulas. This procedure involves taking a second sample, either the same size or smaller than the original survey, to see if the results of the two are roughly similar. In this procedure the first sample, known as the control sample, is prepared rather carefully to insure a high percentage of responses. After this sample has been completed, then a second sample is selected from the elements remaining in the universe.

After the returns of the questionnaires have been tabulated, the answer patterns may be examined for consistency irrespective of the response-ratio variable. If the answer patterns of the second sample survey approach the answer patterns of the control sample with reasonable consistency, the sampling procedure used is satisfactory, and the credibility of the procedure is established without resorting to the complex mathematics of probability testing. For example, a recent survey using two samples selected by random-digit selection procedure produced the following results (each sample represents 10% of the universe):

PERCENT OF RESPONDENTS

Question 1. How will your next year's sales rank in relation to your sales volume for the current year?

	Increase	*Decrease*	*Be About Same*
Control Sample	62%	5%	33%
2nd Sample	58%	13%	29%

Question 2. Will the number employed in your business change next year?

	Increase	*Decrease*	*Be About Same*
Control Sample	33%	5%	62%
2nd Sample	25%	11%	64%

Question 3. What do you think about supply lines? Will order lead times be:

	Longer	*Shorter*	*About Same*
Control Sample	35%	20%	45%
2nd Sample	34%	19%	47%

Question 4. What do you think will be the pace of inflation next year?

	Accelerate	*Slow*	*About Same*
Control Sample	52%	18%	30%
2nd Sample	46%	17%	37%

Question 5. What will be the effect of a federal income tax increase on sales?

	Marked Decrease	Some Decrease	None
Control Sample	4%	60%	36%
2nd Sample	6%	68%	26%

Question 6. What is the effect of the current tight money policy on your business?

	Increasingly Adverse	Moderately Adverse	None
Control Sample	31%	63%	6%
2nd Sample	25%	70%	5%

Though some deviation exists, the similarity of the response-patterns is such that the credibility of a 10% sample is satisfactorily established.

H. SUGGESTED SURVEYS FOR CHAMBERS OF COMMERCE

Some types of surveys have special applicability to Chamber of Commerce activity. The examples outlined in this section are not exhaustive by any means, and are merely cited here for a better understanding of the scope of such surveys.

1. Opinion Surveys

In a public or member opinion survey, respondents are asked to express an opinion or attitude, make an evaluation, or report their judgment on specific issues. The uses of opinion research findings to Chambers of Commerce are almost limitless.

A public opinion survey can provide the organization executive with a wealth of knowledge that is both useful and necessary in developing and carrying out Chamber of Commerce community action programs. The chances for success in any undertaking are greatly enhanced if one knows whether member or public opinion will favor or disapprove of projected activity. If a Chamber executive can refer to information obtained through carefully designed and conducted surveys, he will find his job of solving community problems and developing community projects much easier. Relatively speaking, the more information an executive has gathered through member and public opinion surveys, the better his chances of making the right decisions.

Most Chambers develop their programs of work by surveying the membership to find out what projects are needed and wanted by their members. This is a survey of member opinion. Another use of opinion survey is to test member or public reactions to current issues, whether they be local, state, or national. The results of such a survey can be used to formulate guidelines for establishing the position of the Chamber of Commerce in regard to these issues.

Surveys are important to Chambers of Commerce regardless of size or scope of operation. In smaller communities the job of gathering the survey information may be somewhat easier and less complicated due to the smaller size of the population and the membership of the Chamber itself. For example, in a community of 5,000 people, the sample size needed for a specific degree of accuracy would be smaller than that required in a city of 500,000 people. Thus the task of surveying will be within the capacity of Chambers, regardless of their size, and all Chambers of Commerce should consider the use of opinion surveys in order to gain information which will prove to be most beneficial and necessary in determining the probable success or failure of Chamber endeavors, as well as in helping determine the directions of those endeavors.

2. Wage and Salary Surveys

This is one of the most difficult types of surveys to conduct. Luckily, there are several other organizations which also conduct them, including the Bureau of Labor Statistics, the State Employment Commission, and sometimes the manpower office of the city. However, sometimes a study of a particular industry or category of worker becomes necessary, and the Chamber must stand ready to gather the information.

The procedure for conducting the survey does not differ markedly from that for any other survey. The most difficult facet of the process is deciding on uniform descriptions of particular jobs. The definition must be specific enough to clearly differentiate one type of job from all other types, but it must be general enough to be clearly recognizable by the people who will be responding to the questionnaire, each of whom probably outlines the duties of the job a little bit differently. Usually not only the duties of the job are involved, but also the skill level required to perform it. *The Dictionary of Occupational Titles*[2] helps in defining some of the jobs, but very often is not sufficiently specific for direct application. In such cases the researcher must use his own discretion in defining the range of each position.

---

[2]U.S. Department of Labor, Manpower Administration, Bureau of Employment Security. *The Dictionary of Occupational Titles.* Washington, D.C.: U.S. Government Printing Office, 1965.

3. Business Outlook Surveys

This is a particularly valuable application of the mailed questionnaire technique. Surveys of this type are designed to collect a consensus of
local business leaders about the forthcoming *local* economic climate. National forecasts are certainly important, and there is usually an abundance
of those available, but their focus is too general to apply to most local
predictions.

Local surveys may be taken in any month, but seem to be in greatest
demand toward the year end, when the forecasts are likely to cover all or
part of the coming year. They may be taken by mail and, where a long
series of annual surveys has been conducted by a local Chamber, the cumulative results will yield consistent patterns in the point of view of business
toward the coming year.

In surveys of business outlook, it is best to address your questionnaire
to the local chief executive officer of each firm. It is not necessary to do
this by name, but merely address "Chief Executive Officer." The replies,
however, are to be considered as the responses of the firm rather than the
individual. There should not be two questionnaires collected from any one
firm, unless they clearly represent different operations of the same company.

Questions should be simple, such as "Does the firm expect an 'increase', 'decrease' or 'no change' in their sales, profits, prices, sales promotion expenditures, wages, employment, etc.?" This may be set up as follows
so that their check in the proper box will provide the answer.

	INCREASE	DECREASE	NO CHANGE
Sales	☐	☐	☐
Profits	☐	☐	☐
Advertising and Sales Promotion Expenditures	☐	☐	☐
Employment	☐	☐	☐
Wages	☐	☐	☐
Selling Prices	☐	☐	☐
Opening Inventories	☐	☐	☐
Plant and Equipment Expenditures	☐	☐	☐

If you request a percent change under each of these categories, the
response becomes so cumbersome as to be difficult to handle in the write-
up. While "increase", "decrease" and "no change" are not very specific,
they give good indications of management's thinking.

Business outlook surveys are always of interest to members, public,
press, radio, TV and the Chamber's own magazine. Remember, however,

that the reporting of percentages is *not* the percent of *business increase or decrease,* but rather the percent of the *firms* which have responded in a certain way to the question. It is always in order to ask the type of firm, and to break down the responses by type, such as manufacturing, retail trade, wholesale trade, construction, finance, insurance, real estate, service, etc.

4. Executive Compensation Surveys

This type of survey is not as difficult as a general wage and salary survey because of the narrower range of possible practices. However, unless several arbitrary breakdowns are included in the tabulation, the results of the survey will be of doubtful value. To achieve some kind of consensus on executive compensation practices, the different companies must be divided into somewhat similar groups, such as industry groups or size of company, as measured by number of employees or total revenue or sales. This is necessitated by the obvious fact that the president of a three-man company is not going to make as much as the president of General Motors. A manager of a small retail outlet, similarly, will not be paid as much as the manager of a major department store; and the treasurer of a bank with $1 million of deposits will not make as much as the treasurer of a bank with $300 million of deposits.

Naturally, this is a very sensitive type of survey and confidentiality must be insured before businessmen will respond. One way of obtaining excellent results from surveys of this type is to use a public accounting firm well-known for its strict confidentiality, to whom the completed survey questionnaires will be returned.

5. Personnel Practices and Fringe Benefits

Like the wage survey, this is a very difficult project to complete because of the differences in personnel practices among employers. It will probably require several membership mailings in order to do the whole job. These should go out to all member firms and be directed to the personnel director or the labor relations director.

The questionnaire can be very complex in a personnel practices survey and the resulting report can take equally complex forms with cross-tabulations. Fundamental breakdowns are by type of industry and firm size. Another essential breakdown is between office and plant workers. Surveys of personnel practices may cover such subjects as hours and overtime work, paydays, holidays, vacations, retirement and welfare, hospitalization and medical service, paid sick leave, education, and temporary summer help. Open-ended questions which the respondent may answer in his own words should be eliminated. It is best to have boxes to check or percentages or a single figure to fill in wherever possible. The office and plant breakdown should be maintained throughout the questionnaire, with a single multiple choice question on type of business, and another question on number of employees in the firm. All such questionnaires should have printed on them clearly that the information contained will be held in strict confidence. This will elicit replies from firms that would otherwise not respond.

6. Small-Area or Neighborhood Surveys

The need for detailed social information on a small-area basis has greatly increased in recent years. A partial list of the applications of current demographic data gathered by means of sample surveys includes the following projects:

a. Construction of economic/demographic community profiles;
b. Housing surveys — to determine degrees of deterioration and sub-standard housing, evidence of overcrowding, rent levels, value of structures, age of housing units, percent of new or recent residents, median incomes, and indicators of poverty;
c. City planning — to determine how to allocate expenditures on lighting, streets, sewers, staffing requirements for branch offices of city departments, traffic studies, and need for innovative services; also to determine patterns of migration in the city;
d. Crime surveys — to indicate those areas of the community in which crimes are most prevalent, which types of crime occur most often, and patterns of criminal involvement to reduce the cases of crime;
e. Welfare projects — to determine areas with high concentrations of elderly or underprivileged, where child care centers are most needed, and particular types of health services which would do the most good for the greatest number;
f. Marketing surveys — for example, in determining the optimum site for a shopping center;
g. Mass transit studies — to determine commuter patterns and areas in which preliminary transit lines would be the most rewarding; also, to determine in which areas the need is highest; and
h. Presentations — to demonstrate need for federal funds.

For discussions of sampling procedures that may be used in demographic research, see Section D, Sampling Techniques, in this chapter.

SELECTED READING REFERENCES

American Marketing Association, Committee on Marketing Research Techniques. "Design, Size, and Validation of Samples for Market Research." *The Journal of Marketing,* 1946.

American Marketing Association. *Sampling in Marketing Research.* Marketing Research Techniques Series, No. 3, 1970.

Cassady, Ralph, Jr. "Statistical Sampling Techniques and Marketing Research." *The Journal of Marketing,* Vol. 9 (April, 1945), 317-341.

Clark, Charles T., and Lawrence L. Schkade. *Statistical Methods for Business Decisions.* Cincinnati: South-Western Publishing Co., 1969.

Cochran, William G. *Sampling Techniques.* New York: John Wiley & Sons, Inc., 1953.

Cochran, William G., Frederick Mosteller, and John W. Tukey. "Principles of Sampling." *Journal of the American Statistical Association,* Vol. 49 (March, 1954), 13 - 35.

Croxton, Frederick E., Dudley J. Cowden, and Ben W. Bolch. *Practical Business Statistics,* 4th Edition. Englewood Cliffs, New Jersey: Prentice-Hall, Inc., 1969.

Deming, William Edwards. *Some Theory of Sampling.* New York: John Wiley & Sons, Inc., 1950.

Deming, W. Edwards. *Sample Design in Business Research.* New York: John Wiley & Sons, Inc., 1960.

Erdos, Paul L. *Professional Mail Surveys.* New York: McGraw-Hill Book Company, Inc., 1970.

Ferber, Robert. *Statistical Techniques in Market Research.* New York: McGraw-Hill Book Company, Inc., 1949.

Fisher, R. A. *The Design of Experiments.* London: Oliver and Boyd, 1953.

Frankel, L., and S. Dutka. "How to Get a True Sample of Households." *Printers' Ink,* Vol. 252 (July 15, 1955).

Freund, John E. *Modern Elementary Statistics.* Englewood Cliffs, New Jersey: Prentice-Hall, Inc., 1973.

Griffin, John I. *Statistics Methods and Applications.* New York: Holt, Rinehart and Winston, 1962.

Hansen, Morris H., and William N. Hurwitz. "The Problem of Non-response in Sample Surveys." *Journal of the American Statistical Association,* (December, 1946), 517 - 529.

Hansen, M. H., W. N. Hurwitz, and W. G. Madow. *Sample Survey Methods and Theory.* New York: John Wiley & Sons, 1953.

Hendricks, W. A. *The Mathematical Theory of Sampling.* New Brunswick, N.J.: Scarecrow Press, 1956.

Hoel, Paul G. *Elementary Statistics,* 3rd Edition. New York: John Wiley & Sons, Inc., 1971.

Hyman, H. *Interviewing in Social Research.* Chicago: University of Chicago Press, 1954.

Kendall, M. G., and Babington Smith. *Tables of Random Sampling Numbers.* Cambridge, England: Cambridge University Press, 1954.

Kimball, Andrew E. "Increasing the Rate of Return in Mail Surveys." *Journal of Marketing,* (October, 1961), 63 - 64.

Kish, Leslie. *Survey Sampling.* New York: John Wiley & Sons, Inc., 1965.

Klein, L. R. *Contributions of Survey Methods to Economics.* New York: Columbia University Press, 1954.

Levy, Clifford V. *A Primer for Community Research.* San Francisco: Far West Research, Inc., 1972.

Lorie, J. H., and H. B. Roberts. *Basic Methods of Marketing Research.* New York: McGraw-Hill Book Company, Inc., 1951.

Miller, Irwin. *A Primer on Statistics for Business and Economics.* New York: Random House, Inc., 1968.

Monroe, John, and A. L. Finkner. *Area Sampling.* Philadelphia: Chilton Company - Book Division, 1959.

Moore, P. G. *Principles of Statistical Techniques,* 2nd Edition. Cambridge: Cambridge University Press, 1969.

Neter, John, William Wasserman, and G. A. Whitmore. *Fundamental Statistics,* 4th Edition. Boston: Allyn and Bacon, Inc., 1973.

Parson, Daniel. "The ABC's of Sampling Theory." *American Gas Journal,* (December, 1967), 41, 44.

Parten, Mildred. *Surveys, Polls and Samples.* New York: Cooper Square Publishers, 1966.

Payne, S. L. *The Art of Asking Questions.* Princeton: Princeton University Press, 1951.

Politz, Alfred, and Willard R. Simmons. "An Attempt to Get the Not-at-homes into the Sample without Call-backs." *Journal of the American Statistical Association,* (March, 1949), 9 - 31.

Rand Corporation. *A Million Random Digits with 100,000 Normal Deviates.* Glencoe, Illinois: The Free Press, 1955.

Robinson, R. A. "How to Boost Returns from Mail Surveys." *Printers' Ink,* (June 6, 1952), 35 - 37.

Simon, Raymond. "Responses to Personal and Form Letters in Mail Surveys." *Journal of Advertising Research,* (March, 1967), 28 - 30.

Slonim, Morris James. *Sampling in a Nutshell.* New York: Simon and Schuster, 1960.

Slonim, Morris James. *Sampling.* New York: Simon and Schuster, 1966.

Spurr, William A. *Statistical Analysis for Business Decisions.* Homewood, Illinois: Richard D. Irwin, Inc., 1967.

Stephan, Frederick F., and Philip J. McCarthy. *Sampling Opinions: An Analysis of Survey Procedure.* New York: John Wiley & Sons, Inc., 1963.

Stockton, John R., and Charles T. Clark. *Introduction to Business and Economic Statistics,* 4th Edition. Cincinnati, Ohio: South-Western Publishing Co., 1971.

Stuart, A. *Basic Ideas of Scientific Sampling.* New York: Hafner Publishing Company, 1962.

Sukhatme, P. V. *Sampling Theory of Surveys with Application.* Ames, Iowa: Iowa State College Press, 1954.

U.S. Bureau of the Census. *Sampling Applications of the 1970 Census Publications, Maps, and Public Use Summary Files,* by Margaret Gurney (Technical Paper No. 27). Washington, D.C.: U.S. Government Printing Office, 1972.

U.S. Bureau of the Census. *Who's Home When,* by Dean Weber and Richard C. Burt (Working Paper No. 37). Washington, D.C.: U.S. Government Printing Office, 1972.

U.S. Bureau of the Census. *The Methods and Materials of Demography,* by Henry S. Shryock and Jacob S. Siegel. Washington, D.C.: U.S. Government Printing Office, 1973.

U.S. Bureau of Transport Economics and Statistics. *Table of 105,000 Random Decimal Digits.* Washington, D.C.: U.S. Government Printing Office, 1949.

U.S. Department of Labor, Manpower Administration, Bureau of Employment Security. *The Dictionary of Occupational Titles.* Washington, D.C.: U.S. Government Printing Office, 1965.

Wallis, W. Allen, and Harry V. Roberts. *Statistics: A New Approach.* New York: The Free Press of Glencoe, 1964.

Watson, John J. "Improving the Response Rate on Mail Research." *Journal of Advertising Research* (June, 1965), 48 - 50.

Wonnacott, Thomas H., and Ronald J. Wonnacott. *Introductory Statistics.* New York: John Wiley & Sons, Inc., 1969.

Yates, Frank. *Sampling Methods for Censuses and Surveys.* New York: Hafner Publishing Co., 1960.

Part III

SPOTLIGHTING BUSINESS CONDITIONS AND TRENDS

8 MONTHLY SUMMARY OF BUSINESS INDICATORS

A. INTRODUCTION

After "How are you today?" the question most frequently asked of a businessman is "How's business?" While the first question can be answered with a "Fine, thank you," the second calls for greater documentation, especially if reference is made to the economic health of the local area. Fortunately, an adequate answer is not too difficult to find, if the local Chamber of Commerce has assumed the responsibility for systematically compiling and publishing reports on key factors in the local economy.

It is important for a Chamber, regardless of the size of the community it serves, to be able to provide some type of periodic report on current local business conditions. Though these business-barometer reports have incidental utility in answering casual questions, they are designed primarily to achieve objectives of greater significance. Major goals of a regular report of this type are:

1. Serving as an accurate and prompt measurement of the changes that have taken place in various phases of the local area's business activity;

2. Helping the local Chamber of Commerce monitor the economic pulse of the community, including the identification and study of the causal factors that tend to bring about changes in local business activity;

3. Providing benchmarks by which Chamber members may analyze progress of their respective businesses;

4. Building a storehouse of information useful to various Chamber of Commerce departments in such activities as creating a community image, developing comparative statistics, and preparing other types of reports;

5. Contributing monthly increments to an historical series of local economic information to form an up-to-date base for various program requirements, including local economic projections; and

6. Focusing attention on the local Chamber of Commerce and its Research Department as a viable, authoritative source of local information — an important public relations activity.

Economists track the circular flow of money to producers who in turn become consumers of the goods and services of other producers. Millions of transactions occur daily as money is moved around the circle. It is impossible to follow all transactions, but it is possible to measure the flow of money past some points in the circle, or to at least get some indication of the volume of activity at specific points. If enough indicators are used, researchers can get a fair picture of total economic activity.

Many indicators are used to measure various kinds of economic activity. Indicators thus chosen share three traits: they use some unit of measurement, for some time interval, in some geographic region. For example, car-loadings per month at Central City[1] Depot is one indication of productive activity during the month in the Central City area; dollars of debits to deposit accounts per month at Central City Bank is an indication of the rate at which local depositors are spending their money — further indicating something about what people are earning and what they are spending; spending, in turn, indicates something about sales.

Who cares if the Chamber of Commerce supplies indicators? Do they help the Chamber's members? Do they help anybody? To answer these questions, let's select one indicator and explore whatever conclusions might be drawn from it. Let us suppose that the Chamber of Commerce collected the following data and published it in a newsletter, a magazine, or the local paper:

	June 1972	May 1972	June 1971	Change From May '72	Change From June '71
Automobile sales	13,000	12,000	10,000	Up 8.3%	Up 30%
Truck sales	1,400	1,250	1,000	Up 12.0%	Up 40%

The person most immediately helped is the individual car dealer. He already has his own sales figures for the month but with access to this data, he can compute his share of the market. Suppose one dealer's sales figures are:

	June 1972	May 1972	June 1971	Change From May '72	Change From June '71
Automobile sales	111	108	100	Up 2.8%	Up 11%
Truck sales	54	52	50	Up 3.8%	Up 8%

---

[1] Central City, Midland City, River City, and Moundville are used in this book for illustrative purposes only and do not refer to existing municipalities.

Most retailers would be very pleased to see figures like these: auto sales up 11% and truck sales up 8% in the course of a year. Not bad at all—until he compares his sales with the data the Chamber has given him. His percentage share of the market is:

	June 1972	May 1972	June 1971	Change From May '72	Change From June '71
Automobile sales	0.85%	0.90%	1.00%	Down 5.56%	Down 15.00%
Truck sales	3.86%	4.16%	5.00%	Down 7.21%	Down 22.80%

This dealer's competition is eating him alive. His sales growth has not kept pace with the overall growth in his market. For him, the indicator says he had best take corrective action immediately.

The point to observe here is that if the Chamber of Commerce had not published these statistics, this dealer would be shadow boxing at his competitors, oblivious of the fact that he was not hitting the opportunities the market might offer.

The figures published by the Chamber are also important to other people. An automobile is a "consumer durable good" in the language of economics. When the economy takes a downturn, people will continue to buy the necessities—bread and fuel (consumer non-durables)—but they will postpone purchase of long-term, big ticket purchases such as furniture, major home appliances, automobiles, and other items which carry larger price tags. Thus trends in automobile sales have special meaning for furniture dealers and manufacturers, TV salesmen, carpet installers, finance companies, and many other businesses.

Trucks are "industrial goods," subject to the operation of the "accelerator effect." Suppose a trucking company operates a fleet of 100 trucks, buying 10 new trucks and selling 10 old trucks in a normal year, and suppose they forecast a drop of 10% in shipments for the coming year. The company would probably sell its 10 oldest trucks, buy no new trucks, and operate a fleet of 90 trucks, during the bad year. The trucking company's business is down 10%; the truck manufacturer's business with the trucking firm is down 100%. That is the accelerator effect.

Trends in truck sales are indicators of great interest not only to the people who sell, make, and service trucks, but to people who deal in all kinds of industrial goods as well.

There are many different business indicators. They include statistics on wealth, income, production, transactions, population, taxes, flows of goods, services, and money, sales figures for almost any product, commodity, or service, prices and interest rates. Each indicator measures activity at some point in the many-channeled, circular flow of goods and services in one direction, and the flow of money in the other direction.

B. THREE KINDS OF INDICATORS

Indicators can be grouped into three classes: trailing or lagging indicators, current or roughly coincident indicators, and leading indicators. Trailing indicators tell us how things were last month, last quarter, or last year. Current indicators tell us what is happening now. Leading indicators suggest how the economy might behave in the future. These are general classifications, useful in analyzing data. Some Chambers publish business newsletters with trailing and current indicators and commentary, with the leading indicators grouped into a forecast of things to come. More about the characteristics of indicators can be found in almost any good economics textbook. There are, however, two critical aspects which should be considered here.

First, one man's trailing indicator may be another man's leading indicator. A contractor who builds garages may find that his principal market is among homeowners who wish to convert their attached garages to another use and to build new garages detached from the houses. The average home he serves may be 10 years old. An indicator such as number of new residential electric meters can help him *project his sales 10 years into the future!* The same indicator will tell a residential building contractor how his market has been during the time interval *just past* and will tell an electric appliance salesman something about his market *right now.*

Second, almost without exception there is a lag in collecting and reporting data. What is generally considered a leading indicator by economists may in fact be a current or even a trailing indicator by the time the data are collected and reported. A great deal depends on the agency collecting the data. The Corps of Engineers, for example, is sometimes two years late in supplying statistics on waterborne traffic, whereas the price of a stock transaction is reported within minutes of its occurrence.

Two chapters in this ACCRA manual contain descriptions of the major types of statistical barometers researchers have found to be especially useful in evaluating the economic health of local areas. The first major business barometer — Monthly Summary of Business Indicators — is the subject of the present chapter, and a description of the second barometer — Local Business Index — is presented in Chapter 9.

C. GENERAL CHARACTERISTICS OF A MONTHLY SUMMARY OF BUSINESS INDICATORS

A Monthly Summary of Business Indicators is a collection of statistical information relating to various areas of statistical measure in the local economy. It should, of course, include data on selected phases of economic activity which are significant reflectors of the total economic image of the local area. Major determinants of the contents of this report include the economic characteristics of the individual community and the availability of data on a current basis.

A Monthly Summary need not be too long—a selection of key indicators is better than a long list of data items in which the significance of any single item will likely be buried under massive detail. To be effective, this report also must have continuity—the business indicators selected for presentation in the Monthly Summary must be shown from month to month in a continuous time series of data reflecting changes and trends in the local economy.

The choice of Monthly Summary format is another important decision for the researcher. Some organizations produce only a one-page digest of statistical data for mailing to a selected list of data users in the community, or for reproduction in the local newspapers, Chamber of Commerce newsletter and magazine. Another type of report goes one step beyond the one-page format, adding several pages of back-up data or documentation for the Digest page and thus giving the reader a choice. He may either use only the information presented on the streamlined Digest page or read the Digest page first and then turn to the additional pages for sources of the data reported, plus the tabulations from which statistics for the Digest page were selected.

D. PRODUCING A MONTHLY SUMMARY OF BUSINESS INDICATORS

1. Selecting Basic Indicators

The types of key indicators selected for use in the Monthly Summary do not vary substantially from city to city. Some cities and areas, however, are more heavily oriented toward manufacturing and transportation; some toward recreation, retail and wholesale trade; and still others toward agriculture, military installations, educational or other institutions. Those economic factors that are particularly important to a specific area should be identified and represented in the Monthly Summary.

Indicators selected for this report should relate to the local Standard Metropolitan Statistical Area. However, certain types of information are available only for the corporate limits of cities or for counties within the SMSA; these exceptions should be noted in the Monthly Summary.

A suggested list of indicators to be included in the Monthly Summary is presented below. *This list is intended only to serve as an initial selection of indicators; appropriate changes should be made to this list to reflect local business characteristics.*

1. Financial
   a. Bank debits to individual accounts
   b. Bank demand deposits
   c. Bank clearings

2. Employment
   a. Labor force (total)
   b. Unemployment
   c. Employment (total)
   Manufacturing
   Non-manufacturing
   Agricultural
   d. Ratio unemployment to total labor force:
   Local SMSA
   U.S.

3. Retail trade
   Department store sales (% change)

4. Construction
   a. Corporate limits of Central City
   Building permits residential (no.)
   Building permits residential (value)
   Building permits non-residential (no.)
   Building permits non-residential (value)
   b. County (in which Central City is located)
   Non-residential contracts awarded
   Residential units completed

5. Utilities
   a. Electric current used (M-KWH)
   Non-residential consumption
   b. Electric current customers (total)
   Electric current customers (residential)
   c. Natural gas used (MCF)
   Non-residential consumption
   d. Natural gas customers (total)
   Natural gas customers (residential)
   e. Telephones in service
   f. Watermeters in service

6. Transportation
   a. Port tonnage (short tons)
   b. Rail tonnage (short tons)

   c. Air passengers
      Inbound
      Outbound
   d. Air freight
      Inbound
      Outbound
   e. Motor freight tonnage (% change)

7. Other indicators

   a. Postal receipts
   b. New automobiles and trucks registered
   c. Consumer Price Index
      Local SMSA and U.S. (Base: 1967 = 100)

The use of these suggested indicators in a Monthly Summary is illustrated in Table 8-A.

In addition to the typical indicators listed above, other indicators appear on the business barometer reports of certain cities. A representative list of these special indicators includes real estate transfers; livestock received, processed and shipped (head); savings and loan association total accounts ($000); military payrolls; grain received and shipped (bushels); average weekly hours employment in manufacturing; help-wanted index; average weekly earnings in manufacturing; convention delegate days; spot cotton sales (bales); steel production (tons).

2. Collecting the Data

After selecting the economic indicators to be used in the Monthly Summary, the next step is to develop a systematic flow of appropriate information into the Research Department. Numerous sources of information must be utilized for this purpose, so it is important to develop a list of reliable data sources. Utility companies, railroads, airlines, county clerk, banks, planning commission, tax collectors, Federal Reserve banks, trade associations, and others can all be sources of valuable information. Each potential source should be queried about what information is available; a decision should be made as to what is wanted and needed; and an arrangement whereby the data is reported to the Research Department should be created. Personal contacts with data-source personnel are effective in obtaining their assistance in developing the necessary data input for the Monthly Summary.

After the initial contact with the researcher, some data producers will automatically forward information to the Research Department. Certain items may be obtained by mailing special forms to the data sources each month. Telephone calls may be necessary to get others.

Care must be exercised in gathering data which may be of a confidential nature from private sources. The professional integrity of the local

Chamber of Commerce is important in guaranteeing that such information as sales volume and employment will be used only in compiling aggregates, in which the data contribution of each source will not be identified.

The general categories of desirable data include:

1. *Financial:* Total bank clearings and debits are available from the local Clearing House Association in larger cities and from the nearest Federal Reserve Bank for smaller cities. For local purposes, debits need not be adjusted for seasonal variations.

2. *Employment:* Detailed figures (or estimates) by type of business are almost always available for each county or metropolitan area from state employment security divisions or commissions. If data cannot be obtained from this source, small Chambers can select only manufacturing employment and get totals from personal contacts with local firms.

3. *Retail Trade:* 'Monthly retail sales would be one of the best local business indicators if the figures were readily available. In most areas they are not, but discussion is warranted because some Chambers have found it feasible, with the cooperation of several department stores, to determine weekly percentage changes by obtaining and keeping confidential dollar sales figures from individual stores. Some Federal Reserve districts and the U.S. Department of Commerce accumulate department store sales in key metropolitan areas and report these on a percentage change basis. Additionally, some communities and states are able to produce total retail sales estimates based on sales tax collections. The lag time before figures are available, however, usually makes this type of data impractical for monthly reporting on a current basis.

4. *Construction:* Monthly tabulations of building permits and dollar volume of construction are readily available from local permit issuing agencies. Of particular importance are commercial construction and the types of new residential dwelling units.

5. *Utilities:* Consumption figures as well as customer totals for electricity, gas and water are good monthly barometers. Number of telephone connections or customers is also widely used. Since electricity is used extensively in manufacturing and commercial business, industrial electricity KWH used is an excellent indicator of production activity.

6. *Transportation:* Monthly data on railroad carloadings passing through the local freight yards are fairly easy to obtain from the individual rail lines. Because the size of rail cars has increased in recent years, permitting more net cargo tonnage per car, railroads are being asked to explore the reporting of their tonnage. In securing carloading figures, the Chamber should reach an agreement with the rail lines serving that particular community concerning the inclusion or exclusion of piggybacks as separate cars and demurrage. Total carloadings in and out should be used to mask the volume of any one rail line to prevent individual volume disclosure.

Truck tonnage data from local terminals are a good indicator if the trucking firms are assured that their respective volumes will not be released to competitors. In many metropolitan areas, truck tonnage on a percentage change by week is available from the state trucking association or from the American Trucking Association.

Airline data on passengers carried, totals of cargo handled, and number of aircraft operations are usually available from the local airport management. For port areas, the number of ships and volume of cargo by commodity reflect that important business activity.

3. Recording the Data

Business barometer data received by the Research Department for use in the Monthly Summary should be recorded regularly in a manner which allows them to be added to and expanded upon. A three-ring binder with special tabulation sheets will serve adequately as a Permanent Data Record for this information. Tabs and dividers can be inserted so that each section may be used for recording both current and cumulative data for a single indicator. Sample tabulation sheets are provided in Tables 8-B through 8-F.

To be effective, monthly data should be compared with those of the same month of the previous year. Since large fluctuations may occur in some indicators, it is helpful to maintain cumulative statistics for comparison with the same period of previous years. Percentage changes related to these cumulative totals usually are more meaningful than month-to-month comparisons.

4. Preparing the Monthly Summary for Distribution

The Monthly Summary format selected for discussion in this chapter includes two major sections: (1) a series of back-up or documentary pages prepared from data tabulated in the Permanent Data Record; and (2) a digest page at the front of the report which presents key statistics selected from the report's back-up pages. A typical digest page is presented in Table 8-A.

After the Monthly Summary has been typed in final form, it should be mimeographed or, preferably, printed on offset equipment. In more sophisticated reports, illustrative charts and graphs are used to increase the report's effectiveness, especially in comparing local trends to the state or national economy.

5. Distributing the Monthly Summary

The final important step is to communicate the results of your research. Plan to achieve the widest possible circulation for your Monthly Summary. Decide who should receive the information you have developed, select the media you need to reach those people and publish the report. It may be mailed as a separate report to a special Monthly Summary mailing list prepared by the Research Department, included in the local Chamber of Commerce newsletter and magazine, reproduced by local newspapers — or disseminated through combinations of these publishing procedures.

At this stage the researcher should not consider that the compilation and publishing of his Monthly Summary concludes his research responsibility. Good descriptive copy assessing the community's economic progress should be prepared to accompany the statistical report. The discussion should point out the significance of the indicators in the report, analyze and interpret the statistical data, and spotlight changes and trends indicated by this information — and the problems they represent for the local community.

TABLE 8-A:

Digest Page for a Monthly Summary of Business Indicators

	September - 1972	September - 1971	Percent Change '71-'72	Totals for the First Nine Months - 1972	Totals for the First Nine Months - 1971	Percent Change '71-'72
FINANCIAL						
Bank Debits	$7,378,797,094	$6,350,295,007	+ 16.2	$64,769,042,887	$57,943,797,017	+11.8
Bank Deposits (total)	$1,427,666,491	$1,201,263,898	+ 18.8			
Bank Clearings	$3,718,333,020	$3,306,084,468	+ 12.5	$32,445,574,842	$29,768,375,821	+ 9.0
EMPLOYMENT						
Labor Force (total)	922,000	894,500	+ 3.1			
Unemployment	28,700	24,900	+ 15.3			
	(Ratio of unemployment to total labor force: Central City SMSA 2.9%; U.S. 5.9%)					
Employment	892,900	868,900	+ 2.8			
Manufacturing	148,600	150,200	– 1.1			
Non-manufacturing	736,200	710,500	+ 3.6			
Agricultural	8,100	8,200	– 1.2			
RETAIL TRADE						
Department Store Sales	(Four weeks ending Oct. 2, 1972)		+ 11.0	(Jan. 2, 1972 to Oct. 2, 1972)		+ 11.0
CONSTRUCTION						
Central City Corporate Limits						
Bldg. Permits Res. (no.)	263	314	– 16.2	4,128	2,550	+61.9
Bldg. Permits Res. (value)	$9,940,537	$20,986,823	– 52.6	$173,317,576	$113,385,786	+52.9
Bldg. Permits Non-Res. (no.)	1,011	1,159	– 12.8	14,625	12,552	+16.5
Bldg. Permits Non-Res. (value)	$13,441,311	$23,627,978	– 43.1	$218,759,098	$162,158,499	+34.9
Central County						
Non-res. Contracts Awarded	$52,379,649	$48,992,903	+ 6.9	$520,776,765	$432,969,455	+20.3
Res. Units Completed	3,929	1,107	+254.9	28,179	24,887	+13.2

TABLE 8-A: Continued

	September - 1972	September - 1971	Percent Change '71-'72	Total for the First Nine Months - 1972	Totals for the First Nine Months - 1971	Percent Change '71-'72
UTILITIES DATA						
Electric Current Used (M-Kwh)						
Non-Residential Consumption	1,617,652	1,438,839	+ 12.4	12,430,525	11,326,340	+ 9.7
Elec. Current Customers (total)	575,770	559,382	+ 2.9			
Elec. Current Customers (res.)	504,985	491,977	+ 2.6			
Natural Gas Used (MCF)						
Non-Res. Consumption	49,629,158	45,115,972	+ 10.0	438,346,314	411,008,533	+ 6.7
Gas Customers (total)	476,734	467,022	+ 2.1			
Gas Customers (res.)	440,448	430,649	+ 2.3			
Telephones in Service	1,155,211	1,097,446	+ 5.3			
Water-meter Connections	283,209	278,709	+ 1.6			
TRANSPORTATION						
Port Tonnage (short tons)	5,229,107	4,988,480	+ 4.8	51,772,146	45,085,109	+14.8
Rail Tonnage (short tons)	1,784,320	1,800,812	− 0.9	16,284,359	15,954,266	+ 2.1
Air Freight						
Inbound (lbs)	4,979,770	5,001,587	− 0.4	56,310,839	59,706,274	− 5.7
Outbound (lbs)	4,090,855	3,706,354	+ 10.4	43,690,692	38,374,116	+13.9
Air Passengers						
Inbound	241,758	227,669	+ 6.2	2,904,637	2,693,997	+ 7.8
Outbound	248,548	229,514	+ 8.3	2,914,617	2,715,550	+ 7.3
OTHER INDICATORS						
Postal Receipts	$6,340,765	$5,058,238	+ 25.4	$63,938,558	$62,876,654	+ 1.7
Consumer Price Index	129.9	122.9	5.7			
(All Items: 1967 = 100)						

TABLE 8-B:
Tabulation Form for Bank Debits
To Individual Accounts in _____ County, 1972

Month	Amount	Cumulative Total
January	$8,225,511,038	
February	7,452,059,537	$15,677,570,575
March	8,565,368,587	24,242,939,162
April	7,941,106,594	32,184,045,756
May	8,564,960,307	40,749,006,063
June	9,280,566,685	50,029,572,748
July	8,651,538,369	58,681,111,117
August	9,434,094,992	68,115,206,109
September	8,521,679,792	76,636,885,901
October	9,500,170,958	86,137,056,859
November	9,638,908,035	95,775,964,894
December	10,162,962,473	105,938,927,367

TABLE 8-C:
Tabulation Form for Local Area
Railroad Freight for the Month of _____, 1973

	Railroads			Totals
	No. 1	No. 2	No. 3	All Local RR
1. Carload Freight (short tons, excluding LCL freight):				
2. Received	138,620	106,816	275,135	520,571
3. Forwarded	17,661	8,576	121,398	147,635
4. LCL Freight (short tons):				
5. Received	13	0	813	826
6. Forwarded	4	0	2,788	2,792
7. Total Carload and LCL Freight:				
8. Received (Items 2 & 5)	138,633	106,816	275,948	521,397
9. Forwarded (Items 3 & 6)	17,665	8,576	124,186	150,427
Grand Total Freight Handled by All Railroads Serving Local Area				671,824
10. No. of Loaded RR Cars:				
11. Received	4,780	3,338	6,377	14,495
12. Forwarded	609	268	3,056	3,933
13. Total (Items 11-12)	5,389	3,606	9,433	18,428
14. No. of Loaded Freight Trains:				
15. Received	204	75	514	793
16. Forwarded	143	77	515	735
17. Total (Items 15-16)	347	152	1,029	1,528

TABLE 8-D:
Tabulation Form for Non-Residential Natural Gas Consumption (MCF) in ――――― County, 1972

Month	Gas Companies Reporting					End of Month Total	Cumulative Total
	No. 1	No. 2	No. 3	No. 4	No. 5		
January	2,223,710	6,590,932	12,462,517	14,394,871	3,080,551	38,752,581	
February	2,524,666	5,966,669	10,987,479	13,088,185	2,933,920	35,500,919	74,253,500
March	2,058,380	5,312,319	11,093,434	12,983,232	3,026,566	34,473,931	108,727,431
April	1,825,048	5,427,900	10,747,666	13,038,607	2,849,662	33,888,883	142,616,314
May	1,679,682	5,684,438	11,246,528	13,194,237	2,728,800	34,533,685	177,149,999
June	1,682,549	6,986,252	10,532,855	13,480,980	2,869,855	35,552,491	212,702,490
July	1,667,600	7,835,356	11,183,919	14,065,770	2,944,720	37,697,365	250,399,855
August	1,852,561	8,592,018	11,394,231	15,203,499	2,900,000	39,942,309	290,342,164
September	1,775,331	9,619,146	10,980,396	14,591,559	2,815,019	39,781,451	330,123,615
October	1,808,518	7,959,668	11,713,545	13,998,306	3,002,789	38,482,826	368,606,441
November	2,036,098	5,821,474	12,943,577	12,730,606	2,989,474	36,521,229	405,127,670
December	2,999,392	6,101,338	14,654,711	13,584,847	2,818,677	40,158,965	445,286,635

TABLE 8-E:
Tabulation Form for Telephone Connections
In _____ County, 1972

Month	Number in Service	Net Increase
January	1,114,544	6,520
February	1,120,464	5,920
		12,440
March	1,126,021	5,557
		17,997
April	1,132,747	6,726
		24,723
May	1,136,466	3,719
		28,442
June	1,140,364	3,898
		32,340
July	1,141,426	1,062
		33,402
August	1,148,261	6,835
		40,237
September	1,155,211	6,950
		47,187
October	1,162,713	7,502
		54,689
November	1,168,641	5,928
		60,617
December	1,173,149	4,508
		65,125

TABLE 8-F:
Tabulation Form for Postal Receipts In _____ County, 1972

Accounting Period	Amount	Cumulative Total
1-8-72/2-4-72	$5,508,719	
2-5-72/3-3-72	5,220,399	$10,729,119
3-4-72/3-31-72	5,387,639	16,116,758
4-1-72/4-28-72	5,670,412	21,787,170
4-29-72/5-26-72	5,702,775	27,489,946
5-27-72/6-23-72	5,376,051	32,865,997
6-24-72/7-21-72	5,236,067	38,102,064
7-22-72/8-18-72	5,401,458	43,503,522
8-19-72/9-15-72	5,161,096	48,664,618
9-16-72/10-10-72	7,097,709	55,762,328
10-11-72/11-10-72	5,728,838	61,491,166
11-11-72/12-8-72	6,359,327	67,850,493

9 LOCAL BUSINESS INDEX

A. WHAT A BUSINESS INDEX IS

The types of statistical comparisons useful to Chamber members both in evaluating the economic health of the community and in analyzing the progress of their own businesses are summarized in Chapter 8. The next logical step is preparation of a business index — an effective systematic way to analyze data and to draw an overall picture of the local economy from specific statistics.

The Chamber researcher frequently turns to the types of business indicators described in Chapter 8 to sum up what business is doing in his community: employment up 1%, retail sales off 3%, carloadings up 2%. But what do you do if the indicators are conflicting — carloadings outbound are up 2%, manufacturing kilowatt hours of electricity consumed down 1%? How do you compare apples and oranges? One of the best solutions is to take the indicators of business activity and build them into one or more indexes of activity. Indexes bring together the many hundreds of thousands of business activities and transactions occurring daily in an economy to present a composite picture of a local economy with measurements representing various types of units. They reduce apples and oranges to pure scalar quantities which can be compared directly.

A local business index is essentially a refinement of monthly statistics enabling the researcher to aggregate specific indicators of economic activity into broad generalizations about the entire economy with reasonable accuracy. The use of a variety of statistical tools eliminates most of the guesswork from a comparison of two or more figures chosen for evaluation, making an index a credible data digest.

B. HOW A BUSINESS INDEX HELPS

The major advantage of a local business index to the Chamber of Commerce executive and others involved in community improvement is its ability to measure composite activity. Regardless of statistical series available to measure economic changes in a specific area, the only way to obtain a single overall measurement is through a composite index. If the various data are weighted according to their relative importance within the local economy, the entire business index will be a useful and effective tool: it will indicate where the community stands economically in relation to the past and act as a guide to the community's economic future.

Beyond its utility as a measure of the economic climate, the business index has other practical applications in Chamber of Commerce operations. It is a public relations tool in that it identifies the Chamber as the organization with the ability to provide a comprehensive measurement of cyclical business trends in the community comparable not only with its own previous records but also with national, state, and other area trends. The business index and its component indexes can be persuasive in expanding Chamber support by local business because these are statistical services not readily available elsewhere — a significant asset few Chamber of Commerce staff members would overlook. The trends reflected by such series as employment, payrolls, retail sales, and building construction are essential elements in business planning in the areas of hiring, inventory, marketing, and capital construction.

C. WHO WANTS IT?

Once a business index is made available on a regular basis as a measurement of the local economy, the demand for it may surprise the Chamber executive. Not only will business and industrial managements become dependent on it for the uses indicated above, but government administrators will refer to it in their planning activities as well. And the various news media will tend to give it good coverage, particularly if the index is accompanied by a professionally-composed analysis of trends.

Others finding uses for the local business index include universities and libraries, the State Commerce Department or Development Commission, the area Federal Reserve Bank, and the State Labor Department. It is also a prime subject of interest for new business prospects. A business index graphically demonstrating economic growth can do more to attract new industry to an area than reams of subjective prose.

Business index information can be released in a regular article in the Chamber's magazine, through a special statistical bulletin, or as a combination of the two. The mission here is twofold: to keep the membership informed on the local business climate, and to re-emphasize the Chamber's role as a prime mover of community development.

D. WHO DOES IT?

The preparation of a local business index is basically the responsibility of the Chamber's staff, particularly if it includes economic research personnel. However, to achieve its maximum technical potential, and to ensure its greatest possible acceptability and use, the index should be prepared in consultation with various research elements of the community. In many Chambers these individuals and organizations are already members of an existing Research Committee. In some areas it may be necessary to organize—as a division of the Research Committee—a group of economics-oriented persons to contribute to the extensive examination and analysis of available data, the determination of what to include in the business index, decisions regarding the necessary adjustments and weightings of the various components, and suggestions as to the type of illustrative charts and tables to use in presenting the index.

These statistical and economic technicians may include staff personnel from larger industries, public utilities, and universities. In some communities there may also exist technical personnel in banks, government offices, transportation organizations, social agencies, and retail establishments who are knowledgeable in statistical fields.

Once the business index has been initiated, it is usually better to center responsibility within the Chamber staff for the collection of statistics, calculation of the monthly indexes, and publication of the results. Some Chambers of Commerce include an analysis of current economic trends as a newsletter accompanying the index, plus other selected statistical series. Customarily, these analyses will be written by the staff personnel. Although one person must have responsibility for the written analysis, a joint review has some advantages since a carefully selected economic group can pool the analytical abilities of its members. An incidental benefit to the Chamber of Commerce is the inclusion of community research within the framework of the Chamber organization.

E. CARDINAL REQUIREMENTS FOR THE INDEX

Once a business index has been established, it is important to use the same components and adjustments over a reasonable period. Otherwise users will receive the impression that the index lacks continuity, comparability, and dependability. On the other hand, most statistical measurements can become outmoded in time, particularly if the economic characteristics of the community undergo a marked change. Periodic review is advisable, enabling the committee to evaluate the purposes and composition of the business index and determine whether it is doing an acceptable job in measuring local economic trends. There is no set time for such a review, but once every five years might be regarded as essential, with greater frequency as the base period of federal indexes is revised or as more significant statistical series are developed.

Whatever economic indicators are considered in the composition of a business index, there are four requirements to be met:

1. *Comparability:* A statistical measure must be consistent over an extended period so that it represents the same types of units at all times.
2. *Reliability:* To ensure maximum acceptance, the data sources for the index must be unimpeachable and regarded as authoritative. Be able to document the information.
3. *Regularity:* Economic indicators must be available on a regular basis, preferably at about the same time each month.
4. *Timeliness:* Statistical data lose their value and impact if they are published too long after the period being measured, even if they meet the other criteria.

F. ASSEMBLING THE INDEX

The Consumer Price Index is probably the most familiar index used in the United States. It is based on the consumption habits of the average urban industrial worker. The amounts the average man must pay for the goods and services he purchases are divided by the amount he would have paid during an average month in 1967 and multiplied by 100. The result is an index of consumer prices which reflects the changes in the purchasing power of the dollar since 1967.

The man in the street hears that "the cost of living" went up one-half of one per cent last month. He may be aware that the cost of living report is based on the Consumer Price Index. He certainly is familiar with the terms and knows how to use them, especially if he is employed under a contract with a cost-of-living escalator clause, just as he is familiar with how to use his television set. However, he probably does not know how an index works, any more than he knows the technical details of how his television set works.

What follows, then, is a detailed explanation of how indexes work. While the quantity of arithmetic involved may make the procedure seem formidable, the individual operations are relatively simple. There are just a lot of them. Here is how the Midland City Chamber of Commerce handles the problem.[1]

An economic index is based on economic indicators. The Consumer Price Index is based, in part, on the price of gasoline and the price of baby shoes. Those prices are economic indicators. The Midland City Chamber collects data for the following indicators:

---

[1] The name Midland City is used in this chapter for illustrative purposes only and does not refer to any existing municipalities.

1. Manufacturing kilowatt hours of electricity sold.
2. Freight car loadings—inbound, outbound, and total.
3. Employment—in construction trades and in wholesale and retail services.
4. Department store sales.
5. Automobile and truck sales.
6. Value of building permits for residences.
7. The ATA motor freight index for Midland City.
8. Bank debits and bank loans.

The Chamber has built these indicators into six indexes of economic activity in specific areas of the economy, and then has synthesized these six into a composite index of overall business activity. The six indexes are:

1. *The Industrial Production Index,* based on
   a. Manufacturing KWH, weighted at 70%
   b. Carloadings outbound, weighted at 30%
2. *The Trade and Services Index,* based on
   a. Department store sales, weighted at 35%
   b. Employment in wholesale and retail trade and services, weighted at 50%
   c. Automobile and truck sales, weighted at 15%
3. *The Construction Index,* based on
   a. The average value of residential building permits issued during the past four months, weighted at 30%
   b. Employment in construction trades, weighted at 70%
4. *The Transportation Index,* based on
   a. Carloadings inbound and outbound, weighted at 50%
   b. The ATA motor freight index for Midland City, weighted at 50%
5. *The Financial Index,* based on
   a. Bank debits, weighted at 55%
   b. Bank loans, weighted at 45%
6. *The Employment Index,* based on
   a. Total area employment, weighted at 100%

During the process of developing these indexes, the Chamber's Research Committee met and considered all of the possible indicators of Industrial Production before settling on the two listed above: Manufacturing KWH and Carloadings Outbound. The members then considered the relative reliability of these indicators as measures of industrial production, decided that electricity was considerably better than carloadings as a measure, and weighted electricity at 70% and carloadings at 30%. Similarly, the committee selected indicators for each of the other indexes, and assigned weights to them.

It may well be that in your city other indicators may be more reliable than the ones used in Midland City, and you may wish to weight them differently. The judgments are largely subjective — synthesized judgments of experts who are accustomed to thinking in quantitative terms. Furthermore, the judgments should be reviewed periodically. With the passage of time, the relative importance of the indicators selected may change, in which case their weights should be adjusted accordingly. Also, it may become necessary to drop one indicator and add a new one as their relative values change, a shift brought about by changes in the community's industrial and commercial framework.

The Research Committee also made subjective judgments of the relative importance of each of these six indexes to the overall economy of Midland City to produce a composite index.

The *Composite Index of Business Activity* is based on
1. Industrial Production Index   weighted at 35%
2. Trade and Services Index   weighted at 25%
3. Construction Index   weighted at 5%
4. Transportation Index   weighted at 10%
5. Financial Index   weighted at 10%
6. Employment Index   weighted at 15%

The next subjective judgment to be made was the selection of a base time period. The committee first chose 1957-1959 as the base, because it was being used by the federal government as the base for the Consumer Price Index, the Wholesale Price Index, the Industrial Production Index, and a whole series of other measurements. In 1971, however, the Bureau of Labor Statistics revised its base, selecting the 1967 average to replace the 1957-59 average as the base period for its indexes. During a subsequent review of local indexes, the Midland City Chamber's Research Committee followed suit, and put all local indexes on the 1967 base. This decision made it possible to compare Midland City's economic performance directly with national performance indexes from the government. The Research Committee was able to make this change only because 1967 was not an abnormal year in Midland City.

If something unusual occurred in your city during 1967, such as a flood, a plague, or prolonged strikes in key industries, comparisons of other years with 1967 would be inappropriate and you should therefore select some other base period. Otherwise, 1967 is recommended.

Thus far, the base period had been defined, the indicators for the component indexes had been selected and weighted, and the components of the composite index had been selected and weighted (See Chart 9-A). The next logical step was to begin acquiring the data, the techniques used

**CHART 9-A: Weighted Components of Midland City Composite
Index of Economic Activity**

Manufacturing KWH	70% Industrial Production Index	35%
Carloadings Outbound	30%	
Department Store Sales	35% Trade and Services Index	25%
Employment in Wholesale and Retail Trades and Services	50%	
Automobile and Truck Sales	15%	
Building Permit Value*	30% Construction Index	5%
Employment in Construction Trades	70%	
Carloadings Inbound and Outbound	50% Transportation Index	10%
ATA Motor Freight Index for City	50%	
Bank Debits	55% Financial Index	10%
Bank Loans	45%	
Total Area Employment	100% Employment Index	15%

COMPOSITE INDEX OF BUSINESS ACTIVITY

*Average value of residential building permits issued during the past four months.

being those discussed in Chapter 8. Here are some of the data that the Midland City Chamber collected.

1967	Manufacturing KWH	Carloadings Outbound
Jan.	198,931	8,438
Feb.	196,487	8,137
Mar.	189,785	10,279
Apr.	198,831	9,115
May	201,694	10,328
June	205,704	9,698
July	198,095	8,997
Aug.	202,615	9,650
Sept.	203,276	9,125
Oct.	204,865	9,625
Nov.	204,832	9,005
Dec.	197,528	8,870
Average Month, 1967	200,200	9,272
January 1972	230,585	10,390
December 1972	241,991	11,193
January 1973	252,023	11,241

With these data the industrial production index was computed for January, 1973, for the preceding month and for the corresponding month, one year earlier, as follows:

$$.70 \times \left[\frac{\text{Mfg. KWH (Jan. 73)}}{\text{Mfg. KWH (Ave. Mo. 67)}} \times (100) \right]$$

$$+ .30 \times \left[\frac{\text{Cars Out (Jan. 73)}}{\text{Cars Out (Ave. Mo. 67)}} \times (100) \right]$$

$$= .70 \times \left[\frac{252,023}{200,200} \times (100) \right]$$

$$+ .30 \times \left[\frac{11,241}{9,272} \times (100) \right] = 124.5$$

$$= \text{Industrial Production Index, Jan. 1973}$$
$$\text{Base: 1967} = 100$$

Similarly:

Industrial Production Index, December 1972 = 120.8
Industrial Production Index, January 1972 = 114.2

And so it was that in early February the Midland City News was able to report that "The Industrial Production Index, prepared by the Midland City Chamber of Commerce, reached 124.5 in January, 24 ½ above the average month of 1967, which is the base. This indicates an increase of three percent in overall industrial output since December, and a nine percent increase over January, one year ago."

After similarly computing the indexes of Trade and Services, Construction, Transportation, Finance, and Employment, the Midland City Chamber of Commerce was able to compute the composite index as follows:

Component	Index Number		Weight		
Industrial Production	124.5	×	35%	=	43.575
Trade and Services	129.5	×	25%	=	32.375
Construction	170.9	×	5%	=	8.545
Transportation	151.3	×	10%	=	15.130
Finance	188.7	×	10%	=	18.870
Employment	116.1	×	15%	=	17.415
Composite Index					135.9

The indexes above are not adjusted for seasonal variation. Seasonal variations are those changes in data attributable to the time of year instead of to fundamental changes in economic activity. Everyone knows that department store sales peak in November and December, and remain at fairly high levels during the January "white sales". Suppose February sales are down 10% from the preceding December. Is this good or bad? You expected them to fall, but did they fall more or less than you expected? Adjusting raw data for seasonal variations can answer the question.

Computing seasonal adjustment factors involves staggering quantities of simple repetitive arithmetic. Descriptions of seasonal adjustment procedures are not included in this chapter, but readers interested in this subject will find one method of seasonal adjustment illustrated in Exhibit 9-A.

G. SUMMARY

A local business index goes a step beyond a collection of statistical indicators. It provides the only composite measurement of economic trends in the area. Each series of data is converted into an index and combined with other data to provide a meaningful assessment of the community's economic progress.

Each component index is of particular interest to various segments of the business community, and the complete index commands the attention of planners and the public. The usefulness of these measurements largely depends on the reliability of the sources, the soundness of weighting factors, and the comparability and regularity of the statistics.

The preparation of a business index should be handled by the Chamber research staff with the assistance and counsel of other economic and statistical personnel from local offices. who are frequently brought together in the Chamber's Research Committee. The index should be published regularly and should be reviewed thoroughly about every five years.

The best economic measurement is an index that has been adjusted to remove temporary influences that would otherwise distort an evaluation of cyclical trends. A decision as to these adjustments for seasonal and price elements can be arrived at through an analysis of the relative importance of the various components involved in the structure of the community's economy.

EXHIBIT 9-A:
ADJUSTING RAW DATA
FOR SEASONAL VARIATIONS

The omission of seasonal adjustments to raw data can produce misleading results in the indexes. Consider the Industrial Production Index in the example described in Chapter 9. Seventy percent of it is based on electric power consumption. Manufacturers use electricity for many purposes, only some of which, such as running machine tools and conveyor systems, are concerned with production. Some plants are heated with electricity, but most are not. Many plants use electric air conditioning. Some plants never turn the lights out while others, operating a single shift, turn them out every night. It should be apparent that the consumption of electricity by manufacturers can vary significantly during the course of a year without any change in output, or, conversely, that output can change dramatically with only small changes in electric power consumption. The solution to this difficulty is to adjust the raw data on manufacturing kilowatt hours to eliminate purely seasonal variations before using the data to compute the index. The same holds true for all the other indicators used in all of the other indexes.

Computing seasonal adjustment factors is ideally suited to a computer, which permits subtle changes in the process of computing seasonal adjustments.[2] For example, any given month will have a different number of Saturdays, Sundays, and paydays in successive years. This factor should be taken into account in any automated production of seasonal adjustment factors. Because it adds serious complications to the problem with minimal increase in accuracy, however, it should be omitted from any manual computation of seasonal adjustment factors.

The computer is the ideal tool to use, but you should know what kind of arithmetic the tool is doing for you along with effective use of the adjustment factors. The method of seasonal adjustment most commonly employed is called the ratio-to-moving-average or percentage-of-moving-average method. The theory behind it assumes that there are four factors influencing data in time series: Trends, Seasonal Variation, Cyclical Variation, and Irregular Variations. If the time series is a series of monthly data, a 12-month moving average is an estimate of trends and cyclical influences. Dividing data for a particular month by a 12-month moving average should eliminate trends and cyclical influences, leaving seasonal and irregular factors. That is what we are after.

Some business cycles move up and down with periods less than one year in duration. Others have periods of two years, five years, 10 years

---

[2] A seasonal-adjustment computer computer program is described in *The X-11 Variant of the Census Method II Seasonal Adjustment Program,* Technical Paper No. 15, 4/67:425-0497. Washington, D.C.: U.S. Government Printing Office.

and longer. The longer the base period employed, the more accurate the estimate of cyclical variation will be. In our sample we will use data from six years. A larger sample, 10 years perhaps, would be preferred.

The monthly data the Midland City Chamber has been collecting are all sums of events occurring during the month tabulated as of the end of each month. The first steps in the calculations are aimed at centering the data for a given month on a 12-month moving average. The next step is to compute the percentage of the average month which data for a given month represent. The data in our example represent the number of persons employed in construction trades in Midland City from 1967 to date. It is one of the components of Midland City's Construction Activity Index and is influenced by the seasons.

The information compiled for use in this illustration has been recorded in Table 9-A. The first column in this table lists the number of people employed in construction trades in Midland City by month for each month from January, 1967, to December, 1972. The first number in the second column is the sum of the first 12 numbers in the first column, positioned between the 6th and 7th numbers in the first column. The second figure in the second column is the sum of the second through 13th numbers in the first column, positioned between the 7th and 8th numbers, and so on. Thus the sum of the numbers from January through December is centered on that year, and from February through January is centered in its year, and so on down the line. The numbers in the second column are the 12-month moving total of the numbers of persons employed in each successive 12-month period.

The next step in the process of centering the average on the data for each month is to add the numbers in Column Two together in pairs in a two-month moving total. The sum of the first two numbers in the column is recorded between them in Column Three. Then the sum of the second and third numbers is similarly recorded, and so on. The numbers in Column Four are the corresponding numbers in Column Three divided by 24. Thus we have centered on the data for July, 1972, the average monthly employment for the year January 15, 1972, through January 15, 1973. The numbers in Column Four are average monthly employment figures for a series of successive 12-month periods, centered on each period.

Looking back at the process you can see what has occurred. We started out to compute the average monthly employment for each year, so we computed 12-month totals, preparing to divide by 12. But after we had computed the totals, the totals were not centered on the monthly data we had collected. So we averaged the data for the two 12-month periods that bracketed the month we were after. Instead of adding the two numbers together, dividing by two, and then dividing by 12, we added the two numbers together and divided by 24.

The last step in Table 9-A is to compute the percentage of the average month which the data for each month in Column One represent. To do it we divided each number in Column One by the corresponding number in Column Four and multiply by 100, recording the results in Column Five. As a result of our computations thus far, we can say that construction employment in July, 1972 was 108.6% of employment during the average month; that in December of 1972 it was 95.3% of employment during the average month, and so on.

Using the data from Column Five in Table 9-A, we can make the computations shown in Table 9-B. After arraying the percentages for each month under the respective years, the modified mean of the percentages for each month is computed. This minimizes irregular variations which occur from year to year. In each row, the highest and lowest figures are discarded and the remaining three numbers are averaged. At this stage it helps to review activities and events represented by the data. For instance, in July, 1968, Midland City had a construction strike, and the percentage for that month is significantly lower than that for this month in the other years represented. The strike ended in August, and employment soared as lost time was made up, so August, 1968, shows a much higher percentage than the other Augusts. By first discarding the highest and lowest totals, the extreme irregular variations are eliminated. Then by averaging the rest, the remaining irregular variations, hopefully, cancel each other out. The larger the time span for which data are available, the more likely that this cancellation will occur. The modified mean is our first estimate of an index of seasonal variation.

Since the seasonal index for each month is supposed to be a percentage of the average month, the sum of the 12 modified means should be 1200. Instead it is 1199.2. The fact that it is so close to 1200 is reassuring; it indicates that we have probably avoided gross errors in the preceding arithmetic. Still, it is an error which we can refine. To do this, 1200 is divided by the sum of the modified means, 1199.2, and the quotient, 1.000667, is multiplied by each of the modified means, in turn. These final products are the seasonal index numbers for each of the 12 months.

Seasonal indexes have two principal uses. One is in forecasting. Given a series of data covering a period of time, we can project the trend line into the future. If the data are not subject to seasonal variation, this extrapolation alone may be a sufficiently accurate estimate of things to come, but if the data are subject to seasonal variation, we can multiply the projected data by the seasonal index to predict with reasonable accuracy what will actually occur.

The other use of a seasonal index is our concern here; the seasonal index numbers are used to de-seasonalize data to eliminate changes in the data attributable solely to the time of year. This is done by dividing the data for a given month by the seasonal index for that month. As an example, let us compute the Construction Index for Midland City for December, 1972, using de-seasonalized data. You will recall that the Construction Index is based on the average value of residential building permits issued during the past four months, weighted at 30%, and the number of persons employed in construction trades weighted at 70%. We just computed the December seasonal index for construction employment: 97.8. Similarly the January seasonal index of four-month running averages of residential building permits was computed to be 101.1. The base year (1967) averages are $4,374,061 for building permits and 12,687 for construction employment. During the last four months of 1972, building permits averaging $13,326,620 per month were issued in Midland City, and in December, 13,796 persons were employed in construction trades.

Step One — De-seasonalize the data

Building Permit Value ÷ Seasonal Index = Adjusted Building Permit
Value

$$\$13,326,620 \div 1.011 = 13,182,622$$

Construction Employment ÷ Seasonal Index = Adjusted Construction
Employment

$$13,796 \div .978 = 14,106$$

Note that when the seasonal index figures were computed they were expressed as percentages; here, they were reconverted to decimal fractions before doing the division.

Step Two — Use de-seasonalized data to compute the index number

Construction Index =

$$\text{weight} \times \frac{\text{Adjusted Permit Value} \times 100}{\text{Base Permit Value}}$$

$$+ \quad \text{weight} \times \frac{\text{Adjusted Employment} \times 100}{\text{Base Employment}}$$

$$\left[.30 \times \frac{13,182,622}{4,374,061}\right] \times \left[.70 \times \frac{14,106}{12,687}\right] \times 100 = 168.2$$

Thus we have arrived at a de-seasonalized index of construction industry activity in Midland City in December, 1972. The Midland City Chamber of Commerce, you will recall, computes a Composite Index from six component indexes of which the Construction Index is one. The Component Indexes are based on time-series data for 12 indicators. The indicators must be adjusted for seasonal variation, so seasonal indexes must be computed for each indicator. The volume of simple arithmetic involved makes a computer an indispensible tool.

Here is the full set of formulas used by the Midland City Chamber to compute its seven indexes:

Industrial Production $= \dfrac{.70 \text{ (Mfg. KWH/Seas. Adj.) } 100}{1967 \text{ Ave. Mfg. KWH}}$

$\qquad\qquad + \dfrac{.30 \text{ (Cars Out/Seas. Adj.) } 100}{1967 \text{ Ave. Cars Out}}$

Trade & Services $= \dfrac{.35 \text{ (Dept. Store Sales/Seas. Adj.) } 100}{1967 \text{ Ave. Dept. Store Sales}}$

$\qquad\qquad + \dfrac{.50 \text{ (Trade & Svcs. Emp./Seas. Adj.) } 100}{1967 \text{ Ave. Trade & Svcs. Emp.}}$

$\qquad\qquad + \dfrac{.15 \text{ (Auto-Truck Sales/Seas. Adj.) } 100}{1967 \text{ Auto-Truck Sales}}$

Construction $= \dfrac{.30 \text{ (4 mos. Ave. Res. B.P. Val./Seas. Adj.) } 100}{1967 \text{ Ave. Res. Bldg. Per. Val., 4 Mo. Ave. Totl.}}$

$\qquad\qquad + \dfrac{.70 \text{ (Const. Emp./Seas. Adj.) } 100}{1967 \text{ Ave. Const. Emp.}}$

Transportation $= \dfrac{.50 \text{ (Cars In & Out/Seas. Adj.) } 100}{1967 \text{ Ave. Cars In & Out}}$

$\qquad\qquad + \dfrac{.50 \text{ (ATA Motor Freight Index/Seas. Adj.) } 100}{1967 \text{ Ave. ATA Motor Freight Index}}$

Financial $= \dfrac{.55 \text{ (Bank Debits/Seas. Adj.) } 100}{1967 \text{ Ave. Bank Debits}}$

$\qquad\qquad + \dfrac{.45 \text{ (Bank Loans/Seas. Adj.) } 100}{1967 \text{ Ave. Bank Loans}}$

Employment $= \dfrac{(\text{Tot. Area Employment/Sea. Adj.) } 100}{1967 \text{ Ave. Total Area Employment}}$

Composite Index $=$ .35 (Industrial Production Index) + .25 (Trade & Services Index)

$\qquad\qquad +$ .05 (Construction Index) + .10 (Transportation Index)

$\qquad\qquad +$ .10 (Financial Index) + .15 (Employment Index)

The decimal fractions in these formulas are the weights assigned to the various factors by the Midland City Chamber's Research Committee.

TABLE 9-A:
Computation of the Ratio of Monthly Construction Employment to the Twelve-Month Moving Average for Midland City, 1967 - 1972

Year & Month	Construction Employment	12-Month Moving Total	2-Month Moving Total	Centered 12-Month Moving Average	Percentage of 12-Month Moving Average
1967					
Jan.	11,718				
Feb.	11,153				
Mar.	11,519				
Apr.	12,326				
May	12,887				
June	13,373	152,249			
July	13,794	152,451	304,700	12,696	108.6
Aug.	13,766	153,042	305,493	12,729	108.1
Sept.	13,316	153,413	306,455	12,769	104.3
Oct.	13,125	154,133	307,546	12,814	102.4
Nov.	13,011	154,502	308,636	12,860	101.2
Dec.	12,261	154,266	308,768	12,865	95.3
1968					
Jan.	11,920	152,241	306,507	12,771	93.3
Feb.	11,744	153,253	305,494	12,729	92.3
Mar.	11,890	154,110	307,363	12,807	92.8
Apr.	13,046	154,868	308,978	12,874	101.3
May	13,256	155,398	310,266	12,928	102.5

TABLE 9-A (Continued)

Year & Month	Construction Employment	12-Month Moving Total	2-Month Moving Total	Centered 12-Month Moving Average	Percentage of 12-Month Moving Average
1968					
June	13,137	156,026	311,424	12,976	101.2
July	11,769	155,535	311,561	12,982	90.7
Aug.	14,778	155,706	311,241	12,968	114.0
Sept.	14,173	156,180	311,886	12,995	109.1
Oct.	13,883	156,883	313,063	13,044	106.4
Nov.	13,541	157,975	314,858	13,119	103.2
Dec.	12,889	160,087	318,062	13,252	97.3
1969					
Jan.	11,429	164,042	324,129	13,505	84.6
Feb.	11,915	165,366	329,408	13,725	86.8
Mar.	12,364	166,676	332,042	13,835	89.4
Apr.	13,749	168,379	335,055	13,961	98.5
May	14,348	170,177	338,556	14,107	101.7
June	15,249	172,229	342,406	14,227	107.2
July	15,724	174,637	346,866	14,453	108.8
Aug.	16,072	176,774	351,411	14,642	109.8
Sept.	15,513	178,656	355,430	14,810	104.7
Oct.	15,586	179,734	358,390	14,933	104.4
Nov.	15,339	180,368	360,102	15,004	102.2

TABLE 9-A (Continued)

Year & Month	Construction Employment	12-Month Moving Total	2-Month Moving Total	Centered 12-Month Moving Average	Percentage of 12-Month Moving Average
1969					
Dec.	14,941	178,815	359,183	14,966	99.8
1970					
Jan.	13,837	177,757	356,572	14,857	93.1
Feb.	14,052	176,523	354,280	14,762	95.2
Mar.	14,246	174,911	351,434	14,643	97.3
Apr.	14,827	173,085	347,996	14,500	102.3
May	14,982	171,164	344,249	14,344	104.4
June	13,696	169,287	340,451	14,185	96.6
July	14,666	167,048	336,335	14,014	104.7
Aug.	14,838	164,869	331,917	13,830	107.3
Sept.	13,901	164,023	328,892	13,704	101.4
Oct.	13,760	163,210	327,233	13,635	100.9
Nov.	13,418	162,660	325,870	13,578	98.8
Dec.	13,064	163,723	326,383	13,599	96.1
1971					
Jan.	11,598	163,937	327,660	13,653	84.9
Feb.	11,873	163,937	327,874	13,661	86.9
Mar.	13,400	165,790	329,727	13,739	97.5

TABLE 9-A (Continued)

Year & Month	Construction Employment	12-Month Moving Total	2-Month Moving Total	Centered 12-Month Moving Average	Percentage of 12-Month Moving Average
1971					
Apr.	14,014	167,506	333,296	13,887	100.9
May	14,432	169,407	336,913	14,038	102.8
June	14,759	170,699	340,106	14,171	104.1
July	14,880	171,183	341,882	14,245	104.5
Aug.	14,838	171,045	342,228	14,260	104.0
Sept.	15,754	170,152	341,197	14,217	110.8
Oct.	15,476	169,369	339,521	14,147	109.4
Nov.	15,319	168,559	337,928	14,080	108.8
Dec.	14,356	168,059	336,618	14,026	102.4
1972					
Jan.	12,082	167,782	335,841	13,993	86.3
Feb.	11,735	167,500	335,282	12,970	84.0
Mar.	12,507	166,641	334,141	13,923	89.8
Apr.	13,231	166,070	332,711	13,863	95.4
May	13,622	165,354	331,424	13,809	98.6
June	14,259	164,794	330,148	13,756	103.7
July	14,603				
Aug.	14,556				

TABLE 9-A (Continued)

Year & Month	Construction Employment	12-Month Moving Total	2-Month Moving Total	Centered 12-Month Moving Average	Percentage of 12-Month Moving Average
Sept.	14,895				
Oct.	14,905				
Nov.	14,603				
Dec.	13,796				

SOURCE: State Employment Commission monthly labor force reports for Midland City, 1967 - 1972.

TABLE 9-B

Computation of Seasonal Indexes of Construction Employment in Midland City, 1967-1972

Month	Percentage of 12-Month Moving Average						Modified Mean	Seasonal Index
	1967	1968	1969	1970	1971	1972		
Jan.		93.3	84.6	93.1	84.9	86.3	88.1	88.2
Feb.		92.3	72.9	95.2	86.9	84.0	87.7	87.8
Mar.		92.8	89.4	97.3	97.5	89.8	93.3	93.4
Apr.		101.3	98.5	102.3	100.9	95.4	100.2	100.3
May		102.5	101.7	104.4	102.8	98.6	102.3	102.3
June		101.2	107.2	96.6	104.1	103.7	103.0	103.0
July	108.6	90.7	108.8	104.7	104.5		105.9	106.0
Aug.	108.1	114.0	109.8	107.3	104.0		108.4	108.4
Sept.	104.3	109.1	104.7	101.4	110.8		106.0	106.1
Oct.	102.4	106.4	104.4	100.9	109.4		104.4	104.4
Nov.	101.2	103.2	102.2	98.8	108.8		102.2	102.3
Dec.	95.3	197.3	99.8	96.1	102.4		97.7	97.8
							1199.2	1200.0

Source: Percentages shown in Column Six of Table 9-A.

10 ECONOMIC NEWSLETTER

A. INTRODUCTION

National economic newsletters, in a great variety and number, are available to businessmen, business organizations, labor organizations, and the general public. Statistics are collected and analyzed in publications ranging from the Department of Commerce's *Survey of Current Business,* to magazines such as *Business Week,* to economic newsletters published by regional and local banking institutions. At the state level, economic newsletters are published by universities, state agencies, state organizations, and private companies. Local and metropolitan statistics are published less frequently by the government or other public institutions, if at all. The local area, therefore, has an open-ended need for the newsletter service a Chamber of Commerce can provide.

B. WHO AND WHAT BENEFITS FROM THE NEWSLETTER?

After indicators of local business activity have been documented — in a Monthly Summary of Business Indicators (Chapter 8) and in a Local Business Index (Chapter 9) — the next responsibility of the researcher is to inform Chamber of Commerce members and others of current economic conditions in the local area. The Chamber of Commerce economic newsletter can effectively present the analysis and interpretation of local business indicators, publicizing a general assessment of the local economy on a regular publication schedule (usually monthly). The readership of these economic reports often extends beyond the territorial limits of the community to include government agencies at all levels, outside investors, and prospective new industrial and commercial firms. An economic newsletter is an effective vehicle for interpretative reporting of economic activity reflected by various indicators the researcher discovers.

The Chamber of Commerce researcher is the person primarily responsible for producing the organization's economic newsletter. In many Chambers of Commerce the researcher alone writes this newsletter, while in others a committee or panel assists the researcher in producing the newsletter. Each panel member is responsible for reporting on changes and trends within specific areas of the local economy. The newsletter's full report, then, is a summary of findings from key areas of local business activity. The procedure involving a panel—a division of the Research Committee—is discussed in this chapter.

C. SELECTION OF MAJOR BUSINESS INDICATORS

The Department of Commerce publishes approximately 40 pages of statistics every month in the *Survey of Current Business*. The complete series of data published by the Department of Commerce, assessing the state of the national economy, represents a great volume of detail. If used as a model for the construction of a local index, the data acquisition and dissemination would require facilities far beyond the capacity of a Chamber of Commerce. Although information on every facet of the economy may be ideal, a reliable measure may be developed from limited information. The weekly indexes of *Business Week Magazine,* for example, are based on an assessment of 36 national business indicators.

At the local level, the factors most accurately reflecting business activity in the community must be determined. As a general rule, a local equivalent for gross national product or personal income—the accepted indicators for the national economy—is not available. The selection of local factors must therefore be made within the limits of what can be acquired or developed.

The major divisions of economic activity should be considered as the most important factors in measuring the character of the local economy. These major economic sectors should be used as the foundation for a business activity index for the area covered by the newsletter. As mentioned in Chapters 8 and 9, these factors will vary from one area to another, depending on the economic "mix" of the community and the availability of data for the selected sectors.

Examples of the types of data a local Chamber of Commerce may obtain are shown in the following list of business indicators selected from Chapter 8:

1. *Consumer Price Index.* Both national and local index figures are provided by the regional office of the Bureau of Labor Statistics.
2. *Department Store Sales.* Provided by Federal Reserve Bank in the district.

3. *Bank Debits to Individual Accounts.* Provided by the Federal Reserve Bank in the district.
4. *Bank Clearings.* Local Federal Reserve Bank Clearing House.
5. *Construction.* Contracts awarded as recorded by the Associated General Contractors of America, Inc., and building permits recorded in local incorporated areas. Electrical connections recorded by local electric utility companies can also be used to measure residential construction activity.
6. *Employment.* Record of employment data is provided by state employment office branches. This includes total unemployment and employment by major occupational groups. A ratio between national and local employment statistics can show how the local area shapes up to national figures.
7. *Utilities.* Provided by local utility companies and including the following:
    a. natural gas consumption;
    b. natural gas customers (residential & commercial);
    c. electric current usage;
    d. electric current customers (residential & commercial);
    e. telephones in service.
8. *Transportation.* Includes the following major transportation sectors:
    a. rail carloadings as measured by rail systems serving the area;
    b. port tonnage as recorded by local port authority;
    c. inter-city truck tonnage as recorded by the Weekly Truck Tonnage Report prepared by American Trucking Association, Inc.;
    d. new car and truck registrations recorded by county agencies.
9. *Aviation.* Statistics on the passenger loadings, takeoffs-landings and airmail poundage as recorded by local airport officials.
10. *Postal Receipts.* Record of postal revenues by local post office representatives.

There is no need for the inclusion of numerous economic sectors in a local economic newsletter. They should be chosen on the basis of *quality* and should accurately reflect the characteristics of the community. Each of these business indicators should be assigned to a specific member of the newsletter panel or committee who is responsible not only for reviewing relevant statistical data for his assigned subject matter area, but also for indicating changes and trends in this area and projecting the effects these changes will have on various segments of the local economy.

D. FORMING AN ECONOMIC NEWSLETTER PANEL

The size of the newsletter panel is determined by the number of economic factors to be considered and the availability of current data. The panel nucleus should represent six major sectors: banking, marketing (retail and wholesale), construction. employment, utilities, and transportation. These major sectors can be broken down into as many sections as is feasible for panel presentation.

The selection of panel members is the responsibility of the panel chairman, but the reporting agency for each economic sector should be contacted to assign a representative to the panel. The panel chairman should review the list of recommended panelists with the Chamber of Commerce researcher to make the panel assignments. If an individual is expert in more than one area, his value in a panel discussion session will be more pronounced. A financial analyst, for example, qualified to report on the banking sector as well as to provide an economic overview of the other sectors, is a catalyst to meaningful discussion and interpretation of data.

Examples of selected subjects under each of the six basic newsletter reporting areas—banking, marketing (retail and wholesale), construction, employment, utilities and transportation—and the recommended type of panelist to report on each subject is listed as follows:

1. *Banking.* An officer from one of the larger banks in the area, preferably someone in the investments division who is qualified to discuss the economic impact of financial data.
   a. Debits to individual accounts
   b. Bank clearings
   c. Bank deposits (total demand deposits)
2. *Marketing.* Representative who is familiar with area-wide retail and wholesale activity, possibly someone from the local credit bureau, retail or wholesale trade association, or credit division of a local bank who can interpret and in some cases collect data on sales activity.
   a. Department store sales
   b. Consumer credit accounts activity
   c. Retail sales and wholesale sales for the area
   d. Opinion surveys with representatives of retail and wholesale establishments
   e. Consumer Price Index
3. *Construction.* Staff personnel from the Associated General Contractors, building permits office, or planning commission of the major city area familiar with all types of construction activity.

       a. Number and value of building permits

       b. Contracts awarded

       c. Announced and planned construction projects

4. *Employment.* Reported by someone from the local office of the state employment commission, preferably a labor market analyst familiar with developing manpower planning reports for the area.

       a. Total labor force

       b. Employment and unemployment data

       c. Employment needs in the area

5. *Utilities.* Representatives from each of the local utility companies, preferably personnel familiar with matching future demands to supply of utility services.

       a. Electric current consumption and customers

       b. Gas consumption and customers

       c. Telephones in service

       d. Water meter connections

6. *Transportation.* Representatives from all transportation sectors.

       a. Aviation statistics

       b. Port tonnage statistics

       c. Railroad statistics

       d. Trucking industry statistics

       e. New auto and truck registrations

Important items to be included on the agenda for each meeting of the newsletter panel are a discussion of the Local Business Index (if the local Chamber of Commerce produces an index of this type) and a summary of the economic changes and trends revealed by reports during the panel's meeting.

E. NEWSLETTER PANEL MEETINGS

The schedule of newsletter panel meetings can be arranged to fit the needs of the panel members and to provide for the most effective accumulation of data available. As a suggestion, the panel might meet on the third Tuesday of each month to report on data accumulated during the preceding month.

Prior to each meeting panelists should prepare — and bring to the panel meeting — one-page reports related to their respective assigned sectors. During the meeting, the panel chairman will call on each panelist for a brief report, to be followed by open discussion among the panelists.

If feasible, newsletter panel meetings should be tape-recorded. The tapes may be reviewed later to retrieve interpretative comments by the panelists. These tape-recorded discussions — plus the panelists' written reports — are helpful in preparing the written analysis of economic data presented in the panel meetings.

F. PRESENTATION OF DATA

As the primary goal of the economic newsletter is to inform, effective presentation should be given high priority. Volumes of data can be prepared, but if they are not read and used, they are wasted effort.

A basic technique in the information gathering is the tabulation of time series data. This is the method the Department of Commerce employs in its *Survey of Current Business*. These tabulations, although complete, are not readily assimilated by the average reader. Some abbreviated form of time series must be devised to present current information in a meaningful and readable form. These abbreviated summaries often are comparisons, e.g., comparison of the current month with the corresponding month a year ago, comparison of year-to-date totals to those of a year ago, comparison of current 12-month totals with 12-month totals a year ago, etc. At best, tabular presentations are dull reading and should be used primarily as reference material for the reader who might desire to examine them closely. The short analyses of the data presented by the newsletter panelists in their written reports and tape-recorded sessions are the main input for the economic newsletter, the tabulated time series data being presented alongside the newsletter with references to the time series data included in the newsletter text.

The style, length and depth of coverage of the economic newsletter is determined by the Chamber personnel preparing the material; however, the short, easy-to-read, interesting style of reporting with major points highlighted or underlined for quick reference makes an effective presentation to a larger audience. A copy of the Monthly Summary of Business Indicators may be included with the economic newsletter to provide time-series tabulations with comparisons for further evaluation. For illustrative purposes, Exhibits 10-A, 10-B and 10-C are presented to suggest the content of economic newsletters.

EXHIBIT 10-A:
ECONOMIC NEWSLETTER RELATING
ONLY TO A MONTHLY SUMMARY
OF BUSINESS INDICATORS

There may be fairer weather ahead . . .

. . . if the first quarter gains in Central City's economy are accurate barometers of prevailing conditions. Although prospects of smooth sailing are still overshadowed by inflation, local residents continue to buy goods and services at an accelerating rate, amazing even the members of the Economic Analysis Panel at the most recent tape-recorded session.

Continuing to outshine the national unemployment figure, the Central City SMSA reported a low 2.6% rate for March, compared with the nationwide 5% figure. Nearly all the gains were keyed by rises in construction and miscellaneous business services, with 4,100 reported in trades. The labor force increased by 20,300 workers from Mar/72 to Mar/73 with the total civilian work force increasing by 6,300 workers in March.

Wondering if the price spiral will ever slow down, Central Citians continued to pay more for less, especially for food products. Food prices rose 2.2% in March, raising the retail food price index to 136.6. This means residents were paying $13.66 for food items in March that cost them $13.37 in February and $10.00 during the 1967 base period (1967 = 100).

Positively reflecting Central City's economic outlook, the local banking community turned in an "all systems go" report for March. Bank debits to individual accounts during the month were 12.7% higher than Mar/72 and totaled $10.854 billion, while the year-to-date total was 32.4% above last year with $32.093 billion. Clearings for March were $5.536 billion—up 27.6% over Mar/72—and the Jan-Mar total of $16.233 billion topped the '72 total by 32.4%.

Money may be tight, but local residents continue to spend, almost as if nothing were happening. Retail sales for March were 7% higher than February, and sales for the year beginning January 6, 1972 and ending in March were up 10% over '71.

Central County construction figures were all on the plus side in March, led strongly by non-residential building permits. The permits totaled $58,318,934—up a whopping 123% from February and up 32% from Mar/72. Central City building permits for March totaled $90,447,819—increasing 3.8% over the Mar/72 total of $87,000,242—the highest dollar volume month for the year. Multi-unit residential permits totaled $14,558,999 — up 49.5% from February, but a decrease of 38.9% from Mar/72.

Non-residential natural gas deliveries in the county totaled 47,446,296 MCF for the year, climbing 8.6% ahead of Mar/72. For the first quarter of '73, deliveries totaled 141,480,268 MCF, up 4.5% over the same period last year. An even sharper trend was reflected in residential deliveries: domestic usage of 5,120,854 MCF soared 28% ahead of last year and brought the year-to-date residential sales to a 40.6% gain over '72. At the end of March, 496,902 total gas customers were being served, an increase of 1.7% over '72.

There were 598,905 electric customers in Central County at the end of March. This was 15,213 or 2.6% more than Mar/72 and compares to the 16,482 or 2.9% gain in the 12-month period ending Mar/72. Residential customers increased to 508,170, which is 12,928 or 2.5% over last year. March non-residential sales of electricity totaled 1,511,182 M-Kwh, for 5% increase over Mar/72. This compares to a 16.5% increase in Mar/72 over Mar/71.

The Central City Metropolitan Exchange had 1,274,570 total telephones in service at the end of March — an increase of 20.7% over a year ago. For the year, there was a gain of 24,743 telephones or 19.2% higher than the 20,764 gain during '72.

Airport highlights for March at Central City Intercontinental Airport showed domestic passengers up .3% over '72 and international passengers 28% ahead of Mar/72. At Glenhaven Airport, passenger totals through the airport were up 264% over Mar/72 due to route changes by two major airlines serving the airport.

New car and truck registrations continue in record-breaking numbers: 16,859 vehicle registrations in March, compared with 10,769 in February. March vehicle sales set an all-time record for a single month for Central County, surpassing the previous high last May by 1,943 units. For the year, rail tonnage was up 16.8% over '72. Comparing Mar/73 with Mar/72, truck tonnage figures were up 14.2%.

Despite slowdowns due to continued inclement weather, the local port recorded a big month in March with a total cargo movement of 7,522,574 short tons — a new record for one month's activity. The total was 37.1% more than Mar/72. Heavy bulk grain shipments accounted for much of the gain, with 1,800,000 tons exported during the month.

Postal revenue totaled $5,695,515 for March, compared with $5,387,639 during the same period a year ago. Airmail poundage increased from Jan to Mar, 4,662,594 pounds to 4,758,017 pounds.

EXHIBIT 10-B:
ECONOMIC NEWSLETTER RELATING
ONLY TO A LOCAL BUSINESS INDEX

The Midland City Business Index ran true to form in 1973. It smashed all records to reach a new high point. That's what it's been doing every 12 months for a number of years now.

The Index, compiled by the Research Department of the Midland City Chamber of Commerce, is a composite of all the significant indicators of the area's economic health. The 6% increase posted in 1973 over 1972 reflects the fact that all indicators except construction set new high records.

Whatever economic uncertainties 1974 holds (and they are many), the Midland City area moves into this new year from a position of strength. Moreover, the highly diversified base of the area economy will be a significant stabilizing factor during the coming months of energy crisis, inflation, high interest rates and chronic shortages of raw materials.

All of these disturbing factors began showing up before 1973 ended, but though they were the attention grabbers, the real news of the Midland City economy was its muscle. During 1973:

EMPLOYMENT REACHED A NEW HIGH—

Non-agricultural employment averaged 362,800, an increase of 5.2% over 1972. This increase was broad-based, with workers being added to payrolls in all categories of business. As employment went up, the unemployment rate decreased to its lowest level since 1969, averaging 3.4% of the labor force. This was well below the national average.

Manufacturing showed the largest increase in employment—6.5% over 1972—and the production workers in Midland City's humming industrial plants took home the highest weekly paychecks ever. These high wages and record employment made the retail cash registers ring a happy tune during the year, even though signs of weakness began appearing as the year neared its close.

DEPARTMENT STORE SALES AND NEW AUTO AND
TRUCK SALES SET NEW RECORDS—

Department-store sales are estimated at 8.2% over 1972, setting a new high, while new-car dealers chalked up an 8.3% increase over 1972, again breaking a record only a year old.

CONSTRUCTION, CAUGHT BETWEEN HIGH INTEREST RATES
AND MATERIALS SHORTAGES, WAS THE ONLY SIGNIFICANT
FACTOR SHOWING A DECREASE—

Despite this, local builders are somewhat optimistic about the housing
market for 1974. The dominant factor in new housing starts has always
been availability of money, and builders feel the money market will loosen
up, though interest rates will stay in the 8% to 8.5% range. There are
imponderables here, they admit: consumer pessimism, material shortages
and energy shortages.

However, since only 4,986 housing units were authorized for all of Midland
County (including Midland City) in 1973, a backlog of demand may be accumulating. The housing-permits figure was down 28% from 1972 and is the
lowest total since 1966, while the total for all building was down 25.6%
from 1972.

The weaknesses that began to show up during the last quarter of 1973 may
be signals of what to look out for in 1974. Department-store sales during
the year-end holiday period were higher than in 1972, but not what was expected on the basis of earlier months; industrial production slowed as the
year came to a close; and unemployment began to creep upward.

The months ahead seem to shape up this way:
    Fuel shortages and high fuel costs will continue, limiting travel and
endangering industrial production.
    Prices will be marching higher.
    Demands for higher wages will escalate.
    Profits will be squeezed between rising costs and sluggish sales.
    Interest rates will remain high.
    Unemployment in the Midland City area will increase to perhaps 5%
of the work force.
    The public will spend less on automobiles, travel, home furnishings
and housing. A greater percentage of wages will be spent on necessities and
as much as possible will go into savings accounts and other safe investments.

In short, the year seems full of economic dangers. But, on the basis of the
evidence at hand, the local economy, because of its diversified nature,
should suffer only a mild and brief recession. A year from now, local
economic indicators should be moving upward again—true to form.

EXHIBIT 10-C:
ECONOMIC NEWSLETTER RELATING TO TWO TYPES OF REPORTS: MONTHLY SUMMARY OF BUSINESS INDICATORS AND A LOCAL BUSINESS INDEX

Business activity in the Moundville area for the month of May evidenced leveling or stationary tendencies in some sectors, with continued declines in others. Total employment, estimated retail sales, and the unemployment rate showed improved performance while indexes of industrial electric consumption and help wanted advertising experienced declines. The financial and construction trends have been mixed, but with indications of increased activity in a few of the individual indicators.

EMPLOYMENT

Total employment (non-agricultural) in the Moundville area continued to increase in May and is now 2.2% above the year ago period. The May standing of 514.6 thousand is a record level for this indicator.

The rate of unemployment of 2.9%, after being seasonally adjusted, declined in May to a standing well below the average for the year-to-date of 3.2%. The favorable May report of 19,700 unemployed is entirely due to the sharp increase in the total number employed in the labor force which increased to 571.6 thousand in May.

The help wanted index posted a decline in May, for the third consecutive month. The decline in this indicator for the first five months of 1974, part of a downtrend begun in the third quarter of last year, was to a level more than 16% below the year-to-date level for 1973.

INDUSTRIAL ACTIVITY

Manufacturing employment in the Moundville area declined in May following a decrease the previous month. Although the level of this series is well above the standings of the past two quarters, the May standing of 170.6 thousand was the third month in the last five that this series has declined.

Average weekly hours in manufacturing posted a gain in May for the second consecutive month. The year-to-date average for this series (40.2 hours per week) is slightly below the same period in 1969 (40.8 hours).

Average weekly earnings in manufacturing posted a sharp gain in May to a record level. This series is up more than 5% for the first five months of this year compared to the same period of 1969.

Industrial electric consumption declined in May by an amount nearly equal to the increase of the previous month. However, notwithstanding recent fluctuations, this series is 2.8% above the year-to-date average for 1969.

RETAIL SALES

Estimated retail sales (seasonally adjusted) in the local area continues to exhibit a moderate turn from the reduced levels of the two previous quarters, and is 8.9% above the year-to-date level for 1969.

Estimated "real" retail sales has also continued to experience moderate growth in the past five months and is approximately 2.5% above the same period of last year.

FINANCIAL ACTIVITY

Commercial bank deposits gained in May following a decline in the previous month. This series has experienced much smaller monthly changes in the first five months of this year compared to the same period in 1973, and is almost 2% below the 1969 level for the same period.

The number of checks processed continues to experience wide monthly swings. Notwithstanding the May decline, the average for the first five months of this year is up approximately 7% over the year-ago period.

Commercial and industrial loans at city banks increased in May for the third consecutive monthly gain this year. The year-to-date average of this indicator is up more than 13% over the same period in 1973.

Bank debits to individual accounts declined in May after experiencing a substantial gain in the previous month. This series is 1% above the year-to-date level in 1973.

CONSTRUCTION ACTIVITY

All of the indicators in this section registered declines in May following a pick-up in activity in April.

The total value of building permits averaged a sharp decline in the three months ending with May. For the first five months of the year this series has declined to a level more than 22% below the comparable period in 1973.

Residential permit value has experienced a substantial decline in May following a sharp increase the preceding month. This series is more than 3% below the year-ago average for the first five months of this year.

Non-residential permit value has also experienced decline in May and is approximately 30% below the year-to-date average for 1973.

The number of housing units on building permits in the Moundville area has exhibited renewed strength in the past two months. However, for the first five months of this year, this series has been more than 16% below the year-ago level.

11 INTRODUCTION TO BUSINESS AND ECONOMIC FORECASTING

Foreword

The purpose of forecasting is to improve the quality of current decisions. Planning and deciding for the future have to be done in the present, but they are based on future expectations. Thus every decision-maker is a forecaster in the sense that he has some conception of the future upon which he bases his decisions.

Decision-makers rely increasingly on professional forecasters, whose numbers and techniques have multiplied, while forecasting has seemed to become an arcane science. This brief introduction is intended to provide an eagle's eye view of some of the main elements in forecasting. The nonspecialist needs enough background knowledge to compare and judge forecasts and projections. An awareness of some of the limitations of forecasting and of source materials is necessary to balanced interpretations.

Maintaining prosperity is a primary national problem. Continued prosperity will facilitate the resolution of other domestic problems. A sound economy also will strengthen the initiatives required to meet new international relationships. More accurate forecasts permit better decisions, to the benefit of the manager, his company, and the economy.

Dr. James R. Morris, Senior Associate in the National Chamber's Economic Analysis and Study Group, was responsible for the preparation of this introduction to business and economic forecasting.

Carl H. Madden
Chief Economist
Economic Analysis & Study Group
Chamber of Commerce of the United States

A. IMPORTANCE OF FORECASTING

Business executives and public officials alike must forecast, notwithstanding the hazards of forecasting and the likelihood of errors in some degree. While it is impossible to predict the future with absolute certainty, every decision implicitly involves an estimate of future probabilities. Plans and decisions affecting the future have to be made, and they are determined by expectations about future economic and business conditions. Thus, the real purpose of forecasting is to improve present decisions. Whether to expand facilities, to replace obsolescent plant, to increase inventories, and whether to order new equipment are among the decisions that are based on forecasts.

The prospects of an individual company or of a region or area are heavily determined by the general level of economic activity, and by the trends in the industry or area. Prosperity or depression of the economy as a whole is of vital concern to its constituent parts. General prosperity, however, does not assure the prosperity of an individual firm or an area. The executive therefore must be concerned with the state of the economy as a whole as well as with the specific areas of his active managerial responsibilities.

While business in the aggregate has its ups and down, specific groups such as the construction and textile industries may have their own fluctuations, moving in a different phase or sequence from that of the economy generally. But with this caution it is important to remember that there is usually a close correspondence between a prosperous economy and the welfare of its individual segments.

Politicians also forecast, often seeming to proclaim continuing economic gains if they are in office, and the opposite if they are not. Civil servants forecast, generally confining themselves rather rigorously to factual data and their projections.

Statements by political leaders may be important. They can affect the climate in which decisions are made, and thus may influence the decisions themselves. More important, the forecasts and resultant attitudes of government officials may determine in part actual government policies and actions.

The role of government in shaping the thrust of business and economic activity is of major significance. Total government *purchases* of goods and services in 1971, for example, came to $233.0 billion, 22.3 percent of the nation's total output; total government *expenditures,* which include transfer payments, interest, and subsidies, came to 32.6 percent of the nation's total output ($341.2 billion out of $1,046.8 billion) of goods and services.

Moreover, the Employment Act of 1946 made it the special responsibility of the federal government "to promote maximum employment, production, and purchasing power." The Act provided for the annual Economic Report of the President, which includes facts about the state of the economy (levels of employment, production, and purchasing power) and projections or forecasts of where the economy is heading. Government officials are constantly taking the nation's economic pulse, forecasting, and proposing policies and programs to implement the objectives of the Employment Act.

B. BUSINESS CYCLES

Business conditions are never constant. Change characterizes the level of economic activity as well as the myriad specific business activities that comprise the total. Business cycles refer to the broad ups and downs of business activity as seen through time periods.

An economic "time series" is a collection of numerical information about economic activity (such as output, prices, sales) arranged in chronological order. Typically, business and economic time series include four kinds of movements: trend, seasonal, random, and cyclical.

Secular or long-term *trends* are identifiable movements of a time series over a long period. An example would be the long-term increase in annual sales of power lawn mowers as buyers shifted from hand mowers. Other movements in the time series, such as seasonal variations, fluctuate around the long-term trend. But even trends are subject to eventual and unexpected changes in direction under the influence of changes in underlying forces.

Seasonal fluctuations are typical of economic time series. Periodic recurrences, based on customs or natural forces, take place within the 12-month period. Clothing sales illustrate seasonal fluctuations as does the increase in sales of power mowers as spring and early summer grass grows. Seasonal variations, if inadequately recognized as such, may obscure shifts that portend cyclical turning points. Statisticians adjust the data to remove seasonal influences.

Irregular movements in economic time series are largely random, and tend to be unpredictable. A general strike, an earthquake, and other sporadic occurrences that follow no general patterns may inject substantial random changes in an economic time series.

The *business cycle* is what is left after the statistician has determined the trend factor, deseasonalized the data, and ironed out the random fluctuations in the time series.

Business cycles are wavelike fluctuations in aggregate economic activity. Like waves, business cycles tend to have elements of regularity, but they are by no means identical in length or timing, the movements being broken and uneven rather than rhythmical. The term "business cycles" is still widely used, although most writers now feel it necessary to emphasize their lack of cyclic regularity in timing and amplitude. Forecasting is difficult and subject to much error precisely because business cycles are so irregular in timing and range of fluctuation.

CHART 11-1. Fluctuations in Business Activity

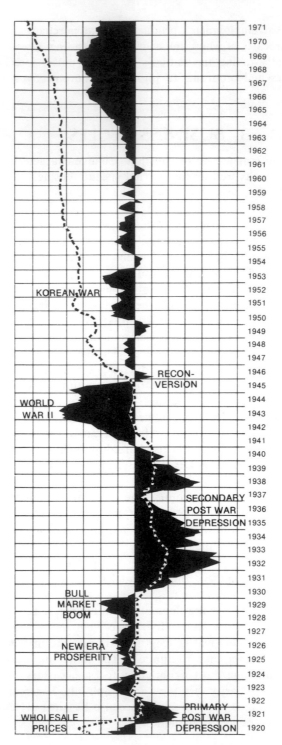

Source: The Cleveland Trust Company. A copy of the full chart is available upon request from the Cleveland Trust Company.

Swings in business activity have plagued us throughout our history. General Leonard P. Ayres originally developed a chart of American business activity back to 1790, which is updated and published by The Cleveland Trust Company. Chart 11-1 shows the record of the business cycle for over 50 years. In addition to the great depression of the 1930's, note the abnormally high level of economic activity during wars, and the long rise in wholesale prices going back to the 1930's.

Not truly cyclic in rhythm, no business cycle is quite like another, and yet they have marked similarities. Business cycles move through characteristic phases as the economy goes into (1) recession, (2) contraction, (3) revival, and (4) expansion.

Of major importance to forecasters are the upper and lower turning points of a cycle marking basic shifts in the direction of the level of economic activity, when expansion gives way to recession, or contraction gives way to revival. Some writers simply emphasize the elements of change, the turning points of the business cycle, believing that economic activity is always in the dynamic process of either expanding or contracting.

Both expansionary and contractive forces and movements are present at all times. During periods of general economic expansion or contraction, some specific sectors of the economy will be expanding while others are contracting. These complementary counter-movements, along with variations among the numerous economic time series, add to the difficulty of forecasting turning points.

The National Bureau of Economic Research (NBER) has dated business cycle turning points, peaks, and troughs, from 1854 through the trough of November 1970. These "business cycle reference dates" mark the dates when aggregate economic activity reached its high and low points. Business cycles have ranged in duration (trough to trough) from 28 months to 117 months. Table 11-1 shows the NBER's figures for cycles for more than a century. The table indicates, among other things, that we should expect changes in cyclical behavior. The pronounced variations suggest the need to be wary of judgments based on comparisons with past conditions.

Expansions have averaged 33 months, and contractions 19 months, i.e., expansions have averaged 74% longer than contractions. Moreover, the average duration of expansions has been lengthening, and the average duration of contractions has been decreasing. The expansion during the 1960's was the longest (105 months) in our history.

Turning points in the business cycle are among the main phenomena predicted in economic forecasts. Thus, most forecasting is concerned with a period of three years or less.

C. KINDS OF CYCLES

Students of business cycles have identified several types of cycles differing in average duration, although scholars disagree about the length as

TABLE 11-1.
Business Cycle Expansions and
Contractions in the United States

Business cycle reference dates		Duration in months		Cycle	
		Contraction (trough from previous peak)	Expansion (trough to peak)	Trough from previous trough	Peak from previous peak
Trough	Peak				
December 1854	June 1857	(X)	30	(X)	(X)
December 1858	October 1860	18	22	48	40
June 1861	April 1865	8	46	30	54
December 1867	June 1869	32	18	78	50
December 1870	October 1873	18	34	36	52
March 1879	March 1882	65	36	99	101
May 1885	March 1887	38	22	74	60
April 1888	July 1890	13	27	35	40
May 1891	January 1893	10	20	37	30
June 1894	December 1895	17	18	37	35
June 1897	June 1899	18	24	36	42
December 1900	September 1902	18	21	42	39
August 1904	May 1907	23	33	44	56
June 1908	January 1910	13	19	46	32
January 1912	January 1913	24	12	43	36
December 1914	August 1918	23	44	35	67
March 1919	January 1920	7	10	51	17
July 1921	May 1923	18	22	28	40
July 1924	October 1926	14	27	36	41
November 1927	August 1929	13	21	40	34
March 1933	May 1937	43	50	64	93
June 1938	February 1945	13	80	63	93

TABLE 11-1 (continued)

Business cycle reference dates	Duration in months			
	Contraction (trough from previous peak)	Expansion (trough to peak)	Cycle	
			Trough from previous trough	Peak from previous peak
October 1945 .... November 1948	8	37	88	45
October 1949 .... July 1953	11	45	48	56
August 1954 .... July 1957	13	35	58	48
April 1958 .... May 1960	9	25	44	34
February 1961 .... *November 1969	9	105	34	114
*November 1970	12	(X)	117	(X)
Average, all cycles:				
27 cycles, 1854-1970	19	33	52	52[1]
11 cycles, 1919-1970	15	42	56	60[2]
5 cycles, 1945-1970	11	49	60	59[3]
Average, peacetime cycles:				
22 cycles, 1854-1961	20	26	45	46[4]
8 cycles, 1919-1961	16	28	45	48[5]
3 cycles, 1945-1961	10	32	42	42[6]

NOTE: Underscored figures are the wartime expansions (Civil War, World Wars I and II, Korean War, and Vietnam War), the postwar contractions, and the full cycles that include the wartime expansions.

*Tentative and subject to revision as more information becomes available.

[1]26 cycles, 1857-1969.   [4]21 cycles, 1857-1960.
[2]10 cycles, 1920-1969.   [5]7 cycles, 1920-1960.
[3]5 cycles, 1945-1969.   [6]3 cycles, 1945-1960.

Source: National Bureau of Economic Research, Inc., as given in *Business Conditions Digest*, April, 1972.

well as the identification of some of these. Among the most commonly noted are cycles averaging about 3 ½ to 4 years in length, and cycles averaging about 8 ½ years. The range of duration of each kind of cycle is considerably greater than the average duration. Kondratieff cycles, named after the Russian economist who identified them, refer to very long "waves" in aggregate economic activity that are 50 to 60 years in length.

Cycles in the level of activity in the construction industry, having an average duration of about 18 years, were first noted by economist Simon Kuznets. These cycles in an important component of aggregate economic activity may be of major significance to the direction and thrust of overall economic activity. Accordingly, construction activity is closely observed by forecasters for signs of impending change that might portend significant alteration in the level of aggregate economic activity.

Some analysts have suggested that the coincidence of several kinds of cycles in the contractive phase may partly explain periods when the economy has been notably sluggish and unresponsive, while coinciding expansive phases of two or more cycles would explain pronounced buoyancy of the economy, with corresponding expansion and growth even in the face of specific depressants.

D. CAUSES OF CYCLES

Early discussions of the causes of business cycles stressed crises and panics such as often followed intense speculative activities in land investments, in canal and railroad construction, and in stocks. Examples are the bursting of the South Sea Bubble in 1720, the Panic of 1819, the Panic of 1837, the Panic of 1857, and Black Tuesday, October 29, 1929, when the stock market plunged, heralding a depression of worldwide scope that lasted well into World War II.

Increasingly, however, it became evident that modern business cycles are more complex, and more pervasive in character, than the economic instability and hardships consequent upon crop disasters, earthquakes, wars, and similar events. The modern business cycle is associated intimately with the rise of free enterprise in Western nations within the past two centuries.

As the causes of business cycles are becoming better understood, the United States and other nations are developing policies and programs to smooth out cyclical fluctuations. But even the elimination of business cycles would leave economic fluctuations resulting from natural disasters, mistakes in monetary and fiscal policies, wars, and so on. The U. S. S. R. and other controlled economies still have economic fluctuations caused by such factors.

Theorists have attributed business cycles to a variety of causes, including, for example, sunspots that were alleged to affect weather and in turn crop production, technological innovations, expansion and contraction of the money supply through the banking system, psychological factors affecting expectations and hence actions, underconsumption, over-investment, and distortions in cost-price relationships. Much emphasis is placed by some economists on changes in investment — in fixed capital especially, but also in inventories.

Rather than holding that there is one cause of business cycles, however, most economists now recognize many causative factors, although they frequently differ as to which factor or set of factors is most important.

E. TOWARD GREATER STABILITY

During the two decades after World War II we appeared to have achieved major gains toward stabilizing the economy. Business cycle swings were less extreme, and some economists confidently proclaimed the end of depressions. An increasing percentage of the labor force was employed in the service industries (now more than half the labor force), where employment is more stable and cyclical disemployment is less common than in durable goods manufacturing industries. Similarly, a larger percentage is employed in white collar occupations, where there also is greater job stability.

The enlargement of the role of government (counted as part of the service industry) has contributed some elements of stability to income flows, and by extension to consumer spending and retail sales. For example, when business activity and employment decline, business and individual tax liabilities decline even more rapidly because the tax structure depends so heavily on the income tax with its graduated rates. As government borrows to offset revenue losses, it can do so in ways that maintain the money supply and encourage aggregate spending. Unemployment compensation, social security benefits, and welfare payments provide a flow of income to recipients and help to stabilize retail sales. Bank deposit insurance has spared depositors losses, but perhaps more importantly, it has also very largely eliminated the runs on banks by depositors that so often in the past culminated in financial disasters. Conservative analysts usually caution, however, that the deposit insurance program has yet to be tested under severe conditions. Paradoxically, it may be countered, its very existence may preclude its ever being put to the ultimate test.

In the private sector, the growth in the corporate practice of paying stable or regular dividends (reducing savings rather than dividends during a business setback), the expanded role of private pensions, and the greater volume of private savings also have stabilizing effects, with personal incomes less directly tied to current fluctuations in production. Consumer confidence, in turn, is maintained, with a stabilizing effect on consumer spending and ultimately on employment levels.

F. TOWARD SECULAR INFLATION

Even while many were asserting our triumph over the vicissitudes of the business cycle, the economy began a major expansion in the early 1960's, and unemployment declined with the accelerating growth. The nation entered the Vietnam War, and at the same time Congress rapidly increased spending for social services and income redistribution. Defense spending increased from $52.3 billion in 1963, to $78.3 billion, or 32% of the budget in 1973. Federal expenditures for human resources, $32.5 billion in 1963, were more than trebled, to $110.8 billion—45% of the 1973 budget.

The new upward fiscal thrust caused by increased government spending was accompanied by pronounced increases in the money supply. Together, the two helped shape the developing economic expansion. By the mid-1960's prices began a sustained rise. By 1971, about 70% of federal budget outlays were classified as "relatively uncontrollable" because they involved previously authorized legal obligations or social insurance trust fund commitments. Both the spending programs and inflation proved hard to curb.

The new economic forces were having results that had been neither widely anticipated nor fully understood. "Stagflation," inflation plus unemployment, was the legacy. Predicting business cycles and the effects of change on economic fluctuations remains an uncertain business.

G. SOME WARNINGS

Forecasting is more precise than an art, yet less so than a science. Careful study of factual data is imperative to the forecaster, but in the end he must reach his conclusions on the basis of his best judgment of the probable meanings of the facts. Indeed, many competent forecasters rely in part on their intuitive judgment, but it is an *informed* intuitive judgment based on careful analysis of current data in the light of past experience.

The past does not repeat itself exactly. No two business cycles are identical. But a knowledge and understanding of previous business cycle history is needed to evaluate the probable effects of new events. At the same time it is equally imperative that the forecaster be perceptive in noting deviations from the past pattern and in assessing their implications for the course of future developments.

Some knowledge of basic economic principles is invaluable. An understanding of the key role of the price mechanism in economic calculation and resource allocation and of other basic economic concepts is vital to the forecaster.[1]

---

[1] An excellent presentation of economic principles for the layman is available in the 10-booklet series entitled *Understanding Economics,* published by the Chamber of Commerce of the United States.

Statistical data are "tools of the trade" to forecasters. However, forecasters are not content to consider only the gross or overall statistics. In their search for significant implications, they strive to look inside or behind the data to consider their components and their definitions.

Statistical data are collected, classified, and reported on the basis of necessarily specific definitions that of themselves tend to shape the direction of interpretations. In short, definitions are based on, or may amount to, hidden premises that underlie the apparently "hard facts." Therefore, constant sifting of and great familiarity with the data are necessary to make valid interpretations. The unemployment rate is an example. It is a key index watched by economists, forecasters, and politicians. Analysts must consider not just the gross rate, but also a variety of other factors, such as the amount of the unemployment that is normally attributable to time lags between job changes, the composition of the unemployed (e.g., in 1971, 26% of the unemployed were teenagers, aged 16-19; 48% were under age 25; 64% of the unemployed were dependents rather than heads of households, etc.), the duration of unemployment (e.g., in 1971, 44% were unemployed less than five weeks), changes in composition of the labor force itself, and shifts and trends in the employment of the labor force. These changes may be more revealing of directional forces than the simple unemployment rate. The analyst also must distinguish between cyclical and other causes of unemployment, such as time lags in re-employment when industry converts from war to peace production.

Forecasts can have important effects on business decisions. And forecasts may set in motion activities that tend either to fulfill the forecast or to counter the expected developments. A widely made and accepted forecast that business is going to worsen could induce "belt tightening" — personal and business decisions to curtail spending — thus becoming a self-fulfilling prophecy. On the other hand, the prediction of worsening business conditions could set in motion a number of compensatory policy actions. Government might cut taxes and ease monetary and credit policies, while business firms might react aggressively, with determined efforts to maintain volume in the face of the predicted general decline, thereby countering the recessive forces. Or, a predicted decline in business activity may lead firms to correct imbalances in labor force and inventories, and increase their efficiency so that they are better able to weather a decline and revival may occur sooner. Under such conditions, is one to assert that the forecaster was wrong, and his forecast futile?

Forecasters keep a sharp eye on each other's forecasts and interpretations. They frequently consult among themselves and often participate in the same meetings where, in the process of discussion and evaluation, they refine their own positions. There sometimes is a tendency to modify interpretations that depart furthest from the norm, thus moving toward a consensus. Such peer-group watching and consultations have the advantage of testing views in a forum, leading to the modification or elimination of those found wanting. On the other hand, sometimes too much weight may be placed on conformity, at the expense of maverick but more accurate interpretations of events and projections.

H. TYPES OF FORECASTING AND EMPHASIS

Forecasts may cover a relatively short-term period of up to two years, a medium-term period of two to five years, or even a longer-term period extending up to ten years. Forecasts may be for specific parts of the economy, for specific industries, or for the economy as a whole. Our discussion is concerned primarily with forecasts for the general economy for periods up to about two years.

There are several types or techniques of forecasting. Sector analysis, which uses the national income accounts, is one of the most widely used. It attempts to estimate probable spending by the different sectors of the economy. Another widely used technique relies heavily on business indicators. The National Bureau of Economic Research analyzed hundreds of economic time series and identified those time series ("leading indicators") whose turning points generally precede business cycle peaks and troughs. The NBER also identified lagging series and coincident series, whose turning points typically lag and coincide with the turning points of aggregate economic activity. The leading indicator series are watched closely for signs of change.

Some forecasters develop models of the economy into which they can insert relevant mathematical data. Projections of economic activity are derived by the simultaneous solution of the various equations included in the forecaster's econometric model.

There now are several econometric models that are used to forecast aggregate economic activity and its components. Among the models in use are the Federal Reserve Bank of St. Louis model, one at Princeton University, and that used by the University of Michigan. One well-known model is that of the Bureau of Economic Analysis (BEA) of the U. S. Department of Commerce. The BEA model is a variant of an early model developed at the Wharton School of Finance and Commerce of the University of Pennsylvania.

The econometric model is constructed on the basis of the builder's conception of the way in which the economy works. The builder then must formulate the component equations of the model. The BEA model consists of about 100 equations, including identities, which may be divided into categories such as (1) components of gross national product, (2) prices and wage rates, (3) labor force and employment-related magnitudes, (4) income components, (5) monetary variables, and (6) miscellaneous equations.[2]

---

[2] A description of the BEA model is given in the *Survey of Current Business,* Vol. 46, No. 5, May 1966, 13-39.

Econometric models and computers provide the means for rapid calculations and projections. But they, too, in the final analysis, are based on judgment from beginning to end. Various assumptions have to be made about the data fed into models, and about the relationships among the data that will prevail in the future, all of which affect the validity and reliability of projections. Econometric models are dependent on constant patterns among variables. There is still no mechanical substitute for human judgment, even with its possibilities for error.

Forecasters today pay considerably more attention to the supply of money and credit than was true only a few years ago. The studies of Professor Milton Friedman and others have served to emphasize and bring to the fore the importance of changes in the supply of money and credit in influencing the course and level of aggregate business activity. These theorists contend that the rate of increase in prices is a "lagged function" of the increase in money supply.

As noted earlier, some monetary school theorists regard the business cycle as being largely a monetary and credit phenomenon. Monetarists, for example, have pointed to the sharp—even unprecedented—contraction in the supply of money and bank credit that characterized the economic collapse of the 1930's—the Great Depression. How money and credit are created, and destroyed, is a fascinating topic that is a "must" for forecasters.[3] Federal government fiscal activities—taxation and spending—are closely noted in terms of their impact on the money supply, as a result of how the deficit is financed, or of what securities are to be retired in the event of a surplus. The Federal Reserve Bank of St. Louis is widely known for its pioneering work in analyzing the impact on the economy of changes in the quantity of money. Its economic projections are widely respected, and many economists and forecasters regularly follow the analyses and data presented in the monthly Review of the Federal Reserve Bank of St. Louis, as well as in its other publications.[4]

Forecasters also keep a close watch on expectations, on the familiar assumption that actions are guided at least in part by what is expected in the future. Consumer buying intentions and expected business capital outlays are closely watched for signs of a change that may herald a general shift in economic activity.[5]

Major attention in this discussion will be devoted to the gross national product or to national income accounts and to the economic indicators. Most forecasters use a combination of techniques and approaches to their forecasts, including elements of "horseback" estimates and intuition.

---

[3] See "Money and Credit," Booklet 4 of Understanding Economics, Chamber of Commerce of the United States, Washington, D. C.

[4] See, for example, the forecast in the February, 1972 Review.

[5] Economic Prospects, published quarterly, includes data on consumer and business spending as well as economic projections and analyses for the economy.

TABLE 11-2.
Gross National Product, 1971
(in billions of dollars)

Gross national product	1,050.4
Personal consumption expenditures	664.9
Durable goods	103.5
Nondurable goods	278.1
Services	283.3
Gross private domestic investment	152.0
Fixed investment	148.3
Nonresidential	105.8
Structures	38.4
Producers' durable equipment	67.4
Residential structures	42.6
Nonfarm	42.0
Farm	.6
Change in business inventories	3.6
Nonfarm	2.4
Farm	1.2
Net exports of goods and services	.7
Exports	66.1
Imports	65.4
Government purchases of goods and services	232.8
Federal	97.8
National defense	71.4
Other	26.3
State and local	135.0

Source: *Survey of Current Business*, September 1972.

I. GROSS NATIONAL PRODUCT AND THE NATIONAL INCOME ACCOUNTS

Forecasting economic conditions is concerned to a great extent with forecasting gross national product. Gross national product and the various national income accounts are aggregate measures of the performance of the economy as a whole and of certain major sectors of the economy. Some understanding of the national product and income accounts is important to seeing how the economy functions, and hence to forecasting.

Gross national product (GNP) is defined by the Department of Commerce as the total market value of the final output of goods and services produced by the nation's economy. GNP includes everything from airplanes to the services of a soothsayer. Illegal activities are excluded. Also excluded are activities that do not enter the market, such as the labor expended in reroofing one's own house and other such work that is not paid for in the marketplace. GNP is concerned with exchange values. It includes all products and services that are bought and sold. GNP is computed in two ways: One way is by adding up the final spending for (1) personal consumption, (2) private investment (including changes in business inventories), (3) net exports of goods and services, and (4) government purchases of goods and services. The other way is by totaling the costs of producing these goods and services (mainly incomes, but also other items such as capital depreciation charges and indirect business taxes). Goods held in inventory are treated as an investment outlay by business; therefore, total spending has to equal total output in a given period of time, since everything produced is either sold or held in inventory. Table 11-2 above shows GNP and its expenditures components.

Net national product, less commonly cited, is GNP minus depreciation and other accounting charges for the wear and tear on business capital equipment.

National income is the total earnings from the current production of goods and services. It is the total of incomes received by or paid to the owners of property and labor. National income is the total of *factor costs* — compensation of employees, proprietors' income, rental income of persons, corporate profits and inventory valuation adjustment, and net interest — of the national output. The components of national income, or types of income, are shown in Table 11-3.

TABLE 11-3.
National Income, by Type of Income, 1971
(in billions of dollars)

National income	855.7
Compensation of employees	644.1
Wages and salaries	573.5
Private	449.7
Military	19.4
Government civilian	104.4
Supplements to wages and salaries	70.7
Employer contributions for social insurance	34.1
Other labor income	36.5
Proprietor's income	70.0
Business and professional	52.6
Farm	17.3
Rental income of persons	24.5
Corporate profits and inventory valuation adjustment	78.6
Profits before tax	83.3
Profit tax liability	37.3
Profits after tax	45.9
Dividends	25.4
Undistributed profits	20.5
Inventory valuation adjustment	−4.7
Net interest	38.5

Source: *Survey of Current Business,* September 1972.

National income does not include all of the costs (e.g., non-factor costs such as indirect business taxes) that are included in GNP. Thus, gross national product less capital consumption allowances equals net national product less indirect business tax and nontax liability (and some minor adjustments), which equals national income, as shown in Table 11-4, which also shows the relation of personal income.

Personal income is the current income of persons (including non-profit institutions, private trust funds, and private health and welfare funds) from all sources. It differs from national income by excluding undistributed corporate profits and other income from production not paid to individuals, and including other income not derived from production such as government transfer payments (e.g., social security payments). Table 11-4 shows these details.

TABLE 11-4.

Gross National Product, National Income,

and Personal Income, 1971

(in billions of dollars)

Gross national product	1,050.4
Less: Capital consumption allowances	93.8
Equals: Net national product	956.6
Less: Indirect business tax and nontax liability	101.9
Business transfer payments	4.6
Statistical discrepancy	−4.8
Plus: Subsidies less current surplus of government enterprises	.9
Equals: National Income	855.7
Less: Corporate profits and inventory valuation adjustment	78.6
Contributions for social insurance	65.3
Wage accruals less disbursements	.6
Plus: Government transfer payments to persons	89.0
Interest paid by government (net) and by consumers	31.1
Dividends	25.4
Business transfer payments	4. 6
Equals: Personal Income	861.4

Source: *Survey of Current Business,* September 1972.

Disposable personal income is the personal income available for spending or saving. It is personal income less personal taxes and nontax payments to government.

Personal saving is disposable personal income less personal outlays. Table 11-5 shows the sources and disposition of personal income, including saving.

J. FLOW OF INCOME AND SPENDING

National income accounting is a way of summarizing some important overall results of market actions. The accounts just reviewed portray relationships between the production of goods and services and the generation of incomes, on one hand, and on the other the spending of those incomes for goods and services. The expenditure of one is the income of another, in

TABLE 11-5.
Sources and Disposition of Personal Income, 1971
(in billions of dollars)

Personal income	861.4
Wage and salary disbursements	572.9
Commodity-producing industries	206.1
Manufacturing	160.3
Distributive industries	138.2
Service industries	105.0
Government	123.5
Other labor income	36.5
Proprietors' income	70.0
Business and professional	52.6
Farm	17.3
Rental income of persons	24.5
Dividends	25.4
Personal interest income	69.6
Transfer payments	93.6
Old-age, survivors, disability, and health insurance benefits	44.5
State unemployment insurance benefits	5.7
Veterans benefits	11.3
Other	32.2
Less: Personal contributions for social insurance	31.2
Less: Personal tax and nontax payments	117.0
Equals: Disposable personal income	744.4
Less: Personal outlays	683.4
Personal consumption expenditures	664.9
Interest paid by consumers	17.6
Personal transfer payments to foreigners	1.0
Equals: Personal saving	60.9

Source: *Survey of Current Business*, September 1972

a circular flow that includes total spending for GNP, the many branch streams such as those that represent tax payments and government spending for goods and services and for transfer payments, and the flow of personal and business savings into the investment stream. Chart 11-2 gives a simplified depiction of the circular flow of the major income and spending streams in our economy.

An expansion of total production in the nation will increase output and the flow of incomes. Conversely, an interruption or reduction in such production will throttle down output and incomes. It is important to recognize that an increase in spending for the nation will result in an increase in *real* income only if unemployed resources are put to work to add to output. If productive resources already are as fully employed as they choose to be, an increase in the national spending stream will not lead to any further output, although price rises will provide increases in money incomes. Because output could not be increased to match the increase in spending, the rise in GNP would be in money terms only, rather than in goods and services. Since inflation is common, a GNP "price deflator" is used to facilitate comparisons of national product and income accounts for different years.

CHART 11-2. Flow of Income and Spending

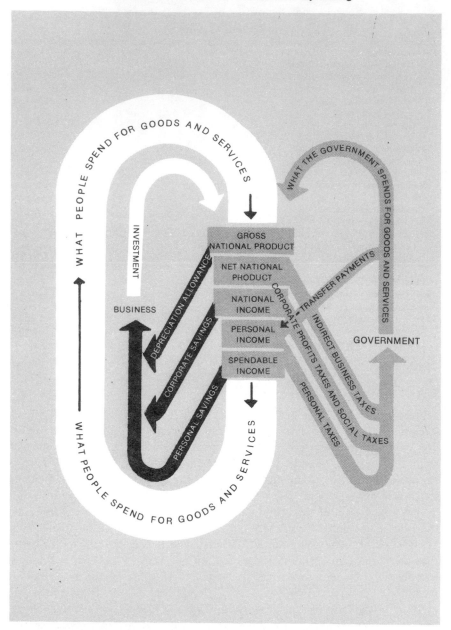

Source: "Discussion Leader's Guide," Understanding Economics, *Chamber of Commerce of the United States, Washington, D.C.*

K. REINFORCING THE BUSINESS CYCLE

Why are there fluctuations in the flow of income and spending, in aggregate economic activity? What are the factors that cause and reinforce changes in employment, output, and income? The national income and product accounts, observed over several years, allow study of the interaction of sectors and types of spending. These national economic accounts are highly valuable in helping us to understand more about what happens during business cycles. Forecasters and policymakers analyze the accounts to improve their record in the future.

Consumption expenditures and savings vary as a proportion of disposable personal income. Savings of 4.9% in 1963 had risen to 8.2% of disposable personal income in 1971. Such shifts may be indicative of significant trend movements with cyclical implications to the level of economic activity. Shifts in consumption and savings frequently reflect consumer expectations or concern about employment and job security, incomes, inflation, investment opportunities, and similar considerations.

More importantly, some series fluctuate more widely than others. The purchase of consumer durable goods generally can be postponed, the consumer making do a little longer with the old refrigerator or other durable product. Likewise, business can postpone the replacement of capital goods, making do with existing equipment. Spending for nondurables, goods that are consumed or quickly used up, allows less leeway, short of a complete cessation of activity.

Consumers and businessmen alike are affected by their expectations, and by psychological reactions to their perceptions of the present and probable future: of personal earnings and income, of labor and other variable costs, of taxation, of interest rates and capital costs, of probable sales and the outlook for profits.

The role of government at all levels—federal, state, and local—has become so interrelated and all-pervasive that governmental decisions may have enormous impact on the market and on business actions. As noted earlier, the role of government also adds some elements of stability to the economy, offsetting tendencies toward cyclical fluctuations. But the role of government is not necessarily benign. It may also have destabilizing influences on the economy, as suggested by the incidence of secular inflation and of "stagflation."

Indeed, secular inflation and its consequent dislocations are interpreted by some analysts as auguries of impending economic crisis, which government now can do less to offset precisely because its existing interventions are so massive that it has little room to maneuver (e.g., the 70% of federal budget outlays now classified as "relatively uncontrollable").

Also of inflationary significance is the selection and definition of estimated potential GNP in contrast to actual GNP for the economy. Chart 11-3 shows the gap between actual and estimated potential GNP.

CHART 11-3. Actual and Potential Gross National Product

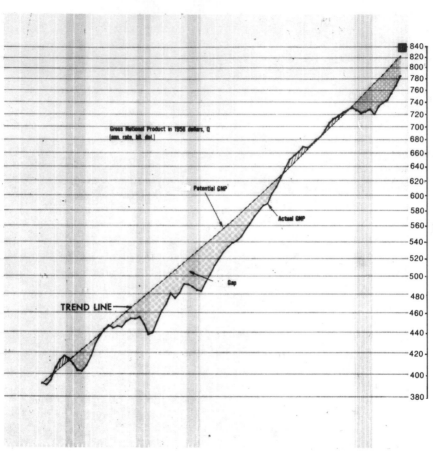

Source: Business Conditions Digest, *September 1972.*

The estimated potential GNP arbitrarily assumes an unemployment rate of 4% as a standard. Conceptually, and from the standpoint of public policy directed toward achieving a dynamic as well as a stable economy, this poses problems since the assumed potential GNP is set so high. Elimination of the GNP gap, with no more than 4% unemployment, is likely to result in serious inflationary pressures and high interest rates such as developed after mid-1965, when the unemployment rate began declining. Since 1929, only three years saw an annual unemployment rate of 4% or less that were not also years of abnormal demand based on wartime emergencies, when the bottom of the manpower barrel was scraped. But not even all wartime years saw such low unemployment as the 4% annual rate.

The vast expansion of federal spending for social services, income redistribution, and defense during the 1960's was not matched by income tax increases. Instead, substantial increases in the quantity of money helped to finance the growing government spending programs. Government fiscal policies and practices (those relating to taxation and spending) are significant not only because of their direct effects, but also because of their impact on the quantity of money, which, in turn, affects incomes, interest rates, investment, and consumption, as well as investment expenditures. Chart 11-4 shows the growth in the money stock (narrowly defined as currency outside banks plus demand deposits) and the growth in time and savings deposits in recent years.

The interrelations among fiscal policy, monetary policy, and the business cycle are of increasing interest to sophisticated economic analysts who have found it necessary to go beyond the model of the circular flow of income and spending streams. Political economists also learned that the complexity of the economy precludes its being effectively "fine tuned" by manipulating fiscal policy, a notion that dominated Washington decision-making for several years during the 1960's.

L. GROSS NATIONAL PRODUCT FORECASTING

Forecasting GNP for a year or two ahead involves estimating future expenditures for consumption, investment, net exports, and for government purchases of goods and services. In practice, many forecasters somewhat intuitively forecast a rough overall GNP figure, and then in a continuing series of interlinked estimates arrive at adjusted estimates for the key components, such as investment expenditures.

As the forecaster includes new factors or assigns different weights to existing items in his analysis, he readjusts other components and the gross estimate.

The forecaster has to examine and appraise the effects on economic conditions of a large number of variable factors, some of which may be moving in opposite directions. Their importance in shaping the direction of

CHART 11-4. The Money Stock

In September the seasonally adjusted money stock rose at a 6.2 percent annual rate, up from a revised 5.7 percent rate in August. Since December the stock of money has increased at an 8.0 percent rate.

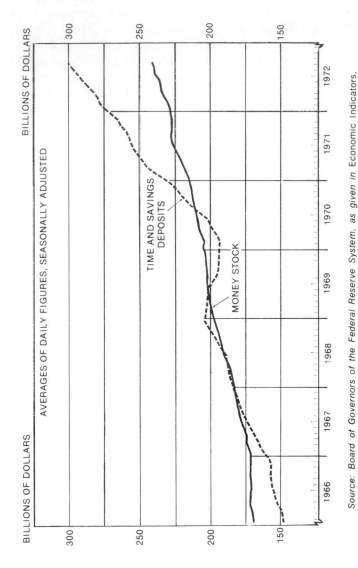

Source: Board of Governors of the Federal Reserve System, as given in Economic Indicators, *October, 1972.*

the overall movement of economic activity has to be evaluated and included in the analysis. The forecaster also must be alert to the fact that the significant factors change both in relative and in absolute terms. Computerized models of the economy can supplement but not supplant human judgment in forecasting.

M. GOVERNMENT EXPENDITURES

Government expenditures for goods and services (omitting items such as transfer payments) are of such magnitude that their impact on GNP and the state of the economy is of fundamental interest to forecasters.

In recent years, the trend of state and local spending has been so nearly in a straight-line upward that a simple extrapolation may be best. In any event, it is impractical to examine the expenditures of the tens of thousands of local governmental units. Analysts also can modify such a projection on the basis of relevant major changes that will influence state or local governmental actions.

At the federal level the major document is the budget itself, which presents recommendations and statements of expectations for the current fiscal year and the forthcoming fiscal year. Chart 11-5 shows government purchases of goods and services, by all levels of government, for more than 20 years.

Budgeted figures have to be weighed within the perspective of the actual functioning of the government and its agencies. An understanding of the terms used in the budget, such as "new obligational authority," is necessary. And experience has shown repeatedly that estimates of the costs of new programs are almost invariably well below realized costs, which mount rapidly as the future flows into the present.

These kinds of figures alone do not suffice, however. The forecaster also needs some familiarity with the political climate, including some perspective on surfacing political issues and probable courses of action. Discussions with knowledgeable government officials and private personnel in Washington can be helpful in evaluating issues and anticipating probable lines of progression. International strife, major strikes, and fundamental shifts, such as those that now appear to be developing with respect to ecology and in the supply-demand equations in the energy industries, are among the kinds of forces that the forecaster must consider.

Government expenditures provide the markets for many producers and suppliers; hence many companies, including subcontractors and suppliers of capital, closely follow government spending and projected expenditures.

Further, forecasters frequently do follow *total* government outlays, including transfer payments, and interest and subsidy payments. While they are excluded from GNP calculations, they do influence the pattern of spending. And, as noted earlier, overall government fiscal operations have

CHART 11-5. Government Purchases of Goods and Services

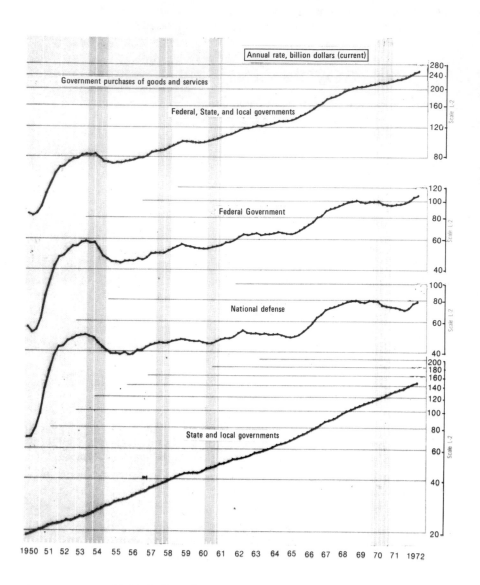

Annual rate, billion dollars (current)

Government purchases of goods and services

Federal, State, and local governments

Federal Government

National defense

State and local governments

Source: Business Conditions Digest, *September 1972.*

implications to and effects on the stock of money, securities markets and interest rates, investment opportunities, and the general price level, among other things. Pronounced increases in world market prices for silver and gold in recent years suggest to some analysts basic shifts not only in currency values but in public attitudes toward governments. Thus forecasting goes beyond the calculation of government expenditures for goods and services, and into the broader realm of political economy. Charts 11-6 and 11-7 illustrate some of these kinds of broader information that forecasters evaluate.

Government purchases of goods and services are a significant proportion of total GNP. Their significance in forecasting lies both in the quantities involved and in the implications to the economic and political climate for business activities.

N. NET EXPORTS

Forecasting net exports of goods and services involves forecasting relations with and among the more than 100 nations of the world. Yet this is the smallest of the expenditures components of GNP, even though it takes into consideration exports and imports of merchandise, transportation services, military outlays, investment returns, et cetera.

International trade is of vital or even paramount value to some firms. And to consumers and business firms alike its impact on competition and market values is positive. Net exports total only a small part of GNP (see the range shown in Chart 11-8), and it is difficult to make detailed estimates. Because of these considerations, some forecasters begin with the assumption that recent performance is likely to be repeated, and utilize the preceding net export figure. They then may scale it upward or downward in light of price movements domestically and abroad, capital flows and balance of payments problems, and the like. Reviewing monthly Department of Commerce figures on exports and imports, and assembling all these kinds of inputs, the forecaster can make an informed judgment that modifies a simple extrapolation of the current net export figure.

International financial and trade patterns provide important clues to the probable direction of future economic activity even though net exports are a small percentage of GNP.

O. GROSS PRIVATE DOMESTIC INVESTMENT SPENDING

Gross private domestic spending is a highly volatile category of the expenditures for national product. It includes business spending for plant and equipment, spending for residential construction, and changes in business inventories. And, because it is volatile and because it exercises a leverage

CHART 11-6. Federal Budget Receipts by Source and Outlays by Function

In fiscal year 1972 both receipts and outlays were $20.2 billion higher than in fiscal 1971. In the first 2 months of fiscal 1973, receipts were $4.5 billion higher than a year earlier while outlays were $1.1 billion higher.

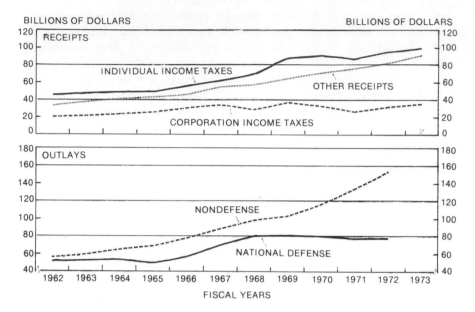

Sources: Treasury Department and Office of Management and Budget, as given in Economic Indicators, *October 1972.*

CHART 11-7. Federal Budget Receipts, Outlays, and Debt

In fiscal year 1972 there was a deficit of $23.0 billion, the same as the deficit in fiscal 1971. In the first 2 months of fiscal 1973 there was a deficit of $5.8 billion; a year earlier the deficit was $9.3 billion.

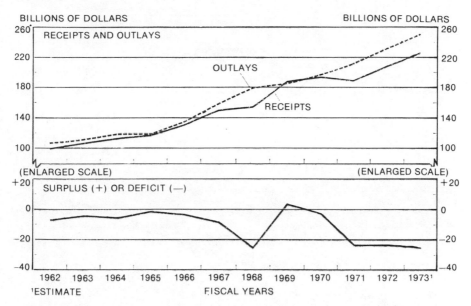

Sources: Treasury Department and Office of Management and Budget, as given in Economic Indicators, *October 1972.*

CHART 11-8. Exports and Imports of Goods and Services

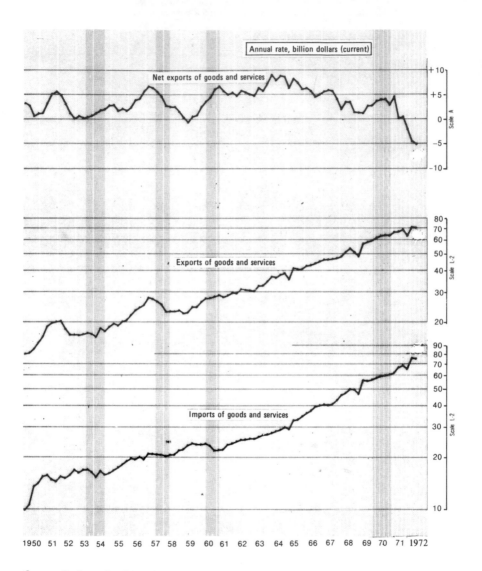

Annual rate, billion dollars (current)

Net exports of goods and services

Exports of goods and services

Imports of goods and services

1950 51 52 53 54 55 56 57 58 59 60 61 62 63 64 65 66 67 68 69 70 71 1972

Source: Business Conditions Digest, *September 1972.*

effect on the economy, forecasting investment spending is both highly important and difficult. Table 11-6 gives a breakdown of gross private domestic investment spending for the years 1929-1971.

Spending for construction includes both public and private construction. Private construction includes both residential construction and business investment in plant.

Public construction is included in the GNP category of government purchases of goods and services, already considered, but since it comprises a substantial proportion — around a third — of total construction spending, a few comments are in order here. Unlike private residential and business construction, public construction is determined mainly by nonmarket considerations that have political implications. Knowledge and awareness of the thrust of political forces can be important, although spending for public construction is relatively stable, following a generally upward trend. However, fluctuations do occur and are especially likely in school building and in highway construction. The forecaster must be alert to changes in public attitudes and planning in addition to reviewing statistical data, such as birthrates and age cohort numbers.

Forecasting business spending on plant involves both commercial and industrial construction. Sales volume, degree of plant utilization, obsolescence, prices and costs, and earnings and profit expectations are among the factors about which judgments must be made.

Commercial construction includes both offices and retail institutions. Population growth and movements as well as income and sales affect commercial construction. Population shifts to suburbs are intimately related to the construction of shopping centers and adjacent office buildings. Industrial construction sometimes is hard to separate from equipment investment because the two have been inseparably merged in a structural unit. Industry by industry analyses may be necessary to achieve accurate perspectives of the total configuration.

Forecasters garner information from McGraw-Hill's F. W. Dodge reports on construction contract awards and from construction planning data in the *Engineering News-Record*. The Department of Commerce's monthly publication, *Construction Review*, contains data on construction expenditures, building permits, housing vacancy rates, housing starts, and other construction series.

Residential construction is vital to the general level of economic activity, and fluctuations in construction can have significant repercussions on employment levels as well as on the housing market as such.

Forecasting residential construction is complicated by cyclical activity in the construction industry. While these construction cycles were found to have an average duration of 18 years, their range precludes any simple assumption about their future incidence. At some times, housing starts have moved countercyclically and at other times they have moved with the busi-

TABLE 11-6.
Gross Private Domestic Investment, 1929-71
(in billions of dollars)

Year or quarter	Total gross private domestic investment	Fixed investment Total	Nonresidential Total	Structures Total	Structures Non-Farm	Producers' durable equipment Total	Producers' durable equipment Non-Farm	Residential structures Total	Residential structures Non-Farm	Residential structures Farm	Change in business inventories Total	Change in business inventories Non-Farm
1929	16.2	14.5	10.6	5.0	4.8	5.6	4.9	4.,0	3.8	0.2	1.7	1.8
1930	10.3	10.6	8.3	4.0	3.9	4.3	3.7	2.3	2.2	.1	−.4	−.1
1931	5.6	6.8	5.0	2.3	2.3	2.7	2.4	1.7	1.6	.1	−1.1	−1.6
1932	1.0	3.4	2.7	1.2	1.2	1.5	1.3	.7	.7	.0	−2.5	−2.6
1933	1.4	3.0	2.4	.9	.9	1.5	1.3	.6	.5	.0	−1.6	−1.4
1934	3.3	4.1	3.2	1.0	1.0	2.2	1.8	.9	.8	.1	−.7	.2
1935	6.4	5.3	4.1	1.2	1.2	2.9	2.4	1.2	1.1	.1	1.1	.4
1936	8.5	7.2	5.6	1.6	1.6	4.0	3.3	1.6	1.5	.1	1.3	2.1
1937	11.8	9.2	7.3	2.4	2.4	4.9	4.1	1.9	1.8	.1	2.5	1.7
1938	6.5	7.4	5.4	1.9	1.8	3.5	2.9	2.0	1.9	.1	−.9	−1.0
1939	9.3	8.9	5.9	2.0	1.9	4.0	3.4	2.9	2.8	.1	.4	.3
1940	13.1	11.0	7.5	2.3	2.2	5.3	4.6	3.4	3.2	.2	2.2	1.9
1941	17.9	13.4	9.5	2.9	2.8	6.6	5.6	3.9	3.7	.2	4.5	4.0
1942	9.8	8.1	6.0	1.9	1.8	4.1	3.5	2.1	1.9	.2	1.8	.7
1943	5.7	6.4	5.0	1.3	1.2	3.7	3.2	1.4	1.2	.2	−.6	−.6
1944	7.1	8.1	6.8	1.8	1.7	5.0	4.2	1.3	1.1	.1	−1.0	−.6
1945	10.6	11.6	10.1	2.8	2.7	7.3	6.3	1.5	1.4	.1	−1.0	−.6
1946	30.6	24.2	17.0	6.8	6.1	10.2	9.2	7.2	6.7	.5	6.4	6.4
1947	34.0	34.4	23.4	7.5	6.7	15.9	14.0	11.1	10.4	.7	−.5	1.3
1948	46.0	41.3	26.9	8.8	8.0	18.1	15.5	14.4	13.6	.9	4.7	3.0
1949	35.7	38.8	25.1	8.5	7.7	16.6	13.7	13.7	12.8	.8	−3.1	−2.2
1950	54.1	47.3	27.9	9.2	8.5	18.7	15.7	19.4	18.6	.8	6.8	6.0
1951	59.3	49.0	31.8	11.2	10.4	20.7	17.7	17.2	16.4	.8	10.3	9.1
1952	51.9	48.8	31.6	11.4	10.5	20.2	17.6	17.2	16.4	.8	3.1	2.1
1953	52.6	52.1	34.2	12.7	11.9	21.5	18.6	18.0	17.2	.8	.4	1.1
1954	51.7	53.3	33.6	13.1	12.3	20.6	18.0	19.7	19.0	.7	−1.5	−2.1
1955	67.4	61.4	38.1	14.3	13.6	23.8	21.2	23.3	22.7	.6	6.0	5.5
1956	70.0	65.3	43.7	17.2	16.5	26.5	24.2	21.6	20.9	.7	4.7	5.1
1957	67.9	66.5	46.4	18.0	17.2	28.4	25.9	20.2	19.5	.7	1.3	.8
1958	60.9	62.4	41.6	16.6	15.8	25.0	22.0	20.8	20.1	.6	−1.5	−2.3
1959	75.3	70.5	45.1	16.7	15.9	28.4	25.4	25.5	24.8	.6	4.8	4.8
1960	74.8	71.3	48.4	18.1	17.4	30.3	27.7	22.8	22.2	.6	3.6	3.3
1961	71.7	69.7	47.0	18.4	17.7	28.6	25.8	22.6	22.0	.6	2.0	1.7
1962	83.0	77.0	51.7	19.2	18.5	32.5	29.4	25.3	24.8	.6	6.0	5.3
1963	87.1	81.3	54.3	19.5	18.8	34.8	31.2	27.0	26.4	.6	5.9	5.1
1964	94.0	88.2	61.1	21.2	20.5	39.9	36.3	27.1	26.6	.5	5.8	6.4
1965	108.1	98.5	71.3	25.5	24.9	45.8	41.6	27.2	26.7	.5	9.6	8.6
1966	121.4	106.6	81.6	28.5	27.8	53.1	48.4	25.0	24.5	.5	14.8	15.0
1967	116.6	108.4	83.3	28.0	27.3	55.3	50.0	25.1	24.5	.6	8.2	7.5
1968	126.0	118.9	88.8	30.3	29.5	58.5	53.6	30.1	29.5	.5	7.1	6.9
1969	137.8	130.4	98.6	34.5	33.7	64.1	59.2	31.8	31.2	.6	7.4	7.3
1970	135.3	132.5	102.1	36.8	35.9	65.4	60.0	30.4	29.7	.6	2.8	2.5
1971	150.8	148.7	108.2	38.1	37.2	70.1	62.6	40.6	40.1	.5	2.1	1.5

Source: *Economic Report of the President*, 1972.

ness cycles. Hence the forecaster has to look to many other factors in anticipating the direction and level of residential building.

One important demand factor is the net household formation rate,
which in turn is affected by population age group changes, marriages, di-
vorces, deaths, and incomes. The availability and cost of mortgage money,
inflation, the second home market, vacancies, land prices, construction
costs and similar considerations combine to influence the housing market.

Vacancy rates have to be evaluated in the light of other considerations.
A high vacancy rate may indicate overbuilding at current prices, and a
probable reduction in construction. However, a high vacancy rate also could
mean that with higher incomes consumers are upgrading the housing inventory, and the high vacancy rate signals a high demolition rate and a continued high level of construction. In many central cities large numbers of
structurally sound housing units are being abandoned under the force of
great social pressures. The forecaster has to examine both the data and the
context to interpret their meaning.

The F. W. Dodge figures on construction contract awards along with
statistical series on construction put in place, housing starts, building permits, construction cost indexes, construction materials output indexes, and
real estate mortgage data are published monthly in the *Survey of Current
Business*. These kinds of data are invaluable in forecasting residential construction activity. Both *Economic Indicators* and *Business Conditions
Digest* also contain useful construction series, as does the *Federal Reserve
Monthly Chart Book*.

Business investment in equipment often is considered along with plant
as part of fixed capital investment. This spending has special significance.
It at once affects the level of economic activity and is an indicator of businessmen's expectations and a determinant of future efficiency and productivity.

Fluctuations in capital goods spending may result from inventions
followed by technological innovation. And changes in demand may induce
"accelerated" fluctuations in investment, insofar as the "acceleration
principle" applies to capital goods spending. A change in consumer demand either upward or downward can lead to a more than proportionate
change in investment demand when firms are operating at or near capacity.
A demand increase of, say, 10% could lead to a 100% first-year increase in
capital equipment demand, assuming a normal replacement demand of 10%
annually. Conversely, a 10% decline in demand could lead to a shrinkage of
replacement demand to zero, in the first year. The acceleration principle
can have an important leverage effect on economic activity. It may be rein-
forced in turn by the multiplier principle, under which people respond to
changes in their incomes by spending or saving more than usual, thereby in
turn affecting the income of others, i.e., total national income, by a multiple
of the original change.

CHART 11-9. Expenditures for New Plant and Equipment

Businessmen have projected a 10 percent increase in plant and equipment expenditures from 1971 to 1972. Outlays are expected to rise from the first to the second half of 1972.

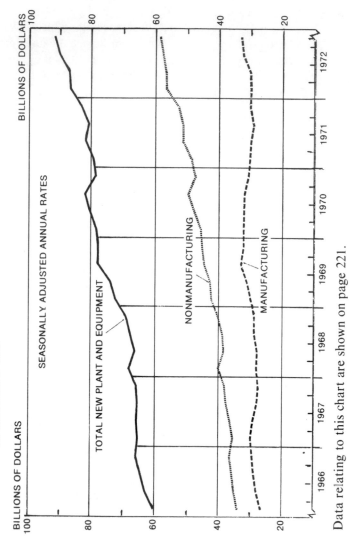

BILLIONS OF DOLLARS

BILLIONS OF DOLLARS

SEASONALLY ADJUSTED ANNUAL RATES

TOTAL NEW PLANT AND EQUIPMENT

NONMANUFACTURING

MANUFACTURING

100

80

60

40

20

1966 1967 1968 1969 1970 1971 1972

Data relating to this chart are shown on page 221.

CHART 11-9 (Continued)

(Billions of dollars; quarterly data at seasonally adjusted annual rates)

Period	Total[1]	Manufacturing			Mining	Transportation			Public utilities	Communication	Commercial and other[2]
		Total	Durable goods	Non-durable goods		Railroad	Air	Other			
1962	38.39	15.06	6.79	8.26	1.40	1.02	0.52	1.65	4.90	3.85	9.99
1963	40.77	16.22	7.53	8.70	1.27	1.26	.40	1.58	4.98	4.06	10.99
1964	46.97	19.34	9.28	10.07	1.34	1.66	1.02	1.50	5.49	4.61	12.02
1965	54.42	23.44	11.50	11.94	1.46	1.99	1.22	1.68	6.13	5.30	13.19
1966	63.51	28.20	14.06	14.14	1.62	2.37	1.74	1.64	7.43	6.02	14.48
1967	65.47	28.51	14.06	14.45	1.65	1.86	2.29	1.48	8.74	6.34	14.59
1968	67.76	28.37	14.12	14.25	1.63	1.45	2.56	1.59	10.20	6.83	15.14
1969	75.56	31.68	15.96	15.72	1.86	1.86	2.51	1.68	11.61	8.30	16.05
1970	79.71	31.95	15.80	16.15	1.89	1.78	3.03	1.23	13.14	10.10	16.59
1971	81.21	29.99	14.15	15.84	2.16	1.67	1.88	1.38	15.30	10.77	18.05
1972[3]	89.10	31.66	15.70	15.96	2.44	1.81	2.50	1.38	17.32	11.99	19.99
1971: I	79.32	30.46	14.21	16.25	2.04	1.46	1.29	1.33	14.64	10.70	17.39
II	81.61	30.12	14.06	16.06	2.08	1.88	2.28	1.40	14.91	11.21	17.72
III	80.75	29.19	13.76	15.43	2.23	1.72	1.68	1.48	15.87	10.73	17.85
IV	83.18	30.35	14.61	15.74	2.30	1.64	2.26	1.33	15.74	10.44	19.10
1972: I	86.79	30.09	15.06	15.02	2.42	2.10	1.96	1.48	16.92	11.71	20.10
II	87.12	30.37	14.77	15.60	2.38	1.88	2.89	1.53	16.60	11.59	19.88
III[3]	90.38	32.62	16.22	16.40	2.46	1.71	2.57	1.49	17.36		32.19
IV[3]	91.84	33.22	16.58	16.65	2.52	1.56	2.59	1.10	18.36		32.49

[1]Excludes agricultural business, real estate operators; medical, legal, educational, and cultural service; and nonprofit organizations.

[2]Includes trade, service, construction, finance, and insurance.

[3]Estimates based on expected capital expenditures as reported by business in late July and August 1972. Includes adjustments when necessary for systematic tendencies in expectations data.

NOTE — Annual total is the sum of unadjusted expenditures; it does not necessarily coincide with the average of seasonally adjusted figures.

These figures do not agree with the totals included in the gross national product estimates of the Department of Commerce, principally because the latter covers agricultural investment and also certain equipment and construction outlays charged to current expense.

Source: Department of Commerce *Economic Indicators*, October 1972.

Close attention is given to anticipations, as reflected by surveys. Forecasters monitor reports on shipments, new orders, and sales and inventories, as well as projected outlays for new plant and equipment. Charts 11-9 to 11-11 show some of the data available. These series include projected estimates for two quarters ahead.

Inventory changes may be the most volatile of the GNP segments, and inventory forecasts are subject to perhaps more error than most estimates. Sharply identifying inventory movements is difficult. The GNP measurement is of the *change* in inventories, not the total level. It is a measure of the change in the physical volume of stocks, at the average prevailing inventory price.

Changes in business inventories are closely linked with business cycles, serving as leading indicators of cyclical movements. Even though inventories may continue to grow in size after a contraction in business has begun, the rate of growth typically will have been declining in advance of the business contraction. And the converse is true in business expansions. Thus, changes in the rate of inventory investment lead the cycle, while investment itself lags somewhat. Inventory changes are intimately related to sales, and a widely used guide to forecasters is the inventory-sales ratios for important industries.

Inventory investments have been reduced in recent years as businessmen have standardized lines, computerized operations, and reorganized practices to that end. Carrying inventories incurs costs, such as transportation and handling, insurance, storage, deterioration, theft losses, possible obsolescence, and alternative opportunity costs.

The forecaster studies the demand for major kinds of goods, including business equipment and consumer durable and nondurable goods.

Possible price changes also have to be considered. Inventories might be increased in anticipation of price increases, or orders reduced in anticipation of declining prices. The forecaster has to evaluate probable price movements and the manner in which both consumers and businessmen may perceive and respond to these price changes. Still other influences may come into play to affect changes in inventories, and the forecaster has to judge their meaning and importance, and adjust for them. Wildcat strikes might affect inventory stocks, for example, while expected strikes at the end of major three-year labor contracts may induce other anticipatory inventory changes. Expected interest rate changes also may influence inventory decisions. Perhaps because of the varied and apparently contradictory responses that are possible, forecasters not uncommonly reach quite different conclusions about future inventory changes.

The *Survey of Current Business* gives monthly figures on sales, inventories, inventory-sales ratios, and orders in a wide variety of categories. Various surveys of inventory trends and anticipations also are available to the forecaster. The Department of Commerce's monthly *Business Conditions Digest* is a valuable source of data.

CHART 11-10. Manufacturers' Shipments, Inventories, and New Orders

Shipments, inventories, and new orders of manufacturers (seasonally adjusted) all showed sizeable increases in August.

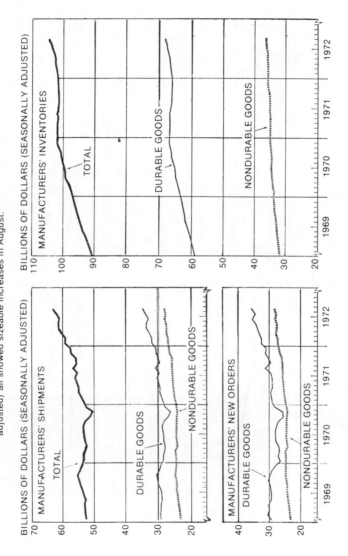

Source: Economic Indicators, October 1972.

CHART 11-11. Business Sales and Inventories

In August, business sales rose 2 percent (seasonally adjusted) while inventories increased by $1 billion. According to advance reports, retail sales declined in September.

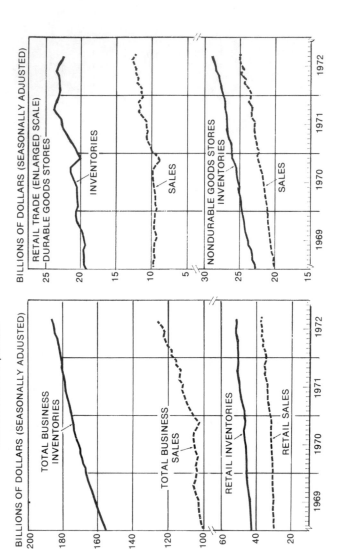

Source: Economic Indicators, October 1972.

P. PERSONAL CONSUMPTION EXPENDITURES

Personal consumption expenditures in 1971 were $662 billion, some 63% of GNP, and by far the largest of the national product accounts. Personal consumption expenditures for durable goods, nondurable goods, and services have been running close to two-thirds of GNP in recent years.

Nondurable goods and services maintain a fairly stable pattern, moving with income. Expenditures for consumer durables, however, fluctuate more widely as consumers can more readily postpone purchases.

As noted earlier, the percentage of disposable personal income that consumers spend (and save) varies from year to year. For example, consumers spent 95.1% of disposable income in 1963, but only 91.8% in 1971, as they stepped up their savings rate. In addition to such short-term shifts, longer-term and possibly more significant changes have been taking place in the distribution of personal consumption expenditures among durable goods, and services.

TABLE 11-7.
Percent of Total Personal Consumption Expenditures

	Durable Goods	Nondurable Goods	Services	Nondurable Goods and Services
1952	13.5	52.6	33.9	86.5
1971	15.2	42.1	42.7	84.8

Two things are striking in the above table. First is the very slight change in the proportion of consumer spending devoted to durable goods vis-a-vis nondurables and services combined. The second is the considerable decline in the proportion spent for nondurable goods, and the corresponding rise in spending for services.

Table 11-8 following shows the details of consumer expenditures since 1929. Of the three categories under durable goods, "automobiles and parts" and "furniture and household equipment" account for the bulk of durable goods expenditures. Food and beverages account for about half of nondurable goods expenditures, with fairly slow but steady growth. Spending for clothing and shoes, however, tends to show greater cyclical fluctuations. Consumer spending for services, like expenditures for nondurables, tends to be relatively stable, but with a substantial growth as noted above, both absolutely and relatively during the past two decades.

Forecasting consumption expenditures entails a consideration of underlying factors that influence consumer demand and spending plans. Employment levels, earnings and incomes, and consumer expectations about future employment and incomes are determinants of spending. Liquid assets, outstanding consumer debt, and credit terms and availability influence consumer buying decisions. The U. S. Bureau of the Census of the Department of Commerce publishes reports of its consumer survey quarterly in "Consumer Buying Intentions."

TABLE 11-8.

Personal Consumption Expenditures, 1929-71 (in billions of dollars)

Year or quarter	Total personal consumption expenditures	Durable goods				Nondurable goods					Services				
		Total	Automobiles and parts	Furniture and household equipment	Other	Total	Food and beverages	Clothing and shoes[1]	Gasoline and oil	Other	Total	Housing[2]	Household operation	Transportation	Other
1929	77.2	9.2	3.2	4.8	1.2	37.7	19.5	9.4	1.8	7.0	30.3	11.5	4.0	2.6	12.2
1930	69.9	7.2	2.2	3.9	1.1	34.0	18.0	8.0	1.7	6.3	28.7	11.0	3.9	2.2	11.5
1931	60.5	5.5	1.6	3.1	.9	29.0	14.7	6.9	1.5	5.7	26.0	10.3	3.5	1.9	10.3
1932	48.6	3.6	.9	2.1	.6	22.7	11.4	5.1	1.5	4.8	22.2	9.0	3.0	1.6	8.6
1933	45.8	3.5	1.1	1.9	.5	22.3	11.5	4.6	1.5	4.6	20.1	7.9	2.8	1.5	7.9
1934	51.3	4.2	1.4	2.2	.6	26.7	14.2	5.7	1.6	5.2	20.4	7.6	3.0	1.6	8.2
1935	55.7	5.1	1.9	2.6	.7	29.3	16.2	6.0	1.7	5.4	21.3	7.7	3.2	1.7	8.7
1936	61.9	6.3	2.3	3.2	.8	32.9	18.4	6.6	1.9	5.9	22.8	8.0	3.4	1.9	9.5
1937	66.5	6.9	2.4	3.6	1.0	35.2	19.9	6.8	2.1	6.3	24.4	8.5	3.7	2.0	10.2
1938	63.9	5.7	1.6	3.1	.9	34.0	18.9	6.8	2.1	6.2	24.3	8.9	3.6	1.9	9.9
1939	66.8	6.7	2.2	3.5	1.0	35.1	19.1	7.1	2.2	6.7	25.0	9.1	3.8	2.0	10.1
1940	70.8	7.8	2.7	3.9	1.1	37.0	20.2	7.4	2.3	7.1	26.0	9.4	4.0	2.1	10.4
1941	80.6	9.6	3.4	4.9	1.4	42.9	23.4	8.8	2.6	8.0	28.1	10.2	4.3	2.4	11.2
1942	88.5	6.9	.7	4.7	1.6	50.8	28.4	11.0	2.1	9.3	30.8	11.0	4.8	2.7	12.3
1943	99.3	6.6*	.8	3.9	1.9	58.6	33.2	13.4	1.3	10.6	34.2	11.5	5.2	3.4	14.0
1944	108.3	6.7	.8	3.8	2.2	64.3	36.7	14.4	1.6	11.7	37.2	12.0	5.9	3.7	15.6
1945	119.7	8.0	1.0	4.6	2.5	71.9	40.6	16.5	1.8	13.0	39.8	12.5	6.4	4.0	16.8
1946	143.4	15.8	4.0	8.6	3.2	82.4	47.4	18.2	3.0	13.8	45.3	13.9	6.8	5.0	19.7
1947	160.7	20.4	6.2	10.9	3.3	90.5	52.3	18.8	3.6	15.7	49.8	15.7	7.5	5.3	21.4

TABLE 11-8 (continued)

Year															
1948	173.6	22.7	7.5	11.9	3.4	96.2	54.2	20.1	4.4	17.5	54.7	17.5	8.1	5.8	23.3
1949	176.8	24.6	9.9	11.6	3.2	94.5	52.5	19.3	5.0	17.7	57.6	19.3	8.5	5.9	23.9
1950	191.0	30.5	13.1	14.1	3.3	98.1	53.9	19.6	5.4	19.2	62.4	21.3	9.5	6.2	25.4
1951	206.3	29.6	11.6	14.4	3.6	108.8	60.4	21.2	6.1	21.1	67.9	23.9	10.4	6.7	26.9
1952	216.7	29.3	11.1	14.3	3.9	114.0	63.4	21.9	6.8	21.7	73.4	26.5	11.1	7.1	28.7
1953	230.0	33.2	14.2	14.9	4.1	116.8	64.4	22.1	7.7	22.7	79.9	29.3	12.0	7.8	30.8
1954	236.5	32.8	13.6	15.0	4.2	118.3	65.4	22.1	8.2	22.6	85.4	31.7	12.6	7.9	33.2
1955	254.4	39.6	18.4	16.6	4.6	123.3	67.2	23.1	9.0	24.0	91.4	33.7	14.0	8.2	35.5
1956	266.7	38.9	16.4	17.5	5.0	129.3	69.9	24.1	9.8	25.4	98.5	36.0	15.2	8.6	38.6
1957	281.4	40.8	18.3	17.3	5.2	135.6	73.6	24.3	10.6	27.1	105.0	38.5	16.2	9.0	41.3
1958	290.1	37.9	15.4	17.1	5.4	140.2	76.4	24.7	11.0	28.2	112.0	41.1	17.3	9.3	44.3
1959	311.2	44.3	19.5	18.9	5.9	146.6	78.6	26.4	11.6	30.1	120.3	43.7	18.5	10.1	48.0
1960	325.2	45.3	20.1	18.9	6.3	151.3	80.5	27.3	12.3	31.2	128.7	46.3	20.0	10.8	51.6
1961	335.2	44.2	18.4	19.3	6.5	155.9	82.9	27.9	12.4	32.7	135.1	48.7	20.8	10.6	54.9
1962	355.1	49.5	22.0	20.5	6.9	162.6	85.7	29.6	12.9	34.4	143.0	52.0	22.0	11.0	58.0
1963	375.0	53.9	24.3	22.2	7.5	168.6	88.2	30.6	13.5	36.3	152.4	55.4	23.1	11.4	62.5
1964	401.2	59.2	25.8	25.0	8.5	178.7	92.9	33.5	14.0	38.2	163.3	59.3	24.3	11.6	68.1
1965	432.8	66.3	30.3	26.9	9.1	191.1	98.8	35.9	15.3	41.1	175.5	63.5	25.6	12.6	73.8
1966	466.3	70.8	30.3	29.9	10.5	206.9	105.8	40.3	16.6	44.4	188.6	67.5	27.1	13.6	80.4
1967	492.1	73.1	30.5	31.4	11.2	215.0	108.5	42.3	17.6	46.6	204.0	71.8	29.1	14.5	88.5
1968	536.2	84.0	37.5	34.3	12.3	230.8	115.3	46.3	19.0	50.2	221.3	77.3	31.2	15.5	97.3
1969	579.6	89.9	40.4	36.3	13.3	247.6	122.5	50.3	21.1	53.7	242.1	84.0	33.7	16.5	107.8
1970	615.8	88.6	37.1	37.4	14.2	264.7	131.8	52.6	22.9	57.5	262.5	91.2	36.1	17.9	117.3
1971	662.2	100.4	46.2	39.5	14.7	278.8	136.6	57.0	24.3	60.9	283.0	99.7	39.3	19.0	125.0

[1] Includes standard clothing issued to military personnel.
[2] Includes imputed rental value of owner-occupied dwellings.

Source: *Economic Report of the President*, January 1972.

Ultimately the forecaster has to pull together all the bits and pieces of facts, projections, political forces, intuition, and judgment, and form an overall pattern, adjusting both the total and its components as he constructs his estimate of GNP.

Q. INDICATORS OF ECONOMIC CHANGE

Implicit throughout the discussion of GNP forecasting, and explicit at points, has been the importance of specific indicators to the forecaster. Forecasters generally meld many elements to arrive at their estimates. Some forecasts are based on easily available data and are relatively simple. For example, figures on the number of employed, labor productivity, earnings, and current price movements may be combined in an intuitive judgment to obtain a rather shrewd projection. Some businessmen and economists seem to have a nose for impending business and economic changes that transcends mere statistics.

Forecasters also find it useful to keep tabs on several series that are generally regarded as important indicators. As noted earlier, increasing attention has been given to federal fiscal operations, with special attention to their impact on debt and the money stock. Stock prices, interest rates, and bond yields are among the closely observed indicants of change. The Federal Reserve Bank of St. Louis is a leader in developing and applying monetary theory in forecasting.

The Federal Reserve System's industrial production indexes provide a wealth of data by market and industry groupings, and include some aggregate selected business indexes, such as the index of "capacity utilization in manufacturing."

The NBER's important work in identifying historical turning points in business cycles has been rounded out by their development of cyclical indicators, as noted earlier. The NBER periodically has reviewed the list of economic time series of leaders, coinciders, and laggers. From its full list of 78 time series it has selected a "short list" of 12 leading, 8 roughly coincident, and 6 lagging indicators.[6] In addition, composite indexes have been constructed of leading, coincident, and lagging indicators. Logic as well as empirical testing supports their use in forecasting, and we are prepared to find that new durable goods orders and housing starts (along with the other leaders) signal an improvement in business activity.

Diffusion indexes are summary measures for particular aggregates, showing the percentages of activities that are expanding and contracting in the face of general expansions and contractions of economic activity. In effect, the diffusion index gives a reading, as it were, akin to that of a rate of

---

[6] See the monthly *Business Conditions Digest* for these indicators.

change for the components of a total. Diffusion indexes tend to lead cyclical changes, but they are erratic and must be carefully interpreted. *Business Conditions Digest* publishes the NBER indicators as well as various diffusion indexes each month.

SELECTED ANNOTATED BIBLIOGRAPHY

Economic Indicators, Council of Economic Advisers, Washington, monthly, about 38 pages, $3.00 per year. Charts and tables showing basic statistics on output, income, employment, wages, production and business activity, prices, money supply and credit, federal finance, and similar series.

Federal Reserve Bulletin, Board of Governors of the Federal Reserve System, Washington, monthly, about 120 pages, $6.00 per year. Analysis of economic and financial developments, statistics on banking, industrial production, credit, trade, international finance, and similar subjects. See also the *Monthly Chart Book,* of Finance and Business Statistics, at $6.00 per year.

Business Conditions Digest, Bureau of Economic Analysis, U. S. Department of Commerce, Washington, monthly, about 125 pages, $15.00 per year. Brings together in charts and tables many of the most important economic time series used by forecasters. Emphasis is given to the leading, roughly coincident, and lagging indicators approach to forecasting, but other key indicators also are given, including anticipations and intentions data, diffusion indexes, international comparisons and related data such as gross national product series.

Survey of Current Business, Bureau of Economic Analysis, U. S. Department of Commerce, Washington, monthly, about 56 pages, $9.00 per year. Brief analysis of the business situation plus a broad coverage that provides hundreds of business and economic statistical series.

Economic Report of the President, Washington, each January, together with the Annual Report of the Council of Economic Advisers, about 300 pages, $1.50. Economic review of the year, analysis, recommendations for improving the economy, and statistics on national income or expenditure, population, employment, wages, productivity, production and business activity, prices, money stock, credit, finance, government finance, corporate profits and finance, agriculture, and international statistics.

Construction Review, Bureau of Domestic Commerce, U. S. Department of Commerce, Washington, monthly, about 60 pages, $6.50 per year. Contains statistical series on construction put in place, housing, building permits, contract awards, costs and prices, construction materials, and contract construction employment.

Each of the twelve Federal Reserve Banks publishes a monthly *Review* or bulletin that is of general interest in addition to being a source of information of special significance within its Federal Reserve district. Also helpful are the monthly letters published by several of the large commercial banks, as well as their annual forecasts of economic activity. *Business Week* magazine publishes several major statistical series weekly. Finally, of daily informational value are newspapers such as *The Wall Street Journal* and *The Journal of Commerce*.

12 ACCRA COST OF LIVING INDEX

A. INTRODUCTION

The American Chamber of Commerce Researchers Association (ACCRA) Inter-City Cost-of-Living Index—today known among Chambers of Commerce nationwide and subscribed to annually by many business firms—is a meaningful measurement of living costs among cities. As outlined by ACCRA, the groups of items forming the basis of this index are priced by capable Chamber of Commerce personnel, at a specified time and by standard specifications, and then are converted to an index by programmed computer processing, providing a useful and reasonably accurate measurement of inter-city cost-of-living differences.

The ACCRA Index is not a precise measurement of living costs between cities, but it can be used effectively as a "reasonable approximation" yardstick of the relative living costs among a large number of U.S. cities. For comparative purposes, no attempt is made by Chamber of Commerce personnel to evaluate the types of purchases made by the consumer. The items selected should not be interpreted on this basis: they have been chosen solely to show price differentials on the same commodities in the reporting cities.

Unlike the Consumer Price Index tabulated by the Bureau of Labor Statistics (BLS), the ACCRA Inter-City Cost-of-Living Index measures the general level of prices at the time pricing is done, in the first week of each calendar quarter. Pricing is done on the first Thursday, Friday and Saturday of January, April, July and October, except when a holiday falls in that period. If a holiday falls within the first Thursday, Friday and Saturday of the month, then the second Thursday, Friday and Saturday are used as the pricing days.

Whereas the ACCRA Inter-City Index shows the relative price levels in participating cities, compared with the U.S. average (equalling 100 for all cities covered), the BLS Consumer Price Index gives reasonably close measurements of living costs within a city and its Standard Metropolitan Statistical Area. This, however, is a measure only of the change in con-

231

sumer prices over time and is restricted to the rise and fall of prices within the SMSA covered. Inter-city comparisons using the Consumer Price Index are available only for a limited number of cities.

The ACCRA Index does not measure price changes in a given period. Each quarterly report is a separate comparison between cities reporting in that quarter, not between cities and prices on previous quarterly reports. While the indexes ideally should be consistent for the prices reported from quarter to quarter, there is no continuity from one quarter to the next.

A major variable in the measurement is the number and mix of cities in each report. New cities volunteer to participate; some contributors, for one reason or another, fail to report. And each quarter some cities file incomplete reports, which are unusable. The Index's character reflects, in many cases, the change of the cities listed in the report from quarter to quarter, and represents only the cities in the Index in the current quarter.

The format of the ACCRA Inter-City Index is indicated in the following illustration:

Column Nos.	#1	#2	#3	#4	#5	#6	#7
Component Weights		20	35	15	12	8	10
City	City Index (All items)	Food	Housing	Utilities	Transportation	Health	Miscellaneous Services
City A	109.0	109.1	110.0	107.5	107.0	111.3	107.7
City B	118.0	112.2	125.4	110.0	113.0	125.1	116.0
City C	97.9	102.4	104.9	86.7	93.3	75.7	105.0

B. PRICES MAKE THE DIFFERENCE

Price level information enables ranking of cities from high to low on the ACCRA Index. The limited number of items priced is sufficient for determining relative price levels, but they fall short as representatives of all prices on the thousands of commodities traded in each city.

Percentages are not valid measurements of the differentials between numbers in comparing cities. The Index is meant to be interpreted as an approximate measurement of average price levels, but not as precise as a percentage differential would indicate. For example: City B may have an index of 100.5 compared to City A's 120.5, showing that City B is substantially lower in price level than City A, but *not* necessarily 20% lower.

What the Index does is *rank* cities from highest to lowest for price levels in an All-Items Index, or in the indexes for any of the components making up the All-Items Index. A close look at the Index in any quarter shows only a few cities with an All-Items Index below 100 having the "sub-100" in every component. The same is true with the "over-100" cities. It is expected that in most cities, at least some of the components vary — and significantly — but even their expected variability is erratic.

The ACCRA Index attempts to cut through these inconsistencies, establishing the rough cost-of-living differentials among cities, or the relative position of any city in regard to another, or to all cities.

Flexibility is probably the best asset in ACCRA's Index where its constantly changing base adjusts to the flux in the U.S. average. Take, for example, the Health component, in which the component prices may remain the same for the two or three quarters. If other cities have an increase in items under this component — such as the price in a hospital room and doctor calls — the city which has remained constant from one quarter to the next will possibly drop in the Index number for that component, as the U.S. average has gone up. In other words, the denominator of the fraction used for the Health Index will rise along with the U.S. average. When the fraction is divided, the constant numerator (the weighted component price for the single city) will show a quarterly decline in the component Index for that city.

Accuracy is especially important in indexes in which the end result, regardless of refining, is as good as the original input. It is assumed that price reports are accurate, but there is a continuous check made on any prices that seem to deviate widely from previous reports. It is believed that the regional coordinators and the central control for the Index preparation now have enough experience to eliminate almost all recording errors in making the Index a reasonable approximation.

C. COMPILING THE ACCRA INTER-CITY INDEX

The ACCRA Index is a product of the 1966 national conference of the American Chamber of Commerce Researchers Association in Columbus, Ohio. At that time, it was first suggested to the ACCRA membership that a study be made to determine the feasibility of an inter-city cost-of-living measurement as an association service.

Chambers of Commerce throughout the United States were invited to participate in this project by collecting price data at a specified time quarterly in accordance with standard specifications. About 140 Chambers of Commerce in 45 states responded to ACCRA's invitation to participate in the pilot project conducted in April, 1967. The information was assembled, published alphabetically by state and city, and distributed to contributing cities and the ACCRA membership. Its potential for becoming a valuable tool led to the formation in 1968 of the ACCRA Cost-of-Living Committee, which has produced the Index since October, 1968, in addition to the Price Report.

The Research Department of the Chicago Association of Commerce and Industry serves as national headquarters for this ACCRA Index. A coordinator is designated by the Index Committee for each of six U.S.

regions. Each coordinator selects researchers in local Chambers of Commerce, who are responsible for compiling and reporting all pricing information relating to their respective cities. Each quarter, a precoded ACCRA Price Report is sent to the researcher for his use in compiling the required information for his area.

After price data are received in the six regional centers, the prices are checked against previous quarters for consistency and any obvious errors. The coordinators often must go back to the city for clarification of some prices. When they have been thoroughly examined, the precoded Price Reports are then sent to Chicago for processing into the Inter-City Index. As a means of detecting errors, the Chicago operation has devised a standard deviation check — a computer printout of the consolidated Price Report in which the computer prints an asterisk behind any price not in line with a two-standard deviation limit on each side of the mean of prices submitted. In all, this would cover 43 items for U.S. cities in the report. The asterisk is used to mark the 2.5% of the highest prices and 2.5% of the lowest prices submitted for each item.

There are over 6,000 prices in the consolidated Price Report each quarter, making the verification of all prices impossible. Extreme prices are easier to locate on the standard deviation test, and upon challenge, are compared to previous quarters or go back to the reporting Chamber of Commerce for verification or correction. When the adjustment, if needed, is made, the information returns to the computer for Index preparation.

Pricing for all items must be checked quarterly to reflect the rising costs of nearly all commodities. When first organized, ACCRA's instructions called for pricing housing and utility items less frequently than foods and other nondurable goods as the general price level seemed more stable. From the experience gathered it has been shown since then that marked differences in housing and other specified items make a quarterly check necessary.

Initially, the Index was based on prices for 44 commodities — 25 for foods, two for housing, three for utilities, four for health, three for transportation, and seven for miscellaneous services.

There were many lessons to be learned early, and almost within a year — from 1967-68 — most of the problem areas were worked out well enough to set a standard that could cope with pricing variables. One of the first outcomes of the project was the deletion of Item 33 — automotive registrations. Legislation affecting this item was different in each state and seriously distorted the rankings of individual cities.

The original Instruction Manual for the ACCRA Index detailed procedures for pricing of individual items and assigning them weights. The first report — for the second, third and fourth quarters of 1967 — was difficult to read. Column headings were used on opening pages with no continuation indicated on following pages. Also, the pre-publication reports covered only 26 commodities and were not, for the most part, the same as those specified at the inauguration of the Index. Early improvements included the expansion of price information from 26 to 44 commodities (and the later deletion of automotive registrations) and a revision of the manual to guide the reporting Chambers as well as the persons preparing the Index.

When the first Price Report and Index Report were published for the first quarter, 1968, the specifications were almost identical to those used today. Earlier reporting had revealed that many brand name items were not available nationwide. There are also some items (such as Item 25 — Soft Drinks), in which a single-bottle price had to be used because the eight-pack, 16-ounce Coca-Cola originally suggested was not found in all stores. Then too, some items were used by chain stores as leaders for attracting the buying public. If a store had a sale on an item, the sale price was used, though some items seemed to be perennially on sale.

In the Foods category, it was decided that the "lowest price" be used rather than a brand name or a specified quality. Round steak was substituted for sirloin when it was discovered to be a more family-type purchase. In the original plans, five pounds of cane sugar was specified. In pricing, it was found that cane and beet sugar were treated similarly in many stores, yet there might be a price differential. This item was dropped.

In the specifications originally proposed in 1967, the Housing portion of the Price Report included three areas of measure — House rent (first class, 3 bedrooms); Apartment (first class, 2 bedrooms); Apartment — (deluxe, two bedrooms). These were combined into the final Housing component items in monthly rent for apartment, and in monthly payment for a purchased house.

D. THE PERIOD OF ADJUSTMENT

The wider acceptance of the Index and the participation of smaller Chambers of Commerce, in addition to early rough spots that needed smoothing out, have brought about several adjustments in Index preparation. Some smaller communities, for instance, do not have bus service. The solution? Combine the weights of bus and taxi fare and use them with the taxi fare alone to produce that part of the Transportation Index. A few cities were "dry" and did not permit liquor sales. The solution: the liquor price average for other cities in the state was taken as the liquor price for that city, and the Index calculated on that basis. The price, however, is not published in the final Price Report.

The most serious problem in compiling the Index is in the Housing component report and in Utilities reporting. Apartment specifications are not easily made universal. The only specifications that seem usable are that an apartment should be in a suitable neighborhood with certain minimum requirements and priced for the executive in a designated income bracket. Housing prices must be detailed as they have the heaviest weighting of any component in the Index.

The Utilities component poses other considerations. Several utility companies previously objected to using the "city average" that covers all types of dwelling units—apartments, single family, etc. The Index instructions specified a new house with certain requirements that was not being priced on utilities services consumed, but was based on a citywide price. The 1969 revision of the Index Instruction Manual specified that the residential utilities rates for electric power and natural gas be in the amount used in the specified house in the Housing component. This too has brought criticism from utility companies that cannot price by this method.

An alternate pricing proposal was made in manual revisions prepared for first quarter, 1971, and beyond. This approach takes a house meeting the requirements specified, as nearly as possible, under five years old. Monthly bills for electricity or gas for that dwelling are averaged, keeping in mind the standard appliances—heating, washing, drying, etc.—used in that city.

The income level of the family specified was raised to $18,000-$20,000 in 1975 from $10,000-$15,000 in the Index's formative stages. This will be weighed against any inflation factor periodically and any needed adjustments will be made.

Procedures for calculating the ACCRA Index are outlined in Exhibit 12-A. In the Index Committee's *Instruction Manual* (available to the local researcher interested in becoming a part of the program) there is information on how to prepare these price reports. The need for additional participating communities continues, to make the Inter-City Index as representative and effective and as useful as possible on a nationwide basis.

EXHIBIT 12-A: METHOD OF COMPUTING THE ACCRA INDEX

Procedures for computing the ACCRA Index are illustrated by means of the following factor-weighting tables and explanation:

TABLE 12-A1

Food

Item	Item Weight	Factor	Sample Item Price		Adjusted Price
Meats (30)					
Round steak	.075	x	1.09	=	.082
Ground beef	.075	x	.59	=	.044
Bacon	.075	x	.79	=	.059
Frying chicken, whole	.075	x	.39	=	.029
Dairy products (12)					
Whole milk, fresh	.05	x	.48	=	.024
Eggs, large	.04	x	.39	=	.016
Margarine	.03	x	.20	=	.006
Produce (9)					
Potatoes	.05	x	.915	=	.046
Bananas	.02	x	.10	=	.002
Head lettuce	.02	x	.39	=	.008
Bakery products (5)					
Bread, white	.05	x	.25	=	.013
Tobacco (4)					
Cigarettes	.04	x	2.39	=	.096
Miscellaneous groceries (40)					
Coffee, vacuum packed	.04	x	.79	=	.0316
Peas, garden	.03	x	.25	=	.0075
Corn, cream style	.03	x	.27	=	.0081
Green beans	.03	x	.23	=	.0069
Tomatoes	.03	x	.17	=	.0051
Peaches, halves	.03	x	.37	=	.0111
Toilet tissue	.03	x	.35	=	.0105
Washing powder	.03	x	.33	=	.0099
Shortening	.03	x	.87	=	.0261
Frozen orange juice	.03	x	.85	=	.0255
Frozen peas	.03	x	.22	=	.0066
Baby food	.03	x	1.47	=	.0441
Soft drink	.03	x	.64	=	.0192
	1.00				

Total adjusted price, Food Index list   0.638

TABLE 12-A2
Housing

Item	Item Weight	Factor	Sample Item Price		Adjusted Price
Apartment	.35	x	175.00	=	61.25
House purchase	.65	x	150.00	=	97.50
	1.00				
Total adjusted price, Housing Index list					158.75

TABLE 12-A3
Utilities

Item	Item Weight	Factor	Sample Item Price		Adjusted Price
Electric Power	.35	x	8.58	=	3.00
Natural Gas	.35	x	8.93	=	3.13
Telephone	.30	x	6.20	=	1.86
	1.00				
Total adjusted price, Utilities Index list					7.99

TABLE 12-A4
Transportation

Item	Item Weight	Factor	Sample Item Price		Adjusted Price
Bus fare	.30	x	0.25	=	.075
Taxi fare	.20	x	0.85	=	.170
Gasoline	.50	x	0.398	=	.199
	1.00				
Total adjusted price, Transportation Index list					0.444

TABLE 12-A5
Health

Item	Item Weight	Factor	Sample Item Price		Adjusted Price
Hospital room	.20	x	24.50	=	4.90
Doctor, office visit	.40	x	8.00	=	3.20
Dentist, office visit	.40	x	6.00	=	2.40
	1.00				
Total adjusted price, Health Index list					10.50

TABLE 12-A6
Miscellaneous Services

Item	Item Weight	Factor	Sample Item Price		Adjusted Price
Man's haircut	.15	x	1.75	=	.263
Woman's shampoo & set	.20	x	3.00	=	.600
Dry cleaning	.20	x	1.50	=	.300
Movie	.05	x	1.50	=	.075
Bowling	.05	x	0.55	=	.028
TV repair	.20	x	7.00	=	1.400
Liquor	.15	x	3.79	=	.569
	1.00				
Total adjusted price, Miscellaneous Index list					3.235

TABLE 12-A7
Adjusted Prices for all Index Groups

Index Groups	Adjusted Price	Group Symbol
Food	0.638	Vf
Housing	158.750	Vh
Utilities	7.990	Vu
Transportation	0.444	Vt
Health	10.500	Vs
Miscellaneous Services	3.235	Vm

(Adjusted prices have been rounded to the nearest .001.)

Central Office processing will involve three steps:

(a) *Computation of the national average of each major group.* Food, Housing, Utilities, Transportation, Health, and Miscellaneous Services.

Where: National averages are represented by the following symbols:

Food - V_{fa} Housing - V_{ha} Utilities - V_{ua}

Transportation - V_{ta} Health - V_{sa} Miscellaneous - V_{ma}

Where: N = the number of cities participating:

Then:

$$V_{fa} = \frac{\sum\limits^{N} V_f}{N} \qquad V_{ha} = \frac{\sum\limits^{N} V_h}{N} \qquad V_{ua} = \frac{\sum\limits^{N} V_u}{N}$$

$$V_{ta} = \frac{\sum\limits^{N} V_t}{N} \qquad V_{sa} = \frac{\sum\limits^{N} V_s}{N} \qquad V_{ma} = \frac{\sum\limits^{N} V_m}{N}$$

Example: Assume 140 cities participating

$$V_{fa} = \frac{\sum\limits^{140} V_f}{140}$$

(b) *Computation of the major group indexes for the participating cities:*

Where: I-No. 16-f = the Food group index for City No. 16

Similarly: I-No. 16-h = Housing group index for City No. 16
I-No. 16-u = Utilities group index for City No. 16
I-No. 16-t = Transportation group index for City No. 16
I-No. 16-s = Health group index for City No. 16
I-No. 16-m = Miscellaneous Services group index for City No. 16

Then, for City No. 16:

$$\text{I-No. 16-f} = \frac{V_f}{V_{fa}} \qquad\qquad \text{I-No. 16-h} = \frac{V_h}{V_{ha}}$$

$$\text{I-No. 16-u} = \frac{V_u}{V_{ua}} \qquad\qquad \text{I-No. 16-t} = \frac{V_t}{V_{ta}}$$

$$\text{I-No. 16-s} = \frac{V_s}{V_{sa}} \qquad\qquad \text{I-No. 16-m} = \frac{V_m}{V_{ma}}$$

These computations produce major group indexes for each city.

(c) *Computation of the city composite all items index for each partici-pating city.* The "all items" index composite of food costs, housing costs, and other categories of living costs, is accomplished by weighting the group component indexes proportionately to the amount of the cost-of-living dollar generally used for each expense category.

In the city composite "all items" index:

Food is weighted at 20
Housing is weighted at 35
Utilities is weighted at 15
Transportation is weighted at 12
Health is weighted at 8
Miscellaneous Services is weighted at 10

Then for each of the participating cities:

The composite all items index, CI, for example, for City I-No. 16 = 20 (I-No. 16-f) + 35 (I-No. 16-h) + 15 (I-No. 16-u) + 12 (I-No. 16-t) + 8 (I-No. 16-s) + 10 (I-No. 16-m)

The computer printout will look something like this:

Column Numbers	#1	#2	#3	#4	#5	#6	#7
Component Weights		20	35	15	12	8	10
City & State	City Index "All Items"	Food	Hous-ing	Utili-ties	Trans-porta-tion	Health	Miscel-laneous Services
City A	109.0	109.1	110.0	107.5	107.0	111.3	107.7
City B	118.0	112.2	125.4	110.0	103.0	125.1	116.0
City C	97.9	102.3	104.9	86.7	93.3	75.7	105.0

Obviously, the average for all cities for each of the components equals 100, which is the base for the index computations.

Part IV

RESEARCH FOR
ECONOMIC DEVELOPMENT

13 ECONOMIC HANDBOOK

A. WHY AN ECONOMIC HANDBOOK?

The Research Department in any Chamber of Commerce provides a multitude of services in its function as the community's data management center. Among the most important of these services is the publication of information on the various aspects of the city, the SMSA, and the surrounding area.

Chamber staff and committee personnel engaged in industrial and business development rely heavily on the Research staff for basic data, and for the compilation and refinement of specific information requested by clients. The information available from the Chamber researcher eliminates most of the guesswork concerning trends of the community's economic activities.

In its role as information purveyor, the Research Department serves as an important liaison office between community interests and those interested in the community. Industry leaders are becoming much more selective in choosing the areas of their future expansion. Due to rising capital investments and long term economic considerations, these leaders must employ more sophisticated selection techniques in making their site location decisions than were previously necessary. Rapidly changing industrial and institutional developments add to the specific information requirements of the corporate decision-makers, calling for a broader range of facts and figures than was formerly needed.

In the very recent past new technological developments and resource limitations, along with quality of life considerations, have initiated an era in which neither a corporation nor a community can any longer blindly pursue growth for its own sake. Corporations now must decide how to allocate limited resources in the most efficient manner. Communities are learning that there is a potentially heavy price to pay for unplanned, undirected growth.

Discussions with corporate executives involved in plant location decisions have identified factors which they consider to be of primary importance as decision aids. It is no surprise that community characteristics often rate high and may have a greater impact on final location choices than many logistical details of operation.

B. AN ECONOMIC HANDBOOK CAN ELIMINATE UNKNOWNS

Effective presentation of information by a Chamber of Commerce in the form of an economic handbook is one of the inducements that helps to promote new business development. One principle of business is that as many of the unknowns as possible should be eliminated when selecting a site for future expansion. A carefully formulated handbook can demonstrate to representatives of small and large businesses alike that the interests of the community are compatible with those of their companies and that planning for the local area is proceeding on a continuous basis to meet the needs of the future. Hence, a Chamber economic handbook can become one of the best sources of quantitative facts with which to eliminate those area unknowns.

Every community has attributes making it particularly suitable for certain types of industrial and commercial activities. Many communities have enough resources to support a variety of economic activities. The purpose of an economic handbook is to pinpoint specifically those qualities of a community which justify the location of a particular type of industry or business within its area. An effective handbook is especially helpful in moving a community through the early elimination rounds which many site locators use in their selection process.

C. HOW TO APPROACH AN ECONOMIC HANDBOOK

Up to this point it has been assumed that the Chamber researcher has already developed his basic library and arranged for regular data input into the organization's research information system. These are such important steps toward the completion of a handbook that they must be explicitly stated: before anyone attempts to prepare a usable economic handbook he must first have become familiar with his community through the constant collection and interpretation of facts within the Research Department. The Chamber has assumed the responsibility for reflecting the attitudes of the community. Any businessman who is seriously considering a community as a possible site for the expansion of his company will certainly be impressed by an alert Chamber of Commerce staff, one that has anticipated his informational needs and can supply answers to most of his questions.

Preparation of an economic handbook is only a small part of the total data collection and interpretation activities performed by the Research staff. Once the primary duties have been completed, the book will almost assemble itself. It is not enough, however, that the staff simply collect data about the community: information must be implemented to become effective. Implementation requires some type of filing system so that the information is easily accessible to all of the Research Department personnel and a capacity on the part of each employee to interpret the information and to document all data collected.

D. ORGANIZATION OF AN ECONOMIC HANDBOOK

A community brochure and an economic handbook are important publications of any Chamber's Research Department. They will often contain similar material, but they are not meant to serve the same purpose and should not be used interchangeably. A *community brochure* is designed to provide condensed information about a variety of subjects and is presented as a two-to-four-page summary of many of the highlights of the community. An *economic handbook* is meant to provide an in-depth analysis of those factors which are of prime consideration to a businessman looking for a location. As such, it should not restrict itself to being a digest of miscellaneous facts, nor should it contain extraneous statistics of no real value to someone interested in a particular subject.

An effective economic handbook should not be a puffed-up piece of propaganda; rather, it should be structured from the viewpoint of those who use it. All too often publications have been designed only to glamorize certain aspects of the community. While these publications probably serve another purpose, they do not accomplish what an economic handbook should, i.e., provide answers to the specific questions put forth by business analysts and site locators.

The creation of an economic handbook involves the preparation of an information sheet — or fact sheet — on each subject relating to the local community that may be required in preparing economic handbooks for specific locational decision-makers. A list of suggested subjects for fact sheets is presented in Exhibit 13-A. To expedite retrieval of information for a handbook, the researcher should file the fact sheets systematically after they have been produced, perhaps placing them in file folders arranged alphabetically by subject.

The small Chamber of Commerce will find that fact sheets are more useful than a complete integrated handbook. Also, the collection of individual, unbound fact sheets will allow each requested handbook to be tailor-made for its intended purpose. This flexibility permits the selection of only that information pertinent to the interests of a client with a specific information request.

People asking questions of or requesting written material from the Chamber of Commerce are often in a hurry to get answers and expect to be able to use the information immediately. If these people represent a firm considering your area for operations, the information provided could be the basis upon which evaluation and selection are made. A Chamber's inability to provide requested information could have an adverse effect on the site locators' decisions. It is therefore of prime importance to be able to provide information as quickly as possible and in the form most useful to those needing it.

The flexibility of composition inherent in the fact sheet system will allow for the constant revision of the material as parts of it become outdated. Additional material can also be added as the community expands and new data are developed.

Organizing the handbook as a collection of separate data sheets will certainly not detract from its usefulness, nor need it detract from its appearance. The use of any of several binding methods with an attractive cover will enable the collected material to be presented as professionally as through a bound volume.

In summary, the objectives of an economic handbook are:

1. To present information that provides the answers to the questions most apt to be asked about the community and the surrounding area;
2. To provide the capacity for quick and easy collection and assembly of those facts which are of particular interest to each individual recipient; and
3. To present the information in a concise, comprehensive form that will serve as an extension of the Research Department's total data collection activities.

Once a comprehensive economic handbook has been prepared, either in flexible book form or as a collection of separate exhibits, it can serve as a source of answers to the many questions asked of all Chambers. When properly maintained and updated, it serves as a continuing reference to anyone interested in the community's trends. Such a handbook will also save a great deal of the staff time otherwise spent searching for answers to the miscellaneous inquiries which consume so much of the day.

E. PROCEDURE FOR ASSEMBLING AN ECONOMIC HANDBOOK

Assume that a commercial or industrial site locator has contacted the local Chamber of Commerce and that you, the organization's researcher, are responsible for preparing an economic handbook tailored for this specific prospect. You should initially review plans for the physical features of the handbook. Its pages should be pre-punched to fit a loose-leaf, three-ring binder. There must be sufficient margin at the punched side to prevent spoilage of any text material. The three-ring binder should not exceed one-inch in thickness (this allows the handbook to be easily filled—no bulk) and in a cover which is business-like in appearance, suitable for an executive to use in a committee or directors' meeting. There is no need for gaudy designs or loud colors on the cover. You are selling your community by the *contents* of the handbook, not by its cover. Personalize the handbook by attaching to the front cover a label indicating that the handbook has been prepared specifically for a designated person or firm.

The pages may be typed and then printed by offset methods, using a clean, sharp type for a neat appearance. It is also possible by offset to reduce the size of the type and thus allow more wordage per page and a professionally typeset rather than typewritten appearance. When using such reduction, do not use paper larger than 11" x 17" for reduction to 8½" x 11". See your local offset printer for assistance; he will be of tremendous help to you in the physical preparation of your handbook.

The researcher's next step in assembling an economic handbook is to select the data items applicable to the site locator's request. Statements in preceding paragraphs of this chapter have indicated the importance of the Research Department's adaptable economic data files as the sources of information for assembling a flexible economic handbook. The specific items selected for use in a handbook, as well as the emphasis given these items, will vary substantially with the requirements of individual site locators. In order to maintain data which are both current and readily available, however, the researcher should be constantly aware of the subject categories which form the basis of a comprehensive economic handbook.

1. Geographic Location

Characteristics of a community's geographic location are usually among the items on a site locator's checklist. Fact sheets in the Chamber researcher's files should point out the location of the community in relation to other major centers and the advantages of its location. There should be information available relating to regional economics and the part the community plays in that economic structure. Any geographic assets of the community's location should also be included. Examples of these would include such factors as close proximity to a seaport, easy access to nearby markets, and a climate favorable to certain types of activities.

2. Climate

Climatic information is available from the Weather Bureau of the U.S. Department of Commerce in monthly and annual summaries of "Climatological Data" for your state. Utilizing the weather station most applicable to the local community, the researcher can enumerate the average temperature by average minimum, average mean, and average maximum for four seasons of the year — as would be indicated by the months of January, April, July, and October — as well as the average for the entire year. For the same months rainfall in inches and the humidity for morning, noon, and evening hours should also be indicated. Other information which can be used includes freeze dates and prevailing wind directions and speeds. The weather information should be based upon an average of several years' observation. In many cases the Weather Bureau is able to provide such information based upon a 20 year average. Do not use a specific month in a specific year . . . you may hit the storm of the century or the drought of the decade.

3. Economic Base

Data on the community's economic base may require the preparation of several readily-available fact sheets, including an inventory of the firms already operating in the area and discussions of the significance of each major type of business establishment in the local area's income-producing activity. Another advantageous item is an indication of the diversification of economic activity in the area.

4. Transportation

The subject of transportation is important to nearly all site locators who come to the local Chamber of Commerce offices for assistance. Use one page for each of the major forms of transportation available to your community. Why? This makes it possible to answer specific inquiries with a single sheet of information. There should be individual pages for RAIL-ROAD, MOTOR TRUCK, AIRLINES, and, if applicable, WATER WAYS. Let's examine the first three for some details:

Railroad: On one side of this sheet supply the names of the railroads serving your area, the location of offices with freight and/or industrial representatives (complete with phone numbers), the frequency of both freight and passenger service to your community, the location of local freight offices, team tracks, etc. On the reverse side present a map of your community areas showing the rail-lines, the location of freight depots and location in shading of zoned industrial areas. Your rail-roads will cooperate with you in this map preparation.

Motor Truck: Again, on one side of the sheet list the motor truck carriers serving the community, the type of service rendered and the type of motor carrier, and the location of the nearest terminal. On the reverse side indicate representative rates in common classes, both truck-load and less-than-truck-load, to overnight points from your community. The American Trucking Association and your State Trucking Association will assist you, as will local motor carriers.

Airlines: This, too, should be a single sheet. On the face, list the scheduled air carriers serving the airport nearest you, the location of offices of these airlines, and information on types of equipment available for handling air-freight. Indicate also the location of airports, the type of service available to non-scheduled air carriers and private aircraft, and information on air-freight handling capabilities. On the reverse side provide maps of local airports showing runways and taxiways and such directional information as may be used by the private aviation user. Remember that a company may wish to fly to your airport for a close look.

5. Utilities

Another major data group relates to utilities—including electricity, gas, water, sewer, and telephone. Your economic handbook will be well-prepared if each page is self-contained, one page each for each utility service. The face of each page should contain the name of the utility, the locations of its main and local offices, and the location of the offices of industrial development representatives. Representative industrial rates should be included on the face of the page. In addition to this information, in the case of industrial water, there should be included a brief summary of water condition from a recognized laboratory's analysis. The *reverse* side of each page should be a map of the zoned industrial area showing the location of lines, sizes of lines, and connections to major facilities in the utility system. A larger Chamber of Commerce with several industrial areas may use a single sheet for each area with facts on one side and a map on the other. The utility companies will assist your Chamber of Commerce in preparing such maps and compiling the required information.

6. Demography

Population data in the "ready" file should exist in both narrative and statistical form, the narrative explaining population trends by recent decades (1950-1960-1970) and within the past five or six years. Reasons for such population trends should be simply stated. There should be a passage on future population projections for the area and a current population estimate with the source indicated. The reverse side can be almost completely statistical, showing population figures for 1950-1960-1970 and projections to 1980 and 1990.

7. Taxation

An important consideration for the location of business and industry is the tax structure of the local and state governments. The researcher's files should include the types of tax information applicable to the local community: rates (state, county, city, school district, water district, etc.), method and basis of assessment, corporation taxes, state income taxes, sales taxes, and other related items.

Like the other component parts, this information should be assembled on individual pages. There should be at least two pages of tax information, one on local taxes and taxing policy-procedures and another on principal state taxes and taxing authorities. A third page could be assembled to show the comparison of taxes in your community with other communities in your economic area. Show the tax rates . . . your prospect will find out later anyway!

8. Natural Resources

Agricultural and mineral resources are important if they lie within the region around the city, or are within a favorable freight rate area for movement from other regions to processing plants within the area.

9. Labor

Labor force statistics are requested by a variety of people. Data for states, metropolitan areas, and cities are generally available through the state employment commission or from federal government publications. An analysis of the labor force by type of industry, occupation, skill, productivity, or average wages is helpful in any type of presentation. A comparison with other communities of like size can be helpful in pointing out the diversification and magnitude of workers in the Chamber's area of influence. Turnover rates, potential of unemployed workers, and perhaps some information about union activity are all appropriate for this section.

10. Government

Government facilities should be described on several pages, including a listing of local city offices, principal city officials, and telephone numbers. List the meeting dates and times for the city council, the planning commission and any other city department involved in approval of industrial or commercial investment. Obtain from the city a summary of local zoning and building regulations. These should be carefully prepared by the responsible city officials with the knowledge that they will be reproduced for general distribution.

A similar listing of information should be provided for county officials, complete with location, names, telephone numbers, meeting dates and times for specific governmental bodies, and, again, a summary of county regulations.

There should also be a listing of principal state and federal offices in the community or within reasonable driving distance from the community, complete with name, address, room number, and telephone number. This will be a useful reference within the office on many occasions.

11. Housing

Housing availability and price information is obtainable from the local Board of Realtors and should be prepared to show the current rentals of two- and three-bedroom houses. Sales prices of homes should be listed for the current calendar year but should not extend to the highest and lowest prices ever paid for homes. There should be a description of suburban areas adjacent to the community and the range of prices available within them. An indication of the hotel and motel situation in the community should also be included. In a small community, the numbers of facilities and total rooms can be listed. The name, address, and phone number of the local Board of Realtors or a similar organization should be listed in this section of the handbook.

12. Cultural Environment

The cultural aspects of the community should be represented as well as the economic characteristics. Fact sheets should be available in relation to theaters, museums, operas, art galleries, and any other civic and cultural presentations that enhance the life of the community.

13. Recreation

Recreation is an important adjunct to culture and can be treated briefly in the handbook if desired. Always of interest are professional sports teams, university athletics, and public facilities for recreation such as golf courses, tennis courts, skating rinks, parks, pools, and nearby resorts.

14. Education

An important feature of any community is its educational facilities. Universities, colleges, and public school systems warrant description. The research facilities of the institutions of higher learning and the current utilization of such research by business and industry should be described on a fact sheet for appropriate use in economic handbooks.

15. Existing Businesses

The economic handbook needs a listing of principal manufacturers and non-manufacturers within the community. This is a good list to type on 11" x 17" paper and have reduced to 8½" x 11". Be sure to include full addresses and telephone numbers (zone numbers and area numbers). If a company is a division of another company or corporation, inquire of management whether such division identification is desired. Give the principal products manufactured—or the principal operation of a non-manufacturer—and the approximate number of employees. SIC numbers should be included if available (SIC = Standard Industrial Classification of the Statistical Policy Division, U.S. Office of Management and Budget) from the companies, the state Chamber of Commerce and/or the state employment service office.

16. Map

A good map is another special feature to be included in an economic handbook. It can be reproduced on a paper 11" x 16", folded once with a one-inch allowance for three-hole punching. An offset printer can show you how the job can be assembled for greatest utility, explaining how to prepare such a map for reduction, with mileage tables, population tables, and—on the reverse side—other information for the community area. This map, by itself, can be a valuable hand-out from your Chamber of Commerce office. It will be as effective in black-and-white as it would be in multi-color. Be sure to secure permission to reproduce a map prepared for another business and to check with your printer on reproduction problems.

F. SYNOPSIS

To summarize the preparation of an economic handbook: First, the preparation of a handbook for a small Chamber of Commerce, a large Chamber of Commerce, a state or an area organization, is essentially the same. Only the complexity of the contents and the number of pages will vary.

Second, establish the ground-rules for preparation of the handbook and the circulation it will be given by your Chamber of Commerce. Specify the physical format: loose-leafed; three-hole punched; one-inch maximum thickness of binder; each page designed to stand alone as an information piece (a dual purpose); offset printed if possible, mimeographed if necessary; maps to illustrate special areas of the facts; emphasis on fact and figure—de-emphasis on words ending in "est." Be prepared to up-date the material annually. Keep a list of recipients.

Third, before assembling any of the material, secure the assistance of your state Chamber of Commerce, state employment service, utilities, railroads, motor truck lines, airlines, city government, state and county government, and local union officials in the collection of data and the preparation of maps and illustrative charts and graphs. Be sure you have permission to reproduce any material from other sources.

Fourth, ask for the loan of economic handbooks already published by Chambers of Commerce and area organizations. Examine them carefully. You will find such economic handbooks featured in the advertisements of development organizations and Chambers of Commerce in *Business Week, Dun's Review, Area Development, Industrial Development,* and similar publications. Your railroads, utilities, banks, and state Chamber of Commerce can assist you in locating representative economic handbooks for examination. Similar assistance is available from the American Industrial Development Council, Inc., and the American Chamber of Commerce Researchers Association.

Finally, be prepared for a continuing Chamber of Commerce activity once you prepare, publish, and distribute an economic handbook. From the moment the outside business world knows that you have prepared a compendium of reliable economic information on your community, you will experience a continuous demand for the handbook or some of its contents. Include in your annual budget a sum for revising and up-dating of the handbook and for the annual correction of mailing lists. This will become a permanent activity of any Chamber of Commerce—small, medium, or large—county-wide or state-wide.

This discussion has presented only a *general outline* of major data categories recommended for the researcher's use in preparing readily available fact sheets for use in economic handbooks. Exhibit 13-A is a list of *specific* data items which the researcher should have on hand to meet the needs of locational decision-makers. Once this information has been compiled, processed, and stored in appropriate files, the researcher is well on the way to having the capability for assembling a specialized economic handbook that will suit almost any specific use.

G. CONCLUSION

While the Research Department does not have the primary responsibility for the Chamber's economic development program, it does play a very significant role in this field. As a group, researchers provide the economic data used by the other staff members in their industrial and commercial development activities. The researchers prepare and publish economic reports and publications and supply statistics as they are needed.

Additionally, it is the research staff which supplies economic information to the businessmen and organizations in the local community to aid in the preparation of their economic presentations. Some of the particular types of industries which rely heavily on this assistance are utility companies, banks, construction and real estate firms, retail stores, mortgage bankers, and railroads. It is also the research staff that provides consulting service to those people who call or write the Chamber's offices or who visit in person.

Whatever the focus of the economic handbook, however it is arranged, it should be neither a collection of statistical tables and charts nor an exhaustive narrative extolling various area virtues without quantitative support. Illustrative additions such as charts and photographs may be included, but should be well-balanced by supportive narrative description and analysis.

It is highly recommended that the comprehensive handbook be organized as a collection of separate sheets of data which can be assembled in any combination and order, allowing them to be included in or deleted from each specialized handbook as desired. This flexibility enables constant revision of the book as parts become outdated, and renders it much more useful to the businessman by providing answers to his questions with a minimum of superfluous material.

A final point to remember when compiling materials to be included in this or any other Chamber publication is that all information should be factual. A high level of business and political integrity must be preserved in these materials. In any event, a detailed investigation by a businessman would reveal any compromise.

The essence of the Chamber researcher's job is response to the constant urgency for immediately available problem-solving information on a wide variety of subjects related to the local community. One of his principal responsibilities is to collect, process, and assemble data that will be useful to those who come to him for assistance. At the same time this information must be available to and appropriate for use by other Chamber staff members who are responsible for the active promotion of the community. The best economic handbook for these dual purposes is one that is assembled as a continuing, integral part of the whole system of research activities.

EXHIBIT 13-A:
CHECKLIST OF ITEMS FOR WHICH FACT SHEETS SHOULD BE PREPARED AND AVAILABLE FOR USE IN ASSEMBLING ECONOMIC HANDBOOKS

This checklist is based upon an analysis of the research information systems of approximately 80 Chambers of Commerce throughout the United States. The list shown here is a composite of the items used generally by Chamber researchers in conducting analyses of their respective communities and in compiling data for use in economic handbooks.

The role of the checklist in this research manual is to present suggestions as to the subjects for which fact sheets should be prepared. The entire list will not be appropriate for use by every Chamber of Commerce. Each researcher who plans to use this list should examine its contents carefully and delete the items that are not applicable to his community.

1. LAND AND CLIMATE
   Location and Area
   > Map of United States Showing Location of State and Region
   > Latitude, Longitude and Elevation
   > Chart of Distances to Other Cities
   Topography
   > Major Terrain Regions
   > Generalized Elevation Map
   > Principal Relief Features
   Climate
   > Temperature, Humidity, Rain, Snow and Wind
   > Historical Extremes
   > Implications for Industry
   Water
   > Selected Water Analysis
   > Average Discharge of Principal Rivers

2. MAPS
   Geographic Location (U.S., State, Region)
   City and County Limits Map
   School District Limits Map
   Industrial Site Map
   Major Thoroughfare Map
   Points of Interest Map
   Immediate Trade Territory Map
   Regional Trading Area Map

Detailed City Street Map
Shopping Centers
Population Base Map
Residential Areas
Land Use Maps
Downtown Development
Census Tracts
Base Map
Air Service
Railroad Service
Postal Zones
Major Suburbs
Standard Metropolitan Statistical Area
Highway Traffic Counts
Highway Construction
Driving Time to Principal Cities
Downtown Traffic Counts
Downtown Streets
Commercial Zone

3. HISTORY
Description
Official State Symbols

4. GOVERNMENTAL ENVIRONMENT
Form of Municipal Government
Mayor
Cabinet
City Council
City Planning
Fire Protection
Fire Insurance Classification
Police Protection
Emergency Services System
Judiciary
Streets and Expressways
Sewers
Garbage Disposal
Industrial Legislation
    Safety Inspections
    Planning and Zoning
Services to Industry
Financing
School Districts
Water Districts

Civic Attitudes
    Attitude Toward Business and Industry
    City-County Cooperation Problem Areas

5. TAXES
    Corporation & Business Taxes
        Corporation Income Tax — State
        Corporation License Tax — Municipal
        Franchise Tax
        Miscellaneous Taxes — State
        Organization & Qualifications Fees
        Property Tax — State, County, City & School
        Sales Use Tax — State
        Unemployment Insurance Tax — State
        Severance and Motor Fuel Tax
        Special Taxes
        Property Valuation
        Assessment Base
    Taxes on Individuals — State & Local
        City, County, Occupational License Tax
        County-Wide School Occupational Tax
        Income Tax Rates
        Personal Income Tax
        Property Taxes
        Sales Tax — State and City
        Property Valuation
        Tax Calendar
        Tax Advantages
        Comparative Tables
        Special Assessments
        Gasoline Tax
        List Tax Rates for Past Years and Show How They Are
          Changing

6. ECONOMIC ENVIRONMENT
    Business Indicators (See Chapter 8 for specific items)
    Personal Income
    Manufacturing
    Retail Trade
    Wholesale and Foreign Trade
    Service Activities
    Agriculture
    Financial Activities
    Economic Growth Trends

7. **RAW MATERIALS AND EXTRACTIVE RESOURCES**
   Forest Resources and Production
   Wildlife
   Mineral Resources and Production
   　　Geology
   　　Commercial Mineral Deposits
   　　Value of Mineral Production
   　　Minerals Produced in Order of Value
   　　Principal Producers

   Fish
   　　Landings
   　　　　Fish
   　　　　Shellfish
   　　Grand Totals (Pounds and Value)
   　　Fish and Seafood Processing Industries

8. **AGRICULTURE**
   Soil Suitability Chart
   Summary of Rating of Soils
   Farm Statistics

9. **MANUFACTURING**
   The Business Climate
   Manufacturing Establishments by Major Industry Groups
   Number of Manufacturing Establishments, Value Added, Payroll, and
   　　Employment
   Value Added by Manufacture for Selected Metro Areas
   Manufacturing New Capital Expenditures & Payrolls
   Employment Trends in Manufacturing
   Distribution of Employment
   Average Hourly Earnings
   Directory of Manufacturers
   Industrial Parks
   Research, Technology and Professional Services
   Natural Resources
   Manufacturers' Representatives
   Research Facilities

10. **MARKETING**
   Primary Retail Market
   Primary Manufacturers and Wholesalers Market
   International Market
   Retail Sales Statistics and Map of Trading Area
   Census of Business Retail Trade
   Census of Business Selected Services

Census of Business Wholesale Trade
Retail Stores — Central Business District
Total Annual New Car Sales
Ranking in Retail and Wholesale Sales
Shopping Center Directory
Department Store Sales
Consumer Price Index ·
Median Family Income
Economic and Demographic Data by Census Tract
Effective Buying Income
Parking Facilities

11. CONSTRUCTION
Construction Contract Awards
Construction by Types (Residential, Industrial, Commercial, etc.)
Building Permit Data — Residential and Non-Residential
Local Construction Cost Index
Housing Units Completed
Absorption Capacity of Multi-Family Residential Projects
Housing Forecast
Residential Demolitions
New Housing Units by Census Tract
Occupancy Rates
Price Ranges

12. UTILITIES
Electric Power
Natural Gas
Water (Sources, Chemical Content and Adequacy of Supply)
Coal
Fuel Oil
Garbage and Trash Disposal
Industrial Waste Regulations
Sewage Services
Telephone Rates
Rate Schedules for All Utilities
Capacity and Planned Expansion of Local Utilities

13. FINANCE
Banks in the Local Area
Industrial Development Amendment
Qualifications of Industrial Revenue Bond Issues for Tax Exempt
    Status
Savings and Loan Associations
Selected Financial Items, Savings and Loan Associations

Selected Indicators of Banking Activity
Liquid Asset Holdings
Commercial and Industrial Loans
Bank Debits
Total Demand Deposits
Total Time Deposits
Total Savings Capital
Business Failures
Availability of Mortgage Loan Money and Prevailing Interest Rates

14. TRANSPORTATION
    Airport and Airlines
        Airport Facilities (including length of runways)
        Airlines Serving Local Airport
        Average Distance Between Major Distribution Centers
        Air Passengers
        Regularly Scheduled Air Cargo Service to Other Major Centers
            from the Local Area
        Air Cargo Shipments
        Transportation Service to and from Local Airport
    Railroads
        Terminals
        Shipping Time to Other Cities
        Railroads Serving the Local Area
        Railroad Cars Loaded and Unloaded
        Railroad Switching Limits and Yard
    Trucking Service
        Terminals
        Highway System
        Motor Carriers Serving the Local Area
        Specialized Motor Carriers
        Express Rates to Other Major Centers
        Freight Delivery Time by Common Motor Truck Carriers
        Express Service
        Traffic Flow Chart
    Water Transportation
        Public Water Terminals
        Port Facilities
        Allowable Draft
        Barge Lines
        Steamship Lines
        Volume of Shipping
    Bus Service
        Terminals

　　　　Intra-City Lines Serving Area
　　　　Schedules
　　　　Bus Passengers
　　　　Volume of Bus Shipping
　　Taxi Service
　　　　Number of Cabs
　　　　Rates
　　Other Transportation-Related Items
　　　　Motor Vehicle Registrations
　　　　Auto Renting and Leasing
　　　　Freight Forwarders
　　　　Public Warehousing Facilities
　　　　Mass Transit Facilities

15. COMMUNICATIONS
Daily Newspapers and News Services
Daily Newspapers within a 150-Mile Radius
Weekly Newspapers of the Local SMSA
Foreign Language Newspapers
House Organs and Publications
Radio Stations
Television Stations
Postal Service
Telephone Service
Telegraph Service

16. RESEARCH
Engineering & Scientific Societies
Contract Research Facilities
Other Large Laboratory Facilities — Limited to Company Research
Industrial Research
Libraries
Engineering & Other Related Services
Medical & Dental Research
Supporting Services — Research & Development
Data Processing Centers
Marine Science and Research

17. POPULATION
General Characteristics
Population Growth
Density
Age and Sex Composition
Population by Census Tracts
Population by County, Minor Civil Divisions

Distribution of Working-Age Population
Marital Status
Households
Racial Characteristics
Projections
Trends, 1900-1970
Comparison of Local Community with Other Cities and/or SMSA's
   in the State, Region or U.S.
Educational Level

18. LABOR FORCE AND EMPLOYMENT
Employment by Major Classification
Characteristics of Labor Market
Availability of Labor
Organization of Labor
Unemployment Compensation
Workmen's Compensation Laws
Comparative Wage Scales – Male
Comparative Wage Scales – Female
Technical and Scientific Manpower
Work Stoppages
Area Wage Survey
Projection of Labor Force
Union Activity
Labor Education
Labor Legislation
High School Graduates
Secondary School Craft Trainees
Vocational Training
College Graduates
Labor Climate
Area Labor Market Map
Job Seekers' Guide
Firms Employing 100 or More
Unemployed as Percentage of Labor Force (quarterly for the
   past ten years)
Distribution of Labor Force by Sex, Age Group, and Ethnic
   Classification
Skills in Short Supply and Abundance
Cost of Living Index
Percentage Distribution of Major Occupational Groups

19. INCOME
Income Characteristics in Cities and Counties in the Local SMSA
Cash Income Breakdown, 30 Largest Metropolitan Areas

Cash Income Breakdown, Selected Metropolitan Areas
Total Effective Buying Income
Effective Buying Income Per Capita
Effective Buying Income Per Household

20. HOUSING
Map of Residential Areas
Residential Building Permits by Census Tract (representing intent to
    build)
New Residential Electric Connections by Census Tract (representing
    new residential units completed and connected with electricity for
    the first time; helps to develop a cumulative inventory of housing)
Residential Construction Cost Index
Residential Units Occupancy Rates
Taxes Applicable to Residential Property
Residential Utility Rates
Housing Forecast
Residential Demolitions
Absorption Capacity of Multi-Family Residential Projects
Price Ranges of Houses Currently for Sale

21. EDUCATION
Public Schools
Private Schools
Parochial Schools
Universities and Colleges
Business and Trade Schools
Qualifications of Teachers
Cost of Education Per Pupil
Capital Investment Per Pupil
Building Expansion Program
Public School Debt Per Capita

22. COMMUNITY AMENITIES
Educational, Medical, Recreational and Civic Data
Educational Facilities
        Elementary and Secondary Schools
        Universities, Colleges and Junior Colleges
Churches
Medical and Hospital Facilities
Proposed Hospital Construction
Residential Housing
Fraternal Organizations
Libraries
Recreational Facilities

Cultural Activities
Historical Attractions
Newspapers
Hotels and Motels
Restaurants and Dining Facilities
Postal Facilities
Parks
Tourist Attractions
Civic, Fraternal, Professional and Social Organizations
Entertainment Facilities
Cost of Living
    Consumer Price Index (BLS)
    Inter-City Cost of Living Index (ACCRA)
    Residential Housing Prices
    Residential Utility Rates
    Public Transit

23. SITE SELECTION
Map of Available Sites
Industrial Parks and Districts
Advantages for New Industry
Plant Location Guidelist
Industrial Team
Commercial and Industrial Brokers
Deed Restrictions
Mill Levies Applicable to Commercial and Industrial Tracts
Industry Zoning Ordinances
Community Attitude
Master Plan for Area
Financing Help Available

14 DIRECTORY OF MANUFACTURERS

A. INTRODUCTION

A manufacturers directory — a publication listing manufacturing plants within a given geographic area — is an important promotional aid to a Chamber of Commerce. The directory can serve as a guide to the established manufacturing industry within this delineated area by listing the types and numbers of manufacturing facilities, the sources of supply for various manufactured products, and the prospective users of certain types of industrial products and services. But its real potential is probably best realized in promoting new industrial development in an area. This type of directory can provide at least a part of the information needed in industrial site location studies. Economic development representatives also will find this directory useful as a sourcebook of new supply sources and users of manufactured products. Specifically, the directory will be useful in developing:

1. Information on area manufacturing potential, including identification of shortages in product supply;
2. Feasibility studies for new plants based on research showing the proximity of customers, suppliers, and raw materials;
3. A list of manufacturing executives, sales managers, and purchasing agents useful in special mailings and sales campaigns;
4. Up-to-date information on new patterns of demand resulting from new materials, new products, and new industries;
5. A list of new prospects on the basis of the products or services manufacturing firms require;
6. Small geographic area data that can be used in setting up sales territories based on census tracts; and
7. Information designed to pinpoint the potential for selected markets by census tract, by customer, and by product use.

For illustrative purposes, assume that you are the researcher for the Central City Chamber of Commerce and that you are planning to publish

267

a directory of local manufacturing plants. Assume also that you have adopted the following guidelines for this project:

1. The proposed directory will contain a listing of manufacturing plants located within the eight-county Central City region.

2. Principal components of this directory will be a company (or firm) section and a product section.

    a. *Company Section* — Each plant will be listed alphabetically by company name with information on location, personnel, organization, and products. This list forms the nucleus of the book with other sections cross-referenced as aids for using it (See Exhibit 14-A).

    b. *Product Section* — Products will be listed under major Standard Industrial Classification (SIC) group category (See Exhibit 14-B). This section can be used to determine which companies manufacture certain products. By referring to the alphabetical company list in the main section of the directory, additional information on the specific manufacturing plant can be obtained.

3. Camera-ready directory copy will be prepared on a typewriter for offset printing.

4. No advertising will be solicited. The directory is to be financed by sale of copies.

5. The directory will include listings of all manufacturing firms in the eight-county area — and will not be restricted to Chamber of Commerce members.

6. The following information will be shown for each firm listed in this directory:

    a. Type of business organization (Corporation, partnership, sole proprietorship, or estate).

    b. Parent company, if a division or subsidiary, and the headquarters address, if different from the plant address.

    c. Date the plant began operation.

    d. Location of plant by census tract or map coordinates.

    e. Name and title of principal officer.

    f. Names of sales manager and purchasing agent.

    g. Approximate number of employees in plant.

    h. Product description by four-digit SIC number.

    i. Area of product distribution.

B. DATA COLLECTION

Data collection begins with the compilation of a list of manufacturing plants within the geographic area to be covered by the directory. The source (or sources) for this list of names will vary somewhat from one area to another, but a list of sources generally should include:

1. State Industrial Commissions.
2. State and local manufacturers' associations.
3. Manufacturing section in area telephone directory's yellow pages.
4. Local and state employment commissions.
5. State Manufacturers Directory.
6. Manufacturers' agents in the area.
7. Banks.
8. Utility companies.
9. Chamber of Commerce membership lists.

The list developed from these and any other sources that may be available should be checked by persons who are familiar with the manufacturing facilities in the area, ideally a division or sub-committee of the local Chamber of Commerce Research Committee. This group should be made up of manufacturers' agents, manufacturing plant managers, utility company managers or research specialists, industrial development managers of local banks, and representatives of various agencies that publish information on segments of the manufacturing industry.

The designated group should review the preliminary list of companies, delete the non-manufacturers, and add any additional companies or information of which they are aware. Because the close review of such a committee will save the time of contacting many firms that would be eliminated later, it is crucial that the members be carefully selected.

C. CONTROLS FOR INFORMATION FLOW

The controls used to guide information through the various steps for processing are as important as the data collection itself. Elaborate control systems should be avoided, if possible; the more simple the control procedures, the more flexibility there will be in the overall information processing sequence.

A control card procedure can be very effective when used in conjunction with an account numbering system. Exhibit 14-C is an example of a control card used to record the dates of completion for various stages of processing. When a particular stage of processing is completed, the date is recorded on the control card. For different listings of manufacturing plants, different color cards can be used. For example, a blue card may represent the firms previously listed in a directory and a yellow card may represent a new listing.

To simplify the operation of recording information on control cards, the procedure should call for placing cards into different files as each operational stage is completed. The date on which a stage is completed should be recorded and the card filed in a separate stack. The remaining cards at the close of a period will represent firms for which the operational stage has not yet been completed.

In addition to a control card system, an alphabetically-sequenced set of file folders should be available for compiling and storing information about each firm to be listed in the directory.

D. COMPILING DATA FOR LISTINGS

Once the mailing list review is complete, the actual survey can begin. The survey will be only as effective as the questionnaire and cover letter which are its instruments; these should be designed to obtain the best possible response from the representatives of the manufacturing firms.

Assuming that you have elected to gather the information noted earlier in this chapter, Exhibit 14-D will provide a good example of an effective questionnaire. This form is to be used to gather initial information on new firms. It is important that the firm name be noted at the top of each sheet, as a company which has enacted a recent name change would not be recognized as the original firm listed on the mailing list.

Another type of questionnaire could be used for firms that have been previously listed in a directory. This form should call for an updating of the information listed in the previous edition (See Exhibit 14-G). Notice how much of the information listed has been coded to abbreviate the directory listing.

Exhibit 14-E is a cover letter relating to the new firms being surveyed with the Exhibit 14-D questionnaire, and Exhibit 14-F is a similar letter relating to the old firms being surveyed with the Exhibit 14-G questionnaire. The wording of cover letters can be changed to fit the circumstances. Exhibit 14-H is an example of a follow-up letter asking for information from a previously listed firm that has not responded to a request for updated information. Other variations of the same letter, such as a personal letter to a particular firm or a letter for special types of information, can be developed to fit special circumstances.

Alternatively, the combination cover letter/questionnaire style can be used to correct or "proof" information already collected and processed. Exhibit 14-I is an example of such a combination style.

E. PROCESSING DATA FOR LISTINGS

As information is received from manufacturing firms, it is channeled into the system for processing. Basic steps in completing this processing include:

1. Recording the receipt of the questionnaire by stamping the date received on the control card and the questionnaire; then checking for duplication of existing firms.
2. Checking information on the questionnaire to see if the firm is manufacturing in the area; if not, mark it non-manufacturer and pull the control card for filing in non-manufacturing group.

3. Recording the account number on the control card and questionnaire.

4. Assigning census tract number or other geographical designation on the questionnaire.

5. Checking the list of manufactured products and assigning four-digit Standard Industrial Classification numbers to products. The reference to be used for classifying products is the latest edition of the *Standard Industrial Classification Manual,* published by the Executive Office of the President, Office of Management and Budget.

6. Assembling on a processing form (Exhibit 14-J) all information for each firm's listing, including all coded items to be included in the listing.

7. Typing listings as prescribed by space limitations designed for printing purposes.

8. Proofreading typed listings by comparing them to the original form questionnaires.

9. Compiling an alphabetical file of typed listings to be part of a complete file on each firm containing original questionnaire, handwritten information, processing form, and typed listing.

10. When the final survey is completed and all firms have been recorded, the typed listings should be in one continuous alphabetical list, with cross-references inserted among the listings.

    a. The company section of the directory is prepared by typing the alphabetical list of companies and cross-references developed from the final survey information (See Exhibit 14-A).

    b. The product section of the directory is prepared by clipping the company listings, and pasting them on cards to be sorted by product classification. From this sorting, companies can be grouped alphabetically under each product classification as shown on Exhibit 14-B, thus identifying firms by types of products manufactured.

11. Electronic data processing of information can greatly expand the flexibility of the directory, but converting the information from a typed listing to key punch cards without lessening control may be time consuming. A data sheet — devised to make the transfer as simple and errorless as possible — will aid the conversion process. Exhibit 14-K is an example of the conversion of information into a usable form for the keypunch operator.

F. DATA CLASSIFICATION

The suggested classification system to be used in preparing listings for the manufacturers directory is the Standard Industrial Classification (SIC) developed to identify establishments by type of activity in which they are engaged. This classification facilitates the tabulation, presentation and analysis of data related to establishments and promotes uniformity and comparability in the presentation of statistical data collected by various agencies.

Features of the recommended classification procedures are described in a number of publications, including:

1. *Standard Industrial Classification Manual,* prepared by the Executive Office of the President, Office of Management and Budget. This publication describes the Standard Industrial Classification and the industrial code assignment procedures. In describing the code assignment the manual states: "Each establishment is assigned an industry code on the basis of its major activity which is determined by the product or group of products produced or handled, or services rendered." The classification makes it possible to identify establishments by industry on a two-, three-, or four-digit basis, according to the degree of detail in information needed. Major groups are identified on a two-digit basis combining groups or industries and further sub-divisions are made for three-digit and four-digit codes.

2. *Alphabetic Index of Manufactured Products,* Census of Manufactures (latest edition), U.S. Department of Commerce, Bureau of the Census. This booklet provides a list of manufactured products, in alphabetical order and coded to the full 7-digit level in the Census of Manufactures, for use as an index to manufactured products.

3. *Numerical List of Manufactured Products,* Census of Manufactures, U.S. Department of Commerce, Bureau of the Census. This numerical list contains the principal products and services of the manufacturing industries in the United States arranged (generally in ascending numerical order) within their respective product classes, the product classes in order with their industries, and the industries within their groups and major groups.

Before searching through any of these publications for a product code, the company in question should be identified as a legitimate local manufacturer of the products listed on his questionnaire (see Exhibit 14-D). The first question to be answered by the firm is: "Do you manufacture a product at this location?" If the answer is "no," then the classification process is completed by listing the firm as a non-manufacturer on the corresponding control card and discarding the firm's data sheet.

If the firm's representative indicates that the firm does manufacture products in the local area, then the products must be identified (normally trade names are not used) and the proper four-digit code applied to the product or group of products. The alphabetic index of products booklet should be used first since the alphabetical sequence of products makes it simpler to locate products and the index number. The *Standard Industrial Classification Manual* should be checked also for verification of the classification code assignment.

G. DIRECTORY FORMAT

The directory should include at least two principal sections.

1. *Alphabetical List of Manufacturing Plants.* This section should include a full description of each plant listed in the directory (See Exhibit 14-A).

2. *Alphabetical List of Manufacturing Plants Classified by Product* (using SIC codes). This section should contain the appropriate SIC manufacturing group categories, with alphabetical lists of manufacturers by four-digit SIC number and key product manufactured by each plant. Each two-digit major group group should include a numerically sequenced list of four-digit SIC codes and an alphabetical list of manufacturing plants classified under each heading. Exhibit 14-B is an example of the product classification list.

In addition to these two sections, the directory should contain a table of contents identifying by page each of the major sections and a listing of the four-digit SIC numbers with a short description of the types of products found under each classification number.

Other important features to be included in the directory are a brief glossary and an explanation of the coding system used for the directory, thereby minimizing confusion for users. Exhibit 14-L is an illustration of this section.

EXHIBIT 14-A:
ALPHABETICAL LIST
OF MANUFACTURING PLANTS

A & B ENTERPRISE: 8315 Manchester; P.O. Box 5254; 77012; 926-1293; CT-321; Corp.; 1970; X-1; C; PO: Bobby H. Hataway; wooden pallets 2499

AB LADDER CO.: 2226 Telephone Rd.; 77023; 926-7448; CT-309; SP; 1954; X-4; B; PO: J. R. Pledger, Pres.; wood ladders 2499; aluminum ladders 3499; wood moldings 2431

A & B METAL MFG. CO., INC.: 1213 Durham; P.O. Box 21198; 77026; 861-9121; CT-518; Corp.; 1956; X-7; C; PO: Gus A. Albers, Pres.; tungsten carbide 3291; tungsten carbide castings, inserts, welding rods 3369

ABC PRINTING & STATIONERY CO.: 321 Franklin; P.O. Box 4202; 77014; 227-8321; CT-121; PO: D. L. Ballich; engraving 2753; printing 2751; plastic laminated cards 3079

ABC VENETIAN BLIND CO.: 1127 Yale; 77008; 862-2208; CT-512; SP; 1960; X-1; B; PO: Wilton W. Varderman; venetian blinds 2591

A AMERICAN STAMP & NOVELTY MFG. CO.: 1031 Richmond; 77006; 524-8243; CT-404; Corp.; 1934; X-7; C; PO: G. A. Burbridge, Pres.; SM: Gifford O. Burbridge; PA: Tillman C. Turner; plastic name plates and tags 3079; metal name plates and tags 3993; badges, decalcomanias 2752

A-1 INCINERATOR: 2814 N. Main; 77009; 225-9503; CT-503; SP: 1971; X-5; A; PO: David Evans, Pres.; commercial & industrial incinerators 3433

A-1 SHEET METAL CO.: 7921 Lyons Ave.; 77029; 672-9721; CT-203; SP; 1946; X-1; C; PO: H. P. Schneider; sheet metal products 3444

AAA LEAD FABRICATING CO.: 503 Melbourne St.; P.O. Box 430; 77028; 692-6168; CT-509; 1966; X-1; B; PO: W. W. Sullivan, Jr., Gen. Mgr.; lead products for plumbing industry 3431

AAA NEON SIGN CO.: 6102 Flintlock; 77040; 462-1892; CT-529; SP; 1953; X-2; A; PO: E. W. McDonald; neon signs 3993

ABCO ALUMINUM & BRASS WORK, INC.: 5235 Griggs Rd.; 77021; 643-4361; CT-314; Corp.; 1946; X-6; D; PO: T. Q. Garrett, Jr., Pres.; aluminum castings 3361; bronze & brass castings 3362

A & D PACKAGING & CRAT-
ING CO.: 6620 Dixie Dr.; P.O.
Box 33088; 77033; 643-9459;
CT-325; SP; 1966; X-7; D; PO:
L. E. Atnip, custom crates 2441

A. E. MACHINE WORKS: 1211
Gibbs; P. O. Box 8866; 77009;
864-2790; CT-511; SP; 1966; X-1;
A; PO: A. E. Herbrich; custom
machined parts 3599

A. I. F., INC.: 6700 Liberty Rd.;
77028; 674-8431; CT-208; Corp.;
1970; X-7; F; PO: R. D. Doesch-
ner, Pres.; miscellaneous steel
fabricators 3443; fired heaters
3567

A & M SHEET METAL CO.: 2109
Lou Ellen; 77018; 682-3696; CT-
518; SP; 1947; X-4; C; PO: Jerry
Mills, Mgr.; sheet metal products
3444

AMF TUBOSCOPE, INC., SUB.
OF AMF INCORPORATED:
2727 Holmes Rd.; P.O. Box 808;
77001; 748-1300; CT-330; Corp.;
1939; X-7; L; PO: R. A. Lahr,
Pres.; SM: R. J. Witten; PA:
Art Levin; plastic coatings
3479

EXHIBIT 14-B:
ILLUSTRATION OF
PLANT CLASSIFICATION BY PRODUCT

MANUFACTURING PLANTS CLASSIFIED BY PRODUCT

MAJOR GROUP 19:
ORDNANCE & ACCESSORIES

1999   *Ordnance & Accessories,*
       Not Elsewhere Classified

Kexplore, Inc.; bullet pullers,
   powder funnels, muzzle brakes
Wanda Cartridge Co.; plastic
   shotgun shells

MAJOR GROUP 20:
FOOD & KINDRED PRODUCTS

2011   *Meat Packing Plants*

Armour & Co.; packing house
   products
B & W Meat Co.; meats
Blue Ribbon Packing Co.;
   dressed beef & veal products
Broussard Packing Co.; meat
   processing
City Custom Packing Co.; custom
   slaughtering
Foster Wholesale Meat Co.; fresh
   & frozen meats
Freedman Bros. Packing Co.;
   meat packing
Hormel, Geo. A., & Co.; meat
   packing
Kay Packing Co., Plt. No. 1;
   meats
M & M Packing Co.; meat
   packing
Main Packing Co.; meat packing

Morehead Packing Plt.; meat
   processing
Nelkin Packing Co.; meat
   packing
Paul & Bills Quality Meats;
   smoked link sausage
Polk Packing Co.; pickled meats,
   sliced ham & luncheon meats
Rath Packing Co.; meat products
Rayner Packing Co.; smoked &
   fresh sausage
Sauer, E. L., & Sons; meat
   processing
Woushatta Packing Co.; sausage,
   wholesale meat

2013   *Sausages & Other Prepared*
       Meat Products

Blue Ribbon Packing Co.;
   sausage
Carlton Food Products, Inc.; of
   Central City; headcheese,
   sausage
Handy Meat Co.; meat
   processing
Hubbell & Sons Food Products,
   Inc., sausage
LaPoblana Food Products;
   sausage
Swift & Co.; meat processing

2015   *Poultry & Small Game*
       Dressing & Packing, Whole-
       sale

City Poultry Processing Co., Inc.;
 poultry processing
Hills Fish & Oyster Co.; dressed
 poultry
Jones Poultry & Egg Co.; processed poultry
Rayner Packing Co.; smoked
 turkeys

2021   *Creamery Butter*

Westmoreland Farm Dairy;
 butter

2022   *Cheese, Natural & Processed*

Stallings Head Cheese Co.; hog
 head cheese

2024   *Ice Cream & Frozen Desserts*

Borden, Inc.; ice cream, ices
Camellia Ice Cream Co., Inc.; ice
 cream, mellorine
Melton Model Dairy, Inc.; ice
 cream, mellorine, ice cream
 sherbets

EXHIBIT 14-C:
CONTROL CARD
FOR PROCESSING LISTINGS

Central City
Manufacturers Directory

Account Number: _____ Old _____ New

- -

Firm _____

Listing Form   Listing Form
   Mailed _____   Returned _____

Processing Form   Processing Form
   Completed _____   Proofread _____

Listing Typed _____   Listing Proofread _____

Listing Mailed for Final Revision _____

Final Revision Returned _____

Final Typing of Listing _____

EXHIBIT 14-D:
SUGGESTED FORM TO OBTAIN INFORMATION ABOUT A PLANT THAT HAS NOT BEEN LISTED IN THIS DIRECTORY PREVIOUSLY

Please Complete and Return This Form to:
Research Department, Central City Chamber of Commerce

1. DOES YOUR FIRM MANUFACTURE A PRODUCT AT THIS LOCATION? _____ Yes _____ No

2. LOCAL PLANT:

Name _____

Street & No. _____ City _____ County _____

Telephone No. _____ Box No. (if any) _____ Zip Code _____

3. LOCAL SALES OFFICE: (Fill out only if different from Number 2 above.)

Name _____

Street & No. _____ City _____ County _____

Telephone No._____ Box No._____ Zip Code _____ State _____

4. HOME OFFICE: (Fill out only if different from Number 2 above.)

Name _____

Street & No. _____ Zip Code ____ City ____ County _____ State _____

5. TYPE OF ORGANIZATION: _____ Sole Prop: _____
Partnership: _____ Corp.: _____ Estate: _____ Other:_____

6. YEAR THIS PLANT WAS ESTABLISHED: _____

7. NUMBER OF EMPLOYEES IN THIS PLANT AT PEAK PRODUCTION: _____

8. EXECUTIVES OF THIS PLANT:

   Principal Officer's Name _____ Title _____

   Sales Manager's Name _____

   Purchasing Agent's Name _____

9. DISTRIBUTION OF PRODUCTS: _____ County; _____ District
   (several counties); _____ State; _____

   Regional (several states); _____ National; _____ International

10. PRODUCTS MANUFACTURED OR PROCESSED AT THIS
    PLANT: (Give complete description; use other side of this sheet if
    necessary.)

   _____

                              Signed _____

                              Title   _____

EXHIBIT 14-E: SUGGESTED COVER LETTER TO PLANTS THAT HAVE NOT BEEN LISTED IN THIS DIRECTORY PREVIOUSLY

To the Chief Executives of Manufacturing
Establishments in the Central City Region:

        Re: Your listing, *at no cost to you,* in the
                Central City Manufacturers Directory.

     The Research Department of the Central City Chamber of Commerce is conducting a firm-by-firm survey of all manufacturing establishments in the Central City region in order to compile and publish an updated edition of this widely used Directory. For your listing, please complete and return to us the attached form within ten days.

     Our Manufacturers Directory lists all plants in Brown, Casper, Fremont, Gaines, Hunt, Llano, Monroe, and Walberg Counties. The Directory, published by the Central City Chamber of Commerce, is a major marketing and promotional tool for suppliers and purchasers of products and services in this region.

     The publication of an accurate listing of your establishment in this Directory is important to your firm and to the continued expansion of the Central City region's economy. *There is no charge for this listing.*

                     Cordially,

_____

EXHIBIT 14-F: SUGGESTED COVER LETTER TO PLANTS THAT WERE LISTED IN THE LATEST EDITION OF THIS DIRECTORY

To the Chief Executives of Manufacturing
   Establishments in the Central City Region:

Re: Your review and revision, as necessary, of your
listing in the next edition of the Central City
Manufacturers Directory, *at no cost to you.*

The Research Department of the Central City Chamber of Commerce is conducting a firm-by-firm survey of all manufacturing establishments in the Central City region in order to compile and publish an up-dated edition of this widely used Directory.

We urgently need your review and revision of your firm's listing as it appeared in the latest edition of this directory. Mark your corrections on the listing form as necessary to bring it up-to-date.

Please return your listing to us by ———————————— *with or without changes.*

Our Manufacturers Directory lists all manufacturing plants in Brown, Casper, Fremont, Gaines, Hunt, Llano, Monroe, and Walberg Counties. The Directory, published by the Central City Chamber of Commerce, is a major marketing and promotional tool for suppliers and purchasers of products and services in this region.

The publication of an accurate listing of your establishment in this Directory is important to your firm and to the continued expansion of the Central City region's economy. *There is no charge for this listing.*

Cordially,

————————————————

EXHIBIT 14-G: SUGGESTED FORM FOR UPDATING A LISTING THAT APPEARED IN THE LATEST EDITION OF THIS DIRECTORY

Please Return This Form
EVEN IF NO CORRECTIONS ARE MADE to:
Research Department, Central City Chamber of Commerce

---

1. THIS IS THE LISTING OF YOUR FIRM THAT APPEARED IN OUR PREVIOUS DIRECTORY. PLEASE CHECK IT AND NOTE ANY NECESSARY CHANGES IN THE SPACE PROVIDED OR ON A SEPARATE SHEET.

(Include Names of Principal Officer,
Sales Manager, and Purchasing Agent)

Information in the Listing is self-explanatory except for the coded items. These coded items indicate the following:

Item One: CENSUS TRACT NUMBER: CT (No verification is necessary.)

Item Two: FORM OF ORGANIZATION:

SP — Sole Proprietorship   Corp — Corporation
Part — Partnership   Est — Estate

Item Three: YEAR PLANT WAS ESTABLISHED AT THIS LOCATION.

Item Four: AREA OF PRODUCT DISTRIBUTION:

X-1 — County-Wide   X-3 — State-Wide   X-5 — International
X-2 — Several Counties   X-4 — National

Item Five: NUMBER OF EMPLOYEES:

A	1 —	3	I	400 —	499
B	4 —	8	J	500 —	749
C	9 —	24	K	750 —	999
D	25 —	49	L	1000 —	1999
E	50 —	99	M	2000 —	2999
F	100 —	199	N	3000 —	3999
G	200 —	299	O	4000 —	4999
H	300 —	399	P	5000 —	plus

Item Six: STANDARD INDUSTRIAL CLASSIFICATION: (The one or more numbers at the end of the product description are the classifications which apply to your products. No verification is necessary.)

___

2. IF YOUR FIRM HAS A HOME OFFICE, OTHER THAN THE LOCATION OF THIS PLANT, PLEASE GIVE THE NAME OF FIRM AND ADDRESS BELOW:

Firm _____

Street & No. or Box _____

City _____

State _____

Zip Code _____

Signed: _____

Title: _____

EXHIBIT 14-H: SECOND REQUEST FOR RETURN OF LISTING QUESTIONNAIRE

To the Chief Executives of Manufacturing
Establishments in the Central City Region:

Re: Your review and revision, as necessary, of your listing
in the next edition of the Central City Area Manufacturers Directory, *at no cost to you.*

The Research Department of the Central City Chamber of Commerce is
conducting a firm-by-firm survey of all manufacturing establishments in
the Central City region in order to compile and publish an up-dated edition
of this widely used Directory.

The listing in the enclosed form has been taken from the previous edition
of the Directory. *Please review the listing, mark on the form to bring it
up-to-date, and return it to us by _____. If there are no
changes, please note "no change" and send the form to us.*

Our Manufacturers Directory lists all manufacturing plants in Brown,
Casper, Fremont, Gaines, Hunt, Llano, Monroe, and Walberg Counties.
The Directory, published by the Central City Chamber of Commerce, is a
major marketing and promotional tool for suppliers and purchasers of
products and services in this region.

This is our second request to your office in our endeavor to compile and
publish an up-dated edition. The information you furnish will determine
the adequacy and accuracy of your listing in this directory. *There is no
charge for this listing.*

Cordially,

_____

EXHIBIT 14-I:
PROOF SHEET FOR DIRECTORY LISTING

Please check the attached proof for your listing. If the proof is correct, it will not be necessary to return it; however, if you wish to make corrections, indicate them and return the corrected proof to: Central City Chamber of Commerce, Research Department. Your listing will be printed as shown here if this proof or other notification has not been received in this office by: _____.

           (date)

Here is an explanation of the symbols used in the listings:

Item One: CENSUS TRACT NUMBER: CT (no verification is necessary)

Item Two: FORM OF ORGANIZATION:

SP — Sole Proprietorship   Corp — Corporation
Part — Partnership   Est — Estate

Item Three: YEAR PLANT WAS ESTABLISHED

Item Four: AREA OF PRODUCT DISTRIBUTION:

X-1 — County-Wide   X-4 — National
X-2 — Several Counties   X-5 — International
X-3 — State

Item Five: NUMBER OF EMPLOYEES:

A	1	—	3	I	400 — 499	
B	4	—	8	J	500 — 749	
C	9	—	24	K	750 — 999	
D	25	—	49	L	1000 — 1999	
E	50	—	99	M	2000 — 2999	
F	100	—	199	N	3000 — 3999	
G	200	—	299	O	4000 — 4999	
H	300	—	399	P	5000 — plus	

Item Six: STANDARD INDUSTRIAL CLASSIFICATION: (The one or more numbers in parentheses in the product description are the classifications which apply to your product. No verification is necessary.)

EXHIBIT 14-J:
PROCESSING FORM
FOR DIRECTORY LISTING

DIRECTORY OF CENTRAL CITY AREA MANUFACTURERS

Firm Name: _____

Street Address: _____

P.O. Box No.: _____

City: _____

Zip Code: _____

County: _____

Telephone: _____

Census Tract: _____

Home Office Name: _____

Home Office Mailing
    Address: _____

Home Office City
    and State: _____

Form of Organization: _____

Year Plant Established
    at this Location: _____

Area of Prod. Dist.: _____

No. of Employees: _____

Prin. Off. and Title: _____

Sales Mgr.: _____

Purchasing Agt.: _____

Product(s) and SIC: _____

EXHIBIT 14-K:
PREPARATION OF LISTING INFORMATION FOR ELECTRONIC DATA PROCESSING

6	6	1	4	1	1	4	
Account Number	Census Tract	Type Bus.	Year Estab.	Dist. Area	No. Empl.	S.I.C.	Description
240100	1116.02	1	1940	7	M	2812	sodium hydroxide
						2815	benzene
						2819	ammonia
						2821	epoxy resins

Doss Chemical Co.

P.O.Box 4391

Central City

45621 (zip code)

238-2951 (tel. no.)

STATE: 039   COUNTY: 141

EXHIBIT 14-L:
INSTRUCTIONS FOR USING THIS
DIRECTORY OF MANUFACTURING PLANTS

HOW TO USE THIS DIRECTORY

Part I of this directory is an alphabetical listing of the Central City Area manufacturing plants. In each of these listings the street address at which the plant is located and/or the post office box number are shown first. The post office zone number appears in parentheses following the address. All addresses are Central City addresses unless the names of other cities are shown.

The next items included in the firm's listing in Part I are telephone number (for plants located in Central County), census tract number (for plants located in Central County; see census tract maps, Figs. 2 and 3), home address (if different from Central City Area plant address), the form of business organization, the year the plant was established in the Central City eight-county region, the area over which the products of the plant are distributed, and an alphabetical symbol to indicate the number of employees.

The type of business organization is abbreviated as follows:

Corp — Corporation   SP — Sole Proprietorship
Part — Partnership   Est — Estate

The code for area of product distribution is as follows:

X-1 — County-Wide   X-4 — National
X-2 — Several Counties   X-5 — International
X-3 — State

The number of employees in a plant is indicated by this code:

A	1	—	3	I	400	— 499
B	4	—	8	J	500	— 749
C	9	—	24	K	750	— 999
D	25	—	49	L	1,000	— 1,999
E	50	—	99	M	2,000	— 2,999
F	100	—	199	N	3,000	— 3,999
G	200	—	299	O	4,000	— 4,999
H	300	—	399	P	5,000	— plus

Other information presented for each firm in Part I includes name and title of principal officer (PO), name of sales manager (SM), name of purchasing agent (PA), description of products, and Standard Industrial Classification number.

Under each classification in Part II of this directory is a listing of the firms that manufacture products included in the classification. The name of the firm is followed by the product description.

15 RETAIL TRADE AREA DELINEATION

A. INTRODUCTION

Today as never before retailers need factual yardsticks to appraise characteristics of their markets. Keen competition and mounting costs, along with many other factors, make it vital that businessmen focus intelligently upon trade area analysis.

If a market area is to be analyzed effectively, researchers must compile and interpret accurate, meaningful data relating to the characteristics of a delineated geographic trade area, including economic base, socioeconomic variables, transportation facilities and topographical features. The currently accepted definition of the term "trade area" is "a district whose size is usually determined by the boundaries within which it is economical in terms of volume and cost for a marketing unit to sell and/or deliver a good or service."[1]

A community's trade area delineation:

1. *Provides a framework for testing a firm's marketing methods.* A retail firm's sales performance in comparison with its sales potential within the trade area indicates the effectiveness level of the firm's merchandising program.
2. *Provides a framework for community comparison.* Retailers want to know if the local community is receiving its share of sales within the boundaries of the territory identified as the local trade area. If the community is not receiving its share, local businessmen want to know why and what can be done to stimulate the market. If the community is receiving more than its share, retailers want to know

---

[1]American Marketing Association, Committee on Definitions. *Marketing Definitions: A Glossary of Marketing Terms.* Chicago: American Marketing Association, 1960.

why, and how the advantage can be retained and improved upon. Since it is possible for a community to be drawing customers from adjacent communities and simultaneously losing sales to the same or other adjacent communities, the businessmen must be aware of current trade patterns. A trade area delineation expedites the accumulation of analytical data needed in studies of these types.

3. *Assists in advertising campaigns.* Retailers may find data compiled for the trade area useful in planning print and electronic media advertising schedules.

4. *Increases the utility of the researcher's data-compilation "tool kit."* The local Chamber of Commerce frequently is confronted with the necessity of assembling data relating to the economic potential of the community's trade area. Such information may be required for a wide variety of industrial and commercial development activities.

Variations in retail sales among adjacent cities have been the subject of systematic mathematical research. The best-known authors in this field are William J. Reilly, Paul D. Converse and David L. Huff.

B. REILLY'S "LAW OF RETAIL GRAVITATION"

Reilly's studies, begun in 1927, were concerned with a method of measuring the retail trade influence of a city. The original law Reilly developed stated that two cities attract trade from a smaller town situated between them in direct proportion to the population of the two cities and in inverse proportion to the square of the respective distances of the intermediate town from these two cities.[2] In other words, the pulling power of a town increases as the population increases: the larger the town, the larger its pulling power. Likewise, as the distance from a large town increases, the pulling power of the town decreases: the farther away from a town a person lives, the less inclined he will be to drive the distance into the town to shop.

Empirically, distance appears to be the more important consideration in measuring pulling power, as a person who lives two miles from the town will be only one-fourth as likely to drive into town as a person who lives one mile from town. A person who lives four miles from town would be only one-sixteenth as likely to make his trip.

In short then, Reilly's evidence indicated that the population of a city and the distance from that city to another city are the most important

---

[2]William J. Reilly, "Methods for Study of Retail Relationships." University of Texas, Bureau of Business Research, Research Monograph No. 4 (1929).

factors that condition the volume of retail trade of the first city. "Reilly's Law" can be expressed by the following formula:

$$\frac{Ba}{Bb} = \left[\frac{Pa}{Pb}\right] \left[\frac{Db}{Da}\right]^2 \quad \text{where}$$

Ba is the proportion of the trade from the smaller intermediate city attracted by City A,

Bb is the proportion attracted by City B,

Pa is the population of City A,

Pb is the population of City B,

Da is the distance from intermediate town to City A, and

Db is the distance from intermediate town to City B.

To illustrate this technique, assume that City A, population 25,000, is located 50 miles from Intermediate City C. City B, population 14,060, is 75 miles from City C. Using Reilly's formula to determine the relative amounts of City C's trade that Cities A and B should draw, the equation would be:

$$\frac{Ba}{Bb} = \left[\frac{25,000}{14,060}\right] \left[\frac{75}{50}\right]^2 = \left[\frac{25,000}{14,060}\right] \left[\frac{5625}{2500}\right] = (1.778)(2.25) = 4.01$$

This means that City A should attract four times as much trade from City C as does City B. Since City A attracts 4/5 of the trade and City B attracts 1/5 of the trade, the relative percentages are 80% and 20%.

The points to be remembered in doing this analysis are that Reilly's formula will give only the relative proportions of trade that two large cities will attract from a smaller intermediate town, not the absolute amounts. Nor does it imply that the larger cities will siphon all the trade away from the smaller town. The formula concerns only the trade that will be going out of the town anyway. Finally, this is only an approximation of how the trade will be distributed, *all other things being equal.*

Reilly based his work on empirical research, but such additional factors as ease of access, types of stores, parking facilities, city image, classes of merchandise, and the price level of each city might alter this theoretical distribution in a given area.

C. CONVERSE'S MODIFICATION OF THE "LAW OF RETAIL GRAVITATION"

A significant modification of "Reilly's Law" was made by Paul D. Converse.[3] By a slight change in the original formula, he made it possible to calculate the approximate point between two competing cities where the trading influence of each is equal. This equality point is the *breaking point*. Once this point is estimated, a city's retail trading area can be delineated by calculating and then connecting the breaking points between it and competing cities in its region. The breaking point formula derived by Converse is:

$$\text{The Breaking Point Between City A and City B in Miles From A} = \frac{\text{Distance in Miles Between A and B}}{1 + \sqrt{\dfrac{\text{Population of City B}}{\text{Population of City A}}}}$$

where City A is the one for which the trade area is being determined.

A sample problem demonstrating how the retail trading area for fictitious City A would be drawn, using calculations based on Converse's formula, is shown in Chart 15-A and Tables 15-A and 15-B. As an additional illustration, the procedure for calculating City A's breaking point in relation to City B follows:

Dab is the distance from City A to City B, or 47 miles,
Pa is the population of City A, or 345,000,
Pb is the population of City B, or 11,900, and
Da is the breaking point between Cities A and B, in miles from A, which must be calculated.

$$Da = \frac{Dab}{1 + \sqrt{Pb/Pa}} = \frac{47}{1 + \sqrt{11,900/345,000}} = 39.7 \text{ miles}$$

This means that the breaking point, or the point where Cities A and B exert equal trade influence, is 39.7 miles from A in the direction of B. Once the breaking points between City A and all other surrounding cities have been computed and placed on a map, the approximate retail trading area for City A can be shown by connecting the points. The actual calculations for computing these breaking points for City A are shown in Table 15-B. Chart 15-A shows the trade area for City A delineated using this method.

---

[3]P. D. Converse, "New Laws of Retail Gravitation." *Journal of Marketing,* (October, 1949), Vol. 14, No. 3, 379-384.

D. HUFF'S ALTERNATIVE SYSTEM FOR DELINEATING RETAIL TRADE AREAS

David L. Huff was another major author who worked on a mathematical trade area delineation technique.[4] Huff felt that there were certain conceptual limitations to the Converse model, and he pointed out specifically that the breaking point system is incapable of providing graduated estimates above or below the break-even point between two competing cities. That is, Converse's formula shows only the point where the two cities exert equal influence; it does not provide a means of calculating the total demand for the products or services of a particular area. Secondly, in multi-trading area delineations some areas would over-lap several times and some areas would not be covered at all.

Huff attempted to correct these limitations by constructing an alternative model the principal focus of which is the consumer rather than the characteristics of the town. His objective is to describe how consumers choose among their alternatives to obtain goods and services.

Variables represented in Huff's complicated formula include the size of shopping areas, travel time involved on shopping trips, and an empirically estimated parameter that reflects the effect of travel time on various kinds of shopping excursions. As a result of his research, Huff re-defines a trade area to be "a geographically delineated region, containing potential customers for whom there exists a probability greater than zero of their purchasing a given class of products or services offered for sale by a particular firm or by a particular aggregation of firms."

The difference between Huff's definition and that given in the beginning of this chapter is obvious. The first operates from the assumption that population and distance determine an area's trading influence and therefore its trade limits. Huff operates from the demand side saying that, ultimately, consumers decide where they will trade, and these decisions determine the strength of an area. If consumers are willing to travel to one trade center more than another, it will be the stronger and will have wider limits.

E. ABC RETAIL TRADING ZONE

As an alternative to using the mathematical techniques, the simplest method for determining a city's retail trade area utilizes the definition supplied by the Audit Bureau of Circulations, usually known as the ABC. The ABC is a tri-partite, non-profit, self-regulatory organization of advertisers, advertising agencies, and publishers formed to verify the circulation figures

---

[4]David L. Huff, "Defining and Estimating a Trade Area." *Journal of Marketing*, (July, 1964), Vol. 28, 34-38.

of member publishers. Before this organization was formed in 1914 newspapers were publicizing inflated circulation figures to lure potential advertisers. The Audit Bureau was formed to correct this unfavorable situation by auditing and verifying the newspapers' circulations, thereby providing assurance to advertisers that they would actually reach the number of readers promised.

In addition to verifying total circulation, one of the services provided by the ABC is a useful area analysis of circulation to households. Using this information, ABC has defined those areas of newspaper "penetration," and subsequent advertising penetration, as *retail trading zones.* These zones, which are defined according to ABC standards using census population reports and proven household newspaper circulation, approximate the trading areas for each town.

ABC's retail trading zones are defined in terms of county and subcounty units. When a county must be split, it is done along census tract boundaries. Delineating zones along those lines makes it easier to place the boundaries on an area map, simplifying further demographic analysis of the trading zone with census data.

For additional information about ABC retail trading zones, contact your local newspaper or write to Audit Bureau of Circulations, 123 Wacker Drive, Chicago, Illinois 60606.

F. USING MAP SURVEYS TO DELINEATE RETAIL TRADE AREAS

Another alternative approach to trade area delineation is to develop a map showing the composite trade area of the retail stores in your community. The best way to do this is to supply representatives of the selected retail outlets with copies of the same map and ask each participant to draw his firm's trade area on the map.

After the individual store maps have been collected, the researcher should transfer the boundary of each store's trade area onto a composite map to determine the community's approximate retail trade area. The extreme or farthest individual trade boundaries will not necessarily circumscribe the right area. The researcher should visually inspect the composite map and then select the consensus boundary—the line that appears to be most representative of the boundaries sketched by the participating retailers.

A gridded map—divided into numbered microgeographic zones— is a useful variation of this technique. Analysis of the gridded map involves counting the number of times each grid section is included in the trade areas of individual stores. The next step is to establish guidelines for delineating primary, secondary and tertiary trade areas. For example, the combination of map-grid zones which is in the trade area of 30% or more of the local retailers might be designated the community's primary trade area. The area serviced by 15% to 29.9% of the sample firms could be referred to as a secondary trade area; "tertiary area" is an appropriate descriptive term for the territory served by 5% to 14.9% of the community's retailers.

G. MISCELLANEOUS TRADE AREA DELINEATION TECHNIQUES

Besides the mathematical delineation techniques, the ABC system, and the composite map method, there are a number of other means for determining approximate retail trade areas. While these methods are less exact than the others, they are worthy of some mention. It is recommended, however, that none of these "miscellaneous" methods be used alone; they should be employed in conjunction with or in addition to the procedures described in other sections of Chapter 15. These additional trade area delineation techniques are listed below in no preferential-use order.

1. *Consumer Sampling:* A percentage of the local community retail customers is surveyed using questionnaires, personal interviews, or both. The information solicited includes the geographic location of the customers' homes. The residences are then related to geographic locations on an area map and, by inspection, serve to delineate a trade area.
2. *SMSA Delineation:* Certain cities use the Standard Metropolitan Statistical Area concept. For each city in this group the territory included within the city's SMSA has been designated to serve as the community's trade area.
3. *Charge Account Technique:* The addresses of charge account customers for selected stores can be organized systematically and located on a map to provide indications of customer concentrations. By means of an arbitrary standard similar to that in the composite map procedure, the researcher can use the charge account data to outline his community's retail trade area.
4. *License Plate Technique:* Some smaller towns periodically place observers at key trading centers to keep records of the license plate numbers on the cars parked there. From these numbers the home addresses of the shoppers can be determined. These residence locations can then be placed on a local map and analyzed as in the charge account technique.
5. *Federal Reserve Bank System:* Some cities define their retail trading area to be equal to the area served by their branch of the district Federal Reserve Bank.

6. *Employment Records Survey:* Some area Chambers sample local businesses to find out the addresses of the employees working in their respective cities. These addresses are then plotted on a map and analyzed for relative concentrations. Again, using an arbitrary standard, the trade area is determined, based on the assumption that the distances people are willing to commute to work are roughly equal to the distances they are willing to travel to shop.

H. ADJUSTMENT OF
THE TRADE AREA BOUNDARY

A final important point to remember when drawing retail trade area boundaries is that, when completed, these delineations should not be shelved as passive information. Instead, these areas can be used as bases for various types of studies and projects. Work on other projects can be greatly expedited if the final trade area boundaries are laid out coincident with the boundaries of previously-existing data-gathering units.

Anyone interested in determining a retail trading area for his city must be careful not to trap himself by drawing a district that appears attractive on the surface, but has limited practical application. This can be avoided by adjusting trade region boundaries to conform to county lines, census tract boundaries, or enumeration districts. There is no part of the country for which one or more of these geographic units are not available. County lines are the most desirable to use, if at all practical, as census data by county are relatively easy to obtain and many types of locally-generated statistics are compiled on a county basis. A county which must be split to be included in a trade area is best divided along census tract or enumeration district boundaries to expedite the compilation and retrieval of project or study information.

Delineation of trade areas in relation to combinations of counties usually is considered to be more desirable and practical by researchers in large cities, while the use of combinations of census tracts and enumeration districts will be more useful for smaller cities. The borders of counties, census tracts and enumeration districts have little or no influence in determining the flow of retail trade. However, the increment of precision lost through the adjustment of the trade area's boundaries to coincide with the borders of pre-existing geographic units is more than offset by the value of the related statistics, many types of which are available only for entire geographic areas of the types indicated above.

CHART 15-A:
DELINEATION OF CITY A'S
RETAIL TRADE AREA
IN RELATION TO SEVEN
OTHER NEIGHBORING CITIES

A-H   Locations of cities

- - - -   Boundary of City A's trade area

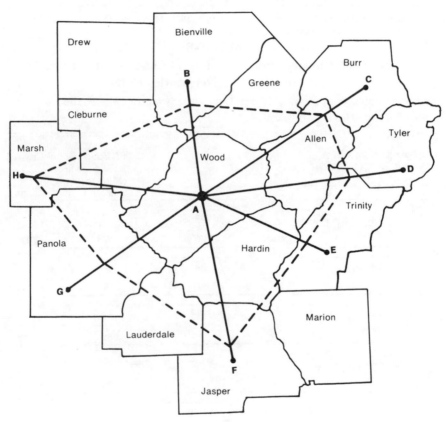

Source: Calculations in Tables 15-A and 15-B.

TABLE 15-A:
Size and Location of Seven Neighboring Cities in Relation to City A

City	Population	Distance from City A (Miles)
A	345,000	
B	11,900	47
C	56,000	55
D	35,000	59
E	19,500	49
F	5,683	51
G	71,000	61
H	4,227	80

Source: Population — U.S. Census of Population, 1970. Distance — State Highway Map.

TABLE 15-B:
Calculation of the Limits (Breaking Points) of City A's Retail Trade Area in Relation to Seven Neighboring Cities

Breaking point = approximate point between two cities where the trading influence of each is equal

Breaking point for City A between City A and each city listed below: Breaking point of City A's retail trade area (Miles from City A)

$$B = \frac{47}{1+\sqrt{\frac{11,900}{345,000}}} = \frac{47}{1+\sqrt{.03449}} = \frac{47}{1+.18571} = 39.7$$

$$C = \frac{55}{1+\sqrt{\frac{56,000}{345,000}}} = \frac{59}{1+\sqrt{.1623}} = \frac{55}{1+.4029} = 39.2$$

$$D = \frac{59}{1+\sqrt{\frac{35,000}{345,000}}} = \frac{49}{1+\sqrt{.1014}} = \frac{59}{1+.3184} = 44.7$$

$$E = \frac{49}{1+\sqrt{\frac{19,500}{345,000}}} = \frac{51}{1+\sqrt{.0565}} = \frac{49}{1+.2377} = 39.6$$

$$F = \frac{51}{1+\sqrt{\frac{5,683}{345,000}}} = \frac{61}{1+\sqrt{.0165}} = \frac{51}{1+.1285} = 45.2$$

$$G = \frac{61}{1+\sqrt{\frac{71,000}{345,000}}} = \frac{}{1+\sqrt{.2058}} = \frac{61}{1+.4537} = 42.0$$

$$H = \frac{80}{1+\sqrt{\frac{4,227}{345,000}}} = \frac{80}{1+\sqrt{.0123}} = \frac{80}{1+.1109} = 72.0$$

SELECTED READING REFERENCES

American Marketing Association, Committee on Definitions. *Marketing Definitions: A Glossary of Marketing Terms.* Chicago: American Marketing Association, 1960.

Applebaum, William. "How to Measure a Trading Area." *Chain Store Age,* (January, 1951).

Converse, P.D. "A Study of Retail Trade Areas in East Central Illinois." *Business Studies.* Urbana: University of Illinois, Bureau of Economic Research, No. 2 (1943).

Converse, P. D. "Consumer Buying Habits in Selected South Central Illinois Communities." *Business Studies.* Urbana: University of Illinois, Bureau of Economic and Business Research, No. 6 (1948).

Converse, P. D. "New Laws of Retail Gravitation." *Journal of Marketing,* (October, 1949), Vol. 14, No. 3, 379-384.

Ferber, R. "Variations in Retail Sales Between Cities." *The Journal of Marketing,* (January, 1958), Vol. 22, 295-303.

Huff, David L. "Determination of Intra-Urban Retail Trade Areas." University of California, Real Estate Research Program, (1962).

Huff, David L. "A Probabilistic Analysis of Consumer Spatial Behavior." *Emerging Concepts in Marketing,* (1964), 444-450.

Huff, David L. "Defining and Estimating a Trade Area." *Journal of Marketing,* (July, 1964), Vol. 28, 34-38.

King, Robert L. "Dilemma of the Small Town Retailers." *Business and Economic Review,* University of South Carolina, Bureau of Business and Economic Research, Vol. XII, No. 3, (December, 1965).

Liu, B. C. "Determinants of Retail Sales in Large Metropolitan Areas." *Journal of the American Statistical Association,* (December, 1970), Vol. 65, 1460-1473.

Mason, Joseph Barry and Charles Thomas Moore. "Traditional Assumptions in Trading Area and Economic Potential Studies: A Dissenting View." *Land Economics,* (May, 1970), 199-201.

Phelps, K. "The Mechanics of Constructing a Market Area Map." *Journal of Marketing,* (April, 1948), 493-496.

Reilly, William J. "Methods for Study of Retail Relationships." University of Texas, Bureau of Business Research, Research Monograph No. 4, (1929).

Reilly, William J. *The Law of Retail Gravitation.* New York: William J. Reilly Co., 1931.

Reynolds, Robert B. "A Test of the Law of Retail Gravitation." *The Journal of Marketing,* Vol. 17, No. 3, (January, 1953), 273-277.

Schwartz, George. "Laws of Retail Gravitation: An Approach." *Business Review,* University of Washington, (October, 1962), 53-70.

16 RETAIL SALES ESTIMATES AND PROJECTIONS

A. INTRODUCTION

A community's aggregate retail trade can serve as a significant measure of economic activity and expansion within the local area. Providing sales data relating to the community—either figures for preceding years or very short-range forecasts for the immediate future—is a responsibility of the local Chamber of Commerce researcher. The present chapter attempts to outline general procedures that should be helpful in this subject area. These broad guidelines are for reference only as there is no procedure currently in use by Chamber of Commerce researchers throughout the United States that is applicable to *all* communities.

Retailing is that part of the distributive process which relates to selling merchandise directly to the ultimate consumer. The *Standard Industrial Classification Manual,* published by the U.S. Office of Statistical Standards, presents this definition of retail trade: "Retail trade includes establishments engaged in selling merchandise for personal, household, or farm consumption, and rendering services incidental to the sale of the goods. Buying of goods for resale to the consumer is a characteristic of retail trade establishments that particularly distinguishes them from the agricultural and extractive industries. For the most part, establishments engaged in retail trade sell merchandise to the general public for personal or household consumption."

Important changes have taken place in the United States since World War II that affect retail trade; these include a substantial increase in per-capita income, a middle-income move to the suburbs, the increased mobility of the general population, and the emergence of a large group of more sophisticated, better educated consumers. Alert downtown department stores have followed the populace to the suburbs with branch retail outlets, and successful retailers generally have made many adjustments in their merchandising activities in the light of changing customer demands.

The sale of goods at retail constitutes a major business activity of most communities. Retail businesses employ a major portion of the area's labor force and distribute goods essential to the community. Though it is important to remember that there is a correlation between retail trade and the amount of income generated by the rest of the community, retailing is not usually a primary catalyst of the area's growth.

The dominant variables determining retail sales are employment, total population, and per-capita income. The U.S. Department of Commerce classifies retailing as a roughly *coincident indicator,* meaning that sales are determined secondarily from other variables, called *leading indicators.* While retail sales totals rank lower than the leading indicators as a monitor of economic activity, the measurement of retail trade within an area is, nevertheless, an important factor in determining an area's level of business growth and expansion.

It is easy enough for anyone with access to the information sources to find historical records of retail sales, but it is very difficult to make reliable short-term projections of sales for year-end periods because any available data are usually three months old. This provides the Chamber with an excellent opportunity to demonstrate its leadership by assuming the responsibility for the publication of retail forecasts.

The procedures outlined in this chapter are proposed to assist the researcher in his attempts to provide retail sales data relating to periods — such as the latter part of a year — for which published information is not available. Specifically, for illustrative purposes, the techniques are designed for a researcher who is called upon in November to make year-end estimates of retail sales with the latest published information available being that for September.

Typical activities requiring sales information of this type include the following:

1. Preparation of a year-end report of local economic conditions for publication in the January edition of the local Chamber of Commerce magazine.
2. Writing newspaper articles on projected Christmas season sales or end-of-year features about the local area.
3. Providing data for year-end reports of banks, utilities, and other businesses.
4. Assisting Chamber of Commerce member stores in comparing their sales performance with that of the aggregate city, county, or SMSA.

There are numerous possibilities of such uses for these estimates, and they all require that the Chamber serve as a credible source of information. It should be remembered, however, that the procedures described in this chapter are designed only for use in the short run; their utility in making estimates for periods longer than six months should be considered in light of their built-in limitations.

The researcher's first step in this analysis is to assemble all relevant information that can be obtained; that is, he should attempt to discover what information has already been collected and make an inventory of this existing information before compiling and processing additional data. There are several sources of retail trade statistics for selected areas. Since these are the most nearly current and reliable reports and publications, they are also the sources used to provide the base information from which illustrative estimates in this chapter are derived. The principal sources are described as follows:

1. *The Census of Business, Retail Trade.* Published by the U.S. Department of Commerce every four years, this comprehensive report covers metropolitan areas, counties and cities within each state. The trade data are complete and relate to the other available information sources. Because it is published for only every fourth year, and even then after considerable delay, there is an important drawback to using this material as a data source. Information provided is outdated almost from the time of its issue, and the relationships represented by the data are thus questionable. These relationships are basic in our estimating procedure, and as the base year gets farther away, this information becomes even less reliable. Therefore, caution should be exercised in using Census of Business reports as sources, especially as the information becomes older. If available, source (4) — described below — might prove to be more useful.

2. *The Survey of Current Business.* Published monthly by the Department of Commerce, this summary contains national industry and total retail trade figures. This is the information source used to calculate national retail sales estimates.

3. *Monthly Department Store Sales.* Published by the Department of Commerce, this pamphlet contains department store sales for selected cities and SMSA's. This is an extremely valuable source because these sales are a determinable percentage of total retail sales. Therefore, given an estimate of department store sales, it is possible to build upon that figure to arrive at a reasonable estimate for total retail sales. The ratio of past department store sales to total retail sales can be computed from the *Census of Business* or *Sales Management.*

4. *Sales Management's Survey of Buying Power.* Published in June or July with figures for the preceding year, this magazine contains a wide range of population, income and sales data for states, counties, metropolitan areas and cities. One of the advantages of this source is that the information provided can be used in relative comparisons of cities and areas, enabling local areas to measure their performance against that of their competitors. A possible drawback to using the data given for estimates is that the sales figures provided by *Sales Management* are estimates, also. However, even if the absolute values of the information given may be questionable, the categorical relationships implied by these values are probably close enough, and with judicious use could provide a fairly accurate base for sales projection.

If available for the local area, other data items that relate to retail trade and should be used as supplementary information in retail sales estimating procedures include: monthly department store sales indexes, monthly labor force tabulations, monthly automobile sales and registrations, retail sales tax data, and year-end population projections.

The problem as outlined for illustration in this chapter is that you, as a Chamber researcher, are near the end of the year, sitting on two-month-old Department of Commerce information, and are called upon to make a defensible estimate of year-end retail sales suitable for publication.

The procedure which has provided the best empirical results — identified as Estimating Method One in this chapter — is based upon computing estimates from published department store sales data, and is therefore available for use relative only to those cities listed in the Department of Commerce publication, *Monthly Department Store Sales*. For all other cities the second best system — Estimating Method Two — must be used.

B. ESTIMATING METHOD ONE

This analysis involves the use of the historical relationship of each month's sales to those of the preceding month — a time-series technique known as the link relative method. Department store sales are tabulated for a period of years, and then each month's sales are expressed as a percentage of sales for the preceding month.

For example, given this sample data, the link relatives would be as follows:

Month	Dept. Store Sales	Link Relative
January	$1000	
February	$1500	1500/1000 = 1.5 or 150%
March	$1200	1200/1500 = .80 or 80%
April	$1600	1600/1200 = 1.33 or 133%

On the basis of the data presented above, February sales were 150% of January sales, March sales were 80% of February sales, and April sales were 133% of March sales. If this trend recurs fairly closely for a period of years, it is reasonable to assume that February sales will probably be around 150% of January sales next year, and one could estimate February sales accordingly, if the January sales were known.

When computing these monthly percentages, it is recommended that data for three years be tabulated to expedite the selection of a median value as a representative link relative. The selection of a median will help decrease the effect of any extreme values due to fluctuations not representative of an average month.

Estimating Method One involves six steps.

Step A

Recall that the researcher in this illustration had received a request for an estimate of the local area's retail sales late in November, 1972. His available reference materials included copies of the *Monthly Department Store Sales,* the latest edition of which included data for September, 1972. From these Department of Commerce reports the researcher tabulated his area's monthly department store sales for all of 1969, 1970 and 1971. These monthly sales totals are shown in Table 16-A.

Step B

Next, link relatives were calculated for the department store sales totals presented in Table 16-A. Each month's sales were expressed as a percentage of the preceding month's; these link relatives are shown in Table 16-B.

Step C

To avoid the effects of unusual fluctuations in the monthly department store sales, the median link relative for each month was chosen to represent that month in this chapter's illustration. These median values are listed in the right hand column in Table 16-B.

The link relatives indicate that it is usually safe to assume that, for the area involved in this illustration, January department store sales were approximately 44.78% of the preceding December sales; February sales were 93.54% of January sales; March sales were 125.73% of February sales; and similarly, sales for each month of the year were expressed as a percentage of sales for the preceding month.

Step D

At this point the researcher in the present illustration observed that he had developed link relatives for all months of 1972 and that he had on hand his area's sales totals (from *Monthly Department Store Sales)* for each month, January through September, 1972. His problem now was to use the link relatives to bridge the gap in his monthly sales data — to obtain sales figures for the months of October, November and December, 1972.

Before proceeding with the remaining calculations necessary to obtain a 1972 year-end sales total, the researcher decided to test the usefulness of his link relatives in the estimating procedure. From the *Monthly Department Store Sales* reports, he compiled his area's department store sales for each month, January through September, 1972. As reported in this Department of Commerce publication, his area's department store sales totaled $511,819,000 for the first nine months of 1972 (Table 16-C). Then he used his link relatives to calculate estimated department store sales for each month in this January-September period (Table 16-C), using December, 1971 sales as the base for the projection.

His estimating procedure produced a total of $506,970,000 for this nine-month period. The total derived from the use of link relatives was within 1% of the sales reported by the Department of Commerce publication, and the researcher concluded that this variance was so small that he must be on the right track and could justify his use of the link relatives in the remainder of his calculations.

Step E

The remainder of the researcher's task involved calculating a sales total for each of the last three months in 1972, adding these amounts to the monthly totals reported for the local area in *Monthly Department Store Sales* for January-September, 1972, and then converting the local area's total department store sales to total retail sales.

In Table 16-D, the link relatives indicate that October sales were usually 105.35% of September sales, November sales were 113.43% of October sales, and December sales were usually 167.39% of those reported in November.

The *Monthly Department Store Sales* publication reported, for the local area, total sales of $58,982,000 for September, 1972. The October estimate was 105.35% of the September total, or $62,138,000. Similarly, estimated sales for November and December were calculated to be $70,483,000 and $117,981,000, respectively. (See Table 16-D.)

The final step in computing total department store sales for the local area in 1972 was the addition of the estimates for the last three months of 1972 to the known values for the first nine months of the year, indicated as follows:

Department store sales, January-September, 1972
(from *Monthly Department Store Sales* reports) $511,819,000

Estimated department store sales,
October-December, 1972
(derived from link relatives) $250,602,000

Estimated total department store sales
for 1972 . . . . $762,421,000

After annual local department store sales have been estimated, there are two ways to convert this number to *estimated total retail sales*. In the first alternative information from the latest *Census of Business, Retail Trade* is a basic component, while the second alternative involves the use of data from the *Sales Management Survey of Buying Power.* The two techniques are basically the same—only the information sources differ. In both publications department store sales are listed as a subgroup under total retail sales. Knowing these numbers, the researcher can compute the relationship between the two totals for his area.

Step F, Alternative 1

If a local area's department store sales were $12,000,000 in 1967 and its retail sales were $42,000,000 for the same year, then retail sales were 3.5 times as great as department store sales. If in 1968 department store sales in the same area were $16,000,000, then retail sales might be assumed (cautiously) to be 3.5 times that number, or around $56,000,000.

To apply this to the illustrative problem selected for this chapter, the input numbers and the procedure to complete the retail sales estimates in Step F are outlined as follows:

Census of Business, Retail Trade, 1967

Local area's total retail sales in 1967	$3,010,993,000
Local area's total department store sales in 1967	$436,415,000

$$\frac{\$3,010,993,000}{\$436,415,000} = 6.8993$$

ratio of retail sales to dept. store sales in 1967

The local area's department store sales estimate for 1972 is $762,421,000 (from page 310)

This total is converted to *estimated retail sales* for 1972 as follows:

$$6.8993 \times \$762,421,000 = \$5,260,171,000$$

As indicated previously in this chapter, the problem with using *Census of Business* data is that this information is always at least two years old and is therefore very probably an unreliable source. There can be no certainty that the implied relationships between these two sales categories—department store sales and total retail sales—will remain unchanged over a period of several years.

Step F, Alternative 2

The second alternative involves the use of similar types of information published in the *Sales Management Survey of Buying Power.* A basic assumption relating to this technique is that the correlation between total retail and total department store sales is probably more nearly accurate since the *Sales Management* sales totals are more recent.

In the use of *Sales Management* data, however, there is always the danger of choosing a base year (for calculating the appropriate ratio) which is abnormal for some reason. This problem can be partially avoided by computing ratios for several years and then using the median ratio, indicated as follows:

Sales Management Survey of Buying Power

	1969	1970	1971
A. Retail Sales (Local Area)	$3,360,576,000	$3,641,866,000	$3,860,328,000
B. Dept. Store Sales (Local Area)	$505,975,000	$514,483,000	$654,290,000
Ratio (A/B)	6.6417	6.3393	5.9000
Median Ratio		6.3393	

The local area's department store sales estimate for 1972 is $762,421,000 (from page 310)

This total is converted to *estimated total retail sales* for 1972 as follows:

6.3393   X $762,421,000   = $4,833,215,000

C. ESTIMATING METHOD TWO

For those cities not listed in the Department of Commerce *Monthly Department Store Sales* publication, the problem of sales estimation becomes slightly more difficult and the procedure involved still less precise. Researchers in those cities and towns not included in the standard government publications used in Method One must employ an alternative procedure utilizing information less directly applicable than that used in Method One and techniques which are relatively subjective and arbitrary. Nonetheless, procedures do exist by which a reasonable estimate of sales may be calculated.

For researchers in small and medium size cities, these suggestions are offered for quantifying subjective estimates of local area sales—with heavy stress on the term "subjective." As in Chapter 19 on population estimation, it is best to use a composite of two or more of the available techniques, weighting them according to reliability and then deriving a weighted average of total retail sales. Approaching the problem from this standpoint necessitates calling upon members of the Chamber's Research Committee for qualified judgments about retail sales to be introduced into all stages of the analysis.

1. Technique Number One: Using Department Store Sales Index Prepared by Federal Reserve Banks

Probably the best alternative sales estimating procedure for a limited number of selected areas involves using the weekly department store sales reports prepared by the Federal Reserve Banks. Each of the 12 Federal Reserve District banks publishes these weekly statistics for selected cities in their respective areas. For those cities listed — and here again, many cities are not listed — the data sheet shows the weekly percentage changes in department store sales from those in the corresponding week of the previous year. Also provided are percentage changes in sales for the year-to-date as compared to those at the same time the year before. This information is especially valuable because there is ordinarily only a two-week lag from data gathering to receipt of published statistics.

As in the analysis using monthly sales, the assumption is that changes in department store sales are proportional to changes in total retail sales. Accepting this assumption, estimates for the year's sales may be made using the estimated percentage change in sales from the previous year and the estimated total of the sales for the current year, available from *Sales Management's Survey of Buying Power*.

Since the type of estimate for which this procedure is designed often will be made in late November or early December, the year-to-date percentage changes in sales are available at least through October. It might validly be assumed that a given percentage change in sales from one October to the next would also approximate the change in sales from one December to the next. However, it is usually best to collect several years' data to see if there is a real correlation.

For example, using sales data for fictitious River City, U.S.A., the historical patterns obtained from the Federal Reserve reports are as follows:

Year	Percentage change through October	Percentage change in sales for year
1969	+11	+12
1970	+10	+11
1971	+12	+12

These figures provide some basis for assuming that changes demonstrated through 10 months of the year will approximate changes through the whole year, and that these October values may be used cautiously. Also, from the latest data sheet received—dated November 27, 1972—the researcher will note that the year-to-date percentage change in sales through November 18 is again 12%, supporting the historical trend and giving a strong indication that sales for the entire year will increase by approximately this amount (See Table 16-E).

From *Sales Management* the 1971 retail sales in River City were $290,803,000. Therefore, estimated sales for 1972 would be computed by:

$$\$290,803,000 \quad \times \quad 112\% \quad = \quad \$325,699,000$$

2. Technique Number Two: Using Panel Samples

For those cities not listed in either the Department of Commerce *Monthly Department Store Sales* bulletins or the Federal Reserve's weekly department store sales index, the interested researcher must work a little harder. The best option left to him is to return to the basics of area analysis, conducting a survey of local businesses designed to provide specific sales information from which projections can be made.

This survey should be done on as systematic and comprehensive a basis as time and funds will allow. Optimally, a wide range of stores should be contacted, including department stores and such specialty stores as automobile dealers, furniture dealers, and appliance stores. The purpose of the survey is to find out from the individual retailers how their sales for the year compare to those of last year and, if possible, what their individual projections are for the remainder of the year. From this information the researcher must determine, to the best of his ability, an estimate of total area retail sales for the year end.

Use of a panel sample will provide a reasonably reliable data source if the same businesses serve as members of the permanent sample and are surveyed every year. An extended period of service on the panel enables these businessmen to become familiar with the goals, techniques, and procedures of the estimating process. As a result of their experience, they can provide the necessary information when it is needed, with a minimum of confusion and delay.

However, complete constancy of panel membership may prove detrimental. Unless precautions are taken to keep a portion of the membership flexible and to draw in new members, the panel could become non-representative of the real economic profile of the area. As the city expands physically, efforts should be made to integrate into the existing panel membership representatives from businesses in the newer suburban areas.

The advantages of using a panel include reductions in the time and expense of data compilation. Also, asking the same questions over a period of years allows significant trends to be more easily pinpointed and measured than if a new sample had to be taken annually.

The goal in surveying selected local retailers is to arrive at some type of consensus figure for the projected changes in total retail sales. Members of the Research Committee should participate in deciding how this figure is to be determined. Some possible techniques include development of a representative percentage change through discussion, the use of a median figure taken from all of the individual business statistics collected, and the use of either a simple or a weighted average. Once again, this decision should be made in light of existing conditions in your particular area.

3. Technique Number Three: Multiple Correlation

Another procedure for calculating a sales estimate requires the analysis of several economic indicators at once, using multiple correlation, and thus takes into account the relationships existing between several economic variables simultaneously. It is overly simplified to assume that there will be a reliable correlation between sales and any one indicator; multiple correlation refines the procedure, allowing examination of several available factors at once. A partial list of suggested indicators to use includes labor force estimates, housing completions, bank debits to individual accounts, auto registrations, and retail sales taxes.

4. Technique Number Four: Graphic Analysis

The next suggested procedure involves the use of economic variables similar to those applicable to Technique No. 3. First, five-year (1967-1971) tabulations of local-area data relating to the selected economic variables should be compiled and plotted on graph paper. Next, the plotted data should be extended to cover those months of 1972 for which this information is available. Also, for the entire period—beginning in January, 1967, and extending into 1972—retail sales data for your area, from appropriate editions of the *Sales Management Survey of Buying Power,* should be plotted.

After preparing these graphic displays, the researcher's task is to estimate roughly the relationship of retail sales to the other variables graphically represented. The easiest method for determining this relationship is to "eyeball" the plotted data—to form visual impressions of this relationship from the lines shown in the researcher's graphs. This observed relationship should then be used to extend the sales line on the graph for all months of

1972 and thus to arrive at an approximation of retail sales for River City in 1972.

D. CONCLUSION

Forecasting total retail sales involves consideration of several economic indicators. Although the local situation is most important, it is in turn influenced by regional and national factors of which the researcher should be aware. National economic information helpful in making local area forecasts includes, among other items, the influences of personal and business taxes on sales, the prospects for new housing construction, expected trends in consumer savings, trends in expenditures, and the outlook for consumer credit.

Regardless of the forecasting methods used, it is essential that the forecasts be checked against the judgment of individuals who are familiar with business in your area. Though the use of statistical data is an attempt to substitute facts for subjective judgments, knowledge gained through business experience should not be completely ignored in favor of quantitative data. The best estimates are those that use a variety of inputs to arrive at one answer. These inputs, both subjective and analytically objective, should be balanced to hit an agreeable mean.

Finally, it is important to emphasize that any forecast should be reviewed frequently and revised in light of the most recent information. Researchers should constantly monitor the data sources to see what has happened to change the outlook. Keeping accurately and fully informed on the current business level is probably the simplest but best insurance against making wrong decisions regarding the future.

TABLE 16-A:
Monthly Department Store Sales for the Central City SMSA
(In $000)

	1969	1970	1971
January	$31,720	$34,323	$41,252
February	28,909	34,363	38,587
March	36,778	42,946	48,515
April	38,356	44,522	53,217
May	42,024	46,554	53,202
June	39,253	46,108	52,414
July	40,394	46,302	53,712
August	44,629	51,098	58,107
September	40,864	45,790	51,513
October	42,093	50,370	54,268
November	47,748	54,351	62,119
December	80,312	88,107	103,980

Source: *Monthly Department Store Sales in Selected Areas,* published by U.S. Department of Commerce, Social and Economic Statistics Administration, Bureau of the Census.

TABLE 16-B:
Link Relatives for Monthly Department Store
Sales for the Central City SMSA[1]

	1969	1970	1971	Median
January	— %	42.74%	46.82%	44.78%
February	91.14	100.12	93.54	93.54
March	127.22	124.98	125.73	125.73
April	104.29	103.67	109.69	104.29
May	109.56	104.56	99.97	104.56
June	93.41	99.04	98.52	98.52
July	102.91	100.42	102.48	102.48
August	110.48	110.36	108.18	110.36
September	91.56	89.61	88.65	89.61
October	103.01	110.00	105.35	105.35
November	113.43	107.90	114.47	113.43
December	168.20	162.11	167.39	167.39

[1]Each link relative represents a month's sales expressed as a percentage of sales for the previous month. Sales totals used in calculating the link relatives are presented in Table 16-A.

TABLE 16-C:
Estimated Department Store Sales for the Central City SMSA
January — September, 1972
(In $000)

Monthly Dept. Store Sales Reported by Dept. of Commerce	Median Link Relatives (From Table 16-B)	Estimated Monthly Dept. Store Sales (Link Relative X Sales)	
December, 1971 $103,980		$103,980	Given
January, 1972 $ 46,105	44.78%	$103,980 × 44.78%	= $ 46,562
February $ 44,730	93.54%	$ 46,562 × 93.54%	= $ 43,554
March $ 60,049	125.73%	$ 43,554 × 125.73%	= $ 54,760
April $ 55,161	104.29%	$ 54,760 × 104.29%	= $ 57,109
May $ 59,345	104.56%	$ 57,109 × 104.56%	= $ 59,713
June $ 60,495	98.52%	$ 59,713 × 98.52%	= $ 58,829
July $ 58,983	102.48%	$ 58,829 × 102.48%	= $ 60,288
August $ 67,969	110.36%	$ 60,288 × 110.36%	= $ 66,534
September $ 58,982	89.61%	$ 66,534 × 89.61%	= $ 59,621
TOTAL $511,819			$506,970

Source: *Monthly Department Store Sales in Selected Areas*, published by U.S. Department of Commerce, Social and Economic Statistics Administration, Bureau of the Census.

TABLE 16-D:
Estimated Department Store Sales for the Central City SMSA
October — December, 1972
(In $000)

Monthly Dept. Store Sales Reported by Dept. of Commerce	Median Link Relatives (From Table 16-B)	Estimated Monthly Dept. Store Sales (Link Relative X Sales)
September		
$ 58,982		$58,982 Given
October		
$ 63,528	105.35%	$58,982 × 105.35% = $ 62,138
November		
$ 74,388	113.43%	$62,138 × 113.43% = $ 70,483
December		
$115,374	167.39%	$70,483 × 167.39% = $117,981
Total, Oct.-Dec., 1972 $253,290		$250,602

Source: *Monthly Department Store Sales in Selected Areas,* published by U.S. Department of Commerce, Social and Economic Statistics Administration, Bureau of the Census.

TABLE 16-E:
Weekly Department Store Sales for Selected SMSA's
in the _____ Federal Reserve District
November 27, 1972

	Percentage change from corresponding period a year ago (Based on retail dollar amounts)					
	One week ended				Four weeks ended	Total Change For Year to
	Nov. 18	Nov. 11	Nov. 4	Oct. 28	Nov. 18, 1972	Nov. 18, 1972
Federal Reserve District	+12	+ 2	+13	+34	+14	+11
Metropolitan Areas						
City A	+12	+ 8	+11	+26	+14	+11
City B	+ 6	+17	+30	+48	+20	+ 6
River City	+14	0	+13	+52	+18	+12
City C	+12	+ 3	+15	+21	+12	+ 9

Source: Research Department, _____ Federal Reserve District.

17 SHOPPING CENTER DIRECTORY

A. INTRODUCTION

Well-developed shopping centers are primary community resources. A directory of these centers, indicating area shopping opportunities, is an excellent community advertisement and a highly useful tool for planners and developers.

As major generators of traffic, shopping centers are focal points of urban development, holding positions of importance far beyond that indicated by the relatively small amounts of land they occupy. These large-scale traffic generators affect various phases of the local Chamber's program, including street and highway planning, retail promotion, zoning, economic and industrial development, and membership.

The residential developer is interested in shopping center location, in quantitative and qualitative shopping opportunities, and in the amenities provided. The industrial developer has much the same interest relative to his concern for general employee welfare. The commercial developer is interested in such detailed information relative to new store location as the competitive problem, class of products, and the size and economic status of market area.

A shopping center directory for a metropolitan area is a listing of the major retail shopping areas outside the central business district. The listings in this publication should represent a variety of shopping center types, including planned regional and neighborhood centers as well as unplanned or intersection shopping facilities and major isolated stores. Information on each center or district should include the tenants within the center by business classifications, the overall size of the center, and the exact address of the center and each of its tenants.

B. SHOPPING CENTER DIRECTORY DESIGN

The scope of the directory can range from a simple alphabetical list of shopping centers and facilities to a complete analysis of shopping trends as they relate to shopping center construction and development. The size of the retail centers also establishes the scope of the directory. The larger the centers to be listed, the fewer listings in the directory.

Inevitably, budgetary considerations affect directory design. Directories for large urban areas with many shopping centers are in great demand and sales revenues substantially defray publication costs, whereas small communities, constrained to publish some shopping center information, may have less sales demand and must absorb most of the cost. Design may vary for these reasons. Chart 17-A is an example of a simple yet satisfactory design for small cities, showing shopping center location and size. Sales volume, or total square footage of store space, may be scaled similarly in map format.

A single-sheet information treatment of shopping facilities costs little, but it does present a good picture of local retail shopping opportunities. Large urban areas with many shopping centers require a more expansive directory treatment. The list of information items required is longer and format design may be as variable as is the creativity of individual art directors.

C. DATA COLLECTION

In compiling the core of the directory — the location and description of what is in a shopping center — it is necessary to pin-point ownership of the center. This can usually be accomplished by contacting the area development departments of local utilities, which usually will have ownership records on shopping centers. Follow-up information, if required, can be obtained by sending questionnaires to the larger commercial realty firms.

After ownership of the various centers is determined, the researcher may employ any of several data-collection procedures:

1. *Mailout-mailback survey* of retail establishments within the metropolitan area involves the use of a questionnaire to gain information on each retail establishment and the compilation of information in such a way as to outline major shopping centers. This method has the disadvantage of being extremely difficult to administer. Additionally, the response of retail establishments may not be large enough to accurately reflect the amount of retail development.

2. *The field research method* provides for teams of interviewers to survey the known retail districts of the metropolitan area. A check with shopping center developers and building contractors may provide leads for shopping center sites. Examination of building permits can also show where new commercial construction is planned. The developer or manager of a center is a good source of such information as size of center, tenants, and parking spaces.

3. *A combination survey* may be used in areas where sufficient information is available on shopping centers and districts, with the researcher both collecting data directly from the developer of centers and deploying research teams to survey unplanned or intersectional shopping districts. Shopping center addresses found in the yellow pages of the telephone book offer leads to shopping centers, and the city directory identifies commercial addresses.

Once commercial districts are identified, researchers can survey the district to establish whether a shopping district exists. The major problem with using a city directory is that often it is out of date and verification of the information is time-consuming and expensive. People in shopping center developments usually can provide an up-to-date list of shopping centers currently under development.

D. CLASSIFICATION OF DATA

Procedures for classifying directory information should be established in advance of collection to insure that all classes of data are collected. Information on the size of centers, available parking areas, classification of map coordinates, census tract location and types of centers should be outlined before an actual survey begins.

1. Size

The minimum size of the shopping center to be surveyed should be established as a guide for data collection. A minimum size of 50,000 square feet would allow most neighborhood centers to be included and prevent the listing of the small strip centers located near major apartment complexes and entrances to medium size housing developments. Centers of over 50,000 square feet—as indicated in Exhibit 17-A—will usually contain one general merchandise store, a major food store, a drug store, a furniture and home furnishing store, and several specialty and service stores. On the average, the typical center will contain from 200 to 500 parking spaces.

2. Types of Business

The retail trade classification in the current edition of the Standard Industrial Classification Manual includes establishments primarily engaged in selling merchandise to customers for personal, household or farm use. The kind-of-business classification that is established and used by the U.S. Department of Commerce, Bureau of Census, Census of Business report is listed below. Not all groups must be used in compiling a shopping center directory, and many can be combined under other major headings such as *other retail stores.*

   a. Building Materials, Hardware and Farm Equipment Dealers: SIC
      Major Group 52.
   b. General Merchandise Group Stores: SIC Major Group 53
        Department Stores: SIC 531
        Variety Stores: SIC 533
   c. Food Stores: SIC Major Group 54
   d. Automotive Dealers: SIC Major Group 55
   e. Apparel and Accessory Stores: SIC Major Group 56
   f. Furniture, Home Furnishings, and Equipment Stores: SIC Major
      Group 57
   g. Eating and Drinking Places: SIC Major Group 58
   h. Miscellaneous Retail Stores: SIC Major Group 59
        Drug Stores and Proprietory Stores: SIC 591
        Liquor Stores: SIC 592
        Sporting Goods, Bicycle Shops: SIC 595
        Jewelry Stores: SIC 597
        Florists: SIC 5992

3. Major Retail Centers

The designation of Major Retail Centers by the Bureau of the Census in *Census of Business* reports can be used to show major trade areas outside of the central business district. Major Retail Centers (MRC's) are defined by the Census Bureau as "those concentrations of retail stores (located inside the standard metropolitan statistical areas but outside of the CBD) having at least $5 million in retail sales and at least 10 retail establishments, one of which is classified as a department store."

MRC's include not only the planned suburban shopping centers, but also the older "string" street and neighborhood developments which meet the listed prerequisites. Frequently the boundaries of a single MRC include stores located within a planned center and, in addition, adjacent stores outside of the planned portion. In general, the boundaries of the MRC's have been established to include all adjacent blocks containing at least one store in the general merchandise, apparel, or furniture-appliance group of stores and, where a planned center is involved, to include all of the center.

MRC information should be noted as such in the directory and a notation should be made of the planned centers within the MRC, with all establishments located within the limits outlined for the MRC included. Total building area for the Major Retail Center would include all retail and non-retail establishments within the designated area.

4. Name and Location of Center

The designated shopping center should show the name by which it is known in the community, and the address should include any intersection and the street address range for the tenants in the center. In the case of a shopping district or Major Retail Center, the address may include several streets, the area should be described as "bounded by" the streets which define these boundaries. Street addresses are not necessary in this instance unless it is the only means available to describe the boundaries. Locating the shopping center by census tract is helpful in compiling census information on population, housing, and other related data.

5. Shopping Center Map

A map of the geographic area covered by a shopping center directory is effective in demonstrating the distribution of the various shopping centers by location. This map can be developed by using a census tract map— Chart 17-B—to show the location of the center by census tract or by using a regular city map showing the major transportation network. The map design will be determined by the geographic limits of the metropolitan area.

The location of the center on the map should be coded to match the directory numbering system. In the case of geographic boundary descriptions, the center should be identified by this geographic boundary description and the number of the center within this area. If the map is quite detailed and a large number of centers are listed, the map should be designed to show geographically only those areas with shopping center facilities. In the case of an extremely large area, the map may have to be divided into several sections to cover all the area with shopping center locations.

E. DIRECTORY FORMAT

The basic directory design should include:

1. A general introduction explaining the directory sections and summarizing the directory information. Subject areas to be summarized should be established to give as complete a picture of the directory findings as is possible.
2. An alphabetical list of all shopping centers found in the directory with as much information about each as is practical within the limited amount of space available. The size of each center and its address are essential to the summary list.
3. The alphabetical list should be followed by the shopping center map to aid in locating each center.
4. Individual shopping centers listed by quadrant (of the city or county) will follow the map, providing detailed information about each center. This section should form the bulk of the directory, with complete information by quadrant for all shopping centers. Each quadrant should be in line with census tract boundaries established for the given geographic area being used.

A summary of the information applicable to each quadrant should precede the entire list of shopping centers. This would include the quadrant number, the name of the center, the overall building area, parking capacity, and the numbers of establishments by types. Totals of each of these categories can be used in the aggregate directory summary—which should be listed in the introductory section of the directory as part of an explanation of the data to be found within the directory. An example of this summary is shown in Exhibit 17-B.

CHART 17-A:
SHOPPING CENTER MAP:
LOCATION AND SIZE BY SALES VOLUME

CENTRAL CITY SHOPPING CENTERS

Annual Sales Volume

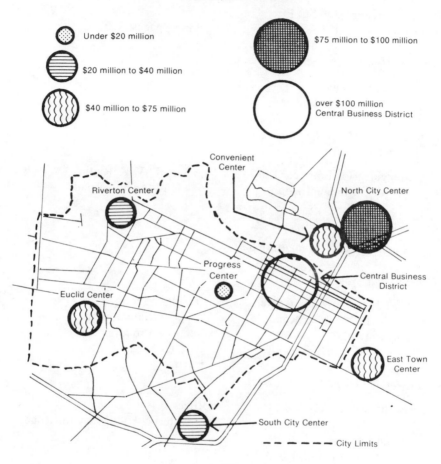

Under $20 million

$20 million to $40 million

$40 million to $75 million

$75 million to $100 million

over $100 million
Central Business District

Convenient Center

Riverton Center

North City Center

Progress Center

Central Business District

Euclid Center

East Town Center

South City Center

— — — — — City Limits

Shopping Center Name and Store Products: Example

Progress Center: Supermarket, Clothing, Drugs, Small Loans, Dry Cleaning

North City Center: Department Store, Supermarket, Beauty Salon, Barbershop, Sporting Goods, Bank, Shoes, Drugs, Variety Store, Furniture, Women's Fashions, Gifts

(Repeat for each shopping center shown on map location.)

EXHIBIT 17-A:
DATA FOR A TYPICAL SHOPPING CENTER

MANGUM SHOPPING CENTER

Mangum Road & W. 43rd
Map Coordinates - L-6　　　　Census Tract No. 526

Building Area: 65,800 Sq. Ft.
Year Established: 1956　　　　Parking Spaces: 330

General Merchandise Stores

> T G & Y Variety,
> 4611 Mangum Road

*Furniture and Home Furnishings
Stores*

> Mangum Hardware & Gifts,　　Mangum T. V. & Radio,
> 4605 Mangum Road　　　　　4513 Mangum Road

Food Stores

> Randall's, 4615 Mangum Road

Other Retail Stores

> Curt Johnson Music Center,　　The Whistle Stop,
> 4511 Mangum Road　　　　　4319 Mangum Rd.
> Dugan Drugs,　　　　　　Wilbank's Liquors,
> 4517 Mangum Road　　　　　4503 Mangum Road

Non-Retail Establishments

> Barber Shop,　　　　　　Offices
> 4501 Mangum Road　　　Washateria, 4509 Mangum Road
> Beauty Salon,
> 4508 Mangum Road
> Laundry,
> 4311 Mangum Road

CHART 17-B:
LOCATION OF SHOPPING CENTERS
BY CENSUS TRACT

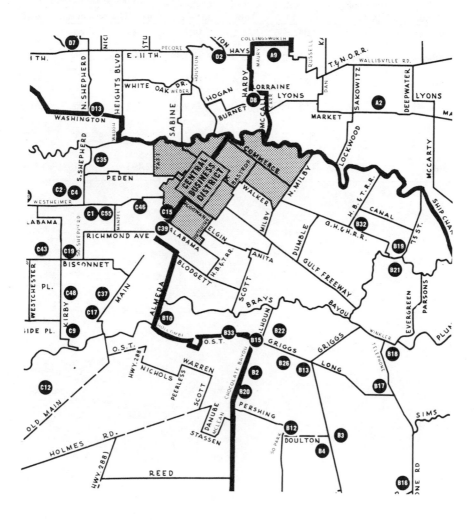

Indicators in circles show the approximate locations of shopping centers. In these indicators, letters of the alphabet refer to quadrants of the county according to this plan: A, Northeast; B, Southeast; C, Southwest; D, Northwest.

EXHIBIT 17-B:
SHOPPING CENTER SUMMARY
BY QUADRANT

Quadrant	No. of Shopping Centers	Quadrant Total (Sq. Ft.)	% of Grand Total	Parking Capacity (Spaces)	Number of Establishments		
					Retail	Non-Retail	Total
Northeast	21	4,041,600	16.5	19,200	333	140	473
Southeast	42	7,172,480	29.2	42,710	603	275	878
Southwest	46	9,651,740	39.3	56,020	993	400	1,393
Northwest	15	3,686,600	15.0	23,960	264	106	370
Grand Total	124	24,552,420	100.0	141,890	2,193	921	3,114

Part V

DEMOGRAPHIC AND
SOCIAL RESEARCH

18 DEMOGRAPHIC DATA FROM THE 1970 CENSUS OF POPULATION AND HOUSING

A. INTRODUCTION

The products of the 1970 Census of Population and Housing provide the richest socio-economic data base ever available to demographic researchers.[1] As might be expected, the change in "richness" implies that other changes have occurred. Such is the case. Even though the items collected in this Census reflected only a limited number of changes beyond those collected in the 1960 Census, the products, in both form and content, have changed tremendously. The number of pages in the printed reports has nearly doubled, due principally to the increased number of "small" areas" for which data are published. Computer tapes are available with several times as much data as are contained in the printed reports, and data are also available on both microfilm and microfiche. Geographic references produced as part of the 1970 Census include several map series and geographic code "lists," and even computer tape files which show the blocks, tracts, and other small areas into which streets and address ranges fall. Computer programs designed to accomplish such tasks as printing data from tapes, assigning geographic codes to data files, and producing computer maps are available to users. Finally, to assist the census data user, a sizable volume of explanatory material has been prepared. This chapter provides a brief guide to all 1970 Census products, computer programs, and informational materials.

---

[1]Prepared by Michael G. Garland, Chief, Data Access and Use Laboratory, Data User Services Office, Bureau of the Census, Washington, D. C. Reprinted from *Population Index*, Vol. 38, No. 4, October—December, 1972.

B. PUBLISHED VOLUMES
AND COMPUTER TAPES

The published volumes continue to be the primary form in which census data are made available. Users will find both the series and their contents quite similar to those from the 1960 Census, although almost every report includes substantially more pages. This results largely from an increase in the number of areas for which data are shown—more standard metropolitan statistical areas (SMSA's), cities of 50,000 population or more, places of 1,000 population or more, tracts, blocks, etc. Changes in page layouts to make the figures more "readable" have also been responsible for expansion of the reports. In addition, more areas qualify for the separate tables showing characteristics of Negroes where there are 400 or more Negroes and, for the first time, separate tables are presented for areas with a Spanish "heritage" population of 400 or more. The principal report series for both population and housing data again are published on a state-by-state basis except for the census tract and block statistics, which are published in separate reports for each SMSA.

Libraries and other institutions that use microform will be interested to know that each of the approximately 1,600 printed reports is being made available on *microfiche* by the National Technical Information Service, a U.S. Department of Commerce agency. Each report is sold separately on one or more fiche (4 x 6 inches—up to 70 pages per fiche).

Similar to the published volumes, summary (aggregated) data are available on computer tape. The Census Bureau closely observed the activities of planners, social scientists, and other researchers during the Sixties in using computer tape released from the 1960 Census. Repeated contact during the decade with these users led the Bureau to create a wide range of 1970 summary data tapes—some 2,000 reels of computer tape separated into six series, called "counts"—for public use. Each count is characterized by: (1) the data from which the tabulations are derived (100-percent or sample), (2) the number and composition of the tabulations, and (3) the geographic areas for which the data are tabulated (census blocks are on one of the counts, tracts are on two, states on four, etc.).

These summary tapes can be viewed as an extension of the printed report program since they contain similar tabulations for the same geographic areas (except as noted below) and are governed by the same rules to insure that no data are released that might identify a specific person or household. However, there are a number of differences between these two data products which users should consider prior to choosing one in lieu of the other. These differences fall into at least five categories:

1. *Detail of Tabulations.* A general principle followed in the preparation of the printed volumes is that the data detail varies with the

type and size of geographic areas: significantly more detailed data are published in any given series of reports for large areas, such as states or large cities (50,000 or more population) than for counties or smaller cities (less than 10,000). In contrast, each summary tape count generally provides the same tabulations for each geographic area presented, regardless of size. Two examples will serve to illustrate the difference in data detail between the printed volumes and the summary tapes. First, the Third Count summary tapes contain 250 cells of data for each census block while the *Block Statistics Reports* present 25 cells for each block. Second, the Second Count summary tapes contain a tabulation of age by sex by race for single years of age (under 1 year to 100 years and over) for census tracts, minor civil divisions, counties, places of all sizes, and states while the same tabulation in the printed volumes, *General Characteristics* − PC(1), is limited to states.

2. *Special Geographic Areas.* Tabulations are presented on the summary tapes for two types of geographic areas that are not included in any of the printed reports. Enumeration district (called "block groups" in the larger metropolitan areas) tallies are contained on the First Count summary tapes, and tallies for all three-digit national ZIP Code areas and the five-digit ZIP Code areas in the SMSA's are presented on the Fifth Count summary tapes.

3. *Cost.* There is, of course, a significant cost differential between acquiring and using the printed reports and the summary tapes. Most printed reports can be purchased for two or three dollars each. In contrast, the Bureau price for summary tapes is $70 per reel, and, in many cases the equivalent of a single report in terms of geographic coverage is two or more reels of tape. But the cost of the tapes is only the "tip of the iceberg." Other costs include the cost of acquiring computer programs to process the tapes − or hiring computer programmers to develop the required programs − and the computer processing cost. The latter must be reckoned with each time more data are required from a set of tapes. It is not uncommon for a summary tape user to invest hundreds of dollars to obtain the desired data in a form tailored to meet his requirements.

4. *Convenience.* Census publications can be acquired from the Government Printing Office and any of the 42 Department of Commerce Field Offices or examined at many university or public libraries, Chambers of Commerce, or local governmental offices. Volumes frequently used can be purchased and kept within easy reach on a desk or bookcase. In contrast, to obtain data from the summary tapes, either a researcher must purchase the tapes, de-

velop or purchase computer programs, and arrange for computer time, or he must deal with someone else who offers summary tape processing services. Experience has shown that either of these routes can take weeks or even months. And, unless the researcher obtains all of the data from the tapes that will meet his current and future needs (which could fill several boxes of paper), he will have to go through this data acquisition process several times.

5. *Data Analysis.* The development of and generally easy access to electronic computers has had a significant impact on the techniques of data analysis. The data processing burden has been greatly reduced and utilization of sophisticated statistical analysis techniques has apparently increased in direct proportion to the accessibility of computers. Correlations, regressions, factor analyses involving many variables and even highly sophisticated modeling techniques can be carried out with relative ease on a computer. Consequently, the demand for computer-readable data has increased substantially; the summary tapes are well suited to meet the processing requirements of this type of analysis.

To briefly summarize these comparisons, the advantages of using the printed publications lie in the areas of cost and convenience, while the merits of the summary tapes include the availability of data for special geographic areas, a greater detail in the data for most geographic areas, and greater processing capabilities for statistical analysis. The prudent user will carefully consider the alternative data sources in relation to his statistical requirements, financial resources, and time commitments prior to launching his census use activities.

C. PUBLIC USE SAMPLES

The data needs of some users cannot be met even by the detailed tabulations on the summary tapes. Generally these users are researchers interested in analyzing the detailed relationships of several person and housing unit characteristics for the larger census areas (states or regions). To meet the needs of these users, the Census Bureau is making available a 1% sample of individual person and housing unit records called a *public use sample.* With such a file in hand, the researcher can develop his own cross-tabulations or statistical analyses without being limited to the tabulations designed for the printed reports and summary tapes.

The public use samples are samples of census records containing the questionnaire responses for a statistically selected sample of households. These data are made available in the form of computer tape files consisting of records on which the census responses appear as numeric codes. No names or addresses appear in the sample and the geographic areas identified in the public use samples are sufficiently large (250,000 persons or more) to avoid disclosure of information for specific individuals.

Six different public use samples are available from the 1970 Census: three from the 5% and three from the 15% data records, one each for the following three categories: (1) County groups, (2) States, and (3) Neighborhood Characteristics. One-in-100, 1-in-1000, and 1-in-10,000 samples are available for each of the six public use samples.

Records on the County Group public use samples carry a code identifying the particular "county group" in which that household was located. Every SMSA having a population over 250,000 is identified, and, whenever possible, subdivisions comprising one or more counties and having over 250,000 population also are identified. Outside these large SMSA's, groups of functionally interrelated counties are identified. State boundaries are not necessarily observed in determining county groups.

The State public use samples identify the state of residence for each household and also indicate whether a household location was urban or rural, metropolitan or nonmetropolitan, and within the central city of an SMSA or not.

The Neighborhood Characteristics public use samples, which identify location of residence by the nine geographic divisions, have two features which distinguish them from the others: (1) location of residence is also identified in terms of size-of-place or urbanized area, and (2) summary characteristics are provided for the neighborhood in which the household is located. The neighborhood characteristics are summary indicators in the form of ratios (e.g., Negro population to the total population, families with income below the low income level to total families) for people living in Census Bureau defined "neighborhoods" of approximately the same size as census tracts.

Historical studies using the State public use samples are possible since the Bureau has created a 1-in-100 State public use sample from the 1960 data files. The form and detail of the 1960 1-in-100 sample parallel that of the 1970 version.

D. SUMMARY TAPE PROCESSING CENTERS

At this point many readers may be attracted by the prospect of using the summary tapes or the public use samples, but at the same time conclude that they must stick with the printed reports due to a lack of experience in using computers. In order to facilitate communication between such users and organizations desiring to provide summary tape processing services, the Census Bureau established the summary tape processing center program.

Since early 1969 the Bureau has recognized over 175 organizations (private, governmental, and academic) that have indicated to the Bureau their intentions to provide services to users of census data. The centers are not established, franchised, or supported by the Bureau, and there are no controls on services or prices. However, as a public service the Bureau provides a public listing of these organizations in its publications, including a description of each center's planned services and tape holdings. Many processing centers offer general services such as tape copying and printouts of data, while others specialize in geographic coding, computer mapping, or data analysis. Tape holdings also vary. Some processing centers hold one count for one state, others hold one or more counts for several states, and a few have the full set of files released by the Bureau.

E. GEOGRAPHIC REFERENCES

Consideration of census data invariably includes reference to some type of geographic area. The name, location, and boundaries of most types of geographic areas (e.g., regions, states, counties, cities) are generally known, but those of census statistical units, such as census tracts and blocks, are more obscure and difficult to remember. Consequently, census users often require maps showing the locations of these census tabulation areas.

The three principal types of maps prepared by the Census Bureau to aid users are the metropolitan, place, and county maps. The metropolitan maps, developed for the urbanized portion of each of the nation's 233 SMSA's, are included in the *Block Statistics Reports* (series HC(3)). Place maps cover incorporated and unincorporated places not included on the metropolitan maps. Generally, these maps must be obtained from the Census Bureau. The county maps, which are reproductions of standard state highway department maps in most cases, show all census boundary information except for those areas covered by the metropolitan and place maps. These maps are also available from the Census Bureau.

The summary tapes present another "geographic" problem to users. Cities, counties, states, and other types of areas are identified on the tapes by numeric codes. Therefore, before data for a specific county can be selected from a tape for printing, the "county code" must be known. The Census Bureau has prepared three reference sources that associate the names of political and statistical subdivisions with the corresponding geographic codes: (1) Master Enumeration District List (MEDList), (2) Geographic Area Code Index, and (3) Geographic Identification Code Scheme.

The MEDList, available on computer tape and microfilm, provides the geographic codes for places, county subdivisions, counties, and states. It also identifies the relationships of these areas as well as enumeration districts to "higher level" areas. For example, a city would be identified as being in county A, SMSA B, and state C. The Geographic Area Code

Index, also available on computer tape and microfilm, is identical to the MEDList except that no reference is made to enumeration districts, reducing the size of this reference source considerably. The Geographic Identification Code Scheme is a four-part publication (one for each census region) presenting a selected hierarchy of codes for counties, county subdivisions, and places.

A final type of geographic reference is the geographic base file, a computer tape file which describes the street network of an urbanized area. Geographic base files were developed for over 200 central cities of SMSA's and their immediate environs for use in the geographic coding operations of the 1970 Census. These files are now available to users for such purposes as manual or computerized geographic coding of local records, computer mapping, and network analysis applications.

There are two types of geographic base files: address coding guides and DIME files. Address coding guides, developed for 147 cities, are basically an inventory of street sides. The inventory consists of records describing each street side in terms of its name, low and high address numbers, and associated census codes including block, tract, place, county, and state. The DIME files, prepared for 194 cities including 113 that had address coding guides, are similar to the address coding guides with the exception of one significant improvement. Street intersections are identified by "node" numbers which are included on each street record. Consequently, street sections are easily linked to each other through the common node numbers. To further increase the utility of the DIME files, x-y coordinates were calculated for each node and included on the computer tapes released by the Bureau.

F. COMPUTER PROGRAMS

For those users who have access to a computer, the Census Bureau has developed several computer programs for processing 1970 Census data files as well as other types of files. The following is a summary of the computer programs currently available from the Bureau:

1. *DAUList.* This is a series of six programs designed to select data from the summary tapes and display it with appropriate annotation.

2. *ADMATCH.* This computer program uses either of the geographic base files as a reference source to assign geographic codes to records with street addresses (e.g., building permits, welfare cases, school enrollment records).

3. *C-MAP and GRIDS.* These two programs produce computer maps on the line printer of a computer using either census or local data.

4. *T-GUIDE*. This computer program is designed to collapse the DIME files from their original state of one record per street per block (e.g., 100 block Main Street, 200 block Main Street, etc.) to one record per street per census tract. This process can reduce a DIME file by as much as 60%, thus making it more manageable for processing.

G. DATA ACCESS AND USE PUBLICATIONS

As the title states, this series was created as a guide to the products of the 1970 Census of Population and Housing. Before a user can use census data with even minimal adequacy, he must be familiar with the definitions of the many demographic, socio-economic and housing terms, geographic concepts, contents of the summary tapes (as compared to the printed reports), and such technical matters as sampling variability and data suppression. To assist the user in this educational process, the Bureau of the Census has prepared several data access and use-oriented publications. Brief descriptions of these publications are provided below.

1. *1970 Census Users' Guide*. This two-part publication is designed to furnish most of the information data users will need for effective access and use of 1970 Census data products. *Part I* covers such subjects as the collection and processing of 1970 data, data delivery media, and geographic reference materials. This part also contains a 1970 Census users' dictionary which provides definitions for more than 200 population, housing, and geographic terms. *Part II* contains the technical documentation for the 1st-4th count summary tapes.

2. *Small-Area Data Notes*. This monthly publication provides up-to-date information on Census Bureau products and programs as well as occasional items on the activities of summary tape processing centers and user applications of census data.

3. *Data Access Descriptions*. This is a series of occasional pamphlets, each issue of which is devoted to a detailed treatment of a particular census topic (examples: contents of Fourth Count summary tapes, public use samples, place-of-work data, low income data).

4. *Census User Bulletins*. This series is designed for quickly announcing progress in releasing printed reports and summary tapes and other matters that require timely notification.

5. *1970 Census and You*. This pamphlet was prepared for potential users of census data to provide basic information on census geogra-

phy, data concepts, data products, and sources for more detailed descriptions of census related topics.

6. *Index to 1970 Census Summary Tapes: Counts 1-5.* This publication presents a comprehensive index to the tape count and tabulation number of each subject variable appearing on these tapes. Subject variables are listed alphabetically along with a description of the appropriate tabulation(s), including the cross-classification variables and the universe.

7. *Census Use Study Reports.* This is a series of 14 reports documenting the Census Use Study's New Haven and Los Angeles projects. The Census Use Study is a small area research activity concerned with determining user needs for data and for tools and techniques for handling census and local data. The Study's activities have included geographic coding and computer mapping research, development of a metropolitan health information system, and surveys of users' data requirements.

H. ADDITIONAL INFORMATION

This chapter was prepared to serve as an *introduction* to the 1970 Census products, and for the sake of brevity, omits many of the details readers may need. Undiscussed topics concern the actual contents of the summary tapes, the number of reels associated with the summary tapes and public use samples, and the sources of the various data access and use publications. Discussion of the procedures for obtaining special tabulation of the basic census records was also omitted, since the results of special tabulations generally are not considered as census products.

A new office has been established by the Bureau to serve as a centralized point to which inquiries such as those cited above can be directed. Users with any questions concerning the 1970 Census, its products, or the procedures for obtaining special tabulations of the basic census records should contact the Data User Services Office, Bureau of the Census, Washington, D.C. 20233.

19 POPULATION ESTIMATES

A. INTRODUCTION

A wealth of demographic detail emerged from the 1970 Census, but what next? Additional census data will not be available until 1980.

Rapid changes are occurring in nearly all communities of the United States, and Chamber of Commerce researchers require data about these changes more often than the U.S. Census offers — once in a decade. Drastic shifts in population distribution have occurred, especially since 1960. Nowhere was this more true than in metropolitan areas. Huge vacant areas along the periphery of metropolitan settlement were gobbled up to provide suburban housing. The inner portions of SMSA's were affected by road building and urban renewal projects, which removed more housing and population dwelling potential.

The result has been a major shift of population out of the city and into the surrounding localities. While the city declined, the population of the remainder of the metropolitan area soared.

Planning for economic development and for expansion of public facilities requires the preparation and maintenance of current population estimates and projections of anticipated growth. Competent population estimates and projections are basic tools in understanding what is happening to a locality, county or region, and in attempting to control and shape changes to benefit its residents.

Since 1967 the Bureau of the Census has been working with agencies and organizations to develop an expertise in the preparation of county population estimates.[1] Recent surveys suggest a rapidly growing sophistication in the methods used to develop estimates. This is reflected in a reduction in the number of poor methods used and an increasing tendency to combine two or more estimates to derive a "best" figure.

---

[1]For a discussion of the origin and evolution of the Federal-State Cooperative Program for Population Estimates, see an article by Meyer Zitter in U.S. Department of Health, Education & Welfare, *The Registrar and Statistician,* Vol. 33, No. 1, January, 1968, pages 4-8.

The principal procedures developed by the Bureau of the Census for preparing postcensal population estimates relating to local areas are described in Section B of this chapter. Section C includes additional procedures which Chamber of Commerce researchers have found to be helpful in preparing population estimates.

B. BUREAU OF THE CENSUS ESTIMATING TECHNIQUES

What sorts of methods are used in preparing population estimates?[2] A wide variety of techniques exist, but the choice of method used may be severely restricted by the symptomatic data available as input to the estimating procedure. Another factor which will influence the selection of methodology will be the side benefits: will the procedure yield population totals only, or will it produce race detail, or age detail, or migration estimates? One method or combination of methods may be used to estimate a county total and a different set of procedures, adjusted to be consistent with the independent county estimate, to estimate the population of the cities and townships in the county.

As a rule the smaller the area being estimated, the fewer may be the methodological options and the fewer the symptomatic indicators available. Consequently there appears to be some advantage to controlling estimates prepared for small areas to independent totals for larger areas where more sophisticated or more varied methods are available.

1. Component Methods

A very commonly used estimating procedure is the *component method*, in which estimates of change in the number of births, deaths, and net migration occurring from the time of the base census to the estimate date are applied to the census population to derive a current estimate. Both births and deaths are commonly obtained by compiling vital statistics from publications and unpublished records of the state and local health departments or the National Center for Health Statistics.[3] The migration component can be estimated in a wide variety of ways, however, and the names of well-known component methods commonly reflect how the migration compo-

---

[2]Adapted from a paper presented by Donald E. Starsinic, Population Division, U.S. Bureau of the Census, at the Population Estimates Conference sponsored by the East-West Gateway Coordinating Council and the Center for Urban Programs, St. Louis University, St. Louis, Missouri, March 4, 1971. Used by permission of the U.S. Bureau of the Census.

[3]The Division of Vital Statistics, National Center for Health Statistics, U.S. Department of Health, Education & Welfare, publishes an annual *Vital Statistics of the United States* showing registered births and deaths for counties and cities of 10,000 and over by white and nonwhite.

nent is derived. The simplest component methods make use of migration trends—either numbers or rates—from a previous period, based on censuses or surveys, and assume a continuation of the past trend or some variation of that trend.

a. Component Method II

A much more complex variation of the component method has been used by the Bureau of the Census for the last 20 years in preparing its state estimates and as one of several methods used for county estimates. Component Method II[4] makes use of school enrollment data to derive the migration component. Basically, it assumes that the relationship on the last census date between the population of compulsory school age and enrollment in the school grades which most closely approximate this age group continues to the estimate date. By applying the census ratio to the enrollment in these same school grades on the estimate date an estimate of the current population of compulsory school age is obtained. This is compared with an estimate of the expected school-age population obtained by aging the school-age cohort (the group of children who would be of compulsory school age on the estimate date) from the census date to the estimate date by use of survival rates. The difference between the estimated and expected school age population is an estimate of the net migration for this age group, which is converted to a migration rate. A national ratio of the migration rate for the total population to that of the school-age population rate is applied to the school-age migration rate to estimate the all-ages migration rate. This in turn is applied to an all-ages migration base to estimate total migration since the last census.

b. Grade Progression Method

Another component method variation, the Grade Progression Method, also uses school enrollment, relating enrollment in specified grades in one year to enrollment in the immediately-next grades the following year. The ratio between these two enrollments is the migration rate for the year.

Other data series such as residential utility data, building permits, school enrollment by age or school census (the Age-Progression Method, for example), labor force data, or automobile permits, might be used in a similar way.

2. Censal Ratio Methods

A second well-known group of estimating procedures is *censal ratio methods*. In the censal ratio methods, current symptomatic data are multi-

---

[4] A general discussion of Component Method II is contained in *Current Population Reports*, Series P-25, No. 436. A detailed step-by-step outline of the method is shown in Series P-25, No. 339.

plied by the ratio of population to the same symptomatic data at the last census for the area for which the estimate is being made. A variation of the method allows for a trend in this ratio between the census and estimate date. Sometimes the initial estimates of population by the censal ratio method for the constituent parts of an area are adjusted to add to an independent estimate for the entire area. A censal ratio method may be simple, using one indicator, or complex, using two or more indicators.

a. Vital Rates Method

A very widely used type of censal ratio method is based upon vital statistics data and is termed the Vital Rates Method.[5] In the Vital Rates Method birth and death rates are computed for the last census date, adjusted to the estimate date by the change in the national birth and death rates, respectively, and divided into the births and deaths for the estimate year. The resultant estimates are averaged to obtain a "best" total.

b. Housing Unit Method

The Housing Unit Method is a censal ratio method in which the estimates of population are based on estimates of housing units.[6] This method is extensively used for urban places and in metropolitan areas because of the general availability of building permit data for these areas — one of the few statistical series that can easily be obtained for cities and often for townships and census tracts. For rural areas, however, the method is generally not practical because of the lack of adequate building permit records to measure changes in the number of housing units.

The Housing Unit Method, although simple in concept, requires the use of broad assumptions concerning change in size of households and change in vacancy rates, which are frequently highly speculative. The use of building permit data also assumes the availability of adequate records on units demolished, a statistic rarely well maintained. Consequently, the error can be quite large for this method except when it is adjusted to an estimate for a broader area using other techniques that avoid the pitfalls of this procedure.

---

[5]Donald J. Bogue, "A Technique for Making Extensive Population Estimates," *Journal of the American Statistical Association,* Vol. 45, No. 250, June 1950, pp. 149-163.

[6]A variation of the Housing Unit Method related to the population 18 and over is described in *Current Population Reports,* Series P-25, No. 427.

c. Ratio-Correlation Method

A complex censal ratio method becoming more widely used is the Ratio-Correlation (or Regression) Method.[7] This method, while relatively untested to date, seems to offer great promise in the estimating of small area populations. In its most common format, the method estimates change in the proportion of an area's share of a larger unit's population total (the dependent variable) by the change in the share that each of several related data series for that area (the independent variables) has undergone over time.

The basic regression can be further refined by stratification, a sorting out of the number of areas to be estimated into groups with similar characteristics.[8] The 115 counties in Missouri, for example, might be separated into three categories: metropolitan counties, nonmetropolitan counties with more than 20 percent urban population in 1960, and remaining nonmetropolitan counties. Alternatively, a separation could be devised by economic base: corn crop, cotton crop, wheat crop, resort and recreation. The one requirement in any such subdivision is that there be at least 20 counties in each category to insure sufficient degrees of freedom for an accurate regression line. In this way regressions are developed for each category rather than one for all Missouri counties, thus presumably improving the accuracy of the estimate.

Even greater refinement within this stratification technique can be achieved by use of dummy variables.[9] For example, within a corn-cotton-wheat-resort stratification, recognition of metropolitan-nonmetropolitan differences might also be given.

Another variation of the Ratio-Correlation Method has been experimented with by Dale Welch of the Maine Department of Health and Welfare. It uses the regression to estimate migration rather than population change.[10] Changes in annual migration rates are estimated by relating them to the percent differences between the expected and actual change in such indicators as births, deaths, and school enrollment.

---

[7]*Current Population Reports*, Series P-25, No. 436 has a brief description of this method. More detailed discussions will be found in David Goldberg, Allen Feldt and J. William Smit, "Estimates of Population Change in Michigan: 1950-1960;"*Michigan Population Studies No. 1*, University of Michigan, Ann Arbor, Michigan, 1960; and Robert C. Schmitt and Albert H. Crosetti, "Accuracy of Ratio-Correlation Method for Estimating Postcensal Population," *Land Economics*, Vol. 30, No. 3, August, 1954, pp. 279-281.

[8]Harry Rosenberg, "Improving Current Population Estimates Through Stratification," *Land Economics*, Vol. 44, No. 3, August, 1968, pp. 331-338.

[9]Donald E. Pursell, "Improving Population Estimates with the Use of Dummy Variables," *Demography*, Vol. 7, No. 1, February, 1970, pp. 87-91.

[10]Maine Department of Health and Welfare, *Population Estimates for Minor Civil Divisions: Maine - 1963 and 1966.*

3. Composite Methods

In another widely used category of estimating techniques, the Composite Method, estimates of various age groups are derived separately and are then summed to secure a total for all ages. One method is to use age-specific deaths and death rates. Another, developed by Bogue and Duncan, uses death statistics to estimate ages 45 and over, birth statistics to estimate ages 15 to 44 and under 5, and Component Method II to estimate ages 5 to 14 years.[11] Other variations of the Composite Method employ other combinations of "indicators" for various age groups. Composite methods permit the choice of those indicators best suited to a given age range and provide some age detail as a by-product.

The Composite Method approach obviously represents a most flexible way of preparing estimates at various area levels. A wide variety of methods can be used to estimate the population in various age groups. For example, in the state estimates for the 1970 decade, the Bureau of the Census may very well abandon its current average of Component Method II and Ratio-Correlation in favor of a component method, with the migration component obtained using the Social Security Administration's one-percent work history sample. The population 5 to 17 would be obtained by a component procedure in which the migration component is derived by relating it to migration in another age group (a procedure similar to that of Component Method II). In this case, however, the migration rate for the group 18 to 64 is converted to a migration rate for the group 5 to 17. The population under 5 would be derived by relating births to women of child-bearing age as commonly used in the Bogue-Duncan Composite Method.

4. Other Estimating Methods

There are a number of widely used but less sophisticated types of estimating procedures that deserve mention despite their limitations. The proration method involves the distribution of an estimated total for some large area among the constituent parts, as an independently estimated state total among counties, on the basis of either the population at the last census or current symptomatic data, such as school data, births, or deaths. This procedure implicitly assumes that the state's population is currently distributed in the same proportion over the counties as at the last census, or that the ratio of population to the symptomatic item is the same for all of the counties. (In this respect, the proration method differs from the censal

---

[11]Donald J. Bogue and Beverly Duncan, "A Composite Method for Estimating Postcensal Population of Small Areas by Age, Sex, and Color," *Vital Statistics—Special Reports,* Vol. 47, No. 6, August 24, 1959. The Composite Method variation used by the Bureau of the Census is described in *Current Population Reports,* Series P-25, No. 427.

ratio method. In the latter the ratio of population to the symptomatic item is derived separately for each county.)

The natural increase method involves adding natural increase (births minus deaths) to the census figure. It assumes, therefore, that net migration since the last census equals zero.

Both arithmetic extrapolation and geometric extrapolation assume a continuation of growth consistent with past amounts of growth or rates of growth respectively. These methods do not bring to bear any current symptomatic data that would reflect change in pattern since the last census.

5. Summary

This provides a brief rundown of some of the many estimating techniques available to the population estimator. Several of the methods require so much manipulation that access to a computer facility greatly eases the burden of working through them on any regular basis. Component Method II and Grade- and Age-Progression Methods, the Composite Method, and certainly the Ratio-Correlation Method fall into this category. The Ratio-Correlation Method, however, once the basic correlations are determined, is one of the simplest methods to maintain.

In addition to the more commonly used symptomatic indicators in the preparation of population estimates which have been mentioned so far (births, deaths, school enrollment, building permits, utility connections), a wide variety of indicators can be drawn upon in estimates work. The prime consideration in using any data series is whether it is reflective of population change. Censal ratio methods, and particularly the Ratio-Correlation Method, can utilize many different indicators. In the Federal-State Co-operative Program literally dozens of different indicators have been utilized by one agency or another. Such items as auto registration, covered employment, votes, sales tax, social security recipients, state income tax, and bank deposits are very commonly drawn upon. In addition, every state or locality is likely to have some indicator data series peculiarly suited to use in estimates for that area.

Methods which use school enrollment data by grade require considerable expenditure of time and effort ensuring consistency of the series from year to year. *All* input used to develop population estimates, however, should be carefully screened for consistency over time. Changes in procedures or in reporting units frequently create breaks in data time series which must be resolved and adjusted. It can *never* be assumed that input data are either accurate or consistent over time simply because they have been published.

Births and deaths can generally be obtained for counties and cities, and possibly for minor civil divisions (townships) and census tracts. School enrollment data normally are available for counties and cities having their own school systems. The next level of availability, the school district, probably will bear no relationship to the smaller units for which population estimates may be desired. In Missouri even county totals may be difficult to obtain because school districts do not respect county boundaries, and school district consolidations make comparison over time very complex.

Building permit data are routinely available in annual reports published by the Bureau of the Census for cities and for many minor civil divisions.[12] Localities frequently maintain permit records by census tract. Demolition data, however, are frequently fragmentary and often relate to structures rather than housing units. Residential electric, gas, and water utility connections have a tremendous advantage over building permit and demolition data in their obvious relationship to occupied units, thus avoiding any assumption concerning a current occupancy rate. These records may not be available, however, for the areal units required. Some of their residential utility connection data may also be reported on master meters, which must somehow be converted to an estimate of the number of residential units served.

Innumerable variations can be indulged in developing population estimates for an area. For example, estimates of the county totals for the metropolitan counties might be developed using an average of Component Method II, the Composite Method, and the Regression Method, with the detail for subdivisions of the area developed by a Housing Unit technique. Age detail could be derived by using a variation of Component II[13] or the Composite Method or by using a regression with certain input detail specific to certain age groups. For subdivisions of the county, lack of age-specific input may prevent the use of any of the above methods. In this case the possible alternative would be to use the Hamilton-Perry Method of extrapolating age detail[14] and then to control the age detail obtained in a more sophisticated manner for broader areas.

Estimates by race are now much in demand, but frequently race detail is not available in most of the symptomatic detail used for estimates. Vital statistics are the most accessible data series available for this work. They may be used in a Vital Rates estimate by race to obtain the necessary racial breakdown. Or the change of racial composition could be estimated by using the birth and death data in a simple regression to estimate change in percent Negro and white.

---

[12]Bureau of the Census, *Construction Reports,* Series C-40, "Housing Authorized by Building Permits and Public Contracts," annual for 12,000 permit-issuing places, monthly for 4,000 large permit-issuing places. See also Bureau of the Census, *Housing Construction Statistics, 1889 to 1964,* for collected statistics for many places.

[13]*Current Population Reports,* Series P-25, No. 436.

[14]C. Horace Hamilton and Josef Perry, "A Short Method for Projecting Population by Age from One Census to Another," *Social Forces,* December, 1962, pp. 163-170.

6. Evaluation of Methods

So far many methods of estimating population have been discussed. How accurate are these methods, however? In the past there has been comparatively little testing of methods below the state level. The Bureau of the Census tested Component Method II, the Ratio Correlation-Method and the Vital Rates Method for states against the 1960 Census.[15] The Bureau found that by combining Component Method II, the procedure used during the 1950's, with the Vital Rates Method or the Ratio-Correlation Method the average error was appreciably reduced. By this last combination the average error was reduced to 1½% as compared with 2% by Component Method II alone and higher percent errors for the Vital Rates Method alone (2.4%) or the Ratio-Correlation Method gives an average error of about 2%, disappointingly higher than the last decade. The rationale for the poorer showing of these methods in 1960 is still being studied.

A number of independent researchers tested county population estimates against the 1960 Census.[16] It is difficult to make direct comparisons between the different pieces of research because of variations in the procedures used in developing the test estimates. The most extensive of the tests was that of James Tarver of Oklahoma State University (covering six states), but six other researchers released findings covering one or more states. Their results indicated a rather discouraging high level of error for most methods tested. Consistently, however, they suggest a considerable improvement in the error rate by combining two or more methods.

At the county level, the Bureau of the Census in the 1950's tested both Component Method II and the Vital Rates Method for about 132 metropolitan counties. Although neither method tested very well by itself (average errors were over five percent), the combination of the two methods reduced the average error to about 4% for counties and 3.3% for whole SMSA's. A preliminary test has been worked up for about 290 SMSA counties in 1970, comparing Component Method II with an average of Component Method II, the Composite Method, and the Housing Unit Method, the latter used only for the central counties of the SMSA's based on preliminary 1969 estimates extrapolated to 1970. The findings suggest that the averaging of methods (with an average error of 3.5% for counties)

---

[15]Meyer Zitter and Henry S. Shryock, "Accuracy of Methods of Preparing Postcensal Population Estimates for States and Local Areas," *Demography,* Vol. 1, No. 1, 1964, pp. 227-241.

[16]Meyer Zitter, Donald E. Starsinic, and David L. Word, "Accuracy of Methods of Preparing Postcensal Population Estimates for Counties: A Summary Compilation of Recent Studies," paper presented at the meeting of the Population Association of America, Boston, April 18-20, 1968. Available on request from Chief, State and Local Population Estimates Branch, Population Division, Bureau of the Census, Washington, D.C. 20233.

is still a considerable improvement over Component Method alone (5.6%), which would not be recommended for use at a small area level by itself.

One of the most exciting prospects in testing the validity of various estimating procedures is the test phase of the Federal-State Cooperative Program now in process which will be completed during the last half of this year. All 47 states participating formally and informally in the program are committed to test a variety of estimating procedures against the 1970 Census to determine their relative accuracy in producing county population estimates. Here for the first time we will have a massive statistical compilation largely standardized for data input and methodology to evaluate such techniques as Component Method II, the Composite Method, the Ratio-Correlation Method, and several other procedures which the individual states desire to test. Based on the findings of this test program, we will be able to judge the appropriateness of these various methods at the county level and the effectiveness of combining them in one way or another. The test will supply us with a basis for laying out estimates programs for the coming decade. At both the state and metropolitan county level the Bureau of the Census will be testing a variety of combinations of methods to learn the advisability and accuracy of these procedures.

As you can see from this discussion, population estimating procedures have not been adequately tested in the past. It is to be assumed that demographers preparing small area estimates will want to test their procedures and to experiment with other procedures to improve their records.

This is a period of considerable flux in the preparation of population estimates at all area levels, and imaginative researchers will have the opportunity to evolve substantial improvement in the procedures employed in population estimates work. The desperate need for accurate estimates of the population at so many different area levels and for estimates of population characteristics in the coming decade should give impetus to a breakthrough in both the quality and quantity of population estimates.

C. ADDITIONAL PROCEDURES FOR ESTIMATING THE POPULATION OF LOCAL AREAS

When the need for population estimates arises, the researcher may not have time to use the more elaborate procedures described in the preceding section of this chapter. Shorter procedures, based upon locally-generated indicators of population change, can be used to provide the necessary data.

The estimating methodology described here is a composite based upon the results of three estimating procedures. Unless it is unavoidable, just a single estimating procedure should never be used, as a combination of procedures can lessen the probability of error. If you have to use just one estimating procedure, it is recommended you use Method One described in subsequent paragraphs.

The general plan outlined here involves estimating the population of a county by each of three estimating methods, weighting each estimate, and then averaging the three weighted estimates to arrive at a composite estimate. The three estimating methods are labeled as follows:

Method One: Labor Force
Method Two: Housing Unit
Method Three: Passenger Car Registrations

For illustrative purposes, assume that, in February, 1974, a reporter for a local newspaper asked the researcher of the Central City Chamber of Commerce for his estimate of Central County's population as of December 31, 1973.

The following description of methods—which the researcher used to arrive at the answer to the reporter's question—is based upon data for a county in which a large city is located, but the same methods can be used for making population estimates for a less populous county, city or SMSA.

1. Estimating Method One: Labor Force

The basic steps involved in estimating the total population of Central County are:

a. Calculate the ratio of Central County's total labor force to its total population on April 1, 1970, the latest decennial census. The appropriate procedure involves adding Central County's total labor force for the months of March, April and May, 1970, and then dividing the total by three. Next, this seasonally-adjusted average should be divided by the figure representing Central County's total population on April 1, 1970.

Below is the formula structure:

Months (1970)	Total Labor Force
March	873,900
April	880,800
May	888,600
Total	2,643,300

$$\frac{2,643,300}{3} = 881,100 = \text{seasonally-adjusted labor force total for April, 1970 (the mean month)}$$

b. Prepare seasonally-adjusted labor force totals (three-month moving averages) for Central County for each month since April, 1970. All of these totals are not needed for the current problem, but this activity should be added to the researcher's work program so that he is prepared to handle future requests for population estimates relating to the local area. Also, these seasonally-adjusted totals can be used in plotting a labor force trend line.

c. Prepare the calculations for the December, 1973 — the period nearest January 1, 1974 — seasonally-adjusted labor force total as follows:

Months	Total Labor Force
November, 1973	950,000
December, 1973	951,000
January, 1974	943,000
Total	2,844,000

$$\frac{2,844,000}{3} = 948,000 = \text{seasonally-adjusted labor force total for December, 1973}$$

d. At this point the researcher should examine carefully the economic indicators for Central County relating to the period April, 1970, through December, 1973. If the results of his investigation point up no significant change in the percentage relationship of Central County's seasonally-adjusted labor force total to its total population, then the following formula may be used in the concluding phase of Method One:

$$\left(\frac{\text{Total labor force, April, 1970}}{\text{Total population, April, 1970}}\right) = \left(\frac{\text{Total labor force, December, 1973}}{X}\right)$$

$$(881,100/1,741,912) = (948,000/X)$$

$$881,100 \; X = 1,651,332,576,000$$

$$x \;=\; \frac{1,651,332,576,000}{881,100}$$

$$x \;=\; 1,874,384$$

Population estimate
for Central County as
of December 31, 1973

2. Estimating Method Two: Housing Unit

The basic assumption of the Housing Unit Method is that changes in the number of occupied housing units in an area reflect changes in the area's population. This procedure includes (1) determining the number of dwelling units constructed in the area since April, 1970; (2) adding the number of new dwelling units to the 1970 Census housing inventory for this area; (3) adjusting the total number of dwelling units to allow for vacancies and demolitions; and (4) multiplying the total number of occupied housing units by a factor reflecting the average household size per dwelling unit.

Suggested data sources to be used in the Housing Unit Estimating Method are listed as follows:

a. *Housing inventory as of April, 1970.* 1970 Census of Housing.
b. *Dwelling units constructed since April, 1970.* Local utilities that compile new residential electrical connections, representing *completed* residential units (both single-family and apartment) and connected with electricity for the first time. Cumulative information of this type is very useful in compiling a continuously-updated housing inventory for the area.
c. *Demolitions.* Records in permit-issuing offices of municipalities in the area.
d. *Vacancies.* Estimates of the local Board of Realtors.
e. *Average number of persons per household unit.* 1970 Census of Population.

The preparation of the population estimates by means of the Housing Unit Method is illustrated as follows:

Total housing units in Central County
April, 1970   587,203

Number of housing units constructed during
the period, April, 1970 - December, 1973 . . . .   +   85,321

Total   672,524
Less demolitions . . . .   -   5,125

Sub Total	667,399
Less vacancies .... -	69,641

Total number of occupied units, Dec. 31, 1973	597,758
Average number of persons per unit .... (X)	3.19

Estimated population	1,906,848

3. Estimating Method Three: Passenger Car Registrations

Passenger car registrations constitute the third symptomatic data series chosen for use in this composite estimating procedure. The first step involved in Method Three is to obtain total passenger car registrations from the Central County tax assessor-collector as of two dates: April 1, 1970, and December 31, 1973. Next, assume that the statistical relationship between population and passenger car registrations has not changed significantly during the period, April 1970 - December 1973. The final step is the application of the following formula—substituting numbers for the components—and generating a population estimate:

$$\left(\frac{\text{Central County passenger car registrations, April 1, 1970}}{\text{Central County population, April 1, 1970}} \right) = \left(\frac{\text{Central County passenger car registrations, Dec. 31, 1973}}{X} \right)$$

$$(777,255/1,741,912) = (907,131/X)$$

$$777,255 \ X = 1,580,142,374,472$$

$$X = \frac{1,580,142,374,472}{777,255}$$

$$X = 2,032,978$$

Population estimate for
Central County as of
December 31, 1973

4. Weighting and Averaging Population Estimates

In the composite procedure which the Central City Chamber of Commerce researcher chose to use, three independent estimates were prepared. These three estimates were weighted—which represented decisions based upon the researcher's analysis of Central County economic and demographic characteristics. The weightings used by this researcher — *which are not necessarily applicable to all local areas* — are shown as follows:

Estimating Method	Weighting
One: Labor Force	6
Two: Housing Unit	3
Three: Passenger Car Registrations	1

Next, the weighted estimates were averaged to derive a final estimate of Central County's population, as indicated:

Estimating Method	Population Estimate	Weighting	Weighting × Pop. Estimate
One	1,874,384	6	11,246,304
Two	1,906,848	3	5,720,544
Three	2,032,978	1	2,032,978
			18,999,826

$$\frac{18,999,826}{10} = 1,899,982$$ or rounded to the nearest thousand, 1,900,000 — the estimate which the researcher in this illustration reported for Central County's population as of December 31, 1973.

The theory behind the use of component weights in population estimates may be summarized as follows:

a. Several factors should be used in the estimating procedure, since fluctuations attributable to one component will probably offset fluctuations attributable to another component.

b. While an estimate based upon the use of only one factor will probably not be completely accurate, some of these factors will be more useful than others in the population estimating procedure.

c. In computing the final composite estimate of population for your area, greater weights should be assigned to the preliminary estimates derived from the components which the researcher and his local advisors believe will be more nearly accurate.

The weighting of estimating components may be tested by comparing an estimate with a reliable benchmark. For example, using data applicable to a county as of April 1, 1970, compute the county's population estimate by means of weighted components and compare the result with the county's population reported by the 1970 Census of Population. If a significant difference is observed, the weightings of the estimating components may need to be adjusted.

Decisions relating to weighting the preliminary estimates are subjective judgments, and this decision-making activity calls for careful consideration and caution. The Chamber of Commerce Research Committee should be quite helpful to the local researcher in deciding which estimating components should be used and how they should be weighted. The area's economic history, the nature of its economic base, employment trends, industry patterns, housing construction and occupancy plus other economic and demographic indicators should be considered in tailoring an estimating procedure to fit the local area.

Broad guidelines may be structured for weighting population components selected for a population-estimating procedure. For example, in an area that has a broad-based economy and has demonstrated long-range economic stability, labor force trends — after adjustment for seasonal variation — are among the most useful symptoms of population change. If an area is heavily dependent upon a very few companies or industries, however, the local economy will likely experience greater fluctuation in economic indicators, including employment. Severe fluctuations in employment lessen the predictability of labor force trends and decrease, therefore, the utility of the labor force method in population estimating. The more erratic and unstable the employment history of an area, the less weight the labor force component should be assigned in the final population estimate.

There are several good measures to determine your area's employment stability. One is the ratio of unemployment to the total labor force in your area. This ratio, calculated as a percentage, can be compared to the national unemployment average for an idea of how well your area is performing relative to the rest of the nation. Viewed historically, this figure can show how well the area has done in the past, which is some indication of what it can expect to do in the future.

An excellent indication of overall area economic strength is the occupational distribution of its workers. A fairly even spread of workers among the different industry groups is evidence of a wide economic base. If there is a heavy concentration of workers in one industry, or working for one company, the evidence points toward dependence upon a limited economic base and potentially unstable growth.

The use of housing units as a base for estimates is generally considered a second best method, while suffering from restrictions similar to those listed for the employment method. While valuable for those areas that have experienced stable, long term growth, housing unit reliability tends to weaken in those areas that suffer from economic instability. To rely on the housing figures necessarily requires good lines of communication between the Research Committee and representatives of the construction industry. Whereas accurate records of housing completions are usually available, these figures do not include indicators of changes in the average number of persons per household; decreases in the housing inventory due to demolitions, fires and other causes; and changes in the rate of housing occupancy. Taken at face value the total housing units figure—if used in a population estimating procedure—would exaggerate the population of an area. It is necessary to rely on local builders, realtors, mortgage bankers and apartment owners and managers to provide additional indicators of the current housing inventory and occupancy rates which the community is experiencing.

The obvious problem is that those cities with heavy economic fluctuations stemming from a weak base are subject to heavier patterns of migration and vacancy, making it more difficult to obtain reliable records of what is really happening in housing. These changes in occupancy are largely independent of normal seasonal variations and are much more erratic. This unpredictability negates in large part the usefulness of housing as a reliable indicator in such an area.

Passenger car registration is a third alternative for a base for population estimation. While still valuable as one of the symptoms of population change, this particular technique must be watched more carefully than the other two. In the case of the Central County estimate, the automobile registration method was assigned the lowest strength in the final average—only one-tenth—because of recent trends in ownership/population ratios.

In the past few years there has been a remarkable shift in the auto-per-capita rate, especially in the urban areas. More people are owning cars, for several reasons. One is that there has been an increase in the eligible population. Another is that there is an increased need for reliable transportation in some areas as mass transit systems become more and more inadequate. There are also the factors of increasing personal income, which allows more people to purchase a car, and the social status attributed to automobile ownership.

The ultimate effect of these trends is that the auto ownership/population ratio is changing at some unknown rate and will not reflect these changes in predictions based upon it. As more people own cars, and as people own more cars, the auto/person ratio increases. The formula given in the sample estimation (Method Three, page 354) assumes that from the base year to the present, the auto/person ratio has remained the same. Mathematically, this means that the calculations will show that population has increased proportionately to auto registration, which is probably not true. From all indications, population has grown at a lesser rate. The result is that this method has a built-in tendency to over-estimate population. If it is necessary to use an estimate based upon this ratio, it should be assigned a lower weight because it is inherently less valuable.

There are varied and active forces at work in each city which make it different from any other. The demographic bases are changing; relationships that once remained stable are now subject to change; periods of instability increase the difficulty of making accurate projections. Any estimating procedure used should allow for these forces. It is the job of the Chamber researcher to be aware of those changes which are acting most strongly in his community and to incorporate allowances for them into his estimating procedure. He must establish his own component weights based upon the reliability of the information supplied and upon any trends in the base relationships which this information implies.

SELECTED READING REFERENCES

1. Population Estimates

Bogue, Donald J. "A Technique for Making Extensive Population Estimates." *Journal of the American Statistical Association,* Vol. 45, No. 250, (June, 1950), 149 - 163.

Bogue, Donald J., and Beverly Duncan. "A Composite Method for Estimating Postcensal Population of Small Areas by Age, Sex and Color." *Vital Statistics — Special Reports,* National Office of Vital Statistics, Vol. XLVII, No. 6. Washington, D.C.: U.S. Government Printing Office, August 24, 1959.

Brown, Hugh H. "A Technique for Estimating the Population of Counties." *Journal of the American Statistical Association,* (June, 1955), 323 - 343.

Morrison, Peter A. *Demographic Information for Cities: A Manual for Estimating and Projecting Local Population Characteristics.* U.S. Department of Housing and Urban Development, RAND Report R-618. Santa Monica, California: The Rand Corporation, June, 1971, 18 - 23, 142 - 149.

Pursell, Donald E. "Improving Population Estimates with the Use of Dummy Variables." *Demography,* Vol. 7, No. 1, (February, 1970), 87 - 91.

Rosenberg, Harry M. "Estimating Changes in Population." *Battelle Technical Review,* Vol. 16, No. 11, (November, 1967), 2 - 6.

Rosenberg, Harry M. "Improving Current Population Estimates Through Stratification." *Land Economics,* Vol. 44, No. 3, (August, 1968), 331 - 338.

Schmitt, Robert C. "Short-Cut Methods of Estimating County Population." *Journal of the American Statistical Association,* Vol. 47, (June, 1952), 232 - 238.

Schmitt, Robert C., and Albert H. Crosetti. "Accuracy of the Ratio-Correlation Method for Estimating Postcensal Population." *Land Economics,* Vol. 30, No. 3, (August, 1954), 279 - 281.

Starsinic, Donald E., and Meyer Zitter. "Accuracy of the Housing Unit Method in Preparing Population Estimates for Cities." *Demography,* Vol. 5, No. 1, 1968.

U.S. Bureau of the Census. "Methods of Population Estimation: Part 1 — Illustrative Procedure of the Census Bureau's Component Method II." *Current Population Reports,* Series P-25, No. 339. Washington, D.C.: U.S. Government Printing Office, June 6, 1966.

U.S. Bureau of the Census. "Use of Social Security's Continuous Work History Sample for Population Estimation." *Current Population Reports,* Series P-23, No. 31. Washington, D.C.: U.S. Government Printing Office, April 10, 1970.

Zitter, Meyer, and Henry S. Shryock. "Accuracy of Methods of Preparing Postcensal Population Estimates for States and Local Areas." *Demography,* Vol. 1, No. 1, (1964), 227 - 241.

2. Population Projections

Commission on Population Growth and the American Future. *Population Growth and America's Future.* Washington, D.C.: U.S. Government Printing Office, 1971.

Friedrich, Otto. "Population Explosion: Is Man Really Doomed?" *Time,* (September 13, 1971), 58 - 59.

Hagood, Margaret Jarman, and Jacob S. Siegel. "Population Projections for Sales Forecasting." *Journal of the American Statistical Association,* (September, 1952), 524 - 540.

Hajnal, John. "The Prospects for Population Forecasts." *Journal of the American Statistical Association,* (June, 1955), 309 - 322.

Hamilton, C. Horace, and Josef Perry. "A Short Method for Projecting Population by Age from One Census to Another." *Social Forces,* (December, 1962), 163 - 170.

Packer, Stephen B. "Population Growth and Market Forecasting." *Financial Analysts Journal,* (March-April, 1966), 13 - 18.

Population Reference Bureau, Inc. *The World Population Dilemma.* Washington, D.C.: Columbia Books, Inc., 1972.

Schmitt, Robert C. "Short-Cut Methods of Forecasting the Population of Census Tracts." *Journal of Marketing,* Vol. 18, No. 3, (January, 1954), 266 - 270.

Schmitt, Robert C., and Albert H. Crosetti. "Short-Cut Methods of Forecasting City Population." *Journal of Marketing,* Vol. 17, No. 4, (April, 1953), 417 - 424.

Spengler, Joseph J. "Population Threatens Prosperity." *Harvard Business Review,* (January-February, 1956), 85 - 94.

U.S. Bureau of the Census. *Handbook of Statistical Methods for Demographers,* by A. J. Jaffe. Washington, D.C.: U.S. Government Printing Office, 1951.

U.S. Department of Health, Education and Welfare. *Handbook of Statistical Procedures for Long-Range Projections of Public Enrollment,* Office of Education Technical Monograph OE-2417, by A. J. Jaffe. Washington, D.C.: U.S. Government Printing Office, 1969.

Part VI

GOVERNMENTAL
RESEARCH

20 EFFECTIVE LEGISLATIVE RESEARCH — WHY AND HOW

A. INTRODUCTION

Business, industry and agriculture—Chamber of Commerce members—are demanding more effective action on legislative issues at the local, state and federal levels.

Chambers which are responding to this demand face real problems. Those which are *not* responding may seem to have fewer problems at the moment, but the odds are that their years are numbered. The squeeze on business is too tight, and businessmen, barraged with requests from other associations, will not put dollars into organizations which ignore their legislative problems.

The demand by business for action by business-supported organizations has resulted from:

1. A phenomenal increase of professional staff in legislative bodies to assist lawmakers to design, evaluate, and consider legislation.
2. A trend toward annual meetings of state legislatures, often resulting in twice as many bills being introduced than would be in biennial sessions.
3. Severe attacks on the American economic system by some politicians at all levels of government—local, state, and federal.
4. Anti-business pressure groups which have turned to legislators at all levels to seek government enforcement of their aims.

The solutions to these problems go far beyond the realm of research, but research plays a vital part because without competent and reliable supporting research it is better for the "voice of business" to remain silent.

It is absolutely essential that Chambers be active in legislative affairs, but it is imperative that they do their homework before they speak on any public issue. Chamber spokesmen must have the facts and have them straight; they must be aware of and prepared to address the pros and cons

363

of the matter at hand; they must be able to present a well-reasoned position that will stand up during every step of the legislative process. Only then will the lawmaker be able to rely on the Chamber as a source of authoritative and dependable information.

In order for Chambers of Commerce to represent business effectively in governmental affairs, they must establish a reputation for credibility, reliability, and honesty. To speak out on the numerous complicated legislative issues which concern business without benefit of adequate research is an open invitation to disaster.

Although having full-time, experienced legislative analysts on the staff is the best way to get results, it is not the only answer. In fact, a Chamber is uniquely equipped to use a combination of methods by virtue of its ability to call on its members.

Moreover, Chambers should not assume that because the halls of legislative bodies are bulging with legislative aides, analysts and researchers (ad infinitum) the quality of legislation proposed is better or that their research is the last word. It would not be difficult to build a strong case to the contrary. Although legislative aides are quick to label everything from a business organization as "special interest," strict objectivity is rare in the halls of the legislature.

There are several ways a Chamber can bolster the quality of its legislative research:

1. *General Research Staff.* All general research should be evaluated with an eye to eliminating that which does not help bolster the bread-and-butter projects of the organization. Pressure on business continues to come from government; therefore, more time and effort of the general research staff should be devoted to work that helps handle legislative problems. The Chamber is uniquely equipped to analyze the impact of proposed legislation on business and the economy.

2. *Shift Priorities.* The number of staff people assigned to legislative and/or governmental affairs should be increased. This may sound like an indirect way to handle research but if Chambers are to send qualified spokesmen to speak before legislatures, city councils, boards of supervisors, boards and commissions, and Congress, staff members representing the Chamber must be knowledgeable and experienced on the subject being considered. Back-up research is indispensable. Before this step—increasing or augmenting the Chamber staff— is discounted for lack of funds, even one-man Chambers should consider developing an appeal, based upon specific work that needs to be done, and turning to businesses with greatest interest to fund the effort. There are numerous case histories to show this can be the easiest money a Chamber ever raised.

3. *Legislative Research Analyst.* Larger Chambers of Commerce should consider employing a legislative research analyst to do in-depth legislative research on top-priority matters.

4. *Staff Work.* Except for the top-priority measures which require extensive research, staff members can improve their work by preparing legislative issue reports which include statements of: The Issue; The Background; Arguments For; Arguments Against; Impact on Business; and The Chamber's Position. With this basic research, the staff man is better prepared to present the Chamber's views and to provide member firms with information they need to speak out effectively on the subject.

5. *Special Counsel.* Counsel should be retained on matters which require special legal background. This enables a Chamber which cannot afford to keep an attorney on its regular staff to engage in extensive legal research on selected, top-priority issues. The attorney then may represent the Chamber before legislative bodies.

6. *Summer Interns.* Graduate students or advanced law students should be employed to undertake research to lay the groundwork for upcoming issues.

7. *Political Science or Law Students.* Credit is given by some universities to students who complete research projects for Chambers on subjects related to the student's field of study. This involves little or no cost to the Chamber.

8. *Task Forces.* Executives may be obtained on loan for important task forces which are needed to obtain research and make recommendations on major programs.

B. LEGISLATION AND LEGISLATIVE RESEARCH

Legislation, throughout this chapter, means any type of law or ordinance promulgated by a governmental unit to require, prohibit or regulate an activity.

Legislative research, especially the digest and explanation of legislative measures, is generally divided into two categories:

1. The analysis of legislative proposals as they are introduced to the law-making unit for action.

2. Research into legislative issues prior to actual introduction so that the business organization may become informed on matters necessary for advocacy or opposition when the legislature convenes.

The necessary *tools* are relatively few and readily available. An analyst needs:

1. Copies of the proposed ordinances and bills as they are introduced and/or printed, with any amendments that are made from time-to-time.

2. A reporting service.

3. The local codes and the compiled state statutes with all amendments.

4. City and county charters.

5. The state constitution.

More important than any of the above "tools" is the analyst himself. He must be able to read and understand complicated, wordy, sometimes technical language so that it can be presented to the interested Chamber member in a brief, simple and easily understood manner.

The analysis of an actual bill encompasses several functions. It involves an initial cursory reading of the bill to determine its possible effect on the Chamber membership. A good reporting service will provide this information by title. Once a bill has been briefly examined for its content and application, and properly classified for convenient reference, it should be marked for a more thorough study. Generally, lengthy legislation can be reduced to a simple paragraph which will allow interested persons to determine whether it needs further study. When the legislation presents serious business implications—as would, for instance, changes in a state's unemployment compensation program or amendments to a metropolitan zoning ordinance—then a detailed analysis of the bill's provisions would be required. On occasion, it may be necessary to project built-in cost factors so that individual firms may make their own estimates of the bill's effect.

During a legislative session—or during continuing meetings of other law-making units—the analysis should be a three-part undertaking:

1. *Original analysis of the legislation should be prepared.* The completed analysis, along with the bill which is its subject, should be classified in two ways: (a) by chronological number or progressing identification, and (b) by subject matter. Inquiries will be made, for instance, about "House Bill 392" as well as on "that bill about Unemployment Compensation." The foremost rule of the legislative analysis is to keep it simple. The inquiring member wants information, not literary style.

2. *A daily record on the status of pertinent bills* should be kept during each session of the legislative body. Many subjects will not be considered at each meeting, but information about current action on

issues of interest to the organization should be readily available. A separate sheet or card should be prepared for each piece of legislation with provisions for all possible action, making it convenient for a clerk to mark the appropriate data in the appropriate space for ready reference. This internal reporting service can be beneficial when a member calls and desires current information on some piece of legislation.

3. The third step in a complete legislative analysis is that of *recording and analyzing all amendments to pertinent legislation.* Frequently, the entire effect of a bill is significantly altered by a clever amendment. The original analysis may need to be completely revised.

C. SUMMARY

Generally, legislative research in which a Chamber is involved includes federal bills, state bills, local ordinances, constitutional amendments, charter amendments, administrative rules and regulations, and in some instances interstate compacts, treaties, and rules of courts.

To the legal researcher, the primary aim of the search is *authority* which the court is bound to respect. The legislative researcher, on the other hand, uses legislative authority and judicial decisions primarily to determine existing law and goes on to find answers to such questions as:

1. What does the proposed legislation do? (Synopsis)
2. Why has the legislation been proposed?
3. Is it really necessary?
4. What are the major arguments for and against the proposal?
5. What additional costs or savings are involved?
6. What are the alternatives?
7. Are there "sleepers" or disguised motives in the bill? If so, what are they?
8. Who supports and who opposes it?

Exhibit 20-A is a sample "Legislative Research Checklist" used in a state legislature by research analysts. It helps guide the researcher in obtaining background, pros, cons, and impact. Sources of information for legislative research are shown in Exhibit 20-B.

EXHIBIT 20-A:
LEGISLATIVE RESEARCH CHECKLIST

Code Section_____   Bill Number_____
Statute Number_____   or   Author_____
Chapter Number_____   Status_____

SUBJECT:_____

BACKGROUND:
□ Committee Hearings   □ Legislative Analyst's Report
□ Committee Reports   □ Departmental/Commission
□ Legislative Journals   Reports
□ Law Reviews   □ Newspaper/Magazine Clippings
□ Legislative Counsel's Reports   □ Committee Files
□ Attorney General's Reports   □ Interim Reports
□ Related Court Decisions   □ Budget Reports
□ Budget Analyses   □ Past Debates

PROS, CONS AND IMPACT:
□ Sponsor's Reports   □ Attorney General's Opinion
□ Opponents' Reports   □ Legislative Counsel's Opinion
□ Legislative Analyst's Opinions   □ Opinions of Special Interest
□ Members' Messages & Releases   Groups
□ Executive Messages & Releases   □ Opinions of Nat'l & State
□ Law Reviews   Chambers
□ Ballot Pamphlets   □ Newspaper Opinions
□ Opinions of Citizens'   □ Polls and Surveys
     Committees   □ Current Debates
□ Opinions of Other Level   □ Departmental Analyses
     Governmental Bodies

EXHIBIT 20-B:
SOURCES OF INFORMATION
FOR LEGISLATIVE RESEARCH

SECTION A: FEDERAL

1. U. S. CONSTITUTION

   a. Literal prints of the U.S. Constitution can be found in many publications which are readily accessible, i.e., in textbooks, some state constitutions, world almanacs, encyclopedias, etc.

   b. *The Constitution of the U.S.A. Analysis and Interpretation. Annotations of Cases Decided by the Supreme Court of the U.S. to June 22, 1964.* Prepared by the Library of Congress. Contains a "literal print" of the Constitution plus principles, interpretations, annotations, histories of each clause or section, citations and quotations of pertinent court decisions, commentaries and treatises on constitutional law, arguments of counsel, and some federal statutes.

   c. Privately published editions such as the *Federal Code Annotated* and *U.S. Code Annotated.*

   — Contain more systematic supplementation than the Library of Congress edition.

   — Cite all important U.S. Supreme Court cases and State Court cases as well as opinions of the Attorney General of the U.S., Presidential Executive Orders and Proclamations, Board of Tax Appeals and Tax Court decisions.

   — Contain occasional law review articles.

   — Provide frequent interim service publications.

   d. Proposed Constitutional Amendments are printed in the *Statutes at Large* (discussed in 2a).

   e. In various notes and journals by and about the originators of the Constitution one can find legislative history and the intent of the Constitution.

2. FEDERAL LEGISLATIVE ENACTMENTS

   a. *U.S. Statutes at Large* published by the government.

   — Published at the end of each Congress.

   — Contains all legislation enacted during the calendar year of each session.

   — Contains public and private laws, joint and concurrent resolutions, proclamations, reorganization plans, Constitutional amendments.

   b. Commerce Clearing House, *Congressional Legislative Reporting*

Service. Supplies an unofficial but accurate text of federal and state laws.

c. *U.S. Code Congressional and Administrative News* is the most generally used unofficial publication. Public laws are collected in semi-monthly pamphlet issues during Congressional sessions and are later cumulated into one volume.

d. Private laws may be secured free from the National Archives.

e. Public laws may be purchased from the bill clerks of the House and the Senate.

f. Statutory compilations can be found in the *U.S. Revised Statutes,* which is in a constant state of revision, and in the *U.S. Code,* which primarily includes general and permanent federal laws.

3. STATUTE INDEXES

a. The Library of Congress in Washington, D.C., keeps a card file on all federal and state statutes; however, due to the volume of this card index, there is little hope of it ever being printed and published.

b. The *U.S. Statutes at Large* and the *U.S. Code* contain excellent indexes of the statutes.

c. To locate federal acts by popular name, i.e., "G. I. Bill of Rights," the following publications are helpful:

   — *Shepard's Acts and Cases By Popular Names: Federal and State.* Contains comprehensive tables of federal statutes by popular names.

   — *U.S. Code* and *Federal Code Annotated* contain tables of codified federal statutes by popular name.

   — *U.S. Code Congressional News and Administrative News* and the *Congressional Index* contain federal statutes by popular name for the current year.

4. FEDERAL LEGISLATION

a. *The Congressional Record* is printed every day that Congress is in session and contains Congressional proceedings and debates, a daily digest and extensions of remarks.

b. *Congressional Index* gives legislative status of bills, is revised weekly and cross-files current legislation by number, author and subject.

c. *Congressional Quarterly* is published weekly and contains background, some pros and cons, and status of major bills.

d. Single copies of federal bills may be obtained from the following addresses at no charge.

        SENATE: Office of the Secretary, U.S. Senate
                    Senate Office Building
                    Washington, D.C. 20510

HOUSE: Document Room, House of Representatives
House Office Building
Washington, D.C. 20575

5. OTHER FEDERAL INFORMATION

a. *Congressional Directory* is printed annually by the government for the use of the Congress and contains names and addresses of key federal cabinet, administrative and departmental staff as well as biographical sketches of Senators and Representatives.

b. *Congressional Staff Directory* is privately printed annually and contains biographies of key staff in Congress, job titles, addresses, phone numbers, assignments to committees, and biographies of members, as well as similar information for key personnel of the Executive Office.

c. *Court decisions* may be purchased, usually for about $1.00 a page, or may be found in the official *U.S. Reports* and in the unofficial *Lawyers Edition* and *Supreme Court Reporter.*

d. Administrative information may be found in three publications: *Federal Register, Code of Federal Regulations,* and *Government Organization Manual.*

e. Legal periodicals provide, among other things, points of view and discussion of issues, court decisions, legislation, and legislative enactments.

f. Congressional members' offices often provide legislative information on request.

g. Congressional committees will often give background and impact information on key legislation in *Committee Prints* which are obtainable through your own Representative or through the appropriate committee.

h. Hearings before committees on key legislation are available from committees or members of Congress.

i. For any type of federal legislative information, especially the business viewpoint and impact, contact the Chamber of Commerce of the United States.

EXHIBIT 20-B:
SOURCES OF INFORMATION
FOR LEGISLATIVE RESEARCH

SECTION B: STATE

1. STATE CONSTITUTION

   a. Proposed Constitutional Amendments.
   b. Ballot Pamphlets.

2. STATE LEGISLATIVE ENACTMENTS

   (Examples of state sources will vary from state to state)
   a. *Summary Digest* is printed for each session and contains a list of all the statutes enacted, resolutions adopted and proposed constitutional amendments.
   b. *Advance Legislative Service* contains full content of legislative enactments as they are chaptered.
   c. Chaptered legislative enactments as they occur during the legislative session.
   d. *Codes* contains the statutes plus annotations including related court decisions and legislative history. Revisions with amendments are also provided.
   e. *Code Commission Reports.*
   f. *Law Revision Commission Reports.*
   g. *Commission on Uniform State Law, Reports.*

3. STATE LEGISLATION

   a. Assembly and Senate Journals record the proceedings of the state legislature.
   b. Assembly and Senate histories give the status of the bills.
   c. Committee reports, interim reports and analyses on key bills are often available from members, the related committee, or Rules Committee.
   d. Committee hearings on major issues or legislation are sometimes available from the committees.
   e. Legislative Counsel's opinions.
   f. Attorney General's opinions.
   g. Governor's messages and releases.
   h. Judicial Council reports.
   i. Departmental Reports and Non-Legislative Commission Reports.

j. State Bar Committee on Legislative Reports.

k. Legislative Analyst's reports.

l. Committees often keep important letters and documents in their files that pertain to current and past legislation.

m. Two copies of state bills may be obtained free from the Bill Room. Additional copies will be forwarded by the Bill Room upon request at a cost.

4. OTHER STATE INFORMATION

a. State administrative rules and regulations.

b. Law libraries.

c. The Government Publications sections of libraries.

d. The Secretary of State.

e. Each state department has public information officers and some reports on its functions and responsibilities.

f. State Chambers of Commerce which have departments that have legislative activities as a primary function.

g. The Attorney General's office is very often helpful in providing legislative information.

h. The Governor's Budget and the Analyst's Report on the Budget provide excellent background on most key legislation.

i. Committee files.

j. Legal periodicals.

k. Many special interest groups issue reports on state legislation.

l. Members' offices will often provide legislative information.

EXHIBIT 20-B:
SOURCES OF INFORMATION
FOR LEGISLATIVE RESEARCH

SECTION C: LOCAL

1. CHARTERS AND NON-CHARTERED GENERAL LAWS

Local bodies normally have general bylaws and principles that are printed in city, county or district charters or formal sets of non-chartered general laws. These charters are usually available through the clerks of the local bodies.

2. LOCAL ORDINANCES

Local ordinances, usually coded, can be found in the clerk or attorney's office of the local bodies. They generally are not annotated and are privately published under the auspices of the city, county or district attorney.

3. LOCAL HEARINGS AGENDAS

The most important source of local information is the hearing agenda. This agenda contains all measures that are being considered and often contains information on past actions. The city, county or district clerks who emit these agendas are also valuable sources of information concerning items on the agenda. On items on which the clerks cannot provide information, they very often can refer you to the proper source.

4. OTHER

   a. Local newspapers are sources of notification of hearings and matters of local interest.
   b. City attorneys and county counsels do at times have legal opinions on key matters.
   c. The State Archives will sometimes keep records of local bodies.

21 FISCAL ANALYSES AND BUDGET REVIEWS

A. INTRODUCTION

During the past 10 years, local taxes have approximately doubled. There is little doubt that local governments will have to increase their spending as inflation expands, population increases and the social and physical compositions of our cities change. Education, highways, health, welfare and provisions for public facilities are major areas of future expenditure. Although these needs must be met, it is necessary that something should also be done to control locally imposed taxes.

Most local governments have needed this money and will continue to increase their spending in reaction to the forces operating on them. Cities are consumers, as individuals are consumers, and experience the same reduction in buying power of the dollar as inflation continues. As the population grows, the support services which a city provides are needed in greater quantity. Cities are experiencing the phenomenon that Alice found in Lewis Carroll's *Through The Looking Glass*: they must run twice as fast as they have been just to stay in the same place. They must continue to spend more money just to provide the same services they have been supplying all along. This increased spending requires more tax revenues.

But even this is not enough. Today the concept of the government's role in our lives is changing as governmental agencies at the state, federal, and local level are providing services which would have been condemned as too socialistic only a few years ago. Changing requirements in education, transportation and mass transit, health care (especially for the very young and the aged), welfare, and environmental control are demanding expenditures which can come from only the taxpayer's pocket.

While it is expected that tax revenues will need to increase for legitimate purposes, they should not be allowed to grow indiscriminately. Even though the increased taxes are to be spent for worthwhile purposes, there is some point at which the increased rates will have an elastic effect upon the economy. This means that although the money is being well-spent, the increased rates would tend to drive away potential new companies and residents which would have otherwise located in the community. When a community reaches this point, it will experience diminishing marginal returns on any new taxes. Further increases would adversely affect incomes, consumption, sales, profits, and some of the incentives for new development by existing or outside companies.

The local property tax rate is still determined by the relationship of two factors: (1) the tax levy, which is the amount of money needed to support the governmental operations other than subvened funds, licenses and miscellaneous imposts; and (2) the amount of assessable and taxable property which exists within the jurisdiction (city, county or special district). Although some cities have additional sales taxes, these taxes have traditionally been within the domain of the state governments.

Tax research at the local level is a relatively new field for Chambers of Commerce. While Chambers have often become vocal at public budget hearings if major tax increases are imminent, this effort is made too late. Reductions in the tax rate can rarely be effectuated after policies are adopted.

The best method for reducing costs is through vigilant expenditure scrutiny and sound policies. Most major policies are made prior to adoption of the local budgets. Therefore, if tax research at the municipal level is to be fully effective, Chambers of Commerce must be in on the decision-making processes. It is during the early stages of this procedure that the Chamber can make its influence felt most strongly.

B. COMMITTEE AND STAFF

Due to the technical nature of the matters involved, taxation research is one of those areas in which the Chamber researcher must rely very heavily on the members of his committee to provide the background information and analysis necessary to develop a viable position on an issue. Perhaps more than on any other committee, it is important that the membership of the Taxation Division of the Research Committee be diversified and well-respected within the community. One might start recruiting by gathering a list of the major industrial and commercial taxpayers in the community, including representatives of financial institutions and major utilities. It is essential that the chief executives of these firms become aware of and interested in this research program.

A representative sample of small businessmen and professional people will round out the committee and provide a cross-section of the community. Tax lawyers and accountants are needed to provide the legal and technical expertise required of any presentation to community officials. It is also necessary to have a staff member who has expertise in the field of local government to direct the program.

C. LOCAL TAX RESEARCH

The area of local governmental finance is one in which the Chamber can maximize its influence through the use and implementation of sound research. The 3,000 counties, 18,000 municipal governments, and 35,000 school districts in the United States had combined annual expenditures of nearly $60 billion in 1970, and so present a wide area for fiscal analysis on the part of Chambers of Commerce. It is at the local level that the community establishes its image and determines its character, attractiveness, and business climate. When the Chamber attempts to represent the business community on questions of education, street planning, rubbish collection, water service, public safety, the judicial system, or any of the other areas of primary interest, it must be able to relate these subjects to the overall budget and tax structure of the local jurisdiction.

D. CONTACT WITH GOVERNMENTAL OFFICIALS

In any local Chamber the chief executive will have frequent contacts with City Hall, its agencies, and various other governmental units. In the area of fiscal policy, he or the research staff must maintain similar liaison with budget officials and administrative heads of tax and other departments. In the smaller Chamber the staff role may be confined to that of providing coordination between the Chamber committee and the local officials. In the larger Chamber the staff research function may be expanded to include extensive independent budget analysis.

Research on fiscal and budgetary matters at the local level will be as diverse as the natures of the communities themselves. A type of non-property tax imposed in a California town may not be permitted by state law or constitutional provision in Massachusetts. The amount of detail in the proposed budget of a municipality in Indiana may be quite different from that submitted for a city in Louisiana. No two cities will have exactly the same problem or exactly the same answer. The researcher must thus be flexible in his analysis and able to apply knowledge gained by counterparts in other communities to similar but not identical circumstances.

E. GUIDELINES

In spite of the variations between communities and problems, a few suggestions can be advanced to provide standard practice items for the research staff concerned with fiscal analysis. These are subject to modification as appropriate for application to any particular locality. These guidelines are as follows:

1. Keep in touch, on a year-around basis, with proposals emanating from responsible quarters relating to the tax structure, new governmental programs, and changes in administrative organization.

2. Keep posted on and analyze the fiscal involvements and the increasing trends to shift functions from one governmental unit to an entirely different taxing entity.

3. Maintain a close working relationship with governmental budget officials, allowing sufficient flexibility so that this relationship can be shifted readily in the event of a change in political control.

4. Always try to obtain as much advance information as possible on any proposed changes that would affect the Chamber and the city. Very often this information will not be ready for release to the public, so efforts must be made to develop a reputation of trustworthiness, discretion, and confidence. Once this is established, the parties on both sides of any question will be more willing to deal with Chamber representatives.

5. As a part of the Chamber's information dissemination service, whenever a new budget has been proposed, (a) distribute copies to those interested members of the Chamber committee and to any other Chamber members who you think might be concerned, (b) prepare summaries of major revenue and expenditures for review by the committee and distribute to committee members for consideration before calling a formal discussion, and (c) arrange your committee meetings as discussions to examine any suggested changes in the tax structure, budget, or city organization, and come up with a definite policy recommendation. Both staff and committee should keep in mind that the ultimate aim of budget studies is the encouragement of appropriate governmental policy to meet the needs of a progressive community in an economically sound manner. This concept goes further than a concentration on tax rates per se.

6. Prepare a statement on this recommendation for review by the Chamber's Board of Directors. This statement should set forth the basis upon which policy might be determined. Ideally, the focus would be on a long term policy rather than one restricted solely to the current fiscal year.

7. Acting upon Board of Directors approval, prepare a statement to be used at public hearings on budget proposals or similar meetings on related subjects. An official Chamber representative's appearance at a public hearing is quite effective. These appearances should not be isolated events, but should be part of a continuing program.

8. Publicize the Chamber's recommendations through the press, radio, television, and house organ media.

9. Follow up the other activities by reviewing administrative procedures during the fiscal year.

10. Attempt to foresee community needs and propose sound financing for those which involve governmental action. The Chamber has an obligation not only to stimulate community progress but to propose realistic means of implementing it.

F. SPECIAL PROJECTS

As the Chamber's fiscal research program becomes better established and recognized as a reliable tool for community enhancement, special projects will emerge. The Chamber Board of Directors may authorize a study of assessment practices; the municipality may ask for a business study of the operations of a certain department; or a debt referendum may require the assembly of facts to be presented to the electorate.

In most of these instances the staff and committee structure provide a ready-made medium for expression of a thoughtful business community view. Sometimes a task force can be formed as a special-purpose study group composed of selected Committee members with the addition of others who may have a particular knowledge of the matter under review.

Once a study is completed and approved by the Board of Directors, it should be released to those concerned in the local government and a related press release should be prepared for the local newspaper. It might be appropriate to feature an article about the report in the monthly Chamber magazine.

Publicizing the Chamber's study through these publications is very important. It provides an opportunity to tell the public and the members what the Chamber is doing in a positive manner to effectuate tax adjustments.

The next step, which is most important, is *to implement the recommendations* contained in the reports. The best method to accomplish this is to have periodic meetings between your task force members and the appropriate governmental officials. Establish a step-by-step procedure for implementation of the recommendations. The task force can be extremely helpful to the governmental officials because of the expert guidance its members can provide in these matters.

Some recommendations can be implemented immediately, while full implementation of others might take several years. *The important thing is to begin.* A procedure should also be established to review and evaluate the progress in each area. Periodic progress reports should be prepared no less frequently than once a year. As implementation takes place your organization may be able to take credit for saving citizens' money and making the community a more profitable place to operate for businessmen.

A positive tax research program will result in many benefits to the community. A major purpose of a Chamber of Commerce is to enact and carry out programs that will improve the economic climate of the community. By representing the views of the business community, tempered by concern for the quality of life in the area, the Chamber can play an important part in deciding the direction of the community, and thereby its economic fate.

Priorities must be established in determining the basis for selecting activities for the local Chamber's program. First, it is important to maintain tax stability and, if possible, even reduce the rate by helping to lower the cost of government. Secondly, the taxable base should be increased, and thirdly, efforts should be made to improve the community to make it a desirable place to live. If these three objectives can be achieved, the community should have a healthy, growing economy.

In summary, there are six important points to follow as a Chamber undertakes a Tax Research program. These points serve as a procedural guide. The first step is to plan the program; second is to organize it; third is to sell it to the local officials; fourth is to perform the necessary studies; fifth is to publicize the project and its results; and sixth is to work to implement your recommendations.

22 DOCUMENTING THE COMMUNITY'S POSITION IN GOVERNMENTAL PROCEEDINGS

A. GOVERNMENTAL RESEARCH VS. ECONOMIC RESEARCH

The presentation of the business community's views on public matters is an important responsibility of a Chamber of Commerce. A public statement of recommendations must be carefully researched and reflective of policy approved by the Chamber's Board after objective committee review. Sound proposals presented in a nonpartisan manner can go far toward establishing the Chamber's leadership position in the community.

The chapters in this manual dealing with the Chamber of Commerce governmental research emphasize a basic difference between this type of analysis and other kinds of economic research which the Chamber may undertake, a difference which the Chamber executive must never overlook. Briefly stated, the distinction is that governmental research, relating as it does to public matters, is inexorably either a precursor or a consequence of established Chamber policy. A Chamber of Commerce may be able to operate an economic research program without a stated policy on economic matters, but it cannot engage in governmental research which neither stems from nor contributes to the development of a written policy on matters in the area of public affairs.

Let us take a case in point. A Chamber executive is of the opinion that his community may fail to develop economically without an improvement in airport facilities. Before making any representations to a governmental agency on the subject, he must gather a large quantity of information on present and potential use of air transportation, alternative competing forms of transportation, estimates of population growth and industrial expansion rates, various methods of financing airport improvement, and the level of government best able to administer the enlarged facilities. He must arrange meetings of the Chamber committee which would normally examine capital needs of the municipality. He must prepare a written proposal for Board of Directors consideration based on committee recommendations. Only after Board approval can the matter be regarded as Chamber policy, and only at that point can the Chamber executive and his officers properly represent the business and professional community in official hearings or otherwise.

B. NECESSITY FOR WRITTEN POLICY STATEMENTS

While much can be done by a Chamber to advance the community's welfare without involving government, some programs of local improvement will inevitably require governmental action on the local, state or federal level. Examples of governmental involvement in economic matters readily come to mind: planning and zoning, tax rate determination, public education, postal service, highway maintenance, public safety and health, parkland development, water service and many others. If the Chamber is to act as spokesman for the business community, it must develop written policy in these areas based on orderly and intelligent governmental research.

The foregoing comments may seem elementary and obvious to the Chamber executive who has been operating in this area for many years, but it cannot be reiterated too often that a Chamber's effectiveness in a political environment depends on the quality of its research and the resulting validity of its policy. A partisan or poorly informed recommendation will discredit the Chamber in the eyes of governmental officials and the public; a factual nonpartisan policy will enhance the Chamber's position as an effective force for community growth.

C. TRANSMITTING POSITION STATEMENTS TO GOVERNMENTAL OFFICIALS

We need not dwell on the processes of fact-finding, committee discussion, statement preparation and policy formation. Assuming that these basic steps have been taken by the Chamber's research director, how are the views of the Chamber transmitted to the responsible public officials? The following are some of the effective ways of expressing Chamber policy:

1. Personal conference with administrative or legislative officials.
2. Letters to these governmental personnel.
3. Representation at official meetings and public hearings held by legislative committees, commissions, or councils.

A word of caution is in order at this point. Since governmental research and policy on public issues, while non-partisan in nature, necessarily takes political realities into consideration, care is required in the presentation of conclusions. A personal conference with a public official is a privileged conversation; release of information regarding it should be left to the discretion of the official rather than the Chamber spokesman. The same stricture applies to written communications. With reference to public hearings, representatives of the news media are customarily in attendance, and copies of Chamber testimony are appropriately released at that time, but not before. While publicity on Chamber action is always desirable, in the field of public affairs the favorable reception of Chamber views by elected or appointed officials must be our major objective.

D. GUIDELINES FOR PARTICIPATION IN HEARINGS

In the presentation of the business community's position at governmental proceedings, a few guidelines will suffice to illustrate effective Chamber action, bearing in mind that flexibility should be maintained to tailor the representation to the circumstances:

1. Present the Chamber's proposals and recommendations in written as well as oral form.
2. Identify the Chamber spokesman at the beginning of the presentation.
3. Indicate the nature and scope of the Chamber organization unless this is already well known.
4. Identify the research group within the Chamber which was responsible for initiating the recommendations.
5. State briefly the business community's interests in the subject of the hearing.
6. Present the Chamber's findings of facts and conclusions.
7. If several points are made, summarize them in the concluding paragraph.
8. Avoid argumentative or provocative statements and confine the testimony to the subject of the hearing.
9. Since there are usually others who wish to present testimony, be as brief as is consistent with the points to be covered.
10. If appropriate, indicate appreciation for the opportunity to appear before the hearing body.

The presentation of the community's position in governmental proceedings can be a vital part of any Chamber's program and can have a lasting beneficial effect on the sound development of the area in which it operates. Illustrations of typical testimony documents are presented in Exhibits 22-A through 22-H.

EXHIBIT 22-A:
REVIEW OF A LOCAL BUDGET

To the Committee on Ways and Means
    of the Board of Supervisors of
    the County of _____ :

    The _____ Chamber of Commerce has reviewed a report from
its Governmental Affairs Committee on State and Local Finance relating
to the 1974 proposed budget of the County of _____ .

    The Chamber presents several recommendations of a general nature
for your consideration, as follows:

1. More time should be allowed for public review of the proposed
   budget.

2. Changes in accounting methods, no matter how praiseworthy,
   should not be put into effect without reconstructing the previous
   year's budget data so that adequate comparisons may be made with
   proposed budget figures.

3. Summaries should be shown for major item categories, such as
   personal services, equipment, supplies, other expense, hospitalization and retirement premiums, debt service, etc.; this should not be
   difficult in a computerized system and would add much to public
   understanding of the County's expenses.

4. Costs of County operation should be examined in the light of established needs rather than in relation to the availability of funds from
   federal, state or surplus sources.

5. With the rapid increase in salaries and wages through across-the-
   board raises, together with the absorption by the County of hospitalization and retirement premiums for its employees, a job evaluation study is now needed to determine whether these personal
   services costs are justified in all instances.

6. While the description of departmental functions in the budget statement is a useful addition, more information would be desirable on the number of personnel involved (as distinguished from the total positions available), the number of items or jobs handled and some measure of the work accomplished.

If the previous recommendations were put into effect, the public would have an improved understanding of County services and a more adequate basis on which to evaluate the price of such services. Under present circumstances both time and information are inadequate for the Board of Supervisors to obtain a well-reasoned response on budget matters from the citizens of the County.

Respectfully submitted,

THE_____
CHAMBER OF COMMERCE

_____
President

EXHIBIT 22-B:
SPECIAL ZONING FOR HOUSING

To the City Council of the
    City of _____ :

    Re: Revised plan for Wilmark Estates as presented to the City Zoning
    Board of Appeals.

    At its latest meeting, the Board of Directors of the _____ Chamber of Commerce passed a resolution regarding several "housing recommendations" which relate to the critical housing shortage in _____ .

    Among these recommendations are those relating to zoning changes which must be made to allow construction of lower middle income housing projects by non-profit corporations.

    The Chamber's Program of Work for the current year states that "full efforts will be put forth to develop the necessary supply of housing, particularly in the lower and middle income brackets throughout the city and suburbs. Joint efforts with other organizations and Chamber groups will seek to develop a community-wide attack on this problem."

    Such is the case here. We actively support the revised plan as now presented by Wilmark Estates and its intent to help relieve our acute housing problem.

    The _____ Chamber of Commerce feels that a special zoning exception for Wilmark Estates will help to meet part of the current shortage.

                  Respectfully submitted for

                  THE_____
                  CHAMBER OF COMMERCE

                  _____
                  President

EXHIBIT 22-C:
SCHOOL DISTRICT TAX POWERS

Dear Senator _____ :

Re: H.B. 264

This letter to you and to each member of the Committee on State Affairs is to present the request of Central City Chamber of Commerce that you *oppose House Bill 264* in the form approved by the House. The bill proposes to authorize the Central City Independent School District to:

(a) set its own tax assessment ratio (now tied to Central City's ratio), and

(b) without prior approval of the voters (as is now required).

It is essential that local-option approval of increased tax assessment ratios be retained.

Local voters have in the past authorized the School Board to increase their assessment ratio, when presented with sufficient justification for meritorious need.

Central City Chamber of Commerce has taken this position because we consistently favor retaining local control over local issues, because we historically have not favored proliferation of taxing powers as may well ultimately result from this proposal, and because the proposal is a move to circumvent present provisions allowing the voters to have their say over the rate of local taxation.

We do not accept the concept that quality education equates with total dollars spent.

If H.B. 264 were to be enacted it would result in an immediate local tax increase of about 25%, probably would result in the expenditure of even more non-teaching dollars through creation of still another tax assessing-collecting agency and would further erode the principle of local control over local issues.

We respectfully request that H.B. 264, in particular the elimination of local-option voting on tax assessment ratio, be disapproved.

Respectfully submitted,

THE CENTRAL CITY
CHAMBER OF COMMERCE

_____

President

EXHIBIT 22-D:
REAPPORTIONMENT OF REPRESENTATION

Chairman Courtney, members of the special Re-apportionment Committee and members of the _____ County Board of Supervisors, I am _____, Executive Vice President of the _____ Chamber of Commerce. I appear before you today as a spokesman for the _____ Chamber of Commerce, its officers, directors and members.

I previously testified before your committee in May of last year regarding the reapportionment of _____County. At that time it was pointed out that the improvement of local government is an integral part of the growth and development of the City and County which is a prime goal of the _____ Chamber of Commerce.

As most of you will recall, the Chamber vigorously supported the modernization of our governmental structure and favored the revision of the County Charter which, at that time, included a proposed reapportionment. Since then we have favored the same points which have recently been adopted as the purpose of the Citizens Committee for Charter Adoption. These principles are:

1. The County Legislature should be a smaller size than presently constituted.

2. Legislative Districts should be of as nearly equal population as practicable.

3. Districts should be represented by one legislator with one single vote.

4. Districting standards, including redistricting procedures, should be written into local law.

5. Legislative Districts should be of compact and contiguous territory.

6. Members of the County Legislature should be elected for the sole purpose of serving on that body.

Recently we have reviewed the proposals of the _____ Bureau of Municipal Research, in which it proposes the reapportionment of the

County into twenty-three voting districts. Eleven of these districts would be located outside the City, eleven within the City, and the twenty-third would be a combination of city and county territory. We, therefore, feel that the proposal for twenty-three districts is as nearly non-partisan as it can possibly be made and that the Bureau's proposal has taken into consideration the interests of the major political parties and minority groups.

In checking the population of the twenty-three districts we learn that the maximum variation in population is well under ten percent. This requirement meets the standard set by the Courts of having voting districts as nearly equal in size as possible.

In practically all cases the division of the county into these twenty-three districts has followed recognized and easily identifiable boundary lines. This accomplishes the general goal of giving all citizens an equal voice in electing their officials and, as a result, the areas are reasonably homogeneous.

The Chamber of Commerce believes that the adoption of an adequate broadly based form of representation on the Board of Supervisors is a necessity if the economic growth of the County is to continue in a healthy manner.

We feel that the reapportionment proposal submitted by the Bureau of Municipal Research, and submitted to the Election Commissioners and the members of your committee, meets these requirements. The Chamber of Commerce therefore urges your favorable consideration, recommendation and adoption of this plan.

I appreciate the opportunity of speaking on behalf of the Chamber and its 5,000 members. We pledge our support to whatever equitable solution can be devised which incorporates the provisions of this proposal for reapportionment.

EXHIBIT 22-E:
CONSTITUTIONAL BAIL-BOND PROVISIONS

TO MEMBERS OF THE COMMITTEE ON JURISPRUDENCE:

Re: SJR 10; SJR 18

Dear Chairman _____ and Gentlemen:

Your successful efforts in securing Senate passage of SJR 18 are commended, and represent a worthy undertaking to eventually tighten up Constitutional bail-bond provisions that now are allowing literally thousands of professional criminals to prey upon our community as repeat felony offenders.

SJR 18 would, if passed by the House and approved by the voters next November, amend Section 8, Article 5 of the Constitution by deleting the provision permitting denial of bail for capital offenses. Substituted therefor would be a provision:

"The Legislature by law may provide rules governing the release or detention of prisoners awaiting trial or during the pendency of an appeal."

We wonder if the voters would adopt such a provision, because they might be persuaded that it would result in removal of all rights to bail.

There presently exists no "capital offense" as a result of the U.S. Supreme Court decision. But if indeed the Legislature does restore the death penalty in this state, would not the loss of the present "no-bail" provisions of Section 8 be detrimental?

We view SJR 10 as an opportunity to "cover all the bases" — would it be at all possible for your Committee to give favorable consideration to this Bill?

SJR 10 would retain present Constitutional provisions (desirable, should the death penalty be re-instated), and add a reasonable and realistic Section 8b to permit the Court to deny bail to a repeat felony offender, under only these conditions:

(a) if there were substantial evidentiary showing of guilt

(b) the accused must be tried within 60 days or the order denying
     bail would be dissolved.

We might comment that a proposal quite comparable to SJR 10 received 31-0 Senate approval in the 71st Legislature and received strong
editorial support in the local newspapers.

The recently-passed SJR 18, on the other hand, has been bitterly
assailed by one prominent local newspaper.

Central City does desperately need relief from present bonding
procedures which allow the professional criminals to perpetrate whole
strings of felonies against our people and their property. More than 60% of
our local felony crimes are committed by these repeaters.

We respectfully urge your consideration of a more effective measure
such as SJR 10.

                                        Very truly yours,

                                        _____

EXHIBIT 22-F:
BUDGET ANALYSIS

My name is _____ . I represent the _____ State Chamber of Commerce, of whose Taxation Committee I have served as Chairman for 12 years. The _____ State Chamber is a federation of 185 local Chambers of Commerce and statewide trade associations with an underlying membership of more than 80,000 business firms.

The budget you are considering represents an increase of more than $600 million above last year. Some of its features we find heartening. Others we find discouraging.

We are heartened by the fact that it proposes no new or increased taxes, that it does not propose another increase in State aid to local schools (which has been an annual event in these past few years), and that there is no straight across-the-board pay raise for all State employees regardless of merit.

We are disturbed, on the other hand, by the fact that this is the third successive year in which the budget is not on a pay-as-you-go basis and by the fact that it proposes substantial increases in many State spending activities as indicated by the schedule of proposed appropriations and by the more than 16,000 new jobs that would be added. These jobs are scattered throughout the State's operating agencies. To some, there would be added only a handful of employees; to others, new employees numbering thousands.

On these points I shall give you specific comments later on. First, however, it is pertinent to make a few comparisons between the rate of State government growth and some of the other factors in our economy.

Personal income has about doubled since 1951, due to the combined causes of population growth, increased productivity and inflation. On a per-capita basis, it has gone up by 75 percent.

However, our State government spending has gone up nearly four and one-half times. Per-capita taxes have increased 360 percent. In other words, in a close parallel to the growth of State government versus private employment, our State taxes have gone up during the same period five times as fast as our people's ability to pay them.

I have referred to the rapid growth in the number of State employees as contrasted with the relatively slow rate of growth in total non-agricultural employment. A comparison with other states is significant. In this connection I use total State and local government employees because of the differences in the way the different states apportion functions among their State and local governments.

The Message characterizes this budget as a "tight budget." This we question. Surely, any budget which would add more than 16,000 new employees to the State payrolls can hardly be characterized as "tight."

All told, 585 new jobs would be created in the Executive Department. It is interesting to review the agencies in that department and note their growth. For example, only a few years ago the Office of Planning Coordination consisted of a small number of people in the Executive Chamber under a different name. Now, through a spinoff, it has become a separate agency within the Executive Department, reporting directly to the Governor. Further, there are other planning activities in Commerce and in the Office for Local Government. Other instances of such proliferation could be cited not only in the Executive Department, but throughout the major agencies of the State government. Duplications and overlapping activities in various fields can be found in various State agencies.

These economy possibilities, these duplications in activities, this continued proliferation of new activities and agencies, all are evidence of the need for a thorough review of the State's administrative operations by an impartial outside agency. In past years we have come before you to urge your support for legislation creating a Commission on Efficiency and Economy in the State Government similar to the two Hoover Commissions which did such constructive service in Federal operations some years ago. Bills to create such a Commission are pending in the Legislature again this year. We urge your support.

The departure of the State from pay-as-you-go and the reliance on various hidden items for debt service indicate the need for establishment of an agency to provide long-range fiscal planning for the State government. This we have suggested on past occasions. Along with it, we recommend that you consider reconstitution of the Capital Construction Fund into a long-range Capital Budget Plan. If debt increase is to be planned on an orderly basis and if periodic crises in State finance are to be avoided, some form of long-range planning activity, in which there are periodic reports to the public and, if necessary, public hearings, is essential for our State government.

EXHIBIT 22-G:
TRANSPORTATION,
HAZARDOUS MATERIALS

TO MEMBERS OF THE
ENVIRONMENTAL AFFAIRS COMMITTEE

Re: H.B. 419

Dear Chairman _____ and Gentlemen:

The Executive Committee of Central City Chamber of Commerce has authorized and directed me to present to you our opposition to H.B. 419, proposed new State regulations to govern reporting requirements by common carrier transportation companies transporting "hazardous materials."

The bill, considered fully by our Freight Traffic Committee, which is a group of industrial freight traffic managers representing the *users* of carrier transportation services, is considered to be

- unnecessary legislation
- duplicative
- vague and ambiguous as drawn.

We respectfully make these points:

1) *Unnecessary legislation: All* (not just common carrier) transportation of hazardous materials and dangerous articles is now governed by rigid regulations and reporting requirements of the Hazzarous Materials Regulations Board of the U.S. Department of Transportation including fully-descriptive placarding and central-reporting requirements. Those controls are made applicable to local trucking, private long-haul trucking and, through the Federal Aviation Agency, to the transportation of hazardous materials by aircraft.

The federal government, by statute, has asserted the enforcement prerogative on all manner of safety requirements on transportation of hazardous materials and dangerous articles; thus, H.B. 419 is *unnecessary* legislation.

2) *Duplicative legislation:* The Railroad Commission of this state has adopted and is enforcing present rules and regulations governing *inter*-state transportation of hazardous materials and dangerous articles, on *intra*-state common carrier traffic.

Common carriers operating intrastate in this state have, by publication in their freight rate tariffs, made all of their services, rates and charges subject to the Department of Transportation regulations as published, typically, in railroads' and motor carriers' "dangerous articles" tariffs.

Contrary to reporting in the media of your Committee's initial hearing, instant reporting of hazardous materials spills and other accidents is now required and observed, as typified by the 24-hour central reporting-response performance that now exists under industry-initiated "Chem-Card" provisions.

H.B. 419 is thus duplicative in nature, and we oppose its enactment for this additional reason.

3) *Vague and ambiguous:* H.B. 419 is so loosely drawn as to be un-enforceable if enacted.

Emphatically, we insist that there could exist *no* reasonable and justifiably definable interpretation of any transported material

> *"capable of causing pollution . . .* to the water, air, or . . . *any place."*

> *"Any place"* is not defined;
> *"Capable of causing"* is not defined;
> *"Pollution"* is not defined.

With the increasing trend of identifying "pollution" to include visual pollution, noise pollution and the like, "spills" under the terms of H.B. 419 could well include a truckload of lumber overturned on a State park road, a piece (or load) of scrap metal deposited or over-turned on the lawn of a museum of fine arts, or a case of household cleaning compound "spilled" from a truck which would be "capable of causing" "pollution" if, for example, fireworks were discharged into the case.

H.B. 419 would apply to common carriers only; most transportation of materials in this state and in the nation is not by common carrier.

Central City Chamber of Commerce contends that H.B. 419 is not deserving of enactment because it is unnecessary legislation, duplicative legislation, and legislation drawn as vague and ambiguous.

We respectfully request that you not support H.B. 419.

Very truly yours,

THE CENTRAL CITY
CHAMBER OF COMMERCE

_____
President

EXHIBIT 22-H:
CONSTITUTIONAL REVISION

To the Members of the Temporary State Commission on
Revision and Simplification of the Constitution:

My name is _____ . I am an attorney with the firm of
_____and_____, located in the city of_____.
I am representing the _____ Chamber of Commerce, an organization with approximately five thousand business and professional members
in _____ County and the surrounding area.

The remarks contained in my testimony are based upon a report of the
organization's Committee on Constitutional Revision, of which I am Chairman, and have been reviewed and approved by its Governmental Affairs
Committee and its Board of Directors. This testimony is therefore a matter
of established policy on the records of the _____ Chamber of
Commerce.

The _____ Chamber of Commerce, cognizant of its responsibilities and opportunity regarding the forthcoming Constitutional Convention, believes that the primary concern of the Convention should be to
simplify the State Constitution. The present Constitution is prolix and
detailed. Many provisions lack the quality of fundamentalism which should
be found in a Constitution. Sections of narrow application should be rele-
gated to specific legislation; they should not encumber the Constitution.
Under our system of government, all powers not expressly delegated to the
federal government are reserved to the individual sovereign states, but the
present Constitution prevents our state from achieving a full realization of
its inherent powers.

Some of the dangers of an unnecessarily detailed Constitution are:

1. Limitation of Inherent Powers

   Specific grants of power in the Constitution contain a negative
   direction against any other type of power, whereas silence in the
   State Constitution implies that the legislature has power to act.

2. Handicapping the State Legislature

Laws needing change or adaptation, if found in the Constitution, cannot be changed by ordinary legislative procedure. The present Constitution can be amended only with attendant delay and difficulty. As a result the capacity for adjustment to unforeseen circumstances is reduced.

3. Constitutional Instability

Many proposals now requiring amendment must be presented to the electorate, and frequently the electorate lacks data or technical information to make a well-considered decision.

4. Duplication and Contradiction

In the present Constitution the same subjects are dealt with in more than one paragraph or article, sometimes with differing results.

Accordingly, the _____ Chamber of Commerce believes that the State Constitution should be greatly simplified. In order to achieve the goal of drafting a meaningful document which will preserve the representative form of government and the fundamental rights of all citizens, it is recommended that an entirely new Constitution be drafted. The alternative piecemeal amendment lends itself to further confusion and complexity and permits the possibility of retention of extraneous matters. A new Constitution, integrated in thought and structure, and directed toward guaranteeing basic rights and principles, seems the logical answer.

On behalf of the _____ Chamber of Commerce, I wish to express our appreciation to the Commission for the opportunity of appearing at this hearing and to assure its members that we are hoping to be of further assistance in the Commission's deliberations on the vital matter of Constitutional revision in this State.

APPENDIXES

Appendix A:

SELECTED
RESEARCH ACTIVITIES

The Appendix B references shown in this exhibit indicate Chambers of Commerce whose research personnel have experience in the particular fields listed. The numbers correspond to individual Chambers as presented in Appendix B, beginning on page 419.

For illustrative purposes, the appearance of 216 in the first list of references below indicates that the Greater Richmond (Virginia) Chamber of Commerce participates in the development of census tracts for the local area and is a source of information relating to this activity.

1. SMALL-AREA DATA FRAMEWORK
AND PUBLICATIONS

a. Census Tract Maps

Related discussion: Chapter 4

Appendix B references: 1, 2, 7, 8, 9, 10, 15, 21, 23, 28, 29, 31, 39, 40, 42, 45, 46, 53, 54, 55, 56, 61, 63, 64, 66, 68, 70, 71, 72, 74, 75, 80, 92, 95, 96, 98, 99, 101, 102, 103, 106, 107, 109, 112, 114, 122, 133, 149, 151, 152, 154, 158, 159, 161, 163, 164, 172, 173, 174, 175, 184, 214, 216, 219, 224, 230, 234, 237, 238, 240, 244, 246, 247, 248, 249, 250, 256, 258, 260, 263, 267, 268, 271, 276, 283, 285, 290, 295, 297, 301, 303, 309, 313, 314, 316, 317

b. Census Tract Boundary Descriptions

Related discussion: Chapter 4

Appendix B references: 1, 2, 7, 10, 15, 23, 28, 29, 31, 37, 40, 42, 54, 55, 56, 59, 64, 66, 70, 74, 75, 92, 99, 102, 103, 106, 107, 109, 114, 122, 126, 149, 151, 152, 161, 164, 174, 216, 219, 224, 234, 237, 240, 244, 247, 248, 250, 258, 260, 263, 267, 271, 276, 283, 290, 297, 303, 309, 313, 317

c. Census Tract Equivalency Tables

Related discussion: Chapter 4

Appendix B references: 1, 2, 10, 15, 28, 29, 40, 51, 54, 56, 64, 66, 75, 99, 102, 103, 106, 109, 114, 122, 151, 164, 174, 216, 240, 247, 250, 258, 260, 263, 271, 276, 283, 285, 303, 313

d. Census Tract Street Index

Related discussion: Chapter 4

Appendix B references: 1, 2, 10, 15, 28, 29, 31, 40, 54, 55, 56, 59, 64, 66, 75, 99, 102, 103, 106, 107, 114, 122, 151, 152, 173, 174, 216, 224, 234, 240, 244, 247, 250, 258, 260, 263, 267, 268, 271, 276, 283, 290, 295, 303, 313

e. Median Family Income by Census Tract

Appendix B references: 1, 2, 7, 8, 10, 15, 21, 25, 29, 31, 39, 40, 42, 45, 46, 51, 53, 54, 55, 56, 59, 61, 63, 64, 66, 68, 71, 72, 74, 75, 80, 92, 95, 96, 99, 101, 102, 103, 106, 109, 114, 116, 122, 140, 149, 151, 152, 154, 158, 159, 161, 164, 172, 174, 186, 197, 199, 205, 216, 224, 234, 237, 238, 240, 242, 243, 244, 247, 248, 249, 250, 255, 256, 258, 260, 263, 267, 271, 276, 278, 283, 285, 290, 295, 297, 301, 303, 309, 310, 313, 314, 316, 317

f. New Residential Electric Connections by Census Tract

Appendix B references: 1, 2, 10, 28, 29, 35, 40, 56, 64, 66, 74, 75, 101, 102, 103, 106, 114, 119, 122, 151, 174, 186, 199, 205, 207, 238, 240, 247, 258, 260, 271, 276, 278, 283, 290, 297, 303, 313, 316, 317

g. Residential Building Permits by Census Tracts

Appendix B references: 1, 2, 10, 21, 28, 29, 31, 35, 40, 54, 56, 64, 66, 74, 75, 80, 95, 102, 103, 106, 109, 112, 114, 119, 122, 153, 174, 179, 207, 224, 234, 238, 240, 242, 244, 247, 258, 260, 263, 271, 276, 283, 290, 297, 303, 305, 313, 316

2. GENERAL INFORMATION RELATING TO THE LOCAL AREA

a. Research Library

Related discussion: Chapter 3

Appendix B references: 1, 2, 3, 6, 7, 8, 10, 11, 12, 15, 17, 18, 20, 21, 22, 28, 29, 31, 35, 37, 39, 40, 42, 45, 46, 47, 48, 51, 53, 54, 55, 56, 58, 59, 60, 61, 63, 64, 66, 67, 68, 70, 71, 72, 75, 77, 79, 80, 81, 83, 89, 92, 94, 95, 96, 97, 98,

99, 100, 101, 102, 106, 107, 109, 110, 112, 114, 115, 116, 117, 120, 122, 125, 128, 129, 130, 132, 133, 134, 139, 140, 141, 142, 146, 149, 151, 152, 157, 158, 159, 161, 163, 164, 169, 170, 172, 173, 174, 175, 176, 182, 184, 185, 187, 191, 192, 194, 195, 197, 198, 199, 200, 201, 203, 207, 208, 211, 214, 216, 221, 223, 224, 225, 227, 228, 231, 234, 235, 237, 240, 243, 244, 246, 247, 248, 250, 255, 256, 258, 260, 262, 263, 267, 268, 270, 271, 272, 276, 278, 281, 283, 284, 285, 286, 290, 294, 295, 296, 297, 299, 303, 304, 306, 308, 309, 313, 314, 317, 318, 321, 323, 324

b. History of the Local Area

Appendix B references: 1, 5, 6, 7, 8, 9, 10, 13, 15, 17, 19, 20, 21, 22, 23, 25, 28, 29, 30, 31, 33, 34, 35, 37, 39, 40, 43, 44, 45, 46, 47, 49, 50, 52, 53, 54, 55, 56, 57, 58, 59, 60, 62, 63, 64, 65, 66, 67, 68, 69, 70, 71, 72, 74, 75, 76, 77, 78, 79, 80, 81, 83, 84, 85, 86, 87, 89, 90, 92, 94, 95, 96, 97, 98, 99, 100, 101, 102, 103, 104, 105, 106, 107, 109, 110, 112, 114, 115, 116, 118, 119, 122, 123, 125, 126, 127, 128, 130, 131, 135, 139, 141, 142, 143, 144, 146, 147, 149, 151, 152, 153, 154, 155, 157, 158, 159, 160, 161, 162, 163, 164, 165, 168, 169, 170, 171, 172, 174, 176, 177, 178, 179, 181, 182, 184, 185, 186, 187, 188, 190, 191, 193, 194, 195, 196, 197, 198, 199, 200, 201, 202, 203, 205, 206, 207, 209, 210, 211, 212, 214, 216, 217, 219, 220, 221, 222, 223, 224, 225, 227, 229, 230, 234, 235, 236, 237, 238, 240, 241, 242, 243, 244, 247, 248, 249, 250, 252, 253, 254, 255, 256, 257, 258, 259, 260, 263, 265, 266, 267, 268, 271, 272, 275, 276, 277, 278, 280, 281, 282, 283, 284, 285, 288, 289, 290, 291, 294, 295, 296, 297, 298, 299, 300, 301, 303, 305, 306, 308, 309, 310, 312, 313, 315, 316, 317, 319, 320, 321

c. Community Brochure

Appendix B references: 1, 3, 4, 5, 6, 7, 8, 9, 10, 11, 12, 13, 14, 15, 16, 17, 18, 19, 20, 21, 22, 23, 24, 25, 27, 28, 29, 30, 31, 32, 33, 34, 35, 36, 37, 39, 40, 41, 42, 43, 44, 45, 46, 47, 48, 50, 51, 52, 53, 54, 55, 56, 57, 58, 59, 60, 61, 62, 63, 64, 65, 66, 67, 68, 69, 70, 71, 72, 73, 74, 76, 77, 78, 79, 80, 81, 83, 84, 85, 86, 87, 88, 89, 90, 91, 92, 94, 95, 96, 97, 98, 99, 100, 101, 102, 103, 104, 105, 106, 108, 109, 110, 112, 114, 115, 116, 117, 118, 119, 120, 121, 122, 123, 124, 125, 126, 127, 128, 129, 130, 131, 132, 134, 136, 139, 141, 142, 143, 144, 145, 146, 147, 148, 149, 151, 152, 153, 154, 155, 157, 159, 160, 161, 162, 163, 164, 165, 168, 169, 170, 171, 172, 174, 175, 176, 177, 178, 179, 181, 182, 183, 184, 185, 186, 187, 188, 189, 190, 191, 192, 193, 194, 195, 196, 197, 198, 199, 200, 201, 202, 203, 204, 205, 206, 207, 208, 209, 210, 211, 212, 213, 214, 215, 216, 217, 218, 219, 220, 221, 222, 223, 224, 226, 227, 229, 230, 231, 233, 234, 235, 236, 237, 238, 240, 242, 243, 244, 245, 246, 247, 248, 249, 250, 251, 252, 253, 254, 255, 256, 257, 258, 259, 260, 261, 262, 263, 265, 266, 267, 268, 269, 270, 271, 272, 273, 274, 275, 276, 277, 278, 280, 281, 282, 283, 284, 285, 286, 287, 288, 289,

290, 291, 293, 294, 295, 296, 297, 298, 299, 300, 303, 304, 305, 306, 307, 309, 310, 311, 312, 313, 314, 315, 316, 317, 319, 320, 321, 323, 324, 326

d. Reference Service

Related discussion: Chapter 3

Appendix B references: 1, 5, 6, 7, 8, 9, 10, 11, 12, 13, 14, 15, 17, 19, 20, 21, 22, 23, 25, 27, 28, 29, 30, 31, 34, 37, 39, 40, 42, 43, 44, 45, 46, 47, 48, 51, 52, 53, 54, 55, 56, 61, 63, 65, 66, 67, 68, 70, 71, 75, 78, 80, 81, 83, 84, 86, 89, 90, 92, 94, 96, 97, 98, 99, 100, 101, 102, 103, 104, 105, 107, 108, 109, 110, 112, 114, 115, 116, 118, 120, 121, 122, 123, 125, 126, 127, 128, 130, 132, 135, 141, 142, 143, 146, 149, 151, 152, 153, 154, 157, 158, 159, 160, 161, 163, 164, 168, 169, 170, 172, 174, 175, 176, 177, 178, 182, 183, 184, 185, 187, 189, 190, 191, 192, 193, 194, 195, 197, 198, 199, 200, 201, 202, 203, 205, 208, 210, 211, 213, 214, 216, 217, 218, 219, 220, 221, 222, 223, 224, 225, 226, 231, 234, 235, 236, 237, 239, 240, 243, 244, 246, 247, 249, 250, 251, 252, 253, 254, 255, 256, 257, 258, 259, 260, 266, 267, 268, 271, 272, 276, 278, 279, 280, 281, 282, 283, 284, 285, 286, 287, 289, 290, 294, 296, 297, 298, 299, 300, 303, 304, 305, 306, 307, 308, 309, 313, 314, 315, 316, 317, 321

e. Index of Library References

Related discussion: Chapter 3

Appendix B references: 1, 6, 7, 10, 17, 20, 21, 25, 28, 29, 30, 31, 37, 42, 45, 46, 48, 51, 53, 54, 55, 56, 66, 68, 75, 83, 89, 97, 99, 101, 102, 103, 106, 109, 110, 114, 116, 122, 125, 140, 142, 146, 151, 161, 170, 172, 173, 174, 176, 182, 187, 194, 199, 200, 203, 221, 222, 231, 236, 237, 240, 247, 250, 255, 267, 268, 271, 272, 276, 284, 285, 286, 290, 297, 299, 303, 310

f. Catalog of Research Products

Related discussion: Chapter 3

Appendix B references: 1, 6, 7, 12, 17, 21, 28, 29, 31, 40, 42, 48, 51, 52, 53, 55, 56, 66, 68, 80, 95, 97, 99, 100, 102, 106, 109, 114, 122, 125, 140, 151, 157, 172, 174, 176, 194, 199, 223, 224, 226, 227, 228, 231, 236, 237, 244, 247, 250, 252, 255, 260, 268, 285, 286, 297, 300, 303, 317

g. Fact Sheets
(On Specific Community-Related Subjects)

Appendix B references: 1, 3, 5, 6, 7, 8, 10, 11, 12, 13, 14, 17, 19, 20, 21, 22, 24, 25, 27, 28, 29, 30, 31, 33, 34, 35, 36, 37, 39, 40, 42, 44, 45, 46, 48, 49, 50, 51, 52, 53, 54, 55, 56, 57, 58, 59, 61, 62, 63, 65, 66, 67, 68, 69, 70, 71, 72, 74, 75, 77, 78, 79, 80, 81, 83, 86, 87, 88, 89, 90, 92, 94, 95, 96, 97, 98,

99, 100, 101, 102, 103, 104, 105, 106, 107, 108, 109, 110, 112, 114, 116, 117,
119, 120, 121, 122, 123, 124, 125, 126, 127, 128, 129, 130, 131, 132, 133,
134, 135, 139, 141, 142, 145, 146, 147, 148, 149, 150, 151, 152, 153, 154,
155, 157, 160, 161, 162, 163, 164, 168, 169, 170, 171, 172, 174, 176, 177,
178, 180, 182, 183, 184, 185, 187, 189, 190, 191, 192, 194, 197, 198, 199,
201, 202, 203, 204, 205, 206, 207, 208, 211, 212, 213, 214, 216, 217, 219,
220, 221, 222, 223, 224, 225, 226, 228, 230, 231, 232, 233, 234, 235, 236,
237, 240, 241, 242, 243, 244, 246, 247, 248, 249, 250, 251, 252, 253, 254,
255, 256, 258, 259, 260, 263, 266, 267, 268, 271, 272, 274, 275, 276, 277,
278, 281, 282, 283, 284, 285, 286, 287, 288, 289, 290, 293, 394, 295, 296,
297, 298, 299, 300, 301, 302, 303, 305, 306, 307, 308, 309, 311, 312, 313,
314, 315, 316, 317, 319, 321, 323, 324, 326

h. Statistical Series
(Economic and Demographic)

Appendix B references: 1, 4, 5, 6, 7, 8, 9, 10, 12, 15, 16, 20, 21, 22, 23, 24,
25, 27, 28, 29, 31, 36, 37, 39, 40, 42, 44, 45, 46, 47, 48, 49, 51, 52, 53, 54,
55, 58, 59, 60, 61, 63, 66, 67, 68, 69, 70, 72, 74, 75, 78, 79, 80, 89, 92, 94,
95, 96, 97, 99, 100, 101, 102, 103, 104, 105, 106, 109, 110, 112, 114, 115,
116, 117, 118, 119, 122, 124, 125, 126, 127, 128, 129, 130, 132, 142, 145,
146, 149, 151, 154, 158, 159, 160, 163, 164, 165, 168, 169, 170, 171, 172,
174, 175, 176, 177, 182, 184, 185, 187, 189, 191, 192, 195, 197, 198, 199,
202, 205, 212, 213, 214, 216, 217, 219, 220, 221, 222, 223, 224, 225, 226,
227, 228, 230, 231, 232, 234, 235, 236, 237, 240, 242, 243, 244, 247, 248,
249, 250, 252, 255, 256, 258, 259, 260, 263, 265, 266, 267, 268, 271, 275,
276, 278, 279, 281, 283, 284, 285, 286, 287, 289, 290, 293, 295, 296, 297,
298, 300, 302, 303, 306, 307, 310, 312, 313, 314, 315, 316, 323, 324

3. ECONOMIC INDICATORS
a. Monthly Summary of Business Indicators

Related Discussion: Chapter 8

Appendix B references: 6, 8, 10, 11, 15, 20, 21, 22, 24, 25, 28, 29, 31, 36,
37, 39, 40, 42, 45, 47, 49, 51, 53, 54, 55, 56, 57, 58, 59, 60, 63, 66, 68, 69,
70, 72, 74, 75, 77, 78, 79, 80, 81, 86, 87, 91, 92, 94, 95, 97, 99, 100, 102,
103, 105, 106, 107, 108, 109, 110, 112, 117, 119, 122, 128, 132, 133, 134,
141, 142, 149, 151, 157, 158, 162, 169, 171, 172, 174, 175, 176, 178, 181,
183, 184, 186, 187, 188, 192, 195, 198, 199, 200, 202, 207, 209, 216, 219,
220, 222, 223, 224, 225, 226, 227, 228, 231, 235, 236, 237, 244, 246, 247,
248, 251, 255, 256, 263, 267, 271, 272, 275, 276, 279, 282, 285, 286, 290,
297, 299, 303, 304, 305, 306, 307, 308, 312, 317, 324

b. Local Business Index

Related discussion: Chapter 9

Appendix B references: 1, 6, 8, 10, 15, 20, 21, 22, 25, 28, 29, 31, 34, 37, 39, 40, 51, 53, 54, 55, 56, 58, 59, 61, 63, 65, 66, 69, 70, 76, 77, 79, 80, 81, 84, 86, 90, 94, 96, 97, 99, 100, 102, 103, 104, 105, 106, 107, 110, 122, 127, 141, 142, 147, 148, 153, 157, 158, 162, 170, 172, 174, 178, 182, 187, 194, 197, 199, 200, 216, 217, 220, 222, 223, 224, 226, 228, 235, 236, 237, 238, 244, 247, 248, 250, 254, 255, 256, 259, 263, 265, 266, 271, 275, 276, 278, 279, 282, 285, 290, 292, 298, 300, 303, 304, 314, 315

c. Business Forecasting

Related discussion: Chapter 11

Appendix B references: 6, 7, 10, 17, 20, 21, 25, 28, 31, 34, 37, 40, 48, 51, 54, 55, 56, 58, 66, 67, 68, 70, 79, 81, 94, 96, 97, 99, 100, 102, 103, 105, 106, 109, 110, 113, 114, 116, 122, 125, 127, 130, 146, 151, 157, 158, 168, 172, 174, 175, 176, 178, 184, 192, 194, 202, 216, 217, 222, 225, 226, 231, 236, 237, 247, 250, 254, 260, 267, 268, 273, 276, 286, 290, 297, 298, 303, 304, 316

d. Economic Newsletter

Related discussion: Chapter 10

Appendix B references: 7, 8, 10, 20, 47, 48, 54, 55, 56, 57, 58, 66, 68, 70, 75, 84, 88, 94, 96, 97, 102, 103, 106, 107, 109, 114, 117, 119, 122, 126, 151, 153, 158, 172, 174, 175, 176, 178, 181, 182, 185, 192, 194, 199, 217, 220, 222, 223, 224, 226, 231, 232, 236, 237, 240, 243, 247, 254, 259, 260, 266, 276, 290, 291, 297, 303, 308, 317

e. Economic Outlook Conference

Appendix B references: 8, 10, 15, 31, 37, 40, 42, 48, 60, 66, 67, 80, 99, 102, 106, 109, 110, 113, 122, 172, 173, 174, 192, 206, 217, 222, 224, 231, 237, 240, 254, 256, 268, 273, 275, 289, 290, 303, 307. 308, 321

f. Construction Activity

Appendix B references: 1, 6, 7, 8, 10, 12, 15, 21, 28, 29, 31, 35, 42, 46, 51, 52, 53, 54, 56, 57, 58, 59, 60, 66, 67, 68, 72, 74, 75, 78, 79, 80, 83, 86, 87, 92, 95, 96, 97, 98, 101, 102, 103, 106, 107, 109, 110, 113, 114, 116, 122, 125, 130, 134, 140, 149, 151, 161, 168, 172, 175, 178, 184, 187, 194, 205, 207, 216, 217, 219, 220, 221, 223, 224, 227, 230, 231, 234, 236, 237, 238, 240, 244, 247, 248, 255, 256, 258, 259, 268, 271, 272, 275, 276, 279, 283, 284, 285, 286, 290, 295, 298, 300, 301, 303, 304, 305, 308, 314, 315, 324

4. DEMOGRAPHIC ACTIVITIES

a. Population Estimates

Related discussion: Chapter 19

Appendix B references: 1, 4, 5, 6, 8, 10, 13, 15, 16, 19, 20, 21, 23, 25, 27, 28, 29, 31, 35, 36, 37, 39, 40, 42, 43, 44, 45, 46, 47, 48, 50, 51, 52, 53, 54, 55, 56, 57, 63, 66, 67, 68, 70, 73, 74, 75, 76, 77, 78, 79, 81, 85, 86, 88, 89, 90, 92, 94, 96, 97, 98, 100, 102, 103, 104, 105, 106, 107, 108, 109, 110, 113, 114, 115, 116, 117, 119, 122, 123, 125, 126, 127, 130, 132, 133, 134, 143, 146, 151, 152, 153, 155, 158, 159, 161, 162, 163, 164, 165, 168, 169, 170, 174, 175, 176, 178, 182, 184, 186, 187, 189, 192, 194, 195, 198, 199, 201, 202, 203, 205, 207, 208, 211, 213, 216, 217, 219, 221, 224, 225, 227, 231, 234, 235, 236, 237, 238, 240, 241, 242, 243, 244, 246, 247, 248, 250, 252, 254, 256, 258, 260, 263, 265, 266, 267, 268, 271, 272, 275, 278, 281, 283, 284, 285, 287, 289, 290, 291, 295, 296, 297, 298, 299, 300, 301, 303, 304, 309, 310, 313, 315, 316, 317, 320

b. Population Projections

Appendix B references: 1, 5, 6, 8, 10, 15, 16, 19, 20, 21, 22, 23, 25, 28, 29, 31, 35, 36, 37, 40, 42, 43, 45, 46, 47, 48, 50, 51, 52, 53, 54, 55, 56, 60, 66, 67, 68, 73, 75, 76, 77, 79, 85, 86, 88, 89, 92, 94, 96, 97, 98, 100, 102, 103, 104, 105, 106, 108, 109, 110, 113, 114, 115, 116, 117, 119, 122, 123, 125, 126, 127, 130, 132, 133, 134, 143, 146, 151, 153, 158, 159, 162, 164, 165, 168, 169, 170, 174, 175, 176, 178, 182, 184, 186, 187, 192, 194, 197, 198, 199, 201, 202, 203, 205, 207, 208, 213, 216, 217, 221, 225, 227, 236, 237, 240, 242, 243, 244, 246, 247, 248, 250, 252, 256, 258, 260, 265, 267, 268, 271, 272, 275, 276, 278, 281, 283, 284, 287, 289, 290, 292, 295, 296, 297, 298, 299, 300, 301, 303, 304, 309, 310, 313, 314, 315, 317

c. Census of Population Data Tabulations

Related discussion: Chapter 18

Appendix B references: 1, 4, 6, 8, 9, 10, 12, 15, 19, 21, 28, 29, 31, 35, 37, 39, 40, 42, 45, 46, 47, 51, 53, 54, 55, 56, 59, 64, 66, 68, 75, 94, 95, 96, 97, 98, 101, 102, 103, 106, 109, 113, 114, 115, 116, 122, 123, 124, 125, 126, 149, 151, 158, 161, 164, 165, 172, 175, 176, 182, 184, 185, 186, 187, 195, 199, 201, 203, 205, 209, 216, 220, 221, 225, 231, 234, 236, 237, 243, 244, 247, 255, 256, 260, 263, 267, 271, 272, 275, 278, 279, 284, 290, 293, 296, 303, 304, 307, 313, 314, 316, 323

d. Tabulations of Vital Statistics

Appendix B references: 1, 5, 6, 7, 8, 9, 10, 12, 20, 21, 28, 29, 31, 37, 39, 40, 42, 46, 51, 53, 54, 55, 56, 57, 60, 61, 63, 64, 66, 67, 68, 75, 78, 79, 80, 85, 92, 94, 95, 98, 101, 102, 103, 106, 109, 110, 112, 113, 114, 115, 119, 122,

125, 126, 130, 148, 151, 159, 161, 165, 168, 169, 172, 174, 175, 176, 182, 186, 187, 188, 192, 194, 195, 199, 201, 203, 205, 211, 213, 221, 225, 231, 234, 235, 236, 237, 243, 247, 254, 255, 260, 263, 267, 272, 275, 278, 287, 290, 292, 293, 295, 296, 297, 298, 300, 301, 303, 312, 313, 317, 320, 321

e. Population Changes (Time Series)

Appendix B references: 1, 6, 7, 10, 15, 21, 24, 31, 37, 39, 40, 42, 45, 46, 47, 48, 50, 51, 53, 54, 55, 56, 59, 60, 63, 66, 70, 75, 80, 101, 102, 103, 106, 109, 113, 114, 115, 116, 122, 125, 132, 151, 159, 169, 170, 172, 182, 187, 194, 205, 225, 243, 247, 248, 258, 267, 268, 271, 275, 276, 278, 279, 289, 290, 297, 300, 303, 307, 309, 314, 317

5. INDUSTRIAL DEVELOPMENT

a. Economic Handbook

Related discussion: Chapter 13

Appendix B references: 1, 3, 6, 7, 9, 10, 12, 13, 15, 20, 21, 27, 30, 31, 37, 40, 42, 44, 46, 48, 58, 59, 60, 63, 66, 68, 77, 80, 88, 94, 95, 99, 102, 103, 106, 109, 110, 113, 114, 117, 122, 125, 133, 139, 140, 142, 151, 152, 157, 158, 162, 169, 172, 184, 187, 191, 192, 195, 199, 203, 205, 216, 217, 224, 227, 228, 231, 237, 240, 243, 248, 250, 256, 258, 265, 276, 282, 284, 285, 292, 297, 300, 303, 312, 319, 321, 324

b. Survey of Industrial Sites

Appendix B references: 1, 5, 7, 8, 9, 10, 12, 14, 15, 18, 19, 20, 21, 22, 24, 25, 27, 28, 29, 31, 34, 35, 37, 39, 40, 42, 46, 47, 48, 50, 51, 52, 53, 54, 55, 56, 57, 59, 61, 62, 64, 65, 66, 67, 68, 69, 70, 72, 74, 76, 78, 80, 81, 83, 85, 86, 92, 93, 94, 96, 97, 99, 100, 101, 102, 103, 105, 108, 109, 110, 112, 114, 115, 116, 117, 118, 122, 123, 125, 126, 128, 129, 130, 131, 133, 134, 136, 139, 141, 142, 145, 146, 147, 148, 149, 151, 152, 153, 154, 155, 157, 158, 159, 160, 161, 162, 164, 168, 169, 172, 174, 175, 176, 178, 183, 184, 185, 187, 188, 190, 191, 192, 194, 196, 198, 203, 205, 207, 209, 210, 211, 212, 213, 214, 216, 219, 220, 221, 222, 223, 224, 226, 227, 228, 234, 236, 237, 238, 240, 241, 242, 243, 244, 246, 247, 248, 249, 250, 251, 252, 254, 256, 258, 259, 260, 263, 265, 266, 267, 268, 270, 272, 275, 278, 281, 282, 283, 284, 285, 286, 287, 290, 291, 293, 294, 296, 297, 298, 299, 300, 303, 305, 306, 307, 309, 310, 313, 314, 315, 316, 317, 319, 324

c. Feasibility Study
for a New Business or Industry

Appendix B references: 8, 9, 10, 11, 14, 15, 18, 20, 21, 22, 23, 25, 27, 28, 29, 31, 33, 34, 35, 36, 37, 39, 40, 42, 45, 47, 48, 51, 52, 53, 54, 55, 56, 58, 59,

61, 62, 65, 66, 67, 68, 70, 71, 75, 81, 83, 85, 86, 88, 92, 94, 97, 99, 100, 102, 103, 104, 105, 106, 107, 109, 110, 112, 113, 114, 115, 117, 120, 122, 123, 125, 126, 130, 131, 132, 133, 140, 142, 145, 146, 151, 153, 155, 157, 158, 159, 162, 165, 168, 169, 172, 174, 175, 176, 177, 178, 184, 187, 188, 190, 191, 192, 194, 196, 198, 199, 200, 202, 203, 205, 207, 208, 213, 219, 221, 222, 223, 224, 226, 228, 231, 233, 234, 236, 237, 238, 240, 241, 242, 243, 244, 246, 247, 248, 252, 254, 256, 258, 259, 260, 265, 267, 268, 270, 274, 276, 277, 278, 281, 282, 284, 285, 286, 287, 290, 291, 293, 298, 299, 300, 303, 309, 313, 315, 316, 317, 321

d. Directory of Manufacturers

Related discussion: Chapter 14

Appendix B references: 1, 3, 4, 5, 7, 8, 9, 10, 11, 12, 14, 15, 17, 18, 19, 20, 21, 22, 23, 25, 27, 28, 29, 30, 31, 34, 35, 37, 39, 40, 41, 42, 44, 45, 46, 47, 49, 50, 51, 52, 53, 54, 55, 56, 57, 60, 61, 62, 63, 65, 66, 67, 68, 69, 70, 71, 72, 74, 76, 77, 78, 79, 80, 81, 83, 85, 86, 87, 89, 91, 92, 93, 94, 96, 97, 99, 100, 101, 102, 103, 104, 105, 106, 107, 108, 109, 110, 112, 113, 114, 115, 116, 117, 118, 121, 122, 123, 124, 125, 128, 129, 130, 131, 132, 133, 134, 136, 139, 141, 142, 143, 144, 146, 147, 148, 149, 150, 151, 152, 153, 154, 155, 157, 159, 160, 161, 162, 163, 164, 168, 169, 170, 171, 172, 174, 175, 176, 177, 178, 179, 181, 182, 183, 184, 185, 187, 188, 189, 190, 191, 192, 193, 194, 195, 196, 197, 198, 199, 202, 203, 204, 205, 208, 209, 210, 211, 212, 213, 214, 216, 217, 219, 220, 221, 222, 223, 224, 225, 226, 228, 229, 230, 231, 232, 233, 234, 236, 237, 238, 240, 241, 242, 243, 244, 245, 246, 247, 248, 249, 252, 253, 254, 255, 256, 257, 258, 259, 260, 261, 265, 266, 267, 268, 270, 273, 274, 275, 276, 281, 282, 283, 284, 285, 286, 287, 289, 290, 291, 292, 293, 294, 295, 296, 297, 298, 299, 300, 301, 302, 303, 306, 308, 309, 311, 312, 313, 314, 315, 316, 317, 319

e. Map of Industrial Parks

Appendix B references: 1, 5, 8, 9, 10, 12, 15, 16, 20, 21, 25, 28, 29, 30, 34, 37, 39, 40, 42, 45, 46, 50, 51, 53, 54, 55, 56, 59, 60, 66, 67, 68, 72, 74, 78, 80, 81, 85, 86, 87, 91, 92, 94, 97, 99, 100, 101, 102, 103, 104, 105, 108, 109, 111, 112, 113, 114, 115, 116, 117, 118, 122, 123, 125, 128, 133, 134, 142, 145, 146, 151, 152, 153, 154, 155, 158, 161, 162, 164, 169, 172, 174, 176, 178, 179, 181, 182, 187, 188, 190, 191, 194, 198, 203, 205, 209, 210, 211, 213, 214, 217, 219, 221, 224, 226, 227, 228, 231, 234, 236, 237, 240, 242, 243, 244, 246, 247, 248, 250, 254, 256, 258, 260, 265, 266, 267, 271, 275, 282, 283, 285, 286, 287, 289, 290, 293, 294, 296, 297, 298, 299, 301, 303, 305, 306, 307, 309, 314, 315, 316, 317, 319

f. Natural Resources Survey

Appendix B references: 1, 10, 15, 20, 22, 25, 29, 37, 52, 55, 56, 65, 66, 75, 81, 86, 88, 97, 100, 102, 103, 106, 122, 125, 155, 172, 194, 197, 199, 205, 209, 213, 236, 240, 248, 250, 260, 267, 268, 276, 285, 303, 309

6. MARKETING ACTIVITIES

a. Retail Trade Area Delineation

Related discussion: Chapter 15

Appendix B references: 1, 6, 7, 8, 10, 11, 15, 21, 22, 25, 28, 29, 31, 33, 37, 39, 40, 46, 51, 52, 53, 55, 56, 61, 66, 72, 75, 78, 80, 81, 86, 89, 96, 97, 100, 101, 102, 103, 105, 106, 107, 109, 110, 112, 116, 122, 123, 125, 126, 128, 130, 131, 134, 143, 146, 151, 153, 158, 161, 164, 165, 171, 172, 176, 186, 188, 192, 194, 197, 201, 202, 207, 210, 211, 216, 220, 221, 222, 225, 228, 230, 236, 237, 240, 243, 247, 248, 250, 252, 254, 255, 256, 258, 260, 266, 267, 268, 271, 272, 274, 275, 276, 277, 279, 284, 285, 290, 291, 293, 296, 297, 298, 300, 303, 305, 306, 307, 309, 315, 316, 317

b. Retail Sales Estimates and Projections

Related discussion: Chapter 16

Appendix B references: 1, 5, 6, 7, 8, 9, 10, 15, 16, 19, 21, 28, 29, 30, 31, 35, 37, 39, 40, 42, 45, 46, 50, 53, 55, 56, 58, 61, 63, 66, 67, 74, 75, 79, 81, 85, 86, 89, 91, 92, 93, 94, 97, 100, 102, 103, 104, 105, 106, 107, 109, 110, 112, 114, 122, 125, 126, 130, 132, 133, 134, 146, 149, 151, 152, 153, 158, 161, 164, 165, 168, 169, 172, 174, 175, 176, 178, 182, 185, 186, 188, 194, 197, 198, 201, 202, 207, 211, 216, 221, 224, 225, 226, 227, 228, 231, 233, 234, 237, 238, 240, 242, 243, 244, 247, 248, 250, 252, 254, 255, 256, 258, 260, 263, 265, 266, 267, 271, 272, 273, 274, 275, 276, 279, 284, 289, 290, 295, 296, 297, 298, 299, 301, 303, 304, 305, 306, 309, 316, 317, 319

c. Shopping Center Directory

Related discussion: Chapter 17

Appendix B references: 1, 6, 8, 9, 10, 15, 17, 19, 21, 22, 27, 28, 29, 31, 34, 37, 39, 40, 43, 44, 45, 46, 47, 49, 50, 51, 52, 55, 56, 58, 67, 68, 72, 75, 79, 80, 81, 86, 87, 90, 92, 94, 95, 96, 100, 102, 103, 106, 107, 109, 111, 112, 113, 117, 120, 121, 122, 125, 131, 132, 133, 134, 140, 142, 143, 147, 151, 152, 153, 155, 161, 162, 164, 170, 172, 174, 176, 177, 178, 181, 182, 184, 188, 192, 194, 197, 199, 202, 203, 205, 210, 211, 213, 216, 219, 220, 222, 228, 231, 234, 237, 238, 239, 243, 247, 248, 249, 250, 255, 256, 257, 259, 265, 267, 268, 271, 272, 275, 277, 282, 283, 284, 286, 289, 290, 295, 298, 300, 301, 302, 303, 309, 310, 314, 315, 316, 321

d. Trade Area Analysis

Appendix B references: 1, 6, 7, 8, 9, 10, 11, 12, 15, 21, 22, 25, 29, 31, 37, 39, 40, 42, 47, 51, 52, 53, 55, 61, 66, 67, 68, 70, 75, 81, 83, 92, 94, 97, 100, 101, 102, 103, 104, 106, 109, 112, 113, 114, 115, 117, 122, 123, 125, 126, 128, 130, 143, 146, 151, 158, 166, 169, 170, 172, 174, 182, 184, 186, 187, 192, 194, 195, 199, 200, 205, 207, 211, 213, 216, 221, 222, 226, 236, 237, 240, 243, 244, 247, 248, 256, 258, 265, 267, 268, 274, 275, 276, 284, 289, 290, 296, 297, 298, 303, 308, 309, 313, 315, 317, 321

e. Wholesale Trade Area Delineation

Related discussion: Chapter 15

Appendix B references: 6, 10, 11, 15, 21, 22, 28, 29, 37, 39, 40, 52, 66, 68, 72, 75, 92, 97, 100, 102, 106, 109, 112, 117, 122, 125, 126, 128, 130, 151, 158, 172, 194, 205, 216, 221, 225, 226, 237, 240, 247, 248, 256, 258, 260, 266, 267, 276, 284, 290, 297, 303, 316, 317

f. Directory of Wholesalers

Appendix B references: 6, 10, 20, 21, 25, 38, 40, 52, 53, 54, 61, 63, 66, 70, 79, 92, 97, 100, 102, 111, 112, 113, 122, 128, 133, 150, 151, 152, 155, 159, 164, 168, 172, 174, 184, 194, 195, 197, 205, 210, 214, 216, 217, 228, 230, 236, 237, 243, 247, 254, 257, 258, 260, 285, 286, 290, 294, 295, 297, 300, 303, 308, 309, 315, 316, 317

g. Directory of Manufacturers Agents

Appendix B references: 9, 10, 12, 20, 21, 25, 31, 39, 40, 42, 52, 53, 56, 102, 113, 150, 151, 153, 157, 159, 164, 174, 188, 194, 195, 197, 199, 205, 210, 214, 216, 227, 228, 236, 242, 254, 257, 265, 271, 276, 285, 294, 295, 300, 303, 315

h. World Trade Directory

Appendix B references: 12, 21, 31, 40, 42, 45, 48, 51, 59, 70, 75, 80, 84, 92, 102, 106, 109, 111, 113, 117, 151, 164, 173, 184, 224, 227, 228, 231, 238, 249, 256, 285, 303, 307

i. Guide for Starting a Business

Appendix B references: 5, 7, 10, 12, 15, 16, 17, 29, 31, 34, 39, 40, 44, 48, 51, 53, 54, 55, 60, 61, 65, 66, 67, 79, 80, 83, 96, 97, 102, 107, 108, 109, 110, 111, 112, 113, 116, 118, 122, 125, 127, 134, 151, 175, 176, 177, 183, 185, 194, 196, 201, 213, 216, 222, 223, 224, 225, 231, 247, 256, 259, 268, 276, 278, 285, 289, 295, 303, 309, 315, 317

j. Central Business District Analysis

Appendix B references: 5, 7, 8, 10, 11, 14, 15, 19, 21, 25, 28, 31, 33, 37, 39, 40, 42, 45, 51, 53, 55, 56, 61, 66, 67, 69, 70, 71, 78, 84, 86, 94, 96, 97, 100, 102, 105, 106, 107, 108, 110, 112, 113, 114, 117, 120, 122, 123, 142, 145, 151, 155, 164, 169, 170, 172, 174, 175, 178, 184, 185, 194, 198, 205, 207, 216, 222, 226, 233, 237, 238, 240, 243, 244, 247, 250, 254, 256, 258, 260, 265, 267, 268, 272, 273, 274, 275, 276, 284, 285, 296, 297, 298, 299, 303, 304, 309, 313, 314, 315, 317, 319

7. GOVERNMENTAL RESEARCH

a. Legislative Research

Related discussion: Chapter 20

Appendix B references: 5, 6, 10, 11, 14, 20, 21, 22, 28, 29, 31, 34, 37, 40, 42, 47, 48, 50, 51, 52, 55, 56, 57, 58, 61, 64, 67, 70, 71, 73, 74, 75, 76, 77, 78, 81, 83, 85, 86, 88, 92, 94, 96, 97, 98, 99, 100, 102, 103, 105, 107, 108, 109, 110, 111, 112, 113, 114, 116, 117, 119, 122, 126, 130, 139, 142, 143, 145, 146, 149, 151, 152, 154, 158, 159, 161, 164, 169, 170, 173, 174, 175, 176, 181, 182, 184, 188, 194, 195, 207, 211, 214, 216, 220, 221, 223, 224, 226, 228, 236, 237, 238, 239, 240, 243, 248, 252, 254, 258, 259, 260, 263, 267, 268, 269, 270, 273, 274, 275, 276, 278, 281, 285, 286, 290, 293, 297, 298, 299, 303, 304, 305, 306, 307, 309, 312, 313, 314, 315, 316, 317, 318, 321, 322, 325

b. Legislative Status and Digests

Appendix B references: 5, 6, 10, 11, 18, 19, 21, 29, 31, 34, 37, 39, 40, 42, 50, 55, 56, 64, 66, 70, 71, 73, 77, 78, 84, 86, 92, 94, 97, 98, 99, 100, 101, 102, 105, 107, 111, 112, 114, 117, 119, 122, 130, 142, 143, 145, 151, 152, 158, 161, 163, 164, 169, 173, 174, 175, 176, 182, 185, 194, 196, 197, 199, 200, 201, 202, 203, 207, 211, 219, 222, 223, 224, 226, 227, 228, 236, 240, 243, 248, 254, 259, 260, 263, 267, 268, 269, 270, 275, 279, 281, 285, 286, 290, 297, 299, 303, 304, 306, 307, 309, 312, 313, 314, 315, 318, 321, 322, 325

c. Fiscal Analysis and Budget Reviews

Related discussion: Chapter 21

Appendix B references: 10, 20, 21, 22, 29, 31, 37, 40, 42, 50, 55, 56, 57, 64, 66, 70, 71, 73, 74, 77, 85, 86, 88, 90, 94, 97, 98, 99, 100, 101, 102, 103, 109, 110, 114, 119, 122, 123, 126, 130, 142, 145, 151, 152, 158, 159, 164, 169, 173, 175, 176, 191, 193, 194, 197, 204, 216, 220, 221, 224, 228, 235, 243, 258, 259, 260, 267, 268, 276, 284, 285, 289, 290, 297, 298, 299, 303, 307, 309, 313, 318, 322, 325

d. Tax Information Relating to Local Area

Appendix B references: 1, 5, 6, 8, 9, 10, 11, 12, 15, 16, 18, 19, 21, 22, 23, 25, 27, 28, 29, 31, 33, 34, 35, 37, 39, 40, 41, 42, 45, 46, 47, 48, 50, 51, 52, 53, 54, 55, 56, 57, 59, 61, 62, 64, 66, 67, 68, 69, 70, 71, 72, 73, 74, 75, 77, 80, 81, 84, 85, 86, 88, 92, 93, 94, 96, 97, 98, 99, 100, 101, 102, 103, 104, 105, 108, 109, 110, 111, 112, 113, 114, 115, 116, 117, 118, 119, 122, 125, 127, 128, 129, 130, 132, 141, 142, 145, 147, 149, 151, 152, 154, 155, 158, 160, 161, 162, 163, 164, 165, 168, 169, 170, 172, 173, 174, 175, 176, 179, 184, 187, 188, 189, 191, 192, 194, 195, 196, 197, 199, 201, 202, 203, 204, 205, 207, 211, 213, 214, 216, 217, 219, 220, 221, 223, 224, 225, 226, 228, 231, 233, 234, 236, 237, 238, 240, 243, 244, 249, 250, 252, 254, 255, 256, 258, 260, 267, 268, 271, 272, 275, 276, 277, 278, 279, 282, 283, 284, 285, 286, 288, 289, 290, 293, 294, 295, 296, 298, 300, 303, 304, 307, 309, 310, 314, 315, 316, 317, 318

e. Local Government Directory

Appendix B references: 1, 5, 9, 10, 11, 19, 21, 25, 27, 28, 29, 31, 39, 40, 41, 42, 51, 52, 55, 56, 61, 65, 66, 67; 68, 70, 71, 72, 74, 75, 76, 80, 81, 84, 85, 92, 97, 98, 99, 100, 101, 102, 103, 105, 107, 109, 112, 114, 117, 121, 122, 127, 132, 134, 143, 145, 150, 151, 152, 154, 155, 158, 161, 162, 164, 168, 169, 174, 175, 176, 177, 178, 179, 181, 182, 184, 194, 195, 196, 197, 199, 202, 203, 205, 212, 217, 219, 220, 221, 222, 223, 226, 227, 235, 236, 238, 243, 250, 252, 254, 256, 259, 260, 263, 265, 267, 268, 271, 275, 276, 277, 278, 283, 284, 285, 286, 287, 289, 290, 293, 294, 295, 296, 300, 301, 303, 309, 310, 313, 314, 315, 321

f. Briefs and Exhibits to Document the Community's Position in Government Proceedings

Related discussion: Chapter 22

Appendix B references: 7, 10, 12, 21, 22, 29, 31, 33, 40, 42, 43, 46, 52, 56, 66, 67, 71, 85, 92, 94, 96, 99, 101, 102, 103, 106, 108, 109, 114, 142, 145, 151, 155, 158, 161, 164, 176, 193, 194, 208, 219, 221, 228, 231, 240, 243, 250, 257, 258, 268, 270, 290, 298, 303, 307, 309, 314, 315, 316, 318, 321, 324

8. LABOR FORCE AND EMPLOYMENT

a. Employment Supply and Demand Projections

Appendix B references: 1, 5, 7, 8, 9, 10, 15, 16, 21, 24, 28, 29, 31, 37, 40, 42, 47, 48, 51, 52, 53, 54, 55, 56, 62, 65, 66, 67, 74, 75, 81, 92, 95, 96, 97, 100, 102, 103, 104, 105, 106, 108, 109, 113, 114, 116, 117, 121, 122, 123, 125, 134, 143, 151, 158, 164, 172, 174, 175, 176, 178, 187, 191, 194, 198, 205,

216, 219, 221, 224, 225, 226, 231, 237, 240, 243, 244, 247, 250, 260, 263, 265, 267, 268, 273, 275, 276, 278, 285, 289, 290, 296, 297, 300, 303, 304, 309, 314, 317

b. Wage Rates

Appendix B references: 1, 3, 5, 7, 8, 9, 10, 11, 12, 14, 15, 16, 20, 21, 24, 25, 28, 29, 31, 34, 37, 40, 42, 45, 46, 48, 49, 51, 52, 53, 54, 55, 56, 59, 61, 62, 63, 66, 67, 68, 69, 70, 72, 74, 75, 77, 78, 80, 81, 92, 96, 97, 100, 101, 102, 103, 105, 108, 109, 111, 112, 113, 114, 116, 118, 122, 123, 125, 126, 128, 129, 130, 133, 134, 142, 143, 148, 149, 151, 152, 155, 158, 160, 164, 170, 172, 173, 175, 176, 177, 178, 184, 188, 189, 194, 195, 198, 199, 200, 202, 204, 205, 209, 219, 221, 223, 224, 225, 226, 227, 231, 237, 240, 243, 244, 246, 247, 248, 249, 250, 253, 256, 260, 263, 265, 266, 267, 268, 275, 276, 278, 279, 281, 282, 283, 284, 285, 286, 290, 296, 297, 298, 300, 301, 303, 304, 305, 306, 309, 314, 315, 316, 317

c. Labor Commuting Study

Appendix B references: 10, 12, 15, 20, 21, 24, 37, 40, 48, 50, 51, 52, 53, 56, 66, 68, 75, 81, 92, 96, 100, 102, 103, 108, 109, 122, 125, 126, 130, 151, 162, 164, 175, 186, 191, 194, 196, 199, 223, 226, 234, 240, 246, 247, 248, 250, 254, 255, 260, 268, 274, 276, 285, 296, 297, 303, 307, 317

d. Directory of Major Employers

Appendix B references: 1, 3, 5, 6, 8, 9, 10, 11, 12, 14, 15, 16, 18, 19, 20, 21, 22, 23, 24, 27, 28, 29, 31, 34, 35, 37, 39, 40, 42, 44, 45, 47, 48, 51, 53, 54, 55, 56, 58, 59, 60, 61, 62, 63, 65, 66, 67, 68, 69, 70, 71, 74, 75, 76, 78, 79, 80, 81, 85, 86, 87, 92, 93, 94, 95, 96, 97, 98, 99, 100, 101, 102, 103, 106, 107, 108, 109, 111, 112, 113, 114, 115, 116, 117, 122, 123, 125, 126, 128, 129, 130, 132, 133, 134, 139, 142, 147, 149, 150, 151, 152, 153, 155, 157, 158, 159, 160, 161, 162, 163, 164, 169, 170, 171, 172, 174, 175, 176, 177, 178, 181, 183, 184, 185, 187, 188, 189, 193, 194, 195, 196, 197, 199, 202, 205, 207, 208, 210, 211, 212, 216, 217, 219, 221, 222, 223, 224, 225, 226, 227, 228, 229, 231, 234, 236, 237, 240, 243, 244, 246, 247, 248, 249, 250, 252, 256, 257, 258, 259, 260, 265, 266, 267, 268, 271, 274, 275, 276, 277, 278, 281, 283, 284, 285, 286, 289, 290, 291, 293, 296, 297, 298, 299, 300, 301, 303, 305, 307, 308, 309, 313, 316, 317, 319, 321

9. TRANSPORTATION

a. Directory of Transportation Facilities

Appendix B references: 1, 5, 6, 7, 10, 11, 12, 16, 20, 21, 24, 25, 28, 31, 34, 37, 39, 40, 42, 51, 52, 53, 56, 59, 61, 62, 63, 65, 66, 67, 68, 70, 74, 75, 80, 81, 92, 94, 97, 98, 100, 101, 102, 103, 109, 111, 112, 113, 114, 115, 117, 122,

123, 125, 128, 130, 134, 151, 155, 160, 161, 162, 164, 169, 174, 175, 176, 178, 187, 189, 194, 195, 197, 199, 205, 207, 208, 209, 210, 211, 213, 217, 220, 221, 222, 223, 224, 226, 227, 228, 231, 236, 237, 238, 240, 243, 244, 246, 247, 249, 250, 252, 256, 257, 260, 265, 267, 268, 270, 275, 276, 277, 278, 282, 283, 284, 285, 286, 289, 290, 293, 296, 297, 300, 303, 309, 313, 316, 317, 321

10. COMMUNITY FACILITIES AND SERVICES

a. Education Facilities Study

Appendix B references: 1, 5, 6, 7, 8, 10, 11, 12, 15, 16, 20, 21, 22, 25, 27, 28, 31, 35, 37, 39, 40, 42, 46, 47, 51, 53, 54, 55, 56, 61, 62, 65, 66, 67, 68, 70, 72, 74, 75, 80, 81, 85, 86, 92, 95, 96, 97, 98, 100, 102, 103, 104, 105, 109, 110, 112, 114, 115, 116, 119, 122, 123, 125, 128, 130, 134, 142, 143, 147, 151, 152, 159, 161, 162, 164, 169, 174, 175, 176, 177, 178, 187, 189, 191, 194, 196, 197, 198, 199, 201, 202, 205, 207, 209, 211, 219, 221, 222, 223, 224, 226, 231, 236, 237, 240, 244, 247, 250, 252, 258, 260, 263, 265, 267, 268, 274, 275, 276, 277, 278, 284, 285, 286, 289, 290, 296, 297, 298, 300, 303, 306, 309, 312, 313, 314, 316, 317, 321

b. Communications Media Directory

Appendix B references: 6, 7, 10, 11, 13, 20, 21, 22, 23, 25, 27, 31, 37, 39, 40, 42, 52, 53, 59, 66, 70, 74, 75, 80, 86, 87, 90, 92, 96, 102, 103, 104, 112, 113, 121, 122, 123, 128, 129, 130, 134, 151, 152, 154, 155, 159, 162, 164, 175, 176, 178, 187, 194, 199, 203, 205, 209, 217, 222, 223, 226, 236, 240, 243, 247, 248, 254, 256, 257, 259, 260, 262, 263, 267, 268, 271, 273, 275, 276, 277, 281, 283, 284, 285, 289, 290, 300, 303, 310, 313, 315, 316

c. Office Space Inventory

Appendix B references: 6, 7, 8, 10, 11, 12, 19, 20, 21, 25, 31, 34, 37, 40, 42, 47, 50, 51, 52, 53, 54, 56, 58, 61, 65, 68, 70, 78, 80, 83, 85, 86, 88, 96, 102, 103, 111, 112, 113, 114, 115, 117, 120, 126, 130, 142, 151, 152, 155, 160, 162, 165, 169, 172, 174, 175, 176, 178, 187, 191, 194, 196, 197, 205, 208, 218, 222, 223, 225, 237, 240, 242, 244, 247, 248, 250, 254, 255, 256, 257, 260, 265, 266, 268, 276, 281, 283, 285, 286, 290, 292, 296, 297, 300, 303, 306, 314

d. Financial Services Directory

Appendix B references: 7, 10, 11, 12, 15, 20, 29, 31, 35, 39, 40, 47, 51, 52, 53, 56, 66, 67, 79, 86, 92, 96, 98, 102, 103, 112, 113, 114, 142, 152, 160, 164, 169, 170, 172, 178, 187, 194, 196, 205, 222, 223, 224, 231, 236, 240, 243, 247, 249, 255, 260, 268, 276, 285, 290, 300, 303, 307, 309, 316, 317, 321

e. Directory of Research, Technology and Professional Services

Appendix B references: 10, 12, 20, 31, 40, 48, 51, 53, 56, 66, 83, 102, 103, 105, 172, 178, 194, 196, 199, 205, 219, 227, 231, 236, 240, 247, 250, 257, 268, 276, 285, 303, 306, 309, 317

f. Data Processing Directory

Appendix B references: 10, 12, 15, 20, 34, 40, 51, 53, 56, 66, 68, 101, 102, 109, 112, 113, 114, 134, 152, 178, 194, 197, 199, 256, 284, 290, 297, 303, 316, 317

APPENDIX B:

IDENTIFICATION OF THE CHAMBER OF COMMERCE CORRESPONDING TO EACH REFERENCE NUMBER SHOWN IN APPENDIX A

Reference numbers shown in Appendix A correspond to the Chambers of Commerce listed below.

The total population of the community served by each Chamber of Commerce (except state Chambers of Commerce) is indicated by means of an alphabetic symbol at the end of the Chamber's listing. These symbols and their corresponding population ranges are presented in the following table:

A	—	Less than 25,000	E —	100,000 - 249,999
B	—	25,000 - 49,999	F —	250,000 - 499,999
C	—	50,000 - 74,999	G —	500,000 - 999,999
D	—	75,000 - 99,999	H —	1,000,000 +

Unless otherwise indicated, each code letter refers to a population total for the local Standard Metropolitan Statistical Area. Asterisks indicate communities for which population totals are available only for incorporated cities.

Information for Chambers of Commerce numbered 291 through 326 was received after the original alphabetical list of participating organizations was prepared.

1. Abilene Chamber of Commerce; P.O. Box 2281, Abilene, Texas 79604; A/C 915, 677-7241; E

2. Alameda Chamber of Commerce; 2437 Santa Clara Ave., Alameda, California 94501; A/C 415, 522-0414; D*

3. Albuquerque Industrial Development Service, Inc.; Convention Center, 401 Second St., N.W., Albuquerque, New Mexico 87101; A/C 505, 842-0220; F

4. Greater Alexandria-Pineville Chamber of Commerce; P.O. Box 992, Alexandria, Louisiana 71301; A/C 318, 442-6671; B*

5. Allentown-Lehigh County Chamber of Commerce; 462 Walnut St., Allentown, Pennsylvania 18105; A/C 215, 437-9661; G

6. Amarillo Chamber of Commerce; Amarillo Building, Amarillo, Texas 79101; A/C 806, 374-5238; E

7. Anaheim Chamber of Commerce; P.O. Box 969, Anaheim, California 92805; A/C 714, 535-2833; H

8. Appleton Area Chamber of Commerce; P.O. Box 955, Appleton, Wisconsin 54911; A/C 414, 734-1491; F

9. Ashland Area Chamber of Commerce; P.O. Box 830, Ashland, Kentucky 41101; A/C 600, 324-5111; F*

10. Ashland Area Chamber of Commerce; Chamber of Commerce Building, Ashland, Wisconsin 54806; A/C 715, 682-2500; A

11. Ashtabula Area Chamber of Commerce; P.O. Box 96, Ashtabula, Ohio 44004; A/C 216; 997-9756; A*

12. Atlanta Chamber of Commerce; 1300 Commerce Bldg., Atlanta, Georgia 30303; A/C 404, 521-0845; H

13. Auburn (Placer County Chamber of Commerce); 217 Maple Street, Auburn, California 95603; A/C 916, 885-4016; D*

14. Augusta (Kennebec Valley Chamber of Commerce); Memorial Circle, Augusta, Maine 04330; A/C 207, 623-4559; A*

15. Austin Chamber of Commerce; P.O. Box 1967, Austin, Texas 78767; A/C 512, 478-9383; F

16. Metropolitan Baltimore Chamber of Commerce; 22 Light St., Baltimore, Maryland 21202; A/C 301, 539-7600; H

17. Beachwood (Heights Area Chamber of Commerce); 2133 Campus Rd., Beachwood, Ohio 44122; A/C 216, 321-3777; E*

18. Beacon-Fishkill Area Chamber of Commerce, Inc.; 442 Main St., Beacon, New York 12508; A/C 914, 831-0150; A

19. Berea Chamber of Commerce; 25 Riverside Dr., Berea, Ohio 44017; A/C 216, 234-2047; A*

20. Big Spring Chamber of Commerce; P.O. Box 1391, Big Spring, Texas 79720; A/C 915, 263-7641; B*

21. Binghamton (Broome County Chamber of Commerce); P.O. Box 995, Binghamton, New York 13902; A/C 607, 729-6344; F

22. Birmingham Area Chamber of Commerce; 1914 Sixth Avenue North, Birmingham, Alabama 35203; A/C 205, 323-5461; F

23. Greater Bloomington Chamber of Commerce; P.O. Box 1302, Bloomington, Indiana 47401; A/C 812, 336-6381; B*

24. Bloomington (Association of Commerce & Industry of McLean County); 212 E. Washington, Bloomington, Illinois 61701; A/C 309, 829-6344; E

25. Greater Boise Chamber of Commerce; 709 West Idaho, P.O. Box 2368, Boise, Idaho 83701; A/C 208, 344-5515; E

26. Greater Boston Chamber of Commerce; 125 High Street, Boston, Massachusetts 02110; A/C 617, 426-1250; H

27. Boulder Chamber of Commerce; P.O. Box 73, Boulder, Colorado 80302; A/C 303, 442-1044; C*
28. Bowling Green Chamber of Commerce; P.O. Box 282, Bowling Green, Ohio 43402; A/C 419, 353-7945; A*
29. Brazosport Chamber of Commerce; P.O. Box 2470, Brazosport, Texas 77541; A/C 713, 265-2505; B*
30. Buena Park Chamber of Commerce & Visitor's Bureau; 6696 Beach Blvd., Buena Park, California 90612; A/C 714, 521-0261; C*
31. Buffalo Area Chamber of Commerce; 238 Main St., Buffalo, New York 14202; A/C 716, 852-5400; H
32. Chamber of Commerce of Burbank; 200 W. Magnolia Blvd., Burbank, California 91502; A/C 213, 846-3111; D*
33. Calais Chamber of Commerce; City Bldg., Calais, Maine 04619; A/C 207, 454-7071; A*
34. Greater Canton Chamber of Commerce; 229 Wells Ave., NW., Canton, Ohio 44703; A/C 216; 456-7253; F
35. Cape May County Chamber of Commerce; P.O. Box 74; Cape May Court House, New Jersey 08210; A/C 609, 465-7181; C*
36. Casper Area Chamber of Commerce; P.O. Box 399; Casper, Wyoming 82601; A/C 307, 234-5311; B*
37. Cedar Rapids-Marion Area Chamber of Commerce; 127 3rd St. Northeast, Cedar Rapids, Iowa 52401; A/C 319, 364-5135; E
38. Charlottesville-Albemarle County Chamber of Commerce; P.O. Box 1564, Charlottesville, Virginia 22913; A/C 804, 295-3141; B*
39. Greater Chattanooga Area Chamber of Commerce; 819 Broad Street, Chattanooga, Tennessee 37402; A/C 615, 267-2121; F
40. Chicago Association of Commerce and Industry; 130 South Michigan Avenue; Chicago, Illinois 60603; A/C 312, 786-0111; H
41. Chula Vista Chamber of Commerce; 298 Fourth Ave., Chula Vista, California 92010; A/C 714, 420-6602; C*
42. Greater Cincinnati Chamber of Commerce; 309 Vine St., Cincinnati, Ohio 45202; A/C 513, 721-3300; H
43. Citrus Heights Chamber of Commerce; P.O. Box 191; Citrus Heights, California 95616; A/C 916, 725-1181; B*
44. Greater Clearwater Chamber of Commerce; 128 N. Osceola Ave., Clearwater, Florida 33515; A/C 803, 446-4081; C*
45. Greater Cleveland Growth Assoc.; 690 Union Commerce Bldg., Cleveland, Ohio 44146; A/C 216, 621-3300; H
46. Clovis Chamber of Commerce; P.O. Drawer C, Clovis, New Mexico 88101; A/C 505, 763-3435; B*
47. Colorado Springs Chamber of Commerce; P.O. Drawer "B", Colorado Springs, Colorado 80901; A/C 303, 635-1551; E
48. State of Colorado, Division of Commerce & Development; 600 State Capitol Annex, Denver, Colorado 80203; A/C 303, 892-2205

49. Columbus Chamber of Commerce; P.O. Box 1200; Columbus, Georgia 31902; A/C 404, 327-1566; E

50. Columbus Area Chamber of Commerce; P.O. Box 29, Columbus, Indiana 47201; A/C 812, 379-9579; B*

51. Columbus Area Chamber of Commerce, P.O. Box 1527; Columbus, Ohio 43216; A/C 614, 221-1321; H

52. Cookeville (Putnam County Chamber of Commerce); 302 South Jefferson, Cookeville, Tennessee 38501; A/C 615, 526-2211; A*

53. Dayton Area Chamber of Commerce; 111 W. 1st St. - Suite 200, Dayton, Ohio 45402; A/C 513, 226-1444; G

54. Decatur (Dekalb Chamber of Commerce); 515 Decatur Federal Building, Decatur, Georgia 30030; A/C 404, 378-3691; H

55. Chamber of Commerce of Decatur, Illinois; P.O. Box 1031, Decatur, Illinois 62525; A/C 217, 429-5167; E

56. Dekalb Chamber of Commerce; 363½ E. Lincoln, Dekalb, Illinois 60115; A/C 815, 756-6306; B*

57. Del Rio Chamber of Commerce; P.O. Box 1388, Del Rio, Texas 78840; A/C 512, 775-3551; A*

58. Denver Chamber of Commerce; 1301 Welton, Denver, Colorado 80204; A/C 303, 534-3211; H

59. Greater Des Moines Chamber of Commerce; Eighth and High Sts., Des Moines, Iowa 50307; A/C 515, 283-2161; F

60. Greater Detroit Chamber of Commerce; 150 Michigan Ave., Detroit, Michigan 48226; A/C 313, 535-0960; H

61. Downey Chamber of Commerce; 8497 2nd St., Downey, California 90241; A/C 213, 923-2191; D*

62. Dresden (Weakley County Chamber of Commerce); P.O. Box 67, Dresden, Tennessee 38225; A/C 901, 364-3787; B*

63. Duluth Area Chamber of Commerce; 220 Medical Arts Bldg., Duluth, Minnesota 55802; A/C 218, 722-5501; F

64. East Chicago Chamber of Commerce; P.O. Box 524, East Chicago, Indiana 46312; A/C 219, 398-1600; B*

65. Eastern Shore of Virginia Chamber of Commerce, Inc.; P.O. Box 147, #1 Court House Sq., Accomac, Virginia 23301; A/C 804, 787-2460; B*

66. Easton Area Chamber of Commerce, Inc.; 62 N. 4th St., Easton, Pennsylvania 18042; A/C 215, 253-4211; B*

67. El Cajon Valley Chamber of Commerce; 190 N. Julian Ave., El Cajon, California 92020; A/C 714, 442-9251; C

68. El Paso Chamber of Commerce; 10 Civic Center Plaza, El Paso, Texas 79944; A/C 915, 544-7880; F

69. Elgin Area Chamber of Commerce; 310 E. Chicago St., Elgin, Illinois 60120; A/C 312, 741-5660; C*

70. Greater Elkhart Chamber of Commerce; P.O. Box 428, Elkhart, Indiana 46514; A/C 219, 293-1531; B

71. Evanston Chamber of Commerce; 807 Davis St., Evanston, Illinois 60201; A/C 312, 328-1500; G*

72. Metropolitan Evansville Chamber of Commerce; Southern Securities Bldg., Evansville, Indiana 47708; A/C 812, 425-8147; F

73. Fairfax County Chamber of Commerce; 8408 Arlington Blvd., Fairfax, Virginia 22030; A/C 703, 560-4000; F

74. Fall River Area Chamber of Commerce; P.O. Box 1871, Fall River, Massachusetts 02720; A/C 617, 676-8227; E

75. Florida State Chamber of Commerce; P.O. Box 8046, Jacksonville, Florida 32211; A/C 904, 724-2400

76. Fontana Chamber of Commerce; 8608 Wheeler, Fontana, California 92335; A/C 714, 822-4433; A*

77. Fort Collins Area Chamber of Commerce; Drawer D, Fort Collins, Colorado 80521; A/C 303, 482-3746; C*

78. Fort Dodge Chamber of Commerce; P.O. Box T, Fort Dodge, Iowa 50501; A/C 515, 576-2108; B*

79. Greater Fort Lauderdale Chamber of Commerce; P.O. Box 1581, 208 S.E. 3rd Ave., Fort Lauderdale, Florida 33302; A/C 305, 522-4721; G

80. Fort Worth Area Chamber of Commerce; 700 Throckmorton St., Fort Worth, Texas 76102; A/C 817, 336-2491; H

81. Chamber of Commerce of Frederick County; Francis Scott Key Hotel, Frederick, Maryland 21701; A/C 301, 662-4164; A*

82. Fresno County and City Chamber of Commerce; P.O. Box 1469, Fresno, California 93716; A/C 209, 233-4651; F

83. Fridley Chamber of Commerce; 6279 University Ave. NE, Fridley, Minnesota 55432; A/C 612, 560-1723; B*

84. Garden City Chamber of Commerce; 29207 Ford Road, Garden City, Michigan 48135; A/C 313, 422-4448; B*

85. Garden Grove Chamber of Commerce; P.O. Box 464, Garden Grove, California 92642; A/C 714, 638-7950; E*

86. Greater Gardner Chamber of Commerce; 301 Central Street, Gardner, Massachusetts 01440; A/C 617, 632-1780;A*

87. Gastonia (Gaston County Chamber of Commerce); P.O. Box 2168, Gastonia, North Carolina 28052; A/C 704, 864-2621; B

88. Globe Chamber of Commerce; P.O. Box 2539, Globe, Arizona 85501; A/C 602, 425-4495; B

89. Goldsboro Area Chamber of Commerce; P.O. Box 1107, Goldsboro, North Carolina 27530; A/C 919, 734-2241; B*

90. Granada Hills Chamber of Commerce, Inc.; 10727 White Oak Ave., Suite 117, Granada Hills, California 91344; A/C 213, 363-4202; C*

91. Grand Island Chamber of Commerce; P.O. Box 1486, Grand Island, Nebraska 68801; A/C 308, 382-9210; B*
92. Greater Grand Rapids Chamber of Commerce; 300 Federal Square Bldg., 29 Pearl St., N.W., Grand Rapids, Michigan 49502; A/C 616, 459-7221; G
93. Chamber of Commerce of the Tri-Cities; 1831 Delmar Avenue, Granite City, Illinois 62040; A/C 618, 876-6400; B*
94. Great Falls Area Chamber of Commerce; P.O. Box 2127, Great Falls, Montana 59401; A/C 406, 453-1441; D
95. Chamber of Commerce of the City of Greensboro, N.C., Inc.; P.O. Box 3246, Greensboro, North Carolina 27402; A/C 919, 275-8675; G
96. Greater Greenville Chamber of Commerce; P.O. Box 10048, Federal Station, Greenville, South Carolina 29603; A/C 803, 235-7411; F
97. Hagerstown Area Chamber of Commerce; 92 West Washington St., Hagerstown, Maryland 21740; A/C 301, 739-2015; B*
98. Hallandale Chamber of Commerce; P.O. Box 249, Hallandale, Florida 33009; A/C 305, 923-0541; A*
99. Greater Hartford Chamber of Commerce; 250 Constitution Plaza, Hartford, Connecticut 06103; A/C 203, 525-4451; G
100. Hattiesburg Area Chamber of Commerce; P.O. Box 710, Hattiesburg, Mississippi 39401; A/C 601, 583-4341; B*
101. Greater Hazleton Chamber of Commerce; Mezzanine, Northeastern Bldg., Hazleton, Pennsylvania 18201; A/C 717, 455-1508; B*
102. Catawba County Chamber of Commerce; P.O. Box 1828, Hickoly, North Carolina 28601; A/C 704, 328-6111; D*
103. Hobbs Chamber of Commerce; P.O. Box 1136, Hobbs, New Mexico 88240; A/C 505, 397-3202; B*
104. Greater Hollywood Chamber of Commerce; P.O. Box 2345; Hollywood, Florida 33022; A/C 305, 920-3330; E*
105. Hot Springs Chamber of Commerce; P.O. Box 1500, Hot Springs, Arkansas 71901; A/C 501, 623-5541; B*
106. Houston Chamber of Commerce; P.O. Box 53600, Houston, Texas 77052; A/C 713, 227-5111; H
107. Huntington Park Chamber of Commerce; 2550-E Gage Ave., Huntington Park, California 90255; A/C 213, 585-3348; B*
108. Hutchinson Chamber of Commerce; 15 East Second, Hutchinson, Kansas 67501; A/C 316, 662-3391; B*
109. Indianapolis Chamber of Commerce; 320 North Meridian Street, Indianapolis, Indiana 46204; A/C 317, 635-6423; H
110. Inglewood Chamber of Commerce; P.O. Box 762, Inglewood, California 90307; A/C 213, 677-1121; D*
111. Jackson Chamber of Commerce; P.O. Box 22548, Jackson, Mississippi 39205; A/C 601, 948-7575; F

112. Jackson Area Chamber of Commerce; P.O. Box 1904, Jackson, Tennessee 38301; A/C 901, 427-3328; C

113. Jacksonville Area Chamber of Commerce; P.O. Drawer 329; Jacksonville, Florida 32201; A/C 904, 353-6161; G

114. Jersey City Chamber of Commerce; 911 Bergen Ave., Jersey City, New Jersey 07306; A/C 201, 653-7400; B

115. Kalamazoo County Chamber of Commerce; 121 W. Cedar St., Kalamazoo, Michigan 49006; A/C 616, 381-4000; E

116. Kankakee Area Chamber of Commerce; P.O. Box 905, Kankakee, Illinois 60901; A/C 815, 933-7721; B*

117. Chamber of Commerce of Greater Kansas City; 620 TenMain Center, 920 Main Street, Kansas City, Missouri 64105; A/C 816, 221-2424; H

118. Kent Area Chamber of Commerce; 540 S. Water St., Kent, Ohio 44212; A/C 216, 673-9855; B*

119. Greater Key West Chamber of Commerce; 402 Wall Street, Key West, Florida 33040; A/C 305, 294-2587; B*

120. Kirkwood Area Chamber of Commerce; 333 S. Kirkwood Rd., Kirkwood, Missouri 63122; A/C 314, 821-4161; B*

121. Kokomo Area Chamber of Commerce; P.O. Box 731, Kokomo, Indiana 46901; A/C 317, 457-5301; B*

122. Greater La Crosse Chamber of Commerce; P.O. Box 842; La Crosse, Wisconsin 54601; A/C 608, 784-4880; E

123. La Grange Chamber of Commerce; P.O. Box 636, La Grange, Georgia 30240; A/C 404, 884-8671; A*

124. Greater Lake Worth Chamber of Commerce, P.O. Box 1422, Lake Worth, Florida 33460; A/C 305, 582-4401; A*

125. Lakeland Area Chamber of Commerce; P.O. Box 3638, Lakeland, Florida 33802; A/C 813, 688-8551; B*

126. Greater Lakewood Chamber of Commerce; 5787 South St., Lakewood, California 90713; A/C 213, 866-2313; D*

127. Greater Largo Chamber of Commerce, Inc.; P.O. Box 326, 395 1st Ave., SW, Largo, Florida 33540; A/C 813, 584-2321/581-4266; B*

128. Laurel Chamber of Commerce; P.O. Box 527, Laurel, Mississippi 39440; A/C 601, 428-0574; A*

129. Leavenworth Area Chamber of Commerce; P.O. Box 44, Leavenworth, Kansas 66048; A/C 913, 682-4112; A*

130. Lebanon Valley Chamber of Commerce; P.O. Box 118, Lebanon, Pennsylvania 17042; A/C 717, 273-3727; B*

131. Greater Lewiston Chamber of Commerce; Ponderosa Lewis-Clark Motor Inn, Lewiston, Idaho 83501; A/C 208, 743-3531; B*

132. Greater Lexington Chamber of Commerce; 249 N. Broadway, Lexington, Kentucky 40508; A/C 606, 254-4447; E

133. Lincoln Chamber of Commerce; 1221 "N" Street, Lincoln, Nebraska 68508; A/C 402, 432-7511; E

134. Little Rock Chamber of Commerce; 500 Continental Bldg., Markham & Main St., Little Rock, Arkansas 72201; A/C 501, 374-4871; F

135. Greater Littleton Chamber of Commerce; P.O. Box 809, Littleton, Colorado 80120; A/C 303, 795-8014; B*

136. Lockport Area Chamber of Commerce; 8 Market St., Lockport, New York 14094; A/C 716, 433-3828; C

137. Los Angeles Chamber of Commerce; 404 South Bixel Street, Los Angeles, California 90054; A/C 213, 482-4010; H

138. Louisville Chamber of Commerce; 300 West Liberty, Louisville, Kentucky 40202; A/C 502, 582-2421; G

139. Chamber of Commerce of Greater Lowell; 178 Church St., Lowell, Massachusetts 01852; A/C 617, 455-5633; E

140. Lubbock Chamber of Commerce-Board of City Development; P.O. Box 561, Lubbock, Texas 79408; A/C 806, 763-4666; E

141. Greater Lynchburg Chamber of Commerce; P.O. Box 2027, Lynchburg, Virginia 24501; A/C 703, 845-5966; E

142. Greater Madison Chamber of Commerce; P.O. Box 71, Madison, Wisconsin 53701; A/C 608, 256-8348; F

143. Mankato Area Chamber of Commerce; 220 Front St., Mankato, Minnesota 56001; A/C 507, 345-4519; B*

144. Mansfield Area Chamber of Commerce; 33 Park Avenue West, Mansfield, Ohio 44902; A/C 419, 522-3211; E

145. Jackson County Chamber of Commerce; P.O. Box 130, Marianna, Florida 32446; A/C 904, 482-8061; A*

146. Marshall Area Chamber of Commerce; 5th and Main, Marshall, Minnesota 56258; A/C 507, 532-4484; A*

147. Martinsville-Henry County Chamber of Commerce; P.O. Box 709, Martinsville, Virginia 24112; A/C 703, 632-6401; A*

148. Mattoon Association of Commerce; P.O. Box 669, Mattoon, Illinois 61938; A/C 217, 235-5661; A*

149. McAllen Chamber of Commerce; P.O. Box 790, McAllen, Texas 78501; A/C 512, 682-2871; E

150. McDonough (Henry County Chamber of Commerce); P.O. Box 92, McDonough, Georgia 30253; A/C 404, 957-5786; A*

151. Memphis Area Chamber of Commerce; P.O. Box 224, Memphis, Tennessee 38101; A/C 901. 523-2322; G

152. Menomonee Falls Association of Commerce; P.O. Box 73, Menomonee Falls, Wisconsin 53051; A/C 414, 251-2430; B*

153. Merced Chamber of Commerce; 505 Twentieth St., Merced, California 95340; A/C 209, 722-4167; B*

154. Merced County Chamber of Commerce; P.O. Box 1112, Merced, California 95340; A/C 209, 722-3864; A*

155. Midland Chamber of Commerce; P.O. Box 1890, Midland, Texas 79701; A/C 915, 683-3381; C

156. Metropolitan Milwaukee Association of Commerce; 828 N. Broadway, Milwaukee, Wisconsin 53222; A/C 414, 273-3000; H

157. Greater Minneapolis Chamber of Commerce; 15 South Fifth St., Minneapolis, Minnesota 55402; A/C 612, 339-8521; H

158. Mobile Area Chamber of Commerce; P.O. Box 2187, Mobile, Alabama 36601; A/C 205, 433-6951; F

159. Mohawk (Herkimer County Chamber of Commerce); P.O. Box 25, Mohawk, New York 13407; A/C 315, 866-7820; C*

160. Greater Monroe Chamber of Commerce; 758 S. Monroe, Monroe, Michigan 48161; A/C 313, 242-3366; A*

161. Monroeville Area Chamber of Commerce; 4099 Wm. Penn Hwy., Monroeville, Pennsylvania 15146; A/C 412, 372-5900; B*

162. Morristown Area Chamber of Commerce; P.O. Box 9; Morristown, Tennessee 37814; A/C 615, 586-6382; A*

163. Mount Prospect Chamber of Commerce; 119 S. Emerson St., Mount Prospect, Illinois 60056; A/C 312, 398-6616; C*

164. Muncie-Delaware County Chamber of Commerce; 500 N. Walnut St., Muncie, Indiana 47305; A/C 317, 288-6681; D*

165. Murray Chamber of Commerce; 118 East 4800 South, Murray, Utah 84107; A/C 801, 262-2253; B*

166. Muskegon Area Development Council Chamber of Commerce; 1065 Fourth St., Muskegon, Michigan 49441; A/C 616, 722-3751; E

167. Nashville Area Chamber of Commerce; 161 Fourth Ave., North, Nashville, Tennessee 37219; A/C 615, 259-3900; G

168. National City Chamber of Commerce; 711 A Avenue, National City, California 92050; A/C 714, 477-9339; B*

169. Chamber of Commerce of Neenah-Menasha; 214 Washington St., Menasha, Wisconsin 54952; A/C 414, 722-7758; B*

170. New Bedford Area Chamber of Commerce; P.O. Box G-827, New Bedford, Massachusetts 02742; A/C 617, 999-5231; E

171. New Britain Chamber of Commerce, Inc.; 24 Washington Street, New Britain, Connecticut 06051; A/C 203, 229-1665; E

172. New Orleans Area Chamber of Commerce; P.O. Box 30240, New Orleans, Louisiana 70190; A/C 504, 524-1131; H

173. New York Chamber of Commerce and Industry; 65 Liberty Street, New York, New York 10005; A/C 212, 732-1123; H

174. Newark Chamber of Commerce; P.O. Box 63, Newark, California 94560; A/C 415, 793-1121; E

175. Greater Newark Chamber of Commerce; 1180 Raymond Boulevard, Newark, New Jersey 07102; A/C 201, 624-6888; H

176. Newark Area Chamber of Commerce; P.O. Box 702, Newark, Ohio 43055; A/C 614, 345-9757; B*
177. Newhall-Saugus-Valencia Chamber of Commerce; P.O. Box 629, Newhall, California 91321; A/C 805, 259-4787; A*
178. Lansdale (North Penn Chamber of Commerce); 324 W. Main Street, Lansdale, Pennsylvania 19446; A/C 215, 855-8414; A*
179. North Royalton Chamber of Commerce; P.O. Box 8208, North Royalton, Ohio 44133; A/C 216, 237-6180; A*
180. Norwalk Chamber of Commerce; 13915 San Antonio Dr., Norwalk, California 90650; A/C 213, 864-7785; D*
181. Oak Creek Chamber of Commerce; P.O. Box 1, Oak Creek, Wisconsin 53154; A/C 414, 762-6600; A*
182. Oak Lawn Chamber of Commerce; 5251 West 95th Street, Oak Lawn, Illinois 60453; A/C 312, 636-2950; C*
183. Oak Ridge Chamber of Commerce; P.O. Box 368, Oak Ridge, Tennessee 37830; A/C 615, 483-1321; B*
184. Oakland Chamber of Commerce; 1320 Webster Street, Oakland, California 94612; A/C 415, 451-7800; H
185. Oshkosh Area Chamber of Commerce; 27 A Washington Avenue, Oshkosh, Wisconsin 54901; A/C 414, 235-3000; C*
186. Greater Ogden Chamber of Commerce; Ben Lomond Hotel, Ogden, Utah 84403; A/C 801, 399-5647; C*
187. Omaha Chamber of Commerce; 1620 Dodge Street, Omaha, Nebraska 68102; A/C 402, 341-1234; G
188. Greater Paducah Chamber of Commerce; P.O. Box 810, Paducah, Kentucky 42001; A/C 502, 443-1746; B*
189. Palatine Chamber of Commerce & Ind. Inc.; 101 S. Northwest Hwy., Palatine, Illinois 60067; A/C 312, 358-3327; B*
190. Paramount Chamber of Commerce; 15357 Paramount Boulevard, Paramount, California 90723; A/C 213, 634-3980; B*
191. Pasadena Chamber of Commerce; 181 S. Los Robles Avenue, Pasadena, California 91101; A/C 213, 795-3355; E*
192. Pensacola Area Chamber of Commerce; P.O. Box 550, Pensacola, Florida 32593; A/C 904, 438-4081; E
193. Perkasie (Pennridge Chamber of Commerce); 607 Chestnut St., Perkasie, Pennsylvania 18944; A/C 215, 257-5067; A*
194. Petaluma Area Chamber of Commerce; 10 Petaluma Blvd. N., Petaluma, California 94952; A/C 707, 762-2785; B*
195. Greater Philadelphia Chamber of Commerce; 1528 Walnut Street, Philadelphia, Pennsylvania 19102; A/C 215, 732-7324; H
196. Phillipsburg Area Chamber of Commerce; 78 South Main Street, Phillipsburg, New Jersey 08865; A/C 201, 859-5161; A*
197. Pine Bluff Chamber of Commerce; P.O. Box 5069, Pine Bluff, Arkansas 71601; A/C 501, 535-0110; C*

198. Piqua Area Chamber of Commerce; P.O. Box 1142, Piqua, Ohio 45356; A/C 513, 773-2765; A*

199. Chamber of Commerce of Greater Pittsburgh; 411 7th Ave., Pittsburgh, Pennsylvania 15219; A/C 412, 391-3400; H*

200. Pittsfield (Association of Business and Commerce); 107 South Street, Pittsfield, Massachusetts 01201; A/C 413, 443-9117; D

201. Placerville (El Dorado County Chamber of Commerce); 542 Main Street, Placerville, California 95667; A/C 916, 626-2344; B*

202. Pocatello Chamber of Commerce; P.O. Box 647, Pocatello, Idaho 83201; A/C 208, 233-1525; B*

203. Greater Port Arthur Chamber of Commerce; P.O. Box 460, Port Arthur, Texas 77640; A/C 713, 985-9373; F

204. Greater Port Huron Marysville Chamber of Commerce; 920 Pine Grove, Port Huron, Michigan 48060; A/C 313, 985-7101; B*

205. Greater Pottstown Area Chamber of Commerce; Griffith Towers - Charlotte & King Streets, Pottstown, Pennsylvania 19464; A/C 215, 326-2900; B*

206. Greater Providence Chamber of Commerce; 10 Dorrance St., Providence, Rhode Island 02903; A/C 401, 521-5000; G

207. Pueblo Chamber of Commerce; Third at Sante Fe, Pueblo, Colorado 81002; A/C 303, 542-1704; E

208. Pulaski County Chamber of Commerce, Inc.; P.O. Box 169, Pulaski, Virginia 24301; A/C 703, 980-1991; A*

209. Quincy Chamber of Commerce; 428 Maine St., Quincy, Illinois 62301; A/C 217, 222-7980; B*

210. Racine Area Chamber of Commerce; 731 Main St., Racine, Wisconsin 53403; A/C 414, 633-2451; E

211. Chamber of Commerce of Reading & Berks County; P.O. Box 1698, Reading, Pennsylvania 19603; A/C 215, 376-6766; F

212. Redwood City Chamber of Commerce; 1006 Middlefield Rd., Redwood City, California 94063; A/C 415, 364-1722; C*

213. Greater Reno Chamber of Commerce; P.O. Box 3499, Reno, Nevada 89505; A/C 702, 786-3030; E

214. Greater Renton Chamber of Commerce; 300 Rainier Avenue North, Renton, Washington 98055; A/C 206, 226-4560; C

215. Richfield Chamber of Commerce; 7011-15th Ave. 30., Richfield, Montana 55423; A/C 406, 869-4813; B*

216. Greater Richmond Chamber of Commerce; 616 E. Franklin St., Richmond, Virginia 23219; A/C 804, 649-0373; G

217. Riviera Beach (Northern Palm Beach County) Chamber of Commerce; 3601 Broadway, Riviera Beach, Florida 33404; A/C 305, 848-3431; A*

218. Roane County Chamber of Commerce; P.O. Box 276, Kingston, Tennessee 37763; A/C 615, 376-6026; A*

219. Roanoke Valley Chamber of Commerce; P.O. Box 20, Roanoke, Virginia 24001; A/C 703, 344-5188; E
220. Rochester Chamber of Commerce; 55 St. Paul St., Rochester, New York 14606; A/C 716, 454-2220; G
221. Rocky Mountain Chamber of Commerce; P.O. Box 392, Rocky Mountain, North Carolina 27801; A/C 919, 442-5111; B*
222. Rosemead Chamber of Commerce; 8780 E. Valley Blvd., Rosemead, California 91770; A/C 213, 288-0811; B*
223. Roseville Area Chamber of Commerce; 700 Vernon St., Roseville, California 95678; A/C 916, 783-8136; A*
224. Sacramento Metropolitan Chamber of Commerce; P.O. Box 1017, Sacramento, California 95805; A/C 916, 443-3771; G
225. Greater Saginaw Chamber of Commerce; P.O. Box 730, Saginaw, Michigan 48606; A/C 517, 752-7161; E
226. St. Joseph Area Chamber of Commerce; 510 Francis St., St. Joseph, Missouri 64501; A/C 816, 232-4461; D
227. Chamber of Commerce of Metropolitan St. Louis; 10 Broadway, St. Louis, Missouri 63102; A/C 314, 231-5555; H
228. Saint Paul Area Chamber of Commerce; 300 Osborn Bldg., Saint Paul, Minnesota 55102; A/C 612, 222-5561; H
229. Salisbury Area Chamber of Commerce; P.O. Box 510, Salisbury, Maryland 21801; A/C 301, 749-0144; A*
230. San Bruno Chamber of Commerce; P.O. Box 713, San Bruno, California 94066; A/C 415, 588-0180; B*
231. San Diego Chamber of Commerce; 233 A. St., Suite 300, San Diego, California 92109; A/C 714, 232-0124; H
232. San Jose Chamber of Commerce; P.O. Box 6178, San Jose, California 95150; A/C 408, 293-3161; H
233. San Leandro Chamber of Commerce; P.O. Box 607, San Leandro, California 94577; A/C 415, 351-1481; C*
234. San Rafael (Marin County Chamber of Commerce); 824 Fifth Ave., San Rafael, California 94901; A/C 415, 454-2520; B*
235. Santa Rosa County Chamber of Commerce; 303 Willing St., Milton, Florida 32570; A/C 904, 623-2339; B*
236. Greater Scranton Chamber of Commerce; 426 Mulberry St., Scranton, Pennsylvania 18503; A/C 717, 342-7711; E
237. Shreveport (Louisiana) Chamber of Commerce; P.O. Box 74, Shreveport, Louisiana 71120; A/C 318, 424-8201; F
238. Skokie Chamber of Commerce; 8322 Lincoln Ave., Skokie, Illinois 60076; A/C 312, 673-0240; C
239. Somerset (Chamber of Commerce of Franklin Township); P.O. Box 1, Somerset, New Jersey 08873; A/C 201, 247-6736; B*
240. South Bend-Mishawaka Area Chamber of Commerce; 320 W. Jefferson, South Bend, Indiana 46601; A/C 219, 234-0051; E

241. South Boston (Halifax County Chamber of Commerce), P.O. Box 399, South Boston, Virginia 24592; A/C 804, 572-3085; B*

242. South Gate Chamber of Commerce; P.O. Box K, South Gate, California 90280; A/C 213, 576-1203; C*

243. South Middlesex Area Chamber of Commerce, Inc.; 109 Concord St., Framingham, Massachusetts 01701; A/C 617, 879-5600; C

244. South Shore Chamber of Commerce; 36 Miller Stile Rd., Quincy, Massachusetts 02169; A/C 617, 479-1852; F*

245. Greater Southington Chamber of Commerce, Inc.; 55 North Main St., Southington, Connecticut 06489; A/C 203, 628-8036; B*

246. Greater Springfield Chamber of Commerce; 818 Myers Bldg., Springfield, Illinois 62701; A/C 217, 525-1173; E

247. Greater Springfield Chamber of Commerce; 1500 Main St., Suite 600, Springfield, Massachusetts 01115; A/C 413, 734-5671; G

248. Springfield Area Chamber of Commerce; P.O. Box 1036, Springfield, Missouri 65805; A/C 417, 862-5567; E

249. Springfield Area Chamber of Commerce; 102 East Main St., Springfield, Ohio 45501; A/C 513, 325-7621; E

250. Staten Island Chamber of Commerce; 130 Bay St., Staten Island, New York 11209; A/C 212, 727-1900; F*

251. Staunton-Augunta County Chamber of Commerce; P.O. Box 389, Staunton, Virginia 24401; A/C 703, 886-2351; A*

252. Greater Stockton Chamber of Commerce; 1105 N. El Dorado St., Stockton, California 95202; A/C 209, 466-7066; F

253. Summit (Berkeley Heights Chamber of Commerce), 57 Union Place, Summit, New Jersey 07901; A/C 201, 277-6800; C

254. Superior Chamber of Commerce; 1215 Tower Ave., Superior, Wisconsin 54880; A/C 715, 394-7716; B*

255. Tallahassee Area Chamber of Commerce; P.O. Box 1639, Tallahassee, Florida 32302; A/C 904, 224-8116; C*

256. Greater Tampa Chamber of Commerce; P.O. Box 420, Tampa, Florida 33602; A/C 813, 229-0911; H

257. Tarzana Chamber of Commerce; P.O. Box 445, Tarzana, California 91356; A/C 213, 343-3687; B*

258. Temple Chamber of Commerce; P.O. Box 158, Temple, Texas 76501; A/C 817, 773-2106; B*

259. Temple City Chamber of Commerce; 5827 N. Temple City Blvd., Temple City, California 91780; A/C 213; B*

260. Texarkana Chamber of Commerce, Inc.; P.O. Box 1468, Texarkana, Arkansas-Texas 75501; A/C 214, 792-7191; E

261. Thousand Oaks (Congo Valley Chamber of Commerce); 401 W. Hillcrest Dr., Thousand Oaks, California 91360; A/C 805, 497-1621; C*

262. Towson (Baltimore County Chamber of Commerce); 305 W. Chesapeake Ave., Towson, Maryland 21204; A/C 301, 825-6200; G

263. Trenton Mercer County Chamber of Commerce; 104 North Broad St., Trenton, New Jersey 08608; A/C 609, 393-4143; F

264. Metropolitan Tulsa Chamber of Commerce; 616 S. Boston Ave., Tulsa, Oklahoma 74119; A/C 918, 585-1201; F

265. Turlock Chamber of Commerce; 140 So. Hwy. 99, Turlock, California 95380; A/C 209, 632-2221; A*

266. Greater Tuscaloosa Chamber of Commerce; P.O. Box 430, Tuscaloosa, Alabama 35401; A/C 205, 758-7588; E

267. Tyler Chamber of Commerce; P.O. Box 390, Tyler, Texas 75701; A/C 214, 592-1661; D

268. Venice Area Chamber of Commerce, Inc.; P.O. Box 937, Venice, Florida 33595; A/C 813, 488-2236; C

269. Vermont State Chamber of Commerce; P.O. Box 37, Montpelier, Vermont 05602; A/C 802, 223-3443

270. Virginia State Chamber of Commerce; 611 E. Franklin St., Richmond, Virginia 23219; A/C 804, 643-7491

271. Waco Chamber of Commerce; P.O. Drawer 1220, Waco, Texas 76703; A/C 817, 752-6551; E

272. Walla Walla Area Chamber of Commerce; P.O. Box 644, Walla Walla, Washington 99362; A/C 509, 525-0850; A*

273. Greater Waterbury Chamber of Commerce; P.O. Box 1469, Waterbury, Connecticut 06720; A/C 203, 757-0701; F

274. Waukesha Chamber of Commerce; 722 North Grand Avenue, Waukesha, Wisconsin 53186; A/C 414, 542-4249; B*

275. Wausau Area Chamber of Commerce; P.O. Box 569, Wausau, Wisconsin 54401; A/C 715, 845-6231; B*

276. Greater Haywood County Chamber of Commerce; P.O. Box 125, Waynesville, North Carolina 28786; A/C 704, 456-3021; B*

277. Wellesley Chamber of Commerce, Inc.; P.O. Box 201, Wellesley, Massachusetts 02181; A/C 617, 235-2446; B*

278. West Point (Valley Chamber of Commerce); P.O. Box 584, West Point, Georgia 31833; A/C 205, 644-3191; B*

279. West Virginia Chamber of Commerce; P.O. Box 2789, Charleston, West Virginia 25330; A/C 304, 342-1115

280. Westfield Area Chamber of Commerce; 260 East Broad St., Westfield, New Jersey 07090; A/C 201, 233-4902; B*

281. White Plains Regional Chamber of Commerce, Inc.; 170 East Post Road, White Plains, New York 10601; A/C 914, 948-2110; C*

282. Wichita Area Chamber of Commerce; 350 W. Douglas, Wichita, Kansas 67202; A/C 316, 265-7771; F

283. Wichita Falls Board of Commerce and Industry; P.O. Box 1860, Wichita Falls, Texas 76307; A/C 817, 723-2741; E

284. Greater Williamsport Chamber of Commerce; 418 William Street, Williamsport, Pennsylvania 17701; A/C 717, 326-1971; B*
285. Winchester-Frederick County Chamber of Commerce, Inc.; P.O. Box 667, Winchester, Virginia 22601; A/C 703, 662-4118; A*
286. Greater Winston-Salem Chamber of Commerce; P.O. Box 1408, Winston-Salem, North Carolina 27102; A/C 919, 725-2361; G
287. Woodland Chamber of Commerce; 520 Main St., Woodland, California 95695; A/C 916, 662-7327; B*
288. Yonkers Chamber of Commerce; 9 Manor House Square, Yonkers, New York 10701; A/C 914, 963-0332; E*
289. York Area Chamber of Commerce; 13 E. Market St., York, Pennsylvania 17401; A/C 717, 854-3814; F
290. Youngstown Area Chamber of Commerce; 200 Wick Bldg., Youngstown, Ohio 44503; A/C 216, 744-2131; G
291. Athens Chamber of Commerce; Security Bldg., Athens, Ohio 45701; A/C 614, 593-5202; A*
292. Billings Chamber of Commerce; P.O. Box 2519, Billings, Montana 59103; A/C 406, 245-4111; C*
293. Beaver Valley Chamber of Commerce; 1215 7th Ave., Beaver Falls, Pennsylvania 15010; A/C 412, 846-6750; A*
294. Berkeley Chamber of Commerce; P.O. Box 210, Berkeley, California 94701; A/C 415, 845-1212; E*
295. Charleston Trident Chamber of Commerce; P.O. Box 975, Charleston, South Carolina 29402; A/C 803, 577-2510; F
296. Cherokee County Chamber of Commerce; P.O. Box 1119, Gaffney, South Carolina 29340; A/C 803, 489-5721; B
297. Harlingen Area Chamber of Commerce; P.O. Box 189, Harlingen, Texas 78550; A/C 512, 423-5440; E
298. Greater Harrisburg Area Chamber of Commerce; 114 Walnut Street, Harrisburg, Pennsylvania 17101; A/C 717, 232-4121; F
299. Henderson Audubon Area Chamber of Commerce; P.O. Box 376, Henderson, Kentucky 42420; A/C 502, 826-9531; B*
300. Euless (Hurst-Euless-Bedford Chamber of Commerce); 1102 W. Euless Blvd., Suite 167, Euless, Texas 76039; A/C 817, 283-1521; A*
301. Kansas City Kansas Area Chamber of Commerce; P.O. Box 1310, Kansas City, Kansas 66109; A/C 913, 371-3070; H
302. Kettering Chamber of Commerce; 40 Southmoor Circle, Kettering, Ohio 45429; A/C 513, 434-7338; C*
303. Greater LaPuente Valley Chamber of Commerce; P.O. Box 327, LaPuente, California 91747; A/C 213, 330-3216; B*
304. Plainfield Area Chamber of Commerce; 119 Watchung Ave., Plainfield, New Jersey 07060; A/C 201, 754-7250; B*

305. Greater Portland Chamber of Commerce; 142 Free St., Portland, Maine 04101; A/C 207, 772-2811; E
306. Santa Monica Chamber of Commerce; 200 Santa Monica Blvd., Santa Monica, California 90401; A/C 213, 393-0825; D*
307. Seattle Chamber of Commerce; 215 Columbia St., Seattle, Washington 98104; A/C 206, 622-5060; H
308. Spokane Chamber of Commerce; P.O. Box 2147, Spokane, Washington 99210; A/C 509, 624-1393; F
309. Greater Westerly-Pawtucket Area Chamber of Commerce; 159 Main St., Westerly, Rhode Island 02891; A/C 401, 596-7761; A*
310. Wheat Ridge Chamber of Commerce; 6470 W. 44th Ave., Wheat Ridge, Colorado 80033; A/C 303, 423-3800; B*
311. Bellingham Chamber of Commerce; P.O. Box 958, Bellingham, Washington 98225; A/C 206, 734-1330; B
312. Galveston Chamber of Commerce; 315 Tremont, Galveston, Texas 77550; A/C 713, 763-5326; E
313. Glendora Chamber of Commerce; 224 N. Glendora Ave., Glendora, California 91740; A/C 213, 963-4128; B*
314. Greater Knoxville Chamber of Commerce; 705 Gay Street, Knoxville, Tennessee 37902; A/C 615, 522-6111; F
315. Kittanning (Middle Armstrong County Chamber of Commerce); Colwell-Arnold Building, N. McKean St., Kittanning, Pennsylvania 16201; A/C 412, 542-2961; A*
316. Minot Chamber of Commerce; P.O. Box 940, Minot, North Dakota 58701; A/C 701, 839-7501; B*
317. Monrovia Chamber of Commerce; 111 West Colorado, Monrovia, California 91016; A/C 213, 358-1159; B*
318. Pennsylvania Chamber of Commerce; 222 N. Third St., Harrisburg, Pennsylvania 17101; A/C 717, 238-0441
319. Redlands Chamber of Commerce; 347 Orange St., Redlands, California 92373; A/C 714, 793-2546; B*
320. Roswell Chamber of Development and Commerce; P.O. Box 70, Roswell, New Mexico 88201; A/C 505, 623-5695; B*
321. Greater Topeka Chamber of Commerce; 722 Kansas Ave., Topeka, Kansas 66603; A/C 913, 234-2644; F
322. Kentucky Chamber of Commerce; 300 West York St., Louisville, Kentucky 40203; A/C 502, 583-2794
323. Delaware County Chamber of Commerce; 6 E. Baltimore Pike, Media, Pennsylvania 19063; A/C 215, 565-3677; G
324. Dallas Chamber of Commerce; 1507 Pacific Ave., Dallas, Texas 75201; A/C 214, 651-1020; H
325. Missouri Chamber of Commerce; P.O. Box 149, Jefferson City, Missouri 65101; A/C 314, 634-3511

326. Northern Middlesex Chamber of Commerce; 100 Riverview Center,
P.O. Box 997, Middletown, Connecticut 06457; A/C 203, 346-
8616; B*

INDEX

438

446